close-up

CLOSE - UP

a critical perspective on film

Marsha Kinder

Occidental College

Beverle Houston

Pitzer College

Harcourt Brace Jovanovich, Inc.

New York   Chicago   San Francisco   Atlanta

The authors wish to thank the following for permission to reprint copy-righted material:

GROVE PRESS, INC., New York: for quotations from "The South" in *Ficciones* by Jorge Luis Borges. Translated by Anthony Kerrigan. Copy-right © 1962 by Grove Press, Inc. Translated from the Spanish © 1956 by Emece Editores, S.A.; for quotations from *Hiroshima mon amour,* text by Marguerite Duras for the film by Alain Resnais. Translated by Richard Seaver 1961. Copyright © 1961 by Grove Press, Inc. Reprinted by permission of Grove Press, Inc., New York, and John Calder Ltd., London.

HOLT, RINEHART AND WINSTON, INC., New York: for quotations from *Steppenwolf* by Hermann Hesse.

HERBERT LIGHTMAN AND *AMERICAN CINEMATOGRAPHER:* for quo-tations from "Creating Special Effects for *2001*" by Douglas Trumbull, and from "Filming *2001*" and "Front Projection for *2001*" by Herbert Lightman, in *American Cinematographer,* June 1968.

LORRIMER PUBLISHING LTD., London, and SIMON AND SCHUSTER, INC., New York: for quotations from *The Rules of the Game* by Jean Renoir.

NEW AMERICAN LIBRARY, INC., New York: for quotations from *Faces* by John Cassavetes. Copyright © 1970 by John Cassavetes. Reprinted by arrangement with The New American Library, Inc., New York, N. Y.

RANDOM HOUSE, INC., New York: for excerpts from *Love's Body* by Norman O. Brown. Copyright © 1966 by Norman O. Brown.

SIGHT AND SOUND, London: for quotations from "Some Ideas on the Cinema" by Cesare Zavattini, in *Sight and Sound,* October 1953.

Picture credits and copyright acknowledgments are on page 395.

ISBN: 0–15–507750–3

Library of Congress Catalog Card Number: 70–187571

Printed in the United States of America

to ralph cohen

preface

We do not attempt to cover the historical development of film in this book; nor do we try to select examples from all periods, countries, and genres. We try instead to present a critical approach that can be applied to any film and to illustrate this approach with as many examples as possible. Our analyses of films are to be taken not as an anthology of "authorized" interpretations, but as examples of the way in which this critical method can expand the experience of movies.

The experience of film, or of any work of art for that matter, is subjective, reaching the gut as well as the head, and is primarily nonverbal. Talking about a film is not the same as or a substitute for experiencing it. Though language is the most efficient and valuable medium for sharing ideas and experiences, its linear nature limits its ability to describe certain phenomena. Cinema can offer a great number of visual events simultaneously, linking them in unpredictable ways. The richer and more complex and innovative a film is, the greater is the difficulty in describing it verbally. Nevertheless we have based this book on the assumption

that critical words can broaden the range of films one can respond to, increase understanding, and ultimately lead to an intensification of subjective response.

All our generalizations are based on our experiencing of specific films. The approach is inductive, though the presentation
may at times appear deductive. General statements are always
subject to refutation. Their value is always tested by their applicability to specific films—not only to films discussed here, but to
films that have been omitted and to films not yet made. One of
the paradoxes in criticism is that in the attempt to develop generalizations inductively on the basis of existing works, critics may
use their findings to limit future experimentation. When a new
work comes along, it is frequently condemned because it does
not fulfill expectations aroused by works of the past. Instead of
questioning the validity and relevance of its expectations, the
audience usually assumes that something is wrong with the new
work: It is not really Art (meaning it differs from the works we
have up to now accepted as art); it is self-indulgent, lacks order
and control (meaning it is not structured according to the conventional ways familiar to us); it is a put-on (meaning nobody is
going to put one over on us). We feel strongly that criticism must
leave room for the unknown; it must be aware that an art form
constantly changes and that predicting what direction that
change will take is difficult. In fact, criticism does not really
predict. Its generalizations are usually retroactive—that is, they
apply to existing works not presently under consideration. Repeatedly through history, works of art—Shakespeare's plays,
Stravinsky's *Rite of Spring,* the paintings of the French Impressionists, *Un Chien Andalou, Performance*—come along and challenge the current critical assumptions. By redefining art, the artist
forces the critic to rethink his critical approach. One of our goals
is to develop a critical approach based on the awareness of this
process.

Here, then, we present a theoretical approach to film, but one
expressed primarily through practical criticism. Most recent
books of film criticism offer unrelated essays of practical criticism, a discussion of particular kinds of cinema, or theoretical
ideas about space, time, color, sound, illustrated with many brief
examples. We try to combine these approaches. The overall organization of this book grows out of esthetic issues, illustrated
with extended analyses of specific films.

One of our basic assumptions about cinema is that its power as
a medium derives from its unique capacities to represent the ex-

ternal, objective world and to express the subjective reality of a personal vision. After an introductory chapter explaining our critical method, we discuss several films in the context of different esthetic questions, always relating them to the mimetic and expressive capacities of cinema. In Chapter 2 we trace the silent cinema as it develops these capacities through visual composition, camera movement, and editing. Chapter 3 is an exploration of some of the technical advancements that promised to improve the medium's recording ability but, in the hands of imaginative filmmakers, actually liberated its powers of expression. Documentary, the genre that normally stresses the recording function of the camera, is the subject of Chapter 4; the films we have chosen, however, depend upon a combination of both powers in order to achieve their specialized intentions. Three movements (Italian, French, and American) that develop different kinds of realism are the focus of Chapter 5. In Chapter 6 five films made in the 1960's that take as their subject matter the creative process in general and filmmaking in particular and that ultimately offer the director's personal statement are examined. Chapter 7 is a discussion of the various ways in which films can be mythic—through symbolism, genre, and personal vision. The special problems of evaluation raised by politically controversial films, an important issue in contemporary art, are explored in Chapter 8. Finally, in Chapter 9 we incorporate all the issues discussed in the preceding chapters into a full treatment of one film, *Performance*.

The theoretical assumptions we discuss in Chapter 1 are always operating implicitly in the other chapters. We are always concerned with the relationship of form and content, assuming that they work together and that they cannot be evaluated separately. We are constantly engaged in evaluating films, implicitly and explicitly, through trying to describe the qualities that make them unique.

M. K.
B. H.

acknowledgments

We wish to extend out sincere thanks to those who helped us in creating and preparing the manuscript: Occidental College, Pitzer College, Ann Manning, Cliveden Chew, Merton Rapp, Albert Richards, Robert Ryf, Douglas Trumbull, Bob Curtis, Monte Hellman, Beverly Walker, Susan Wladawsky, and the senior film class of spring 1971 of the Oakwood Secondary School. For enabling us to screen films, we are also grateful to Bill Moritz and Beverly O'Neill of the Los Angeles Filmmakers Cooperative, Bob Pike of Creative Film Society, Leacock-Pennebaker, Contemporary Films, Warner Brothers, Aaron Sloan, Jack H. Harris, and John Cassavetes. Special thanks to the following who helped us obtain photographic stills: Helen Nathan, Robert Laemmle, Bob Pike, Chick Strand, Pat O'Neill, Jack Harris, the UCLA Research Library, and the Library of the Academy of Motion Picture Arts and Sciences.

contents

contents

3

technology and illusion
pressures from within the medium   49

4

the expressive documentary   101

contents

5
three cinema movements
views of realism

contents

xiv

contents

9

the ultimate performance

appendix 1

appendix 2

index

close-up

1

the
reel
experience
and the
critical
perspective

Our approach to film is experiential, inductive, and open-ended. Its main goal is evaluation, based on the comparative method. It results in long, detailed discussions of films, designed to reveal the nondiscursive qualities of a filmmaker's use of the medium to express his unique vision. We approach a work of cinematic art armed with our own experience of life and of other works, which will necessarily affect our response to the one under scrutiny. But the film to be explored is always an unknown quantity: We have no preconceptions about what we are looking for; that is determined by the work itself. The uniqueness may be in the use of space or time, structure, editing pace, camera movement, visual composition, imagery, sound. Every filmmaker makes choices in all these areas, and the choices, conscious and unconscious, are bound to create implications about the universe of a film. We can never know in advance which aspects of a film are going to be particularly important in shaping its unique vision; hence we can have no absolute criteria when approaching any of a film's components. What we know about them is what we learn from observing how they have been handled in this and other films —how they work in a particular context toward a particular intention. Such insights about filmic qualities define the realized potentialities of the medium, but certainly not all the ones that are possible. Therefore, we assume that the justification for theoretical statements about film lies in their applicability to individual works, in their ability to expand our experience, understanding, and appreciation of the film; specific works must not be reduced to data manipulated to support a theoretical structure.

Our approach assumes that art is constantly reshaped by innovation and hence anticipates the changing definitions of art, cinema, and genre. One way of defining art is to start by investigating its function, shifting emphasis from a metaphysical focus on being (what is the nature of art?) to an existential focus on the process of becoming (how does art function?). Obviously several purposes are operating simultaneously: to teach, to delight, to express, to communicate, to persuade. But the question is which of these approaches is most fruitful for an understanding of the creation and experience of works in a particular medium and is least likely to lead to a prejudiced valuing of one kind of art over another. For example, one who adopts the view that the primary function of art is to persuade will be likely to rank neo-realism quite high and to question the value of directors like Méliès, Buñuel, and Fellini; and he might totally ignore filmmakers like Léger, O'Neill, and the Whitneys, who stress visual experimentation.

Two main views of the function of art have prevailed through history: art as imitation or mimesis, the idea Aristotle introduced in his *Poetics;* and art as subjective expression, the idea dominant in criticism since the nineteenth century. In the former, the emphasis is on a work's relationship to the outside world, which it imitates, and its effect on the audience. In the latter, art expresses something in the artist—a private vision or an accurate imitation, political propaganda or visual abstraction—and the critical emphasis is on the work of art itself.

Any work can be approached from either perspective: It always has a relationship to the outside world and is always an expression of its creator. The expressive view has tended to replace the mimetic because it is more open to all kinds of art, regardless of style, subject, or intention. The mimetic view has tended to favor realistic

2

and didactic art and to be limited in dealing with nonobjectivism, a major force in the twentieth century. It tends to limit the responsive capacity of the popular audience by developing an exclusive taste for verisimilitude. Since the mimetic view assumes that art is valuable because it provides knowledge about the world, it makes art compete with history, philosophy, and science. If "truthfulness" or knowledge is to be the main criterion, then all art is bound to come off second best. The mimetic view also implies that art is a substitute for or imitation of the "real thing"—that is, a way of experiencing things vicariously.[1] If one assumes that the primary function of art is imitation, then undoubtedly going to Paris is better than seeing a film about Paris—"better" in the sense of providing more information and a fuller experience of Paris itself. But such a view totally ignores the uniqueness of the esthetic experience. One might go to Paris a thousand times. Each visit would be different from the others; they would all be different from the experience of seeing Godard's *Two or Three Things I Know About Her.* The esthetic experience does not "imitate" any other experience in life any more than eating an apple imitates swimming.

The conflict between the imitative and expressive views of art has been particularly relevant to cinema. The camera is an objective instrument capable of recording sensory data. It is a machine —impersonal, detached, invented by scientists, not by artists. One of the biggest breakthroughs—the photographing of natural motion—came when Leland Stanford, in order to win a bet, commissioned Eadweard Muybridge to "prove" photographically that at one point in the stride of a galloping horse all four feet are off the ground. Muybridge met the challenge in 1872 by using twenty-four cameras in a row to make rapid successive photographs of a running horse. Only the "objective" camera could collect the evidence and reach the "truth." In 1895, when the Lumière brothers first effectively projected moving pictures before an audience in the basement of the Grand Café in Paris, they were documenting common sensory experiences: a train entering a station, factory workers leaving work, waves breaking on the shore. Their *actualités* were the basis of the documentary tradition.

It was immediately apparent that cinema, of all art media, was best equipped to achieve verisimilitude, far surpassing painting in

---

[1] In the *Republic* Plato presents this view as an argument against allowing art a place in his Utopia. Susan Sontag, in *Against Interpretation* (New York: Farrar, Straus and Giroux, 1964), cited this attitude as an argument against the mimetic view of art.

3

this capacity.[2] When a filmmaker decides to include a physical object such as a table or chair in a scene, he, unlike a writer, cannot make his reference vague or abstract but is forced to select a chair of a certain size, shape, style, color, and to place it in a specific position. This gives a remarkable particularity to the physical texture of reality in cinema, a quality that novelists like Robbe-Grillet have tried to incorporate in their writing.

But there is another side of cinema. The images on the screen are flickering shadows; they are larger than life. The motion is an illusion caused by a peculiarity in human perception called persistence of vision. When we are in a theater, we actually see a series of consecutive still pictures flash very rapidly on the screen. But since the human eye retains a visual image for approximately one-tenth of a second after an object has disappeared from sight, as long as we see at least ten pictures per second we will not perceive any gaps and therefore experience still pictures as continuous motion.[3]

One of the first artists in filmmaking, Georges Méliès, exploited film's capacity for illusion to express his own dreams and fantasy. He assumed complete control over his films, creating the first fictional plot and scenario, casting the actors, designing the costumes and scenery, and setting up the camera. Many of his films were fairy tales and science fiction—for example, *Cinderella* (1900), *A Trip to the Moon* (1902), and *An Impossible Voyage* (1904). One day in 1896 when he was out shooting in the Place de l'Opéra, his camera happened to jam. Later when he projected the film he saw a bus suddenly transformed into a hearse. The bus had been on the street before the camera jammed, and by the time he resumed shooting, it had moved on and a hearse had taken its place. This accident made Méliès realize that the camera had a capacity to create tricks and illusions far greater than the stage magic he had been practicing and encouraged him to experiment and discover other devices for this purpose, such as the fade-in and fade-out, the dissolve, reverse shooting, slow and accelerated motion, animation, stop action, mask shots, superimposition, matt shots, and underwater shots. In *The Magic Lantern* (1903), he introduced a film within the film, the first in cinematic history. Méliès

[2] André Bazin offers an important discussion of this question in *What Is Cinema?* (Berkeley: University of California Press, 1967). He argues that the capacity for accurately capturing reality is the unique and most significant aspect of the medium.

[3] For a fuller discussion of the illusory aspects of cinema see Rudolf Arnheim, *Film as Art* (Berkeley: University of California Press, 1966), ch. 2.

4

never pretended to imitate reality; he liked to remind his audience that they were watching an expressive medium.

The history of film can be examined in terms of the polarity between the medium's recording and expressive capacities. Repeatedly we find filmmakers, critics, and historians calling one or the other the unique aspect of the medium. But neither by itself can account for the full range of cinematic achievement. A director may proceed as if he is exploring only one capacity, but he can never really avoid aspects of the other.

This conflict is related to polarities that apply to all media—between subject and form, between centrifugal and centripetal meanings.[4] A film based on a mimetic view of art tends to stress subject matter or theme. Its style or technique is likely to seem invisible or at least unobtrusive; hence, it will draw one's attention to centrifugal meanings—those leading out to the world beyond the film. In contrast, a film based on an expressive view of art tends to stress the formal aspects. The style or techniques are usually conspicuous and self-conscious, reminding us that we are watching a film; hence, it will draw our attention to centripetal meanings—those leading in toward the autonomous world of the film.

Form and subject, or centripetal and centrifugal meanings, are not separate properties or "things" existing within a work of art; they are ways of approaching or talking about it. Any work can be approached through either of these polarities. If, for example, an artist like Méliès, with an expressive view of art, reminds his audience that they are watching a film, he is calling their attention to the actual experience they are having. Paradoxically, then, perhaps a self-conscious style that reminds the audience of the filming process can be more appropriate for a documentary than the mimetic approach, which tries to create an illusion of objectivity.

This is one of the central issues in Godard's films. A character in his *La Chinoise* gives a lecture on cinema in which he corrects all previous film historians who have labeled Méliès as the father of expressive cinema and the Lumières as the creators of the documentary. Instead, he insists that Méliès was making documentaries, for he was shooting trips to the moon, which have become the reality of the 1960's and 1970's, and the Lumières were treating the same expressive subjects, such as waves breaking against the shore, painted by the impressionists of their era. If we focus only on the subject matter of films, we might agree with Godard's char-

[4] This terminology derives from Northrop Frye, *The Anatomy of Criticism* (New York: Atheneum, 1969).

5

acter. But as soon as we look at the way these subjects are treated, the question becomes more complicated. The Lumières use the camera's potential for documenting reality in order to create an illusion. Méliès, on the other hand, purposely creates a world remarkably different from the one we normally inhabit and realistically documents the camera's potential for illusion. We are not implying that one approach is inherently better than the other, but rather we are trying to discover the particular way in which a specific film uses this double potentiality for mimesis and illusion, because the combination determines the film's relationship with reality.

Our approach focuses on evaluation, which is often used to establish arbitrary hierarchies of films, directors, and genres, or merely to allow the critic/reviewer to condemn the films that offend his moral or esthetic sensibility. Our intention, however, is to use evaluation to define the unique characteristics of each work, thus discriminating among various kinds of esthetic value in film, and to perform the social function of making these values more accessible by expanding the range of films to which people can respond. Therefore, we tend to discuss films that we regard as effective, often discriminating between what a particular film does and does not do well, evaluating films in terms of their intentions rather than arranging them in a hierarchy of value.

Our procedure defines a particular view of evaluation, which may be contrasted with other ways of conceptualizing value in art. The word "art" is sometimes used as a value term, implying that an unsuccessful work is not art. This assumes a prescriptive definition of art, in which all its characteristics, past and potential, are known. It denies that art is open-ended, evolving out of specific works that continue a process of experimentation, some of which succeed while others fail. It implies that people readily agree on what is art and bases this agreement on qualities that have been commonly recognized. However, this view (like similarly based social positions) supports the status quo and makes it impossible to deal with contemporary experimentation, such as pop art, happenings, rock music, conceptual and found art, the esthetic values of which may be perceived only by those who experience these phenomena as art. Though these innovations teach us that art can be defined only as what is perceived as art, each one demands the recognition of its unique esthetic components so that it may be fully experienced and evaluated.

Another similar conception of value in art assumes that goodness is an absolute, a Platonic form toward which art must strive but which it can never fully achieve. This kind of evaluation, therefore, would proceed by comparing works with this ideal model, never accepting the work of art on its own terms. This view forms the basis of hierarchies—"the perfect western," "the great American novel," "the greatest epic of them all." These models, which are infused with autonomous life, actually develop from qualities in specific works that are transformed into prescriptive formulas. Such an absolute view gives rise to definitions of goodness based on several absolute criteria, which are often derived from the Platonic triad of truth, beauty, and virtue (expanded in modern life to include complexity, universality, and organic unity), but which usually disguise the critic's hidden preferences. Some of these qualities (unity and universality) are to be found in every work; others are as vague and subjective as "goodness" (beauty and virtue); and some (complexity) are values only in certain contexts, as is the case with their opposites (simplicity). Hence, these criteria cannot provide a basis for distinguishing good works from bad. Other approaches to evaluation may depend on criteria from systems or disciplines outside of film. Criteria from one medium are sometimes imposed on another, requiring films to be like literature or painting. The imposed values may derive from moral and political ideologies such as Marxism, Maoism, Freudianism, feminism, and Christianity. While these perspectives can be illuminating, the doctrinaire critic assumes that all works can be interpreted and evaluated exclusively within his particular framework, regardless of their own intentions.

Our view assumes that evaluation is relativistic, that goodness must be considered in relation to a particular end and context. Art in general can be seen as valuable because it fulfills man's apparently innate need for controlled expression. But a "good" work is one that transforms its medium to realize fully its expressive possibilities for the work's intention. The problem of determining a work's intention is complex. We cannot simply ask the artist. Even if he were willing and able to answer, he could not reveal the role of the unconscious in creation, nor could he deny the emergence of patterns and relationships that he did not formerly perceive. This problem is particularly difficult in film, which is a collaborative medium giving rise to effects unintended by a single participant and in which it is frequently impossible to determine who did what. Any statement of a work's intention can only be a hypothesis, based on a critic's experience of qualities observable in the work, which can be confirmed or refuted by others. Calling a critical statement hypothetical is not the same as saying it is subjective. Though its truth cannot be absolute, the value of an hypothesis depends upon how much of the work it can explain, whether it is supported by commonly observable evidence, and whether it omits elements by which it might be contradicted.

The hypothesis that forms the basis of evaluation must somehow take into account the four elements of every esthetic experience: the audience, the work, the artist, and the outside world. We all begin as members of the audience, responding subjectively with a full range of emotions. We may offer statements of taste ("I liked the film." "I hated it!")—that is, statements about ourselves. But once we begin to ask what in the film evoked our reactions, we have selected our object of scrutiny and have begun the critical process. Our focus now is on the work. We explore the striking and unusual ways in which the film uses components of the medium to create its unique nondiscursive qualities. We examine the parts in relationship to each other as they form an autonomous structure. We are always concerned with both form and content, for together they comprise the film's meaning. The arrangement of formal elements like time, space, narrative continuity, camera movement, editing pace, and visual composition implies an attitude toward experience, the various choices creating an interpretation of the events and ideas comprising the content and establishing a universe unique to the film. If, for example, two filmmakers treat the same subject, or even the same story (Renoir and Buñuel's *Diary of a Chambermaid; Seven Samurai* and *The Magnificent Seven;* Olivier's and Kozintsev's *Hamlet*), their formal choices transform the contents and ideas. No subject matter or technique is inherently more valuable than any other; each contains an expressive potential. Both must be evaluated by how they are used in a particular context and by how they are developed in relation to each other. They are not separable because their relationship actually forms the true "meaning" of the work; in fact, "form" and "content," as the terms are used analytically, only suggest ways into the work, perspectives or emphases in approaching the totality that is the film. Through selecting and describing significant elements of the film's sensuous texture, we are engaged in evaluation, implying that these elements rather than others are essential in revealing what is unique and valuable in the work of art. Hence, declarations of value ("the picture of the year!" "* * * *," "good but not great," "absolutely worthless!") are far less meaningful than descriptive reasons given to support the judgment. We can always learn a great deal from a responsible critic even if we disagree entirely with his final judgment. This exploration of particular works may lead us to consider the career of a filmmaker as an object of scrutiny that can reveal the development of his esthetic vision. Finally, investigation moves toward the outside world to which the film refers and in which it is created and experienced. A film's social value may depend upon its ability to influence the culture or to weaken its values through exploitation.

Our approach assumes comparison to be the basis of all evaluation. In the words of Samuel Johnson:

> As among the works of nature no man can properly call a river deep or a mountain high, without the knowledge of many mountains and many rivers; so, in the productions of genius, nothing can be styled excellent till it has been compared with other works of the same kind.[5]

Comparison to distinguish among similar phenomena is the basis not only of esthetic criticism but of the historical study of events, the anthropological study of cultures, and the sociological study of groups. As ordinary-language philosophers study the ways in which words change meaning in different contexts, so the critic examines the shifting meanings of conventions in changing artistic contexts. In fact, this kind of comparison is an important epistemological tool for every individual as he acquires experience in the world.

Each work we absorb becomes part of us and affects our understanding of the next work, forming an experiential basis for the comparative method. We want to maximize the positive carry-over from one film to another, not to form prescriptive rules but to broaden experience, so that the next film will be approached with an awareness of new questions and possibilities. Sometimes it is difficult to deal with a work and define its unique qualities until later works emerge that are similar and can provide a basis for comparison. For example, we can only understand the unique qualities of *Monterey Pop* as a rock documentary from the perspective of *Woodstock* and *Gimme Shelter,* later works in the same genre. T. S. Eliot describes this relationship between past and future works as an aspect of formal and historical criticism:

> No poet, no artist of any art, has his complete meaning alone. . . . You must set him, for contrast and comparison, among the dead. I mean this as a principle of aesthetic, not merely historical, criticism. . . . What happens when a new work of art is created is something that happens simultaneously to all the works of art which preceded it.

[5] Samuel Johnson, *Preface to the 1765 Edition of Shakespeare's Works.*

> The existing monuments form an ideal order among themselves, which is modified by the introduction of the new (the really new) work of art among them. Whoever has approved this idea of order . . . will not find it preposterous that the past should be altered by the present as much as the present is directed by the past.[6]

In an esthetic context, the goal is to compare works that are as similar as possible in order to reveal the most subtle distinctions. For this reason we classify works into genres (the western, the horror film, the gangster thriller, the documentary), considering them not as fixed categories by which films should be systematized but as shifting combinations of conventions. The definitions of genre, like the definition of art, are empirically based and change with the introduction of new works. Every work of art combines the conventional and the unique, mixing the old and the new. We can recognize an innovative use of the fade only because we know that conventionally it indicates the passage of time. Similarly, all conventions are based on knowledge common to artist and audience; innovation changes slightly the terms of this agreement. If a work were completely new, we could not possibly understand it. If it had nothing new, it would simply re-create an existing work. But innovation or departure from convention is not inherently valuable; its effectiveness depends on whether it works toward the integrated fulfillment of a film's specific intention. The critic's task is to discover the particular combination of the unique and the conventional in any work of art. Northrop Frye has perceptively observed:

> The possession of originality cannot make an artist unconventional; it drives him further into convention, obeying the law of the art itself, which seeks constantly to reshape itself from its own depths, and which works through its geniuses for metamorphosis, as it works through minor talents for mutation.[7]

This unique combination may be discovered through several kinds of comparison. We compare films made in the same country, period, and movement; experimenting with the same technology; belonging to the same genre; taking a similar attitude toward genre; treating the same basic subject; created by the same director; incorporating mythic dimensions; and raising related problems. However, we can never give a "complete" view of any film

[6] T. S. Eliot, "Tradition and the Individual Talent," *Selected Essays* (New York: Harcourt Brace Jovanovich, 1932), pp. 4–5.
[7] Frye, p. 132.

or genre, for we are limited by our own experience in films, in art, and in life. Therefore we try to make our approach as experiential, as empirical, and as open as possible, bringing together our various efforts through the techniques of comparison and evaluation.

2

the silent cinema becomes an art form

During the first three decades of the twentieth century, cinema was transformed from a scientific novelty and commercial fad into a new art form with exciting possibilities. Paradoxically, some of the most important breakthroughs resulted from the use of conventions of other media, particularly theater and painting. As Méliès first approached cinema as an art form by trying to adapt conventions from magic and the theater, he discovered many techniques that were uniquely cinematic. Yet, like the Lumière brothers and other contemporaries, he faced several important limitations: The smallest unit in his films was the scene rather than the shot; his camera sat in a fixed position like a spectator in a theater; and his range of visual composition was very narrow. The art of the silent film grew out of experimentation primarily in visual composition, camera movement, and editing. The results of these experiments were used to develop both conceptions of cinema— as an objective recording of sensory data and as a subjective expression of fantasy and illusion.

Experimentation was going on all over the world, but the major contributions came from the United States, the Soviet Union, Germany, and France. In the United States, the editing principle was introduced by Edwin S. Porter and developed by D. W. Griffith, both of whom used it for melodramatic effects. The Soviet filmmakers transformed American cutting, learned from Griffith, into dialectic montage, which reshaped experience and expressed a subjective vision, thus becoming a valuable technique for propaganda. Germany also made important strides in controlling point of view by experimenting with visual composition in expressionist films and with camera movement in realist films. The avant-garde movement in France launched the nonliterary film and used visual composition and editing to create analogies with painting, music, dance, and architecture. Thus, within a relatively short period, the silent cinema was established internationally as a respected new medium with a number of artful practitioners.

united states

Edwin S. Porter

A cameraman for the Edison Company, Porter was the first filmmaker after Méliès to take an important step in developing the art of cinema. The Edison catalogue of 1904 claimed that the aim of Porter's film *The Life of an American Fireman* (1902) was to portray the subject "without exaggeration and at the same time to embody the dramatic situations and spectacular effects which so greatly enhance a motion picture performance." As a way of fusing these two lines of action—the documentary footage of firemen on the job and the melodramatic situation of a woman and child threatened by the fire—Porter devised the technique of editing. Although he used it to adapt narrative conventions from literature and drama, editing enabled him to treat the shot, rather than the scene, as the basic cinematic unit, and to achieve motion not only within individual shots, as Méliès had done, but also in the continuity between them. His film demonstrated that one of the most important creative tasks in filmmaking would be the assembling of shots, taken at different locations at different times, into a continuous unified action.

The Great Train Robbery (1903) showed marked advances in editing technique. Instead of using dissolves, Porter introduced flat cuts that jumped directly from one scene to the next. More importantly, for the first time in films he used cross-cutting between two actions remote in space but simultaneous in time—bandits escaping and a telegraph operator being untied by his daughter. The camera work is much less impressive than the editing, yet Porter used panning quite effectively, as when some bandits are escaping down a hill.

To understand Porter's significance, it is helpful to compare his work with that of Méliès. Both have been credited with introducing the story film, but their stories were quite different, both in subject and in structure. Méliès' stories usually dealt with fantasy; Porter's represented common experience. Although the subject of *The Life of an American Fireman* was exciting and adventurous, Porter strove for realism by filming real firemen in their actual setting. All the scenes in *The Great Train Robbery* are contrived and rehearsed, yet the film contains shots of authentic locomotives. Although it was the first western, a genre that would develop many elements of fantasy and myth, these elements are not present in Porter's film.

To Méliès a story was a series of tableaux arranged in chronological order. The visual appeal of Porter's individual scenes could seldom rival that of Méliès, but by editing Porter effectively combined scenes to create a straightforward narrative lacking in Méliès' work. These differences in narrative structure imply different conceptions of experience. Méliès creates an unpredictable visual spectacle within conventionally limited space. His approach is linked to his conscious borrowings from magic and the stage. As the viewer sits in his theater seat and watches the rectangular screen, he sees a series of surprising illusions that expand his conception of reality. Méliès' approach implies that the visual texture—the way in which incidents are uniquely portrayed and experienced—is far more important than the incidents themselves or the way they fit into a conventional plot. It also implies that the viewer's mind should focus on the key moments in experience, having great pictorial value, which are then playfully elaborated. Méliès purposely frustrates conventional expectations: The usual causative links are omitted because they are irrelevant.

Porter's approach to film narrative is closely linked to the novel in its emphasis on time, causality, and details creating the illusion of reality. Porter assumes that verisimilitude will be achieved by creating and satisfying conventional expectations in the chronological development of common events.

Atlanta, which expand the scale of destruction and the sense of personal loss resulting from the war. Through his editing, Griffith emphasizes some important comparisons. The close-ups of the family juxtaposed with the long shots of the soldiers suggest the contrast between a personal view of war (which brings loss to individuals) and the historical overview (which reduces men to the scale of indistinguishable insects). He also contrasts the feminine principle—linked with fertility, emotion, and passivity—with the masculine—associated with action, movement, and destruction.

The homecoming scene, in which Ben Cameron returns to his family in the South after having been wounded and captured in the war, opens with a series of interior close shots of the house where the family is preparing for the celebration. Griffith cuts to a long shot of the exterior of the house, front yard, fence, and street—all shabby, empty, and waiting. The first sign of the returning son is his shadow, which we see on the left. He then appears in a long shot as a small, lone figure, tired and stooped,

Birth of a Nation

moving slowly forward along the fence and hesitating at the gate—only a shadow of what he had been before the war. Intercut with this image are contrasting close shots of the interior of the house where the family is cheerfully preparing for Ben's return. Finally the two scenes are joined when Ben meets his sister Flora on the steps. Without speaking a word, they experience a range of emotions: first a shy awkwardness, then joy at the meeting and laughter at their attire, then a moment of sadness when they both acknowledge the shabbiness and destruction around them, and finally a passionate embrace, which heightens Ben's anger at the forces that have altered the Old South. With Flora's arms around him, he moves with her toward the front door. Another arm extends from within the house, touches Ben, embraces him around the neck, and brings him inside, where the camera does not follow. We know without being told that this arm belongs to his mother, who offers him the comfort and rest he so badly needs. The contrast between the two embraces is effective: Flora's embrace arouses the whole range of turbulent emotions growing out of the war, while his mother's is all-soothing. In this brilliant sequence Griffith has visually defined home in a variety of ways: in the exterior long shots as a physical dwelling that haunts the memory; in the interior close shots as a lively atmosphere of familiar domestic activity; and in the final shot as a mother's love and comforting embrace.

These scenes and several others (especially the battle scenes) are as impressive today as they were in 1915 when the film was released, for they successfully exploit the visual potentialities of cinema. Yet despite the considerable value of many sequences, *Birth of a Nation* does have serious weaknesses, many of which are linked to Griffith's literary sources. Contemporary audiences are usually shocked by his racism, saccharine sentimentality, and melodramatic characterization. Perhaps we can distinguish more clearly between the faults and values of the film by focusing on one central theme—the attraction of a forbidden love. Griffith supported the Southern myth that the Confederates were fighting the Civil War to save their women from rape by repeatedly showing black men lusting after white women. This theme is fully developed in two parallel incidents involving two couples—Silas Lynch and Elsie Stoneman and Gus and Flora Cameron. Lynch, the mulatto lieutenant governor of South Carolina during the Reconstruction period, wants to marry Elsie Stoneman. The encounter between them is bad melodrama with stereotyped characterization and exaggerated acting, though Lynch is potentially an interesting character. Because Lynch is a mulatto, Griffith could have had him combine black and white qualities and transcend the stereotype. He has been assured by Stoneman, Elsie's father, that he is the equal of any white man, and so he is justified in "aiming rather high." But, instead of granting Lynch the sympathy he seems to deserve on the film's own terms, Griffith's titles label him as "a traitor to his white patron and a greater traitor to his own people."

The parallel relationship between Gus, a renegade black, and Flora Cameron is more successfully handled, for Griffith develops its implications cinematically. One of those implications is that the gulf between Gus and Flora is not so great as that between Lynch and Elsie. In one sense, they are both childlike primitives—he because of uncontrollable lust and she because of her natural playfulness. From the very beginning she is seen as a flighty little creature, running and jumping, unable to suppress her excitement and enthusiasm. Although we see her undergo the transformation to young womanhood, her childlike spirit is undiminished. He, like all blacks in the film, is a child with evil passions and impulses who must be controlled by his white superiors; once he is given his freedom and told he is equal, his impulses run wild. This similarity is expressed visually in the scene that first brings them together. In the foreground Flora is jumping about and embracing Elsie; lurking in the background between the trunks of two trees, with the sun glistening overhead, Gus resembles a wild animal stalking his prey. Later, when Flora goes to the spring alone, she is breaking her brother's rule; she is distracted from her task by a squirrel, who is as playful and innocent as she. Her flight from Gus is the instinctive act of a frightened little creature, and her suicide is impulsive. The chase is presented mainly as physical movement, in contrast to Lynch's more verbal and sophisticated pursuit of Elsie. Although this incident is more filmic than the one between Lynch and Elsie, both are based on a prejudiced view of the black, and both develop the theme of forbidden love into a conflict between evil (lust) and good (honor), between black and white.

The theme of forbidden love is also central to the union between the North and the South, but it is treated quite differently. Instead of a conflict between irreconcilable opposites, it is a choice between positive values temporarily at odds because of an unnatural separation. The theme is again dramatized in two sets of parallel relationships—between Phil Stoneman and Margaret Cameron and between Ben Cameron and Elsie Stoneman. Although these couples are natural pairs, their union is temporarily forbidden by the circumstances of war, which demands their patriotism and loyalty to family honor. In both situations, reunion results from a common struggle against the true natural enemy, the black man, or, to quote the titles, "The former enemies of North and South are united again in common defense of their Aryan birthright." The ride of the Klan brings an identical solution to both plots; the final parade demonstrates the harmonious reconciliation of love, family, country, and honor and brings about the reunion of the two pairs of white lovers.

In analyzing this theme, we have seen that Griffith continually employs contrast. This dualism exists not only in the plot structure and in the construction of individual scenes such as Sherman's march but, as Eisenstein later emphasized, also in the cross-cutting or parallel montage. It is also revealed in Griffith's unsuccessful attempt to blend factual history (frequently represented by static tableau facsimiles of actual events) with a melodramatic plot. A throwback to Méliès, the tableaux work against the fusion, for the titles that provide the audience with the pertinent historical data set these staged scenes apart instead of integrating them with the fictional story. Whether such an approach could ever adequately handle the complexities of the Civil War is questionable. However, what distinguishes *Birth of a Nation* from Griffith's other films is that in it he developed innovations specifically suited to express a dualistic conception of the world.

the soviet union

The rise of the Russian film was linked to the 1917 Revolution, a connection realized not only by the filmmakers but also by Lenin, who in 1918 observed, "Of all the arts, the cinema is the most important for us." [2] In the following year he transferred the entire photo and cinema industry to the People's Commissariat of Education, putting it in charge of organization and materials. Thus from the beginning of the new regime there was an awareness that film could be an important political tool, that it could serve

[2] For more detailed information about the political background of cinema in the Soviet Union see Jay Leyda, *Kino: A History of the Russian and Soviet Film* (New York: Macmillan, 1960); Paul Babitsky and John Rimberg, *The Soviet Film Industry* (New York: Praeger, 1955); and George A. Huaco, *The Sociology of Film Art* (New York: Basic Books, 1965).

the masses by documenting their struggle and shaping their political beliefs.

Dziga Vertov and Lev Kuleshov were particularly important in preparing the way for the important contributions that were to come from Soviet cinema between 1925 and 1930. Vertov helped to realize Lenin's beliefs by organizing a group of filmmakers who shot footage at the front during the civil war in an attempt to keep the people informed. Gradually he developed *Kino-Eye,* a theory rejecting the fiction film and arguing that the main function of cinema is to record every step toward socialism and every fact needing public attention. He initiated *Kino-Pravda,* a weekly newsreel, which put his theory into practice. Kuleshov was important for his technical contributions to editing. Founding a film school in Moscow (whose students included V. I. Pudovkin), he studied Griffith's cutting techniques in *Intolerance* and conducted experiments that demonstrated the importance of editing in creating meaning. He took a shot of an actor's face and paired it with three different images: a bowl of soup, a coffin, and a child with a toy bear. Although the shot of the actor's face was in each case the same, viewers swore that his expressions in the three scenes were different and that he was a great actor. Each piece of unedited film has two possible meanings: its meaning in isolation and its meaning in relationship to other pieces of film. An important extension of Griffith's steps toward montage, this was the most important contribution of Russian cinema.

Montage, a French word meaning "mounting" or "putting together," was adopted by Sergei Eisenstein to describe the Russian conception of editing. He wanted to distinguish it from "the American cut," which referred primarily to the cross-cutting techniques the Russians had studied so carefully in Griffith's *Intolerance.* Most simply, montage is the technique by which a filmmaker combines individual shots so that the effect of the whole is greater than the sum of its parts. It is a combination that leads to a creative remolding of experience rather than an objective recording of reality.

Eisenstein linked montage with the Russian Revolution of 1917. We can see this by examining his analysis of how Soviet montage differed from Griffith's cross-cutting:

> Montage thinking is inseparable from the general content of thinking as a whole. The structure that is reflected in the concept of Griffith's montage is the structure of bourgeois society. . . . And this society, perceived only as a contrast

21

between the haves and the have-nots, is reflected in the consciousness of Griffith no deeper than the image of an intricate race between two parallel lines. . . . He is the greatest master of "parallel montage"—montage constructions that have been created in a direct-line quickening and increase of tempo. His is a school of tempo rather than of affective rhythm. True rhythm presupposes above all organic unity.[3]

While Griffith's "parallel montage" expresses a dualistic view, Soviet montage is based on a world view that is both monistic and dialectical. Contrasting images (thesis and antithesis) lead to a new organic synthesis. The result is monistic, the process dialectical. Eisenstein argues that Griffith's editing technique remains on a level of juxtaposition and quantitative accumulation, that there is no new quality created out of the whole. Thus Griffith is also limited to representation because his combinations of images merely "show" or "present," whereas in the Soviet Union they "signify, designate or give meaning." According to Eisenstein, the unique contribution of Soviet montage is "a means of achieving a unity of higher order—a means through the montage image of achieving an organic embodiment of a single idea conception, embracing all elements, parts, details of the film-work."[4]

Montage was also revolutionary in another sense. In stressing the primacy of the visual image and the individual shot as the basic unit, those who used it were consciously rebelling against cinema's dependency on the theater and literature. They were consciously valuing cinema for its newness because this would make it an appropriate medium to express the values of a new society. And just as the unique values of that society had to be distinguished from the corrupt values of capitalism, cinema had to discover its unique potentialities apart from its roots in other media. Montage was one potentiality—particularly dialectical montage, which was naturally linked to the dialectical materialism of Marx and Engels.

Interestingly, Eisenstein traced the Soviet idea of dialectical montage back to the montage structure of Griffith's literary sources—Dickens' novel *Oliver Twist,* Walt Whitman's poetry, and American melodrama. He acknowledged that montage, the essential cinematic resource, was basically rooted in literature:

Let this past be a reproach to those thoughtless people who have displayed arrogance in reference to literature,

[3] Sergei Eisenstein, "Dickens, Griffith, and the Film Today," *Film Form: Essays in Film Theory* (Cleveland: World, 1957), pp. 234–35.
[4] *Ibid.,* p. 254.

which has contributed so much to this apparently un-
precedented art and is in the first and most important
place: the art of viewing—not only the eye, but viewing—
both meanings being embraced in this term. . . . This esthetic growth from the cinematographic eye to the image
of an embodied viewpoint on phenomena was one of
the most serious processes of development of our Soviet
cinema in particular.[5]

Typically, Eisenstein insists on the inseparability of form and content, an assumption basic to the Soviet idea of montage. Although Soviet cinema grew out of documentary rather than the
fiction film, it rejected the idea that the primary function of film
was to record external reality objectively. Rather, its goal was to
reshape reality creatively through montage and, by doing so, to
help reshape society. This was its revolutionary mission. To demonstrate these characteristics, we will examine Eisenstein's
Battleship Potemkin (1925), which was commissioned by the government to commemorate the abortive 1905 revolution.

BATTLESHIP POTEMKIN (1925)

Instead of having a dramatic plot, *Battleship Potemkin* is divided
into five separate sections, each titled and numbered, covering
five incidents in chronological order. Considered in isolation,
each incident appears to be a minor act of rebellion against authority: a complaint against eating maggoty meat, which leads
to rebellion; a refusal to shoot fellow sailors, which leads to mutiny; a procession of mourners who pay respect to a dead sailor,
which leads to a massive demonstration; a massacre of people on
the Odessa steps, which leads the *Potemkin* to fire on military
headquarters; and, finally, a decision by another ship to join the
Potemkin mutiny, which ultimately leads to revolution. When
combined in this order, the incidents create a pattern of escalat-
ing revolution, a tiny stream that builds into an immense flood
that is impossible to stop. The flood is hastened by corrupt authority. The initial refusal to eat the spoiled meat is minor and at
first seems apolitical. But this mild protest elicits an extreme
over-reaction from the authorities—the decision to kill many men
—which, in turn, radicalizes large numbers and makes them join
in more extreme revolutionary action. This conception of how a
revolution grows is embodied in the structure of the film. Not

[5] *Ibid.*

only the division into five episodes but all the film's structural components are concerned with an accelerating relationship between the one and the many.

Although Eisenstein rejects the individual hero and focuses on collective mass action, the rebellion is initiated by the actions of one man, Vakulinchuk the sailor, who is killed in battle and whose dead body becomes the rallying point for the masses. Collectivity is shown in recurring imagery. Shots of people gathering to pay homage suggest a flowing stream. In a shot of the empty steps, the two sides of the screen are blocked out in order to emphasize the vertical line (like a shot in *Intolerance*); then there is a dissolve to an image of the steps covered with crowds of people. People are moving in all directions, horizontally crossing a bridge, vertically forward along the water. The steady addition of bodies and directions of motion also creates a feeling of escalation or crescendo.

The principle of the one leading to the many is best expressed in Eisenstein's masterful use of montage, which is most brilliantly employed in the Odessa steps sequence. In the original scenario for the film, Odessa was to be the location of a strike after the *Potemkin* mutiny, a minor episode that was to consist of only forty-two shots. But once Eisenstein saw the steps, he decided to make the *Potemkin* mutiny the central episode. He prepared for the sequence very carefully, building a camera trolley along the steps and using several cameras simultaneously, strapping one to the waist of an assistant who was falling down the steps. He knew from the beginning that the full effect of the sequence would be created by editing and thus made sure that he had all the elements necessary to express the maximum conflict. The overall experience is comprised of many individual shots. Eisenstein constantly cuts back and forth between various scenes and various angles, leading to an effect of confusion, panic, and disorientation, suggesting that many more unseen atrocities are taking place. A conflict between peace and violence is suggested by a shot of a parasol just before the violence begins. The cutting moves back and forth between individuals—a mother and her child, a baby in a carriage, a woman whose glasses are smashed—and the masses of people; between the orderly, synchronized soldiers who move like one great machine and the disorderly movements and confusion of the human beings they are slaughtering. Within individual shots, there is a play between light and shadow, between vertical and horizontal lines, between a slow-motion fall and the rapid scrambling of a fleeing cripple.

Battleship Potemkin

The arrangement and accelerating pace of these fragments, to-gether with the beauty of composition, create one of the most powerful sequences on film.

In response to the massacre, the *Potemkin* fires on the military headquarters. This action is followed by three shots of stone lions—one sleeping, the second awakening, and the third rising. Here we have a relatively simple example of dialectical montage —the contrast among the three positions of the lions, between the implied motion and the stationary quality of the marble forms, and between the literal and symbolic meanings. The parts are merely three shots of three statues, but the sum or effect of the whole is a synthesis creating the new idea that the stone lion is leaping up to protest against the firing. Again, it is the principle of the one and the many.

Comparison of Griffith's and Eisenstein's use of editing dem-onstrates how the same basic technique can be used in different ways to express quite different conceptions of experience. Both *Birth of a Nation* and *Battleship Potemkin* have political themes. Griffith used editing in an essentially apolitical and melodramatic way, whereas Eisenstein transformed it into a political tool to ex-press a revolutionary idea.

germany

During the 1920's, Germany experienced a golden age of cinema that experimented with point of view, mainly through visual com-position and camera movement. The movement had two significant parts, expressionism and realism, each concerned with the relationship between subjective vision and external sensory data, each linked to a movement in the related art of painting, and each emphasizing one aspect of cinema's dual nature.

The Expressionist Film

The expressionist film, which was dominant from 1919 to 1924, experimented with sets, visual composition, and lighting to express a subjective reality. On the surface, such films are concerned with madness, identity, and evil, but they also have implications about society. Expressionism was, of course, not limited to cinema but was current in painting, literature, and drama. Essentially, it focuses on the subjective inner world as expressed through distortions of external reality. Hence, point of view is extremely important. Cinema was a particularly good medium for this movement because it had so many potentialities for distortion. Expressionist films were shot inside a studio, with stylized, painted sets (like those of Méliès) that usually incorporated the distorted forms of expressionist painting. Lighting techniques created tension between light and shadow, sometimes evoking fear. Acting style, make-up, and costumes all tended to be highly stylized and exaggerated. Human figures were frequently arranged into meaningful but abstract visual patterns. A film would usually have at least one or two recurring visual images that might take on symbolic implications. Sometimes camera tricks such as superimposition were used to create supernatural effects, as in *Nosferatu* (1922), but technical innovations with the camera itself were rare. In their concern with the set, geometric form, and light and shadow, the expressionist films of this period strengthened cinema's ability to make purely visual and symbolic nondiscursive statements.

THE CABINET OF DR. CALIGARI (1919)

The first and probably the best expressionist film was *The Cabinet of Dr. Caligari*. The story of its genesis is particularly interesting, for it confirms the expressionist idea that art is based on the emotional experience of an individual. The original idea grew out of separate personal experiences of the two writers, Hans Janowitz and Carl Mayer. One day in Hamburg, Janowitz's attention was attracted by a pretty young girl with a typically bourgeois gentleman. Later he saw the man emerging alone from a wooded area. Shortly afterward, when Janowitz read in the newspaper of a horrible sex crime, he realized that he had seen both the victim and the murderer. This experience haunted him and became the "seed" of the film, but it also needed "the mother who conceived and ripened it."[6] According to Janowitz, this role was performed by Mayer. While in the First World War, Mayer had psychological difficulties and developed a strong hatred for the military psychiatrist who was in charge of his case. After the war, he met Janowitz and they shared their feelings against the war and authority. One night, they went to a side show together, the setting of which provided the coalescing element for their story.

Erich Pommer, the head of Decla Studios, assigned the story to director Robert Wiene and three designers—Hermann Warm, Walther Reimann, and Walther Röhrig—all of whom were affiliated with the Berlin Sturm group, which advocated expressionism for all art forms. The painted sets were covered with jagged Gothic forms, which created an ominous environment. Painted shadows on the canvases contrasted with the lighting effects and created additional tension.

The original story was about Francis, a young man who suspects Dr. Caligari and his somnambulist Cesare (played by Conrad Veidt), who are appearing at a local fair, of murdering his best friend Alan and the town clerk. While Francis is watching Caligari, Cesare kidnaps Jane, Francis' fiancée. Francis pursues Caligari to a mental institution, where he learns that the doctor, the chief psychiatrist, is trying to revive the ancient myth of a priest named Caligari, who gained power through murders committed by his somnambulist. When the psychiatrist is confronted with the dead body of Cesare, he goes mad and is confined in a strait jacket. The distortions of the film seem to reflect an evil world headed by corrupt authority. Caligari appears to be a criminally insane tyrant who is supported by social institutions (the church in the ancient myth and the asylum in the contemporary setting). But Wiene and Pommer added a frame at the beginning and end of the story, changing the function and meaning of the distortions. The frame opens with Francis' telling his story to a man (the listener) who has just finished telling one of his own. The ending reveals that Francis (along with the listener, Jane,

[6] Siegfried Kracauer, *From Caligari to Hitler: A Psychological History of the German Film* (Princeton, N.J.: Princeton University Press, 1947), p. 63.

27

The Cabinet of Dr. Caligari

and Cesare) is an inmate in the asylum headed by Dr. Caligari, who altruistically wants to cure him.

The visual distortion in *Caligari* represents not a society marked by corruption and chaos, but the subjective vision of a demented mind. The entire film, except for the frame, is developed from Francis' distorted perspective, implying a subjective use of the camera. Yet there is some question about whether the altered version is really so conventional. As Kracauer has pointed out, despite the shift to a safe view of authority, the film has revolutionary implications: "Even though Caligari had become a conformist film, it preserved and emphasized this revolutionary story—as a madman's fantasy. Caligari's defeat now belonged among psychological experiences." [7]

Throughout the film there is a conflict between the rational explanation of the frame and the inner vision, which has the more powerful emotional impact on the viewer and is presented in the expressionist style. The meaning of the film is in part created by this conflict. In fact, there are two conflicting views of practically every character and incident in the film. The most obvious example is, of course, Caligari. In the frame, he is a respectable authority figure, but Francis sees his hidden side as tyrant

[7] *Ibid.,* p. 67.

28

and madman. This conflict is best expressed in a scene where Francis get Caligari's assistant to help him seek the truth. While Caligari is peacefully sleeping, Francis and the others probe his mind by going through his diary—again, the split between the external and the inner man. Francis and Caligari are linked—one is the victim and the other the persecutor—but the assignment of role depends on one's point of view.

This doubleness applies to the other major characters. Cesare, for example, is victim and murderer, seer and madman; he arouses both pity and fear in the viewer. When Francis is watching the box containing the dummy while the real Cesare is kidnaping Jane, there is again a conflict between misleading external appearance and the acting out of inner impulse. The dummy in the box is analogous to the sleeping Caligari in the asylum and the external Calagari in the frame of the movie. Because Francis is fooled by this dummy, he refuses to believe that Cesare was Jane's kidnaper and begins to think Jane is having hallucinations, a doubt confirmed by the frame, which reveals that Jane is an inmate of the asylum. Similarly, when the viewer sees Caligari in the frame story, he comes to doubt Francis' sanity.

Other minor characters who have this doubleness are the town clerk, the criminal, and the listener. The town clerk is both a tyrant and a victim of Caligari. The criminal, who is unjustly accused of the murder, is both an aggressive criminal and an innocent victim trapped by authority. The doubleness of the listener is more complicated. At the beginning of the frame, we have no idea that Francis is in an asylum, and so we tend to identify with the listener, for we, too, are hearing Francis tell his story. But at the end, when we learn that he is also an inmate, the film begins to suggest that this doubleness might apply to us. As Kracauer has pointed out, the setting in the final scene of the frame story, which supposedly restores the normal perspective, remains visually distorted as before and thereby raises the question of whether the distortions represent only Francis' subjective view.

This tension between two possible views of the characters is also expressed visually in the contrast between black and white: between Jane's stark white face and her black eyes and hair; between Cesare's skeletal white face and black leotard; between the black shadows and the white walls, streets, and sky. There is also a conflict between the shadows painted on the sets, which seem to come from the inner world, and the shadows cast by the external lighting. Threatening diagonals and verticals with their

29

sharp points and angles contrast with safe, self-enclosed circles, usually associated with unity and eternity. Kracauer quite arbitrarily links the circle with chaos, particularly in the carnival sequence. The carnival appears to be a place of fun, but murder and grotesque horror lurk beneath its surface. The circular movements of the organ grinder and the merry-go-round belie the danger of the underlying angles. The circle pattern, however, is not confined to the fair, as Kracauer seems to imply, but is one of the dominant shapes in Jane's home. One scene opens with a circular iris shot, which sharply contrasts with the strong verticals of the previous scene. The one scene in which the circle is not associated with Jane's house occurs when Cesare enters through the sharply vertical windows and breaks the circle of security. The pattern of the frame story is circular; it encloses the inner narrative and provides a safe, self-contained explanation. The scene that perhaps best illustrates the conflict between geometric shapes occurs when Francis arrives at the asylum. He is standing on a small circle with verticals projecting outward to form the spokes of a much larger circle. The ambiguity of the asylum and of the minds within it is reflected in this combination of shapes. Francis is unsure whether the asylum is a safe place or a hostile prison. This ambiguity lies at the heart of the film and at the heart of its attitude toward society, skillfully expressed through visual means and through a carefully controlled point of view.

The Realist Film

Unlike expressionist films, realist films (dominant between 1921 and 1929) focus on the external world. They are full of real objects and textures; they show a new interest in the social setting, particularly of the lower middle class. Kracauer and others have linked this change to *die neue Sachlichkeit* (the new objectivity), a term coined by Gustav Hartlaub in 1924 to describe the new realism in painting that followed expressionism. He felt that the positive side of this movement was expressed in an "enthusiasm for the immediate reality as a result of the desire to take things entirely objectively on a material basis without immediately investing them with ideal implications." [8] Yet the objects in these new realistic films were full of psychological, as well as social and political, implications.

The camera begins to move through space like a person, shift-

[8] Letter from Gustav Hartlaub, quoted in Kracauer, p. 165.

ing its focus and angle. It becomes identified with the actor rather than with a detached spectator. Suddenly the cinema had a new means of expressing a subjective point of view, not through distortions of setting or ~~visual tricks, as in the expressionist films, but~~ through the "natural" movement of the camera. The subjective view was no longer limited to fantasy or aberration but was compatible with cinematic rather than theatrical realism. Although these films were also shot within the studio, the sets were realistic rather than fantastic or obviously artificial. The acting, make-up, and costumes were less stylized. In every respect, sensitivity to the camera and to its ability to record subtlety was greater.

p. 36.

We will examine these characteristics in two films—*The Last Laugh,* directed by F. W. Murnau and written by Carl Mayer, who wrote several of the best realist and expressionist films of the period, and *The Love of Jeanne Ney,* directed by G. W. Pabst, one of the most important directors to emerge from this movement.

THE LAST LAUGH (1924)

A simple story with few characters, *The Last Laugh* is set in a working-class world. The hero (played by Emil Jannings) is an old man whose neighbors admire him as long as he has his job as doorman at a nearby palatial hotel and as long as he wears the uniform that symbolizes his position. But when the hotel manager decides that the hero is too old to handle large trunks and demotes him to lavatory attendant, making him exchange his glorious uniform for a white coat, his world is destroyed and he loses his self-respect and the respect of his neighbors.

Since both *The Last Laugh* and *Caligari* were written by Carl Mayer, it is valuable to compare them. Mayer's realist films—*Backstairs, Shattered, New Year's Eve,* and *The Last Laugh*—were all written between 1921 and 1924. Unlike the later films of this movement, they tend to share many characteristics with expressionism. Usually they explore the psychological effects of the external world on a human personality. Like *Caligari, The Last Laugh* was shot entirely within a studio. The sets by Robert Herlth and Walther Röhrig (who also worked on *Caligari*), though not fantastic, were exaggerated slightly to emphasize the vast difference between the drab, monotonous working-class tenement and the splendor of the luxurious hotel, the two poles in the old man's world, reconciled only by a glorious uniform that gave him access to and respect in both.

The universe of this film, defined spatially by the hotel and the tenement, is as narrow as that in *Caligari.* Time is concretized in changing light and shadows creeping across buildings; rain is expressed by umbrellas and wet luggage and by the haste of people rushing into the hotel. The fall from power is localized in the move from the lobby to the basement restroom, in the change from the highly decorative uniform to a simple white coat. Outside world opinion is embodied in neighbors who are eager to attack and ridicule the fall of any authority figure. Making everything local and concrete gives the film its intensity and symbolic power.

Another similarity with *Caligari* is the psychological interest. Just as most of *Caligari* is seen through Francis' eyes, most of *Last Laugh* is presented from the old man's point of view. At times, distortion achieves this. There is a scene where the camera whirls around when the old man is drunk, and in another scene the walls of the hotel seem to be pursuing him as he runs away in terror. But throughout most of the film, point of view is achieved by the camera's moving freely and naturally through sets built especially to allow mobility through corridors and down steps, into rooms, and in an elevator. Though the common goal of both expressionistic and realistic films is to reveal the subjective state, the movement of the camera in the new realist films frees them from dependence upon distortion, creating a greater appearance of disinterest.

As he did with *Caligari,* Erich Pommer, the producer, insisted on adding an ending to *Last Laugh* that would substantially alter it. This time it was a happy ending: The old man inherits a million dollars from an American patron whom he had attended in the lavatory. In 1962, Pommer explained that he convinced Mayer to add this ending only after ten conferences. Pommer's motive was clear and familiar:

> We added the happy ending because without it the film would have been too much like real life, and would have been a commercial failure. After the war, many former businessmen, kings, etc. were occupying menial jobs. What is left if you take the uniform away from a general? Nothing. The head porter was the most important man in the hotel. This was the story of thousands and thousands of people in Germany to whom this had happened. But the audience did not catch on. The happy ending said: by chance, tomorrow you might go up again.[9]

Although this may have been Pommer's motive, his statement is

[9] Huaco, pp. 55–56.

certainly not the last word on how this sequence functions in the film. The ending is introduced by the only title in the film, a note from the author explaining that he is going to lead the old man to a better, though unreal, future because he pities the fate he would meet in *real* life. On one level, it parodies the unrealistic happy endings found in American movies. The millionaire who leaves the money is, significantly, an American. Second, the shift in the film's tone to farce and comedy is analogous to the disintegration of the old man's personality. In going from realism to fantasy in a film where the point of view is primarily identified with the central character, that shift must also imply something about his consciousness. Third, we might relate the ending to the historical background. The old man is a working-class figure who desires authority and superiority over his peers. His neighbors both respect and hate him because they would like to take his place as an authority figure. This pattern is expressed by the ending; the fantasy demands not the destruction of the system but rather a simple reversal of roles to put the lowly on top. As in *Caligari,* the attitude is both revolutionary and conformist, implying that the German hates not the system but only his position within it. The pattern supports Kracauer's description of the ambivalent attitude of the middle class toward those in power.

Films like *The Last Laugh* also differed from the expressionist films in their relationship to events in the real world. As Huaco has pointed out, and as Pommer has confirmed, this film is linked to a specific period in history: "After the elections of May 6, 1924, the right-wing Nationalist party captured the largest number of seats in the Weimar Parliament. This was the year in which reparation payments were nationalized through the Dawes Plan, and there was a massive influx of U.S. investment funds." [10] If the old man is associated with former businessmen, kings, and generals (as Pommer suggests), then his restoration to power by means of American aid seems to be a significant parallel to contemporary events. But the farcical treatment seems to suggest a cynical attitude. As Kracauer concludes: "Through its second ending the film underscores the significance of its first one, and moreover rejects the idea that the 'decline of the West' could be remedied by the blessings of the West." [11]

Although one can find ironic justifications for the ending, one should not forget that Mayer was forced to add it. It jars the audience primarily because it shifts the mode of reality, and this is

[10] *Ibid.,* p. 56.
[11] Kracauer, p. 101.

an effective reminder of the essential difference between the conceptions of experience expressed in *Caligari* and in *Last Laugh.* The frame of *Caligari* futilely tries to restore normalcy to a totally distorted world; the ending of *The Last Laugh* tries to distort the normal. Both attempts are jarring and at least partially unsuccessful for reasons that do credit to each film. The world view of each is expressed cinematically with such power that it is impossible to reverse it at the last minute.

THE LOVE OF JEANNE NEY (1927)

G. W. Pabst was one of the most important filmmakers to emerge from the realist movement. He came from the theater, like Griffith, and was unfortunately influenced by melodrama. Yet he turned out to be perhaps the most cinematic German director of his time. Although he made important innovations in camera movement, his most impressive achievement was his ability to synthesize the potentialities of cinema developed to that time—editing, composition, and camera movement—in order to express visually a more complex view of the world.

Like Mayer, Pabst used external details with psychological implications—with an important difference. Where *Last Laugh* portrays the influence of the external world on personality, the richness of external details in the films of Pabst gives insight into character; these details evoke a complex view of reality that is large in scope and subtle in its political and psychological implications. These qualities suggest a comparison with the work of Antonioni and Resnais.

The Love of Jeanne Ney, Pabst's best silent film, presents European postwar society on a scale larger than that of any other German film of the period. Based on a novel by Ilya Ehrenberg, the plot is melodramatic, but the visual treatment is brilliant. It presents a world full of particulars. Rooms are crowded with people and things; they have interior recesses and a sense of depth. They are linked to the outside world by details such as the wind entering through a crack in the door. The exterior shots are full of people, vehicles, and movement. Yet among all these particulars, Pabst always leads his audience to focus on the important details, primarily through the close-up. The film is full of marvelous faces, even in the smallest roles. Close-ups of hands and eyes are particularly important in revealing character—the exploring hands of a blind girl, her prime means of making contact with a strange and frightening world; the expressive hands of a woman who comes to warn the blind girl that Kalibiev is going to strangle her; the hypocritical hands of Kalibiev, sensuous and possessive although hidden in genteel gloves. Although Kalibiev is basically the stereotyped villain of melodrama, Pabst gives him another dimension through the visual details that surround him. In the opening shot, he is in a cluttered room; the general state of disorder and specific objects like the obscene cigarette holder reveal his slovenliness and lust. When we later see him foppishly dressed in new clothes, we understand his hypocrisy. But we respect his intelligence; he is observant, always noticing the details in the room, taking advantage of whatever opportunities arise. Throughout the film, we always sense the presence of a masterful control, an omniscient perspective that leads us through this world full of particulars, making sure that we observe what is important and interpret it correctly.

As in the films of Antonioni, the physical arrangement of characters in *Jeanne Ney* frequently tells a great deal about their rela-

The Love of Jeanne Ney

tionship. The best example is the parting between Jeanne and her lover after the death of her father: Pabst visually expresses the distance between them. In the first shot, the lover is standing in the rain, the stark composition of the image powerfully emphasizing his desolation. When the couple meets, the surroundings of smoke, ruins, rubble, and rain are just as crucial in creating the emotional tone of the scene as the expressions on their faces. They stand apart, limp and immobile, as if gaining strength for the embrace. As they move toward each other, other people walk between them, delaying the meeting.

Control is also present in camera angle and movement. For example, in an overhead shot in the bar the camera looks down on the crowded room, and part of a banister provides a diagonal line across the composition. The line seems almost to point, from this overview, to the significant details of the decadent scene below. There is a shot in the cathedral where the omniscient camera looks down from the altar at Jeanne and her lover. As the lovers walk out into the sunlight, the camera remains in the darkness of the cathedral so that their outlines are silhouetted against the light. The camera movements frequently involve considerable complexity. In one of the shots in the bar, the camera moves to the left while the people are moving horizontally to the right, thereby creating tension and a sense of complex and varied motion. When the eyes of Jeanne and her lover first meet after he helps to kill her father, there is a rapid pan between close-ups of their two faces before a cut to a flashback of their past. In this scene the fast panning helps to suggest the sudden flood of emotions that the lovers must be experiencing. In another meeting between them, tracking shots are combined with effective editing to create one of the best scenes in the film. Jeanne is in a car moving horizontally to the right with the camera tracking behind her. Then the film cuts to a tracking shot of her lover running horizontally to the left. The cross-cutting between the two accelerates in pace, building the emotional tension, until finally they meet and move vertically forward.

One of Pabst's most important contributions was a subtle blending of camera movement and editing. Previously, editing had been used to develop the expressive aspects of film rather than its potential for documentary. Porter used it to fuse documentary with an artificially constructed fictional plot, Griffith to express his dualistic world view, and Eisenstein to reshape experience. In each of these instances, juxtaposition gave the artist opportunity to ex-

36

The Love of Jeanne Ney

press his vision. Although Pabst effectively employed this kind of editing, he also developed a new editing principle that is capable of producing considerable verisimilitude but is not dependent on unadulterated "realism." In the scene where Kalibiev sells the list of Bolshevist agents to Jeanne's father, there are forty cuts within three minutes, yet the audience is hardly aware of any of them. Pabst achieved such fluid and unobtrusive movement by cutting during a physical movement or gesture. In that way, the audience's attention would be focused on the movement that was carried over into the next shot and thus would hardly notice that a cut was taking place. Although this technique might contribute to the illusion of verisimilitude, it actually allowed the filmmaker greater selective emphasis by increasing the fragmentation of the scene.

While making skillful use of the cinematic techniques developed by the masters who had preceded him, Pabst offered film the means of expressing a richer, subtler, more mature view of human experience. The richness of detail enhanced the potentiality of the camera as a recorder of objective reality, but Pabst's uniquely effective camera angles, movement, and editing allowed omnis-

37

cient control of emphasis and tone. Thus he was able to draw on both sources of cinematic richness; he could offer his audience a controlled and complex interpretation of events without denying or minimizing the camera's great realistic power.

france

The first conscious attempt to make "art" films occurred in France in 1907. A company called Film d'Art produced films featuring great stars of the French stage such as Sarah Bernhardt. This attempt was doomed because the company tried to film stage plays, and hence the films were seriously restricted by the conventions of the theater and by lack of sound. But the attempt shows that from cinema's inception French artists in other media looked to it as a serious art form. A later movement was successful. The avant-garde cinema, a period of filmmaking from 1921 to 1931, centered in Paris, drew people from all over Europe to take part in the movement: Max Ophuls from Germany, Alberto Cavalcanti from Italy, Luís Buñuel and Salvador Dali from Spain, and Carl Dreyer from Denmark. Many of the best films were made by artists famous in other media, especially painting, who were trying to apply their experiments in cubism, futurism, expressionism, surrealism, and dada to the new medium.

The experimentation in this movement was based on assumptions about cinema that contradicted those underlying other films being produced at that time. One was that a film should be the personal expression of an individual artist rather than the product of a commercial industry. Like Méliès and the German expressionists, avant-garde filmmakers rejected the notion that the primary function of the camera was to record external reality. In rejecting literary and dramatic analogies, they also avoided the conventional notion of plot. Instead, they stressed perception. They forced their audiences to watch what was on the screen—not its symbolic meaning but its visual form and the actual patterns of movement. Although they frequently considered their own films "pure" or "absolute" and felt that they, unlike those who relied heavily on literary conventions, were developing the unique qualities of cinema, they were actually creating new analogies to painting, music, dance, and architecture. We will explore these qualities as they appear in Léger's *Ballet Mécanique*, Buñuel and Dali's *Un Chien Andalou*, and Dreyer's *Passion of Joan of Arc*.

BALLET MÉCANIQUE (1924)

When Fernand Léger, the cubist painter, turned to cinema, he was consciously trying to extend the experimentation of his painting: "In this medium I worked as I had done before in painting. To create the rhythm of common objects in space and time, to present them in their plastic beauty, this seemed to me worthwhile, this was the origin of my *Ballet Mécanique.*" [12] But he also realized that cinema had something new to offer. Since the camera itself was a machine, it had a new capacity for expressing through composition and editing the fragmentation that was an essential element in the new reality of the mechanical age:

> The war had thrust me, as a soldier, into the heart of a mechanical atmosphere. In this atmosphere I discovered the beauty of the fragment. I sensed a *new* reality in the detail of a machine, in the common object. I tried to find the plastic value of these fragments of our modern life. I rediscovered them on the Screen in the close-ups of objects, which impressed and influenced me. [13]

In *Ballet Mécanique,* Léger transforms common objects into pure visual form and mechanical motion. The images, all moving, can be divided into four categories: abstract forms (geometric shapes such as triangles and circles, numbers, letters), machines (gears and pistons), common objects (bottles and pots), and human beings. By treating all these in the same way, without arranging them in any hierarchical order, and by stripping them of their conceptual meaning and function, Léger forces his audience to perceive their *visual* relationships. The techniques of repetition and fragmentation facilitate this process. By constantly repeating the image of a woman walking upstairs, Léger makes the viewer forget she is a human being. Since she never reaches the top of the stairs, we cease to think of the narrative possibilities of the image (who she is, where she is going, when she will get there, why she is going there, and so on) and instead concentrate on the rhythm of her motion or on the visual relationship between the vertical stripes of her blouse, the horizontal lines of the stairs, and the diagonal lines of the brick wall on her right. We see only what Léger wants us to see, which he controls through his selection of camera angle, composition, and editing pace. By presenting only part of an object, such as an extreme close-up of a smiling mouth

[12] Léger, quoted in Arthur Knight, *The Liveliest Art* (New York: New American Library, 1959), p. 102.
[13] *Ibid.*

Ballet Mécanique

or blinking eye, he forces his audience to perceive it in a new context, as an autonomous object having its own composition and motion. We no longer think of the mouth or the eye as part of a human being who exists in the real world, or even as part of a face; it becomes an object as self-contained as a bottle, with a motion as regular as a pendulum, with a form as abstract as the circle or the triangle, existing on a two-dimensional screen.

Léger presents a world in which the presence of the camera is always obvious, primarily because of his pervasive use of close-ups. The viewer is reminded that only by means of the camera is he able to see and analyze these objects and fragments from this new perspective. Léger reminds us that a machine is needed to reveal the mechanical aspects of experience, an idea underscored by the recurrent image of the blinking eye. When the camera follows the swinging pendulum, it forces the eye to participate in the mechanical dance. Léger's insistence on the filmic importance of objects and motion for their own sake reemphasizes cinema's purely visual possibilities and urges the medium toward greater freedom from sentiment and from narrative itself. This contribution to cinema was, of course, particularly appropriate for a point in time when civilization was moving rapidly toward mechanistic fragmentation with the same inevitability as Léger's own images.

UN CHIEN ANDALOU (1928)

Probably the most famous film to come out of the avant-garde movement, and certainly the one to arouse the most controversy, *Un Chien Andalou* was the product of a collaboration between Salvador Dali, the noted Spanish surrealist painter, and Luís Buñuel, who at that time was a young assistant director. They collaborated on the basic conception and on the screenplay, but Buñuel did the actual directing. In surrealistic painting, particularly in the work of Dali, there is an ironic incongruity between the precise literality of the style and the symbolic irrationality of the conception or subject. Although the subject is from the bizarre world of dreams (for example, a melting clock), it is presented in a style of photographic realism. Film offered the perfect medium for achieving this incongruity. The camera automatically recorded the external appearance of physical objects with a visual accuracy that far surpassed the capacity of painting, yet it could also present (mainly by means of the tricks discovered by Méliès) the irrational world of dreams.

Like *Ballet Mécanique*, *Un Chien Andalou* forces us to attend to what we actually see, boldly demonstrating that we cannot predict what will happen. In the opening sequence, a man (whom the knowing will recognize as Buñuel) is standing near a window sharpening his razor. He looks through the window and sees a cloud moving toward and eventually passing in front of the full moon. The man then takes the razor and slits open the eyeball of a young woman. The image is both visually and emotionally shocking, particularly because of the photographic realism. Understanding the image's relationship to the other elements of the sequence depends on acts of visual recognition: the recognition of Buñuel, the director, who is performing the action; the visual association between the angular cloud passing across the round moon and the long, narrow razor slitting the round eyeball (a visual pattern that recurs throughout the film). This image is like a prologue to the film, warning the viewer that it is going to assault his vision, force him to see in new ways, make him give up his conventional expectations, violate his senses—in short, it is going to open his eyes.

The rejection of conventional expectations and patterns is particularly important. Buñuel claims that *"Nothing* in this film *symbolizes anything."* He explains that he and Dali purposely rejected any idea or image that was derived from memory or from their cultural pattern or any that had conscious association with earlier ideas or images. They accepted as valid only the representations that, though profoundly moving, had no possible explanation. But

Un Chien Andalou

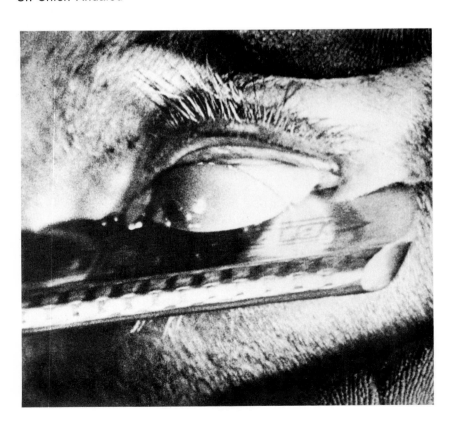

this argument does not necessarily deny that the film develops a pattern of its own—not an external pattern imposed onto the film, but one that can be derived from close attention to the specific images. This film evokes not the objective world of external reality but the bizarre subjective world of dreams. In order to discover the nature of this world, we must examine things such as the conception of time and space and the nature of the images.

Time is nonlinear. *Un Chien Andalou* begins with a title "once upon a time" as in a fairy tale (and in one sense this is a tale about a fairy) or myth, which immediately tells us that we should not expect verisimilitude. Practically all the titles refer to shifts in time, yet they do not function like conventional narrative links because they are not chronological. This device simultaneously parodies the conventional narrative plot in the literary film and evokes the nonrational time incongruities of the dream world. The incongruities of time are visual as well as verbal, as when the film cuts from a nighttime interior to a daytime exterior shot, or when the title's cue of "16 years earlier" is followed by no visual shift.

Like the treatment of time, the shifts in space are abrupt and dreamlike. The door to the upstairs apartment leads directly to the sea. The spatial composition of individual shots is not particularly striking. Much more important is the jarring juxtaposition of images through the editing, which forces us to realize that space in cinema lacks the continuity it has in external reality. The film's structure works not by plot or chronology but by the association of incongruous images whose recognizable connections are primarily visual. We find that the circle and the vertical line are repeated throughout the film: the moon, the eyeball, iris shots, a crowd standing in a ring, a collar, a hole in the hand, a sea urchin, breast and buttocks; vertical lines of striped clothing, a tie, a striped box, the razor, guns. Frequently the two forms come together, as in the linking of clouds, moon, razor, and eye; the forming of the striped tie into a circular collar; and the insertion of the vertical pen into the circular inkwell. The shapes obviously suggest male and female sexual organs; their fusion implies not only sexual intercourse but a confusion of sexual identity.

The film also has recurring images whose connections are more complicated. Perhaps the most important are transformation images, which merge various parts of the body and various images of the same person. The visual linking between a hairy armpit, a mouth, a sea urchin, and a hand with ants crawling out of a hole in its center suggests the further link with the female sex organ; the Méliès trick transformation of breasts into buttocks supports this pattern. There is also a transformation of characters; practically all the "male" characters are played by the same actor, something the audience must recognize visually. All these images seem to focus on the problem of sexual identity: A swaggering masculine figure in a hat is shot by a pouting, effeminate boy; a man who unsuccessfully attempts rape looks down into the street at a young man in drag riding a bicycle with a striped box (containing a striped tie) hanging on his abdomen. All four figures are the same person. There are also castration or dismemberment images: the eye slit open; a hand caught in a door; the hand with a hole in its center; a dismembered hand in the street; a lost mouth; the disappearing armpit hair; and the final image of the man and woman, ironically set in springtime, who are both buried to the waist in sand after they have broken the box and thrown away the belt, giving up their sexual organs altogether.

This recurring pattern is not the same as a rational explanation that stands in place of the visual experience. It is impossible to develop a neat, allegorical interpretation that represents the "real meaning" or "latent content." Yet the images in the film are rich with association. Even Buñuel admitted that the only possible explanation of *Chien Andalou* would be psychoanalytical—not one that imposed an external theory but one that explored the associations of the particular images that comprise the film.

Like *Ballet Mécanique,* this film moved cinema away from the conventions of theater and literature by forcing an intensification of visual experience. But, while Léger's film tended toward a focus on the mechanized aspect of cinema and of modern life, Buñuel and Dali helped to open cinema to a vision of the timeless and nonrational as they might be experienced in dreams.

THE PASSION OF JOAN OF ARC (1928)

Showing the international character of the avant-garde movement, *The Passion of Joan of Arc* was made in France by the Danish director Carl Dreyer, with sets by Hermann Warm, the German who worked on *Caligari.* It starred Maria Falconetti, an Italian stage actress. Unlike *Ballet Mécanique* and *Un Chien Andalou,* it is a dramatic film, with a conventional narrative plot, of feature length. Yet Dreyer shares the three basic assumptions about cinema that underlie the avant-garde movement: A film should be personal expression of an individual artist; it is not the primary function of the camera to record objective external reality; and film should force the audience to focus on visual perception, on the images actually seen. These assumptions underlie his emphasis on a self-conscious style that will express his own vision and control every detail perceived by the viewer.

> The style of a film that is a work of art results from many different components, such as the effect of rhythm and composition, the mutual tension of colour surfaces, the interaction of light and shadow, the gliding rhythm of the camera. All these things, combined with the director's conception of his material as something that can be expressed in terms of creative film, decide his style. If he confines himself to the soulless impersonal photography of what his eyes can perceive, he has no style.[14]

One could also apply this statement to *Ballet Mécanique* and to *Chien Andalou,* but there is a quality in Dreyer's film that was rejected by Dali, Buñuel, and Léger—a conscious level of symbolic meaning. Dreyer's main technique for achieving this quality is abstraction and simplification:

> This abstraction through simplification, so that a purified form emerges in a kind of timeless, psychological realism, can be practiced by the director in a modest way in the actual rooms of his films. How many rooms without souls have we seen on the screen. . . . The director can give his rooms a soul through simplification, by removing all that is superfluous, by making a few significant articles and objects psychological witnesses of the inmate's personality.[15]

Hence, the images have not only associations like those in *Chien Andalou,* and plastic, formal value like those in *Ballet Mécanique,* but also controlled psychological meanings, the kind of meanings Godard consciously rejected in *Vivre Sa Vie* (1962), which includes a long film clip from Dreyer's *Passion of Joan of Arc* to underscore the contrast. One feels that most of the images within Dreyer's room have "definite" implications, like the shadow of the cross from the window, which Joan interprets as a sign from God about her interrogator's lack of sincerity. Similarly, we in the audience interpret images as definite signs from Dreyer, the divine creator of this fictional world. The dramatic contrast between black and white expresses the moral dichotomies operating in the film; the spikes on the instruments of torture are ominously black. The

[14] Carl Dreyer, "Thoughts on My Craft," in *Film: A Montage of Theories,* ed. Richard Dyer MacCann (New York: Dutton, 1966), p. 313.
[15] *Ibid.,* p. 315.

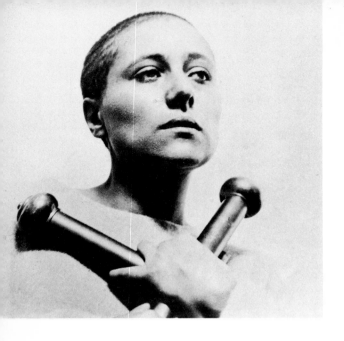

The Passion of Joan of Arc

camera angles reveal the power relationships as low-angle shots fill the screen with the threatening forms of the judges.

Dreyer also gets at inner life by composing his film almost entirely of close-ups of the human face. The actors are not wearing make-up so we see a large range of textures. The faces of the judges include odious moles, hair that looks like devilish horns, narrow slit eyes under ominous, heavy brows, and inflated, fat cheeks above a spitting mouth. Through the close-ups we, like Joan, experience the overbearing pressure of these physically repulsive faces as they loom around us and cramp our space. Falconetti's face is unforgettable. It registers her pain and the intensity of her feeling so vividly that we almost feel trapped by its power. It is hard to believe that she is acting as tears fill her eyes and roll down her cheeks throughout the film. We see her soul. Dreyer anticipates Bergman and Fellini by recognizing the human face as one of the most important resources for cinema:

> Nothing in the world can be compared to the human face. It is a land one can never tire of exploring. There is no greater experience in a studio than to witness the expression of a sensitive face under the mysterious power of inspiration. To see it animated from inside, and turning into poetry.[16]

He accomplishes this amazing transformation with Falconetti in *Passion.* Although the film has a narrative structure, the plot is relegated almost completely to the long titles. The visuals are not

[16] *Ibid.,* p. 317.

really dependent upon the literary analogy. We are frequently so close to Falconetti's face that we can read her lips as well as her emotions, and we resent cutting away to the intrusive titles. We are interested not so much in what characters say or do but in how they feel and in the quality of their inner life, and we can read this more easily in their faces and bodies than in their words.

The images of the film suggest connections with other art forms. The many long panning shots across posed figures remind us of huge tableau paintings. Particularly in the burning sequence, the running soldiers, scurrying people, and flying birds suggest the choreographed movement of dance. But the art form that is most consistently evoked by the film and by Dreyer's own comments is one rarely compared to cinema—architecture. Dreyer's conception of architecture is most closely linked to the insistence on absolute control over every detail, especially in its relationship to the overall structure: "In all noble architecture the details are so finely balanced and harmonized as to fit in with the whole. No detail, however small, can be changed without giving the impression of a flaw in the harmony." [17] Architecture is also a static art form, more concerned with space than with time. Dreyer's style, too, is primarily dependent not on cutting rhythm but on static elements like composition of individual shots, camera angles, interaction of light and shadow, modulated shades of gray, and formally arranged groups of figures.

This static quality has frequently been perceived as a flaw in the film, preventing it from being "cinematic." But we must consider whether this criticism is justified in terms of what the film is trying to accomplish, whether the static quality contributes to the architectural harmony of the whole, whether it helps to express Dreyer's particular conception of his material. One aspect of the static quality is the restriction, for the major portion of the film, to very limited space—small rooms, often with tiny windows and narrow doors. Restricting the scope of the space limits the mobility of the camera. Yet the spatial limit Dreyer imposes on himself is part of his simplification technique; it becomes a way of expressing Joan's sense of confinement, something we in the audience are also forced to experience. The slow pace through most of the film is also linked to Joan's experience. It is as if she needs time to think about the questions and actions of her judges; she needs time to get in touch with her soul, time to decide what kind of action on her part will be in harmony with God, time to get in tune with the absolute. Her spiritual experience has drawn her out of

[17] *Ibid.,* p. 314.

time. The most threatening gestures are performed with exaggerated speed and motion: the attempts to get her to sign the recantation, the speeded-up motion of the torture sequence, the fast-moving lips of the judge who pours invective in her ear, and the rapid cutting and uneven panning of the burning sequence. The predominantly static quality of the film tends to draw more attention to any motion that does occur and makes the climactic sequence particularly powerful. The sequence is introduced by a transitional shot through the grillwork of the prison (which encloses the static world) down to the carnivallike movements that precede the burning and anticipate the later violence. Joan remains the static element in this sequence, tied to the post, with the flames and spectators moving around her. It is a perfect visual metaphor for the moral and metaphysical vision of the film.

Dreyer's film, like most architecture, stresses being rather than becoming, for he chooses to portray not Joan's heroic actions in battle or her transformation from the simple peasant girl to the military hero and saint but her trial, in which her being is subjected to evaluation. We in the audience judge her by reading her feelings and inner nature as they register on her face. Throughout her various experiences in this film, Joan's face reflects her sincerity, passion, and faith. This static view of human nature is defined by the stylistic qualities of the film. Hence, to argue that this film is not cinematic because it is static is to argue from a very limited conception of what film must be and to prescribe not only a certain style but also a certain conception of experience.

The first thirty years of cinema saw its development from a crude device into a complex and artful medium, capable of expressing a tremendous range of attitudes toward human experience. Early filmmakers like Dreyer, emphasizing the medium's recording or interpretive, emotional or visual possibilities, created and refined techniques of composition, camera handling, and editing that brought the silent cinema to maturity.

3

technology
and
illusion
pressures
from within
the medium

Cinema is the art form of the twentieth century, and the twentieth century is the age of technology. While the development of most art forms has been influenced by technological discoveries (for example, perspective in painting, movable type in literature, new instruments in music, new materials in sculpture and architecture, and the recent "art and technology" movement), cinema owes its very existence to a sophisticated technology. Its birth depended on several inventions that were part of the increased scientific activity of the late nineteenth century: the discovery of persistence of vision, which was the basis of many toys that created the illusion of motion (Nollet's "whirling top" in 1765; Plateau and Stampfer's magic disk in 1832, which used a shutter; and Horner's Zoetrope, or wheel of life, in 1834); photography, which required the prior invention of the camera obscura, the discovery of the effect of the sun on silver salts, the discovery of a suitable supporting material for the negative, and a camera that could photograph motion; and the projector, based on the seventeenth-century magic lantern. Each of these inventions had its independent history, some of which predated the nineteenth century. But they had to be combined to create motion pictures. The principles of the shutter and persistence of vision were first combined with the projection of photographs in 1870 when Henry Renno Heyl projected his eighteen posed pictures of a waltzing couple before an audience of fifteen hundred people in the Academy of Music in Philadelphia. The first real moving pictures (rather than posed photos) projected before an audience were Muybridge's running horses, which he showed in San Francisco in 1880 and in Paris in 1882. There were other modified versions of motion pictures in the 1880's and 1890's—by LePrince and Marey in France, the Skladonowski brothers in Germany, Friese-Greene and Robert Paul in England, and the Lathams in America.[1]

From the beginning, movies have appealed to the audience's interest in "miraculous machinery." For example, when movies were introduced in Japan in the late nineteenth century, a popular part of the performance was an explanation by the *benshi* (lecturer) of how the projector worked. Some enterprising Japanese theater owners went so far as to put the projector on the stage—although this meant that few in the audience were able to see the images on the screen—because they realized that many people were interested more in seeing how the technological aspect worked than in experiencing the illusion.

Throughout the history of the medium the filmmaker has turned to the scientist for the technological breakthroughs that would guide the new directions of cinema—whether it be the introduction of sound and color or holography. Although new discoveries are usually intended by their inventors to increase the capacity of film to record sensory data, they are soon exploited by others to create more fantastic illusions and to express a more subjective vision. The pattern frequently goes like this: A technological breakthrough expands the recording power of film, but the exploitation of the technical discovery soon leads to the establishment of rather artificial conventions, which in turn evoke rebellion and parody from the most experimental filmmakers. They take the

[1] For a fuller discussion of the development of the early inventions see Kenneth Macgowan, *Behind the Screen: The History and Techniques of the Motion Picture* (New York: Delacorte Press, 1965); Ernest Lindgren, *The Art of the Film* (New York: Macmillan, 1963); Roger Manvell, *The Film and the Public* (Baltimore: Penguin Books, 1955); Lewis Jacobs, *The Rise of the American Film* (New York: Harcourt Brace Jovanovich, 1939); Martin Quigley, Jr., *Magic Shadows* (Georgetown University, 1948).

new potentiality beyond the conventions and ultimately free it for use in either documentation or subjective expression.

sound

We can see this pattern quite easily in the case of sound, the first technological discovery that revolutionized the medium. The story is well known. From the beginning, inventors were hoping to match sound with the filmed image. In fact, Edison got the idea of making motion pictures after his invention of the phonograph in 1877; he wanted to add photographs to his sound recordings. As early as 1891, his kinetoscope included a phonograph, making it possible to listen to a recording of music through earphones while watching a movie. In France, Germany, and England, similar attempts were going on. But in order to go beyond music and sound effects and to introduce language and integrated visual and audio experience as in real life, perfect synchronization was required. One necessary step was a system of recording sound vibrations photographically, on the film itself, a process first patented by Eugene Lauste in 1906. When combined with the electrical amplification of sound to produce adequate volume, this system became the basis for talking pictures. In the United States, General Electric, Westinghouse, and Bell Laboratories were all experimenting in this area. Warner Brothers went to Bell with the rather conservative goal of finding a way to put a musical background directly on the film. In 1926 they had a showing of *Don Juan,* a silent feature with sound effects and a mechanically reproduced musical accompaniment. But also on the program were some short films with music and synchronized dialogue, which were to have far more interesting effects. The following year, Fox Film Corporation introduced its Movietone Newsreel, which used sound to record the voices of important figures in the news. The sound film in this case was definitely being used to increase cinema's capacity to document external reality. But the implicit potentiality for a synchronized sound, full-length fictional film was not realized until later in 1927 when Warner Brothers scored a hit with *The Jazz Singer.* The sound film became a commercial reality, almost immediately replacing the silent film all over the world.

Suddenly the screenplay became more important. But who knew how to write for the "talkies"? The common solution was to turn to literary sources. If a filmmaker was adapting a play, now for the first time it was possible to incorporate the language. Overnight, then, language became an important new resource for the medium. It was no longer absurd to think of recording a great actor's performance of a certain role, as it had been in 1912 when the Film d'Art company recorded Sarah Bernhardt's *Camille* and *Queen Elizabeth* on silent film. One might argue that cinema was being reduced merely to a recording device for a special performance in another art medium, as it is still being used in Richard Burton's *Hamlet* and Laurence Olivier's *Othello*.

With the introduction of sound, most filmmakers were so absorbed with the problems of learning how to handle the new resource of language that they seemed to forget the artistic accomplishments of the silent cinema. Since early methods of picking up sound were very primitive, a new series of technical restrictions on the filmmaker developed and, ironically, led not to the greater verisimilitude that sound had promised but to more artificial conventions: The actors had not only to follow the script but to stand near microphones, which considerably limited their movements and spontaneity as well as the visual composition of the shot; scenes could be cut only after the dialogue was completed; locations tended to be restricted to indoors, where it was easier to control the conditions for sound recording. Thus the three elements that had been so crucial to the artistic development of the silent cinema—visual composition, camera movement, and editing—were severely restricted. As filmmakers became more technically competent with sound, these restrictions were overcome. But another problem that came with language still has not been solved. The "talkies" limited the international appeal of films by introducing a need for translation, which ultimately led to the inadequate solutions of dubbing and subtitles.

Not all early filmmakers were trapped into making mediocre films because of the advent of sound. A few such as Alfred Hitchcock and Fritz Lang effectively exploited the expressive possibilities of sound and avoided the artifical conventions. In their first sound films both Hitchcock and Lang combined the visual resources developed in the silent cinema and the new possibilities of sound to express their own views of the world.

BLACKMAIL (1929)

Hitchcock started making *Blackmail* as a silent film but changed his mind and took on the challenge of sound. It was the first sound film with dialogue to be made in England. Although it is a psychological melodrama revolving around a murder, its visual and auditory power transforms the film into an exploration of the failure of various kinds of communication. The heroine, Alice White, has committed a murder while defending herself against rape. She first will not confess and later is ironically prevented from doing so.

Hitchcock focuses on the limitations of verbal communication by emphasizing visual values. He makes full use of the visual possibilities of the silent film. Many of the strongest sections in *Blackmail* have no dialogue at all. The opening sequence, long, exciting, and full of action, has only music on the sound track. It begins with a close-up of the spinning wheel of a police van and then cuts quickly back and forth between an exterior shot of the van speeding down the street, the buildings whizzing by, and the interior of the van where policemen work intently over the radio. However, when information is passed among the men inside the van, it is written. The men get out of the van under a dramatically arched bridge. When they rush upstairs to arrest the suspect, he looks out at them from between the metal bars of the footboard of his bed. The room is in bright sunlight, barred by slatted windows. The shadows are not only esthetically pleasing, but they also advance the narrative. We see a close-up of the policemen's faces striped by shadows from the slats. Then we cut to the shadow of the suspect's arm moving slowly toward the gun. The shadow alerts the policemen, who grab him. Although the characters' lips are moving, we hear only "chase" music. Once back at Scotland Yard, the passing of time is conveyed without the help of sound, as a close-up of a cigarette in an empty ashtray dissolves into an ashtray full of butts. An elegant close-up of the suspect dissolves into a close-up of his fingerprint, giving us two aspects of his visual identity. As the men deliver the prisoner to his cell and conclude the excitement of this silent sequence, they move down the corridor toward the most mundane of settings, the men's washroom. The dialogue begins.

Another powerful sequence without dialogue is the final chase in the British Museum. Hitchcock emphasizes the limitations of verbal communication by framing the film with two silent sequences. This sequence also begins with the spinning wheel of the police van. The pattern of shots of the van on the street closely parallels that of the opening sequence. In the chase through the British Museum Hitchcock is at his best, anticipating the visual brilliance that characterizes his use of space and famous settings in later films. The figure of the fleeing blackmailer is reduced to insignificance by the great stairway and columns of the museum. This interpretative perspective is continued with the shot of an ancient carved head, the size of which is unknown to the viewer until the suspect begins to lower himself down a chain along the face of the sculpture and reveals its immense proportions. The long columns, mazelike room, and angular staircase recall the distorted sets of German expressionist films. The sequence is intercut with shots of Alice struggling to write her confession; as she stands up after finishing, the wall behind her is barred with shadows in the sunlight. Like *Caligari,* the film then includes a roof-top chase across the dome, ending with the blackmailer's plunge to death.

Even in the sequences including dialogue, which is usually minimal and often trivial, the visuals are very strong. The link with German expressionism is present also in the sequence where Alice goes to an artist's studio. As they walk up the stairs, the camera rises to follow their ascent and the angular shadows on the walls. Later the staircase is shot straight-on from overhead, flattening it out into a two-dimensional shape. As the artist prepares to steal her dress, they have a banal exchange: "I'd better go," says she. "I see," he replies. Then to undercut the neutrality of his response, an ominous arabesque shadow like a spider appears on his cheek, anticipating symbolically his evil designs.

Hitchcock's control of space is also demonstrated by his anticipation of the split screen as he divides the studio with a folding screen, behind which Alice puts on a costume as the artist plays the piano on the left. Hitchcock shows that he is aware of the visual appeal of this scene by drawing it out, an effect he repeated in the washerwoman sequence in *Marnie* (1964). His confidence in the evocative power of visual effects is emphasized in the murder scene, where all the action is expressed by the thrashing of bodies behind drawn bed curtains, the shadows of the struggle on the wall, punctuated by the shocking details of two arms outflung—first hers to grasp the knife, then his in death.

Hitchcock also demonstrates in the painting of the harlequin with the pointing finger that context changes the meaning of an image, an idea that Kuleshov had made the basis of Russian montage. First the harlequin leers at Alice, then it laughs derisively, and finally it accuses, always in relation to her changing situation.

Once again verbal communication is inadequate as the landlady tries to describe the blackmailer, now suspected of murder. However, when she expresses herself by pantomiming his expression, we in the audience can recognize him. The visual dimension provides identification within the film as well when we see an impressive montage of pages of mug shots being turned rapidly, like the pages of a riffle book, with cross-dissolves, until the blackmailer's face finally zooms forward.

Not only is verbal communication limited, but sound itself is frequently mocked; it is either subordinate or inappropriate to the visuals. The opening dialogue as the men go to the washroom is trivial and largely inaudible. At other times the sound is absurdly inappropriate, as after the murder, when Alice returns to her room in a panic and moves around aimlessly in shock as her pet bird chirps with insane gaiety. The misleading quality of sound is also mocked as the various characters hum and whistle, unaware

Blackmail

of ironic reversals that are to follow: The artist hums confidently, anticipating a seduction that ends in his own murder; Frank whistles casually before discovering Alice's incriminating glove at the murder scene; and the blackmailer hums and whistles with pleasure, toying with his victims before they turn the tables on him. Another means of demonstrating the inadequacy of verbal communication is the omission of dialogue that seems to carry important information. The source of a strong outburst of laughter remains unknown to Frank and to the audience as we watch a policeman whisper a joke in Alice's ear. Significantly, the first time we meet the blackmailer, we hear only snatches of his conversation with the artist. Alice's screams for help are futile because the policeman passing outside cannot hear them.

Hitchcock repeatedly explores the limitations of the telephone, a prime instrument of verbal communication. When Frank receives the important call from Scotland Yard, we hear him say only, "What? Who?" Then he closes the door, turns his back to the camera, and we can hear only murmurs, although the change in his expression and manner shows that he has received a significant message. In the shot where the landlady is calling the police to report the murder, both speakers are shown in a single frame using a single telephone. While the policeman garbles the verbal message, the visual image proves effective in connecting them spatially. However, the most powerful use of the telephone comes in the final sequence, when Alice's attempt to confess is interrupted by the ring of the telephone, and the truth is obstructed forever.

The characters do not use speech to express the truth. Alice responds with stunned silence as Frank asks her, "What happened last night?" She does not speak out when the blackmailer is accused of the murder; she puts her confession in writing and does not speak until she is out of danger. Frank does not confront Alice with his suspicion; he does not report what he knows to Scotland Yard; and he is willing to shift the blame to the blackmailer. He argues, "Our words are as good as or better than that of a jailbird." The truth is, in this film nobody's word is very valuable.

Such emphasis on visual values and the mocking of sound might suggest that Hitchcock was questioning whether sound really was an important contribution to film. A conversation between Alice and Frank about movies supports this view:

Frank: We're only going to the pictures, there's no rush.

> Alice: I don't think I want to go to the pictures; I've seen
> everything worth seeing.

Yet Hitchcock experiments with the expressive possibilities of sound that had been implicit in some of the early silents. The German expressionist filmmakers had used visual distortion to suggest a character's emotional state, but Wiene had resorted to the actual word. In one scene in *Caligari,* there is a shot of the mad doctor calling the name of his ancient predecessor. The word "Caligari" is written on the screen and grows larger and larger as if to suggest the doctor's growing madness and desperation. This anticipated the expressive possibility of sound distortion. Hitchcock in *Blackmail* was the first to develop this potentiality.

The best example of a scene where sound distortion dominates is the morning after the murder, when Alice, distraught by her guilt, is breakfasting with her family. Also present is a customer who is talking about the murder and dwelling on the brutality of using a knife. The volume rises each time the word "knife" is repeated over and over (anticipating the sound loop), effectively revealing Alice's mental state as the distorted sound hammers away on her consciousness.[2]

There are many other instances when a loud and rather irritating sound track reveals the character's psychological sensitivity. In the restaurant, for example, the violin music and background noise of conversation and dishes contribute to the tension and friction between Frank and Alice. In the sequence where Alice is walking home after the murder, her disturbed emotional state is expressed both visually and auditorily. As she walks down the street, the images of people passing her in both directions are superimposed over hers, suggesting oppressiveness, which is intensified by the loud, irritating honking horns of passing cars. The quick cuts to the hands of a mannequin and a policeman remind her of the victim's hand and the murder. Finally, when she comes to a drunk lying in her path and sees his motionless hand, we hear a bloodcurdling scream, which is a sound bridge to the next sequence, where the landlady discovers the body of the dead artist. Although the scream may have come from the landlady's mouth, it expresses Alice's emotional condition.

[2] In responding to a question about this scene, Hitchcock observed, "I think this kind of effect may be justified. There have always been occasions when we have needed to show a phantasmagoria of the mind in terms of visual imagery. So we may want to show someone's mental state by letting him listen to some sound—let us say church bells—and making them clang with distorted insistence in his head." Quoted in *Film: A Montage of Theories,* ed. Richard Dyer MacCann (New York: Dutton, 1966), p. 59.

The power of the final scene also relies on expressive sound. As Frank and Alice enter the waiting room after her confession has been interrupted by the telephone call, they both realize that she is home free and they begin to laugh. At first we interpret this psychologically; the laughter is a means of releasing their tension and anxiety. But as one of the officers picks up the painting of the harlequin with the pointing finger and carries it down the corridor, Hitchcock raises the volume of the laughter and it echoes through the halls. Perhaps we recall an earlier scene on a subway, where Hitchock, sitting next to Frank and Alice, blatantly faces the camera while a naughty child pulls his hat down over his eyes. A broad joke, visual this time, identifies him as a jester and blatantly announces the dark comic tone of this unconventional movie. We begin to suspect that the harlequin and Hitchcock too are laughing as they mock the conventions of poetic justice and the effectiveness of verbal communication in Hitchcock's first sound film.

M (1931)

Another highly effective early use of sound occurs in Fritz Lang's *M*. The story is about an insane child-murderer pursued by the police and the criminal underworld, yet it focuses on the nature of social order. It sets up a comparison between two groups normally perceived as opposites and reveals their underlying similarities. The most obvious comparison is between the police— the traditional good guys who are the protectors of order in society—and criminals—the bad guys who bring chaos. Lang exposes their similarities of organization and efficiency. They are united by their pursuit of Beckert, the child-murderer (brilliantly played by Peter Lorre), who is overcome by an uncontrollable desire to kill. Both the police and the underworld want to purge society of an evil force that threatens reason and order. Yet in their pursuit they reveal that they are subject to the passion that controls him. The criminal members of a kangaroo court decide that Beckert must die because he kills not for rational reasons like greed and gain but because he is overcome by an irresistible impulse. They begin to shout, "Crush him, the brute," "Bleed the beast," and "Beat him down," and their rational goal of restoring peace to society is suddenly transformed into blood lust. When the police arrive at the last minute, prevent Beckert's death, and grant a lawyer's request that "this man be granted the protection of the law, which is everybody's right," we wonder whether this distinction is ironic. Can we really expect a different kind of behavior from the authorized court? The parallels between the law and the underworld stressed throughout the film seem to make this unlikely. Thus, capital punishment becomes as brutal as the acts of the child-molester, and society is even more guilty than Beckert because it kills willingly and tries to justify the act with rational explanations.

Lang effectively exploits sound to develop this comparison. In the opening overhead shot, a group of children are singing a bizarre song about the child-murderer:

> Just you wait a little while,
> The evil man in black will come.
> With his little chopper,
> He will chop you up.[3]

Besides immediately introducing an ominous tension and incongruity, the song makes the first reference to Beckert, who combines childlike innocence with evil. When one mother complains about the song, another replies, "As long as they're singing, at least we know they're still there." The sound a person makes is a projection like a shadow, a means of identification like fingerprints. Lang fully exploits these functions of sound in identifying Beckert. His first appearance is as a shadow moving across a pillar on which appears a poster asking, "Who is the Murderer?" Then we hear a voice off-screen saying, "What a pretty ball! What's your name?" As he speaks, we see his shadow bending down toward a little girl who is standing in front of the poster. The voice functions like his shadow, but we still have not seen his face. When he buys little Elsie Beckman a balloon from a sightless beggar, he whistles an off-key tune from Grieg's *Peer Gynt.* This becomes another of his projections; later, when we see him in his room and see his face for the first time, we recognize him as the murderer because he is whistling the same tune. Later, a beggar will recognize the murderer by means of this same sound clue. Unlike the whistling in *Blackmail,* which signals a false nonchalance and an illusion of control, Beckert's whistle signifies that his irrational impulses are about to overpower him. He whistles to retain control over his will; yet whenever we hear this tune, we expect him to commit a murder because we know the inner struggle is taking place. Sound also leads to his final

[3] Fritz Lang, *M,* ed. and trans. Nicholas Garnham (New York: Simon and Schuster, 1968), p. 15.

59

capture, when his tapping on a door gives him away to his underworld pursuers, whose presence, ironically, is also revealed to the police by means of a sound alarm. In the final sequence, where Beckert is being tried before the underground kangaroo court, we hear the music of *Peer Gynt* once again, this time not in the idiosyncratic off-tune whistle, but melodiously played by a full orchestra, as the police enter and shout, "Police . . . Hands up . . . In the name of the law." [4] Since we already associate this tune with Beckert's irrational impulse to kill, its new link with the police must underscore the irrationality they share not only with the underworld court but also with Beckert.

These examples demonstrate that Lang did not restrict himself to dialogue but effectively used many sounds as important elements in the narrative structure of his film. Perhaps this is most apparent in the incidents surrounding Elsie's death. A variety of sounds signal the passing of time and Elsie's absence. The striking of the cuckoo clock in the Beckman home merges into the ringing of a church bell near the schoolyard, signaling the end of

[4] This music does not occur in all versions of the film but is noted in the screenplay in Lang, p. 108.

M

the school day. The ringing of the doorbell presents the paperboy instead of Elsie. Mrs. Beckman mistakenly interprets the sound of anonymous footsteps as a sign of Elsie's return, and she calls Elsie, her voice echoing through the halls, as we see a montage of shots that reveal the child's absence: an empty stairwell, a deserted courtyard, her place-setting at the table, her ball rolling out of the bushes, and a balloon caught in the telephone wires. This combination of visual and audio cues makes the murder seem inevitable. Reaction to the murder is effectively expressed in a sound montage. Mrs. Beckman's echoing cries of Elsie's name merge into the sounds of the paperboy shouting "Extra, Extra, Extra," and we recall that she had mistaken his ring for Elsie's. Next we cut to reactions to the murder: the sounds of a crowd reading a new poster, which has replaced the one under which Elsie and Beckert had stood; their conversation merging into the voice of a radio announcer speaking of the murder, which is then transformed into the voice of a middle-class man reading aloud from his newspaper in his club and then into an argument in a bar.

This early film also makes use of one of the most complex possibilities of the new sound—its ability to control structure. Sound is used to unify important sequences. A good example is a telephone conversation between the minister and the chief of police, which unifies the sequence covering the rational efforts of the police to catch the mad killer. We immediately sense the high degree of emotion in the minister's comments; he is terribly upset by the fact that the newspaper has printed the murderer's letter, more upset, in fact, than by the murder itself: "It's an unheard of scandal. . . . What a deplorable effect this will have on public opinion, Inspector. It is a serious error, very serious." [5] The inspector responds by stressing the insanity of the killer and the rational efficiency of the police methods, the implication being that reason must prevail: "The guilty man is a mental case. He must get pleasure out of seeing his actions reported in the papers. We immediately got in touch with the editor to obtain the original letter. The laboratory is already busy on it." [6]

The inspector's comment leads into a large close-up of fingerprints that are further blown up by a magnifying glass. As the inspector continues to describe the organized efforts of the police, his comments are illustrated by scenes of the police performing the actions, as if these visuals were supporting evidence in a

[5] *Ibid.*, p. 29.
[6] *Ibid.*

rational argument. But on the minister's side there is only the feeling of anger and frustration and fear for his own career. The conflict between reason and passion, so basic to the theme of the movie, is reflected in this conversation. It is expressed most obviously in the battle between the killer and society and between the law and the underworld, but more subtly it is a conflict among all these elements. The framing telephone conversation shows it within the law, but the entire sequence shows that the conflict is everywhere. There is the irrational argument between the two witnesses in the police station who disagree vehemently on the color of a hat. Following a shot of the police archives, the film cuts to Beckert making grotesque faces in a mirror—as if his rational self is trying to examine the madman who obsesses him— a shot that is almost a parody of the rational efforts of the police. There is a close-up of the minister in his office saying into the telephone, "Results . . . results . . . *your* police are failing," which obviously emphasizes his desires and fears and demonstrates that he is unaffected by the rational arguments of the police chief. This conversation is the background for the subsequent raid of the underworld hangout, which makes the comparisons of the three elements more complicated.

As Inspector Lohmann enters the noisy cafe, we first see his shadow and then hear his voice: "Come on now, children. Let's not do anything silly . . . be reasonable." The underworld characters call him Pop Lohman; they whistle and chant his name, which is reminiscent of the opening scene of the children singing about the child-killer, whose appearance is also introduced by his shadow and voice. Like Beckert, Lohmann poses a threat to these people, but unlike the killer he is shrewd, efficient, and in control. Like Beckert he whistles a tune, but as a sign of his control. He ironically whistles "Where did you get your beautiful blue eyes?" as he discovers false papers on one of the underworld characters.

The underworld is not totally made up of confused children. It has Schranker, who is as cool and efficient as Lohmann. He is also capable of controlled irony: Witness his whistling of "Be faithful and honest" as he breaks into an office building. Following the raid, a meeting of the underworld, with Schranker in control is intercut with a meeting of the police; in these meetings gestures and discussions are similar. Both groups are highly organized and bourgeois. Both are concerned with their reputation and want to influence the general public. Both are part of the establishment and believe in the values of work and business. The underworld claims of Beckert:

> There is an abyss between him and us. . . . We are doing our job . . . because we have a living to make. But this monster has no right to live. He must be exterminated, without pity . . . without scruples. Gentlemen, our members must be able to carry on their business normally without being handicapped by the growing nervousness of the police.[7]

Both groups fear irrationality and "nervousness" in themselves and in each other. Both are nervous about relying on chance and want to use reason to capture Beckert. Their strategy assumes the existence of rational patterns. The police focus on the past (anyone capable of committing such murders *must* have a record of insanity) and look for material evidence (the Ariston cigarette wrapper, the scrapings of the red pencil, and the marks made by his writing). The underworld looks to the future (he *must* strike again, and when he does, the beggars' union will be watching). Although both groups ultimately succeed in capturing their man, their final desire to "exterminate" him is a denial of their reason.

Like Hitchcock, Lang effectively uses the visual resources of the silent cinema to present this view of society. He makes particularly effective use of recurring imagery, camera movement, and camera angles. Throughout *M* there is a pattern of entrapment that particularly threatens Beckert and the children, thereby linking them as victims of the orderly society. For example, in the opening sequence the irate mother leans over the bars of a railing to tell the children in the enclosed courtyard below to stop their singing; the setting looks like a prison. Later, Elsie's balloon, which is shaped like a man, is trapped in telephone wires. Beckert is usually enclosed by the brick columns and iron gates of the office building in which he hides, or by the cagelike room inside. On the street we see his face peeking out from behind foliage that partially hides him. At times he is entrapped by reflections from store windows, which reveal his inner tumult: the diamond pattern of knives that encloses his face and that of the little girl who is his intended victim; the downward-pointing arrow and the perpetual whirlpool that frame his image; and in a toy shop the bobbing legs of a puppet, reminiscent of the balloon man caught in the telephone wires.

Camera movement is also used effectively, particularly to express point of view. Frequently it operates efficiently—like the

[7] *Ibid.*, p. 47.

M

police—investigating a setting and moving in to find significent
details that may be important clues. For example, when the detectives are exploring the house in which Beckert lives, the camera pans the room and then moves in for a close-up of the waste
basket. It works this way even when the detectives are not present,
as in the scene where the camera zooms in through the window to
show the beggars being organized, each assigned an area to
scrutinize. Lang frequently varies the camera movement to create
suspense and control the audience's emotional sympathies. Perhaps the best example of this is the brewery scene, where the
motionless camera is focused on the empty stairway. Then we
see men running down the steps and moving out of camera range.
Again we see the empty stairway but begin to hear screams that
arouse our curiosity. Then we see the men carrying Beckert, again
moving out of camera range. We are confused and curious, like
Beckert, about what is going to happen. When the film finally cuts
to the room where the trial is to take place, the camera slowly
pans the huge crowd of criminals, who remain silent and motionless. We sympathize with Beckert because the camera presents

his point of view; we, too, are shocked and frightened by the grotesque spectacle slowly unfolding.

One of the dominant visual characteristics of *M* is the extensive use of overhead camera angles. Frequently these angles express a subjective point of view. The person whose view is taking over the camera is temporarily in control and more powerful than the person he is observing. For example, the overhead shot of the children in the courtyard is presented as the point of view of the chiding mother; the downward shot of Beckert and the little girl in the candy store is from the perspective of the beggar who is following them. Just as the overhead shot implies control, the upward-angle perspective implies victimization or entrapment. We watch neutrally from a straight-on angle as a little girl asks an old man for the time and people on the street begin to suspect that he is the child-killer. The camera cuts to a downward-angle shot of the old man, who shrinks in size and becomes a pathetic figure, then cuts upward to the looming bully who is wrongfully accusing him. During the raid of the underworld bar, in which the police look down upon the criminals, one man, in an attempt to escape, looks up at the towering figure of a policeman standing on the bars of a grating.

The overhead angle also expresses the omniscient view of the film as it examines the nature of society, stressing the similarities between the police and underworld. For example, after the raid there is an overhead shot of the tools, weapons, and stolen goods uncovered by the police. In the sequence in the beggars' headquarters, there is a similar overhead shot of their haul of cigarette butts and discarded food, implying that both groups are involved in similar activities.

Probably the most effective use of both functions of the overhead shot occurs in the sequence where the police capture Franz, the burglar who is left in the offices after the other criminals have fled. The scene opens with a downward shot into the hole he has cut through the ceiling in the second floor. Thinking that the other criminals are still there, Franz is talking. The camera remains still as we see hands lowering a ladder into the hole and then Franz's head and shoulders emerging from the opening. It is clear that the camera sees from the point of view of the police who have tricked Franz and caught him red-handed. Yet, as he claims that he is innocent, the camera tracks backward until it looks down at the entire scene from the ceiling of the third floor. Now the camera represents the overview of the filmmaker, as it looks with detached amusement at the bafflement of both the police and their captive. Throughout the film we in the audience are invited to share with Lang the power that such omniscience gives us, a power that might be used to fight against capital punishment and to improve society.

depth focus

Other important technical breakthroughs were the introduction of panchromatic stock and the development of lenses that made depth focus easily attainable in interior and exterior shots.[8] Now the camera was able to approximate human vision even more closely than before, but it took imaginative directors like Jean Renoir and Orson Welles to exploit fully the expressive power of this new technical capacity. Both Renoir and Welles are fascinated by the ambiguity and complexity of experience. Both are concerned with evaluating human beings, who are made up of contradictory qualities; they both assume that such evaluation depends upon a complete knowledge, inaccessible to any one person. Thus the problem of point of view—who is observing, where he is standing, from what angle he is observing, what other things are taking place in the environment at the same time, when the observation is taking place—becomes extremely important in making such evaluations. One of the ways in which both directors expressed this view of complicated reality is through depth of field. The characters must always be evaluated in relationship to the context in which we find them; and the audience can never know all there is to be known, for these directors create the illusion that a space exists beyond the two-dimensional movie screen. There are rooms beyond the rooms we see, and the characters move freely in and out of them. Sometimes long tracking shots allow us to enter these spaces, but more frequently we only catch glimpses of them, although they are always sharply in focus. Both directors make frequent use of mirrors to heighten the illusion of great depth.

In Renoir's films there is a feeling of omniscience; behind the film there is an artist who creates order, and is able to see the multifaceted nature of the characters and, despite the

[8] For a discussion of the implications of this technical innovation see Rudolf Arnheim, *Film as Art* (Berkeley: University of California Press, 1967); André Bazin, *What Is Cinema?,* trans. Hugh Gray (Berkeley: University of California Press, 1967); and Ralph Stephenson and J. R. Debrix, *The Cinema as Art* (Baltimore: Penguin Books, 1965).

follies and cruelties he observes, lovingly accepts all human beings. Full knowledge in depth leads to human benevolence. His characters dream of romantic freedom, but they are enmeshed in the petty rules of society. Welles's characters, on the other hand, try to control. They try to become both omniscient and omnipotent, but Welles's vision of the world shows that such control is impossible, even to the filmmaker. Limits are inherent in human nature and in the individual rather than in society.

THE RULES OF THE GAME (1939)

In *Rules of the Game* Renoir is dealing with European society in the period between Munich and the outbreak of World War II. He is concerned not with individuals but with their interaction. Renoir has said of this film, "My preoccupation is with the meeting: how to belong, how to meet." [9] This preoccupation is emphasized by the characters and the plot. André Jurieu (Roland Toutain), the aviator, is the outsider who tries to break into society and ultimately is destroyed by it. He is a romantic, Lindbergh-type hero who makes a solo flight across the Atlantic. Competent and brave in individual feats, he is very naive and incompetent in dealing with the rules of society and its many nuances. He is the kind of hero who can only be sacrificed—applauded for his brave deeds and sent out to die for the society in which he really does not belong. The film opens with his heroic arrival at Le Bourget aerodrome after his successful flight. The crowds, the press, the radio corps, are there waiting to receive him, to perform the public ritual. But once he gets out of his plane, Jurieu begins to alienate them. He has been disappointed by Christine (Nora Grégor), the woman he loves, who is not there, and he ingenuously announces this to the radio audience. He doesn't understand his role in the ritual or what is expected of him. He embarrasses and angers everyone there except his friend Octave.

Octave is the antithesis of Jurieu. He is the anti-hero, the comic failure who started out with dreams of being a musician but who ended up a critic. He too loves Christine but is willing to be her friend or the confidant of her lover. Of all the characters in the film he has the greatest social mobility, for he is confidant to practically all the major characters and takes an active role in

[9] Jean Renoir, "A Certain Grace," in *The Rules of the Game,* trans. John McGrath and Maureen Teitelbaum (London: Lorrimer, 1970), p. 13.

the main plot and the subplot involving the servants. Because of this universal involvement, he never condemns anyone. Of the views of all the characters, his comes closest to that of the omniscient filmmaker behind the action, a similarity underscored by the fact that Renoir himself plays the role and by speeches such as this:

> I feel like... like disappearing down a hole... it would help me not to see anything more, not to search any more, for what's good, and what's bad. Because, you see, on this earth, there is one thing which is terrible, and that is that everyone has their own good reasons.[10]

How ironic that at the end of the film it is Octave whom Schumacher, the jealous husband from the subplot, means to kill. Although Octave may be the one who is most responsible for what happens because he has the most knowledge, it seems highly inappropriate for such a character to be the victim. Conveniently, the heroic Jurieu accidentally takes his place as victim. Octave gives up Christine to Jurieu, the hero, an unselfish action that contributes to Jurieu's death. In this film, it matters less that neither Octave nor Jurieu actually commits adultery than that the socially appropriate victim be chosen. Facts and details of events matter less than the formalized social patterns.

Robert LaChesnaye (Marcel Dalio), Christine's husband, is full of contradictions: respected because he is a rich marquis, but looked down upon because he is a Jew; at times modest and at other times vain; in love with his wife yet involved with his mistress; basically insecure yet confident of how to move within his society; selfish in pursuing his own goals and playing with his mechanical toys, yet capable of empathizing with everyone else, even with Marceau, who tries to poach on his land, and with Jurieu, who tries to steal his wife. In response to Octave's observation that "everyone has their own good reasons," he replies: "But, of course, everyone has their own good reasons—and I, I want everyone to give them freely. I am against barriers, you know, I am against walls. Anyway, that's why I'm going to invite André." [11] Thus, although it might work against his own interest, he is willing to invite Jurieu to La Colinière for the weekend.

Christine, the heroine, is a foreigner—the daughter of a famous Austrian conductor. She is from an earlier, more elegant, and simpler world and is transplanted into a society of great tensions and complications. She has a marvelous sense of grace that dem-

[10] *Ibid.*, p. 53.
[11] *Ibid.*

onstrates how it was once possible for the social rules to work. For example, when Jurieu arrives at the chateau, she manages to transform a potential fiasco into a graceful social gesture, an accomplishment that everyone greatly admires. Yet, as Renoir points out, her limitation is that "she thinks that everything is simple, that she has only to follow the impulses of her heart. . . . But it is much more complicated than that." [12]

Thus the four major characters are outsiders for one reason or another: Jurieu is from a different world; Christine is a foreigner; Robert is a Jew; and Octave is a failure. However, all get involved in a web of complications that far exceed what they had anticipated. We can be sympathetic with them all, for they have their own good reasons for their actions; yet each is partly responsible for Jurieu's death and the war that follows. They are all members of a dying race.

Depth focus is one of Renoir's most important techniques for developing the uncontrollable events that grow out of the complicated interactions among individuals. In the entire film there are only 337 shots,[13] which means that Renoir lets the events unfold uninterruptedly before the camera instead of restructuring experience through montage. He is interested in showing that each character has his own justified perspective, which must be seen in relationship to his environment and the people with whom he interrelates. It might be argued that there is so much within each scene that every viewer must employ his own selectivity in deciding what is important, instead of having Renoir predetermine the significance through close-ups and cutting. Such directional choice, in a sense, would be an oversimplification, a narrowing of perspective, and would run counter to Renoir's intention.

The technique is particularly well illustrated in the first sequence, at the aerodrome. Instead of isolating Jurieu, Renoir shows him in relation to his surroundings—the mobs waiting for for him, his meeting with Octave, his disappointment over Christine's absence, and his interaction with the news media. The newsmen's method of covering the event is contrasted with Renoir's. While depth focus allows us to see these complicated interactions and to select our own perspective, a radio announcer tries to make the event fit her conventional expectations, which are based on what has happened at similar events (like Lindbergh's landing) and on what she thinks her audience expects to

[12] Jean Renoir, "The Birth of *The Rules of the Game*," in *ibid.*, p. 7.
[13] Joel W. Finler, "An Intimate Chamber Piece," in *ibid.*, p. 17.

see and hear. The sequence opens with a low-angle medium close-up of the radio recording truck. The camera follows the cable until it reaches the radio announcer and then follows her as she moves through the crowd to get closer to the approaching airplane. We are following Renoir, the camera, the cable, and the announcer; the screen is crowded with images. Renoir shows Jurieu embracing Octave in an overhead shot that includes the whole scene. The news photographers, however, are taking conventionally posed close-ups of the embrace. One of Renoir's comments is particularly relevant to this contrast:

> The more I advance in my craft, the more I feel it necessary to have the scene set in depth in relation to the screen, and the less can I stand having two actors carefully positioned in front of the camera in a "plan Americain" as though posing for a photographer. Rather I prefer to set my actors freely at different distances from the camera, to make them move about.[14]

The contrast is also underscored in this scene by the different reactions of Octave and the announcer. Octave represents Renoir's attitude toward Jurieu; "It's splendid to see you! Oh, not because of your little trip . . . I couldn't give a damn for that! . . . just to see you standing there." Renoir ignores the conventional excitement over the flight by excluding it and attending instead to what Jurieu will do now that he is "standing there." The radio announcer steps between them and begins to ask him conventional questions. She is interested in the trip: "Listen, you have just made a flight over the Atlantic. You were alone in the aeroplane for a whole day. You must have something to tell us. Find something. Tell them anything. Tell them you're happy!" To deliver this speech, she steps in front of Octave, but despite her visual centrality they both ignore her.

Depth focus is also used effectively in many interior scenes. In Robert's Paris townhouse, doors and mirrors make the rooms seem quite spacious and accentuate the variety of actions taking place within them. In La Colinière there are several shots down the long hallway, with its checkered floor, that connects the bedrooms of the guests; characters enter the hall from various doorways, moving in different directions as though they were pieces on a checkerboard. When Geneviève, Robert's mistress, arrives at La Colinière, a depth shot into the chateau includes the rain and the doorway in the foreground and rooms beyond the foyer in the background. Probably the best example of depth focus is

[14] Jean Renoir, quoted in *ibid.*, p. 17.

the scene in which Jurieu arrives at La Colinière and Christine gracefully explains away the awkwardness of his presence. The camera moves around behind Christine as Jurieu enters the door, as if shifting momentarily to her perspective. Then she moves forward into camera range to embrace Octave, who enters behind Jurieu. Robert enters the foyer from another direction, and soon guests are converging into this space from every angle, heightening the sense of social pressure on Christine. She is the last to greet Jurieu, but all eyes are on her. The camera focuses on Christine in the foreground with Jurieu in the background. As she begins to speak to the assembled group, she moves toward him and they stand facing each other. Then Octave and Robert move around behind and exactly between them, both listening intently as she explains her relationship with Jurieu. All three men are in love with Christine, and Renoir uses depth focus and choreographed movement to show that all three are deeply affected by what she says and to allow the audience to select its own focus of attention or to explore all reactions simultaneously.

In the outdoor sequences in the country at Sologne, the importance of depth shots is also apparent. Renoir described these scenes and what he was trying to achieve in this way:

> I wished to capture that strange kind of poetry, both calm and dramatic at the same time, which emanates from the landscapes of Sologne—I wanted it to have just as important a part in the film as one of the characters. For this reason I tried to modify my technique. For the exterior scenes in *The Rules of the Game* I used a very simplified technique. I tried not to move the camera too much; I had very few panning shots and avoided high angle shots, and other unusual angles, as much as possible.
>
> I also wanted to use lenses which would capture the pure and "revealing" qualities of the Sologne countryside. I wished to show that depth of characterization cannot be separated from the setting of the film, that the characters must be considered as part of an entire world—each element in this world influences all the other elements.[15]

Another characteristic of the film closely related to the use of depth focus is the masterful control of pace. After the initial sequence at the aerodrome, the pace of the film seems to be rather slow. It is a drawing-room comedy, in which one of the primary activities is conversation. In Robert's townhouse, instead of seeing events, we hear people talk about them. In retrospect, we realize that this approach has been taken with Jurieu's flight,

[15] Jean Renoir, "Interview in Sologne," in *ibid.,* p. 10.

which we do not actually see. But later, when Octave visits the Paris townhouse, the physical movement becomes much more spontaneous and playful as he frolics on the bed with Christine and chases Lisette around the table. We welcome this action because there has been little so far. Instead we have been finding out about relationships—between Christine and Jurieu, Christine and Octave, Robert and Geneviève, Lisette and Octave —the conventional concerns of comedy of manners.

Once the scene shifts to the chateau of La Colinière, both the pace and the complications in plot begin to accelerate. We see the new setting for the first time in a long shot of two cars driving up to the chateau. We are struck not only by the physical movement of the cars but also by the mobility of the camera, which tracks along beside them and continues moving around to the front of the chateau. Along with this shift in setting is an expansion of space; yet we soon learn that this space is governed by the same tight code of social rules. There is also an increase in the number of characters, and with new characters come new complications—relationships between Saint-Aubin and Christine, Jackie and Jurieu, Lisette and Marceau.

The next marked shift in pace comes with the hunting sequence, for suddenly Renoir turns to a heavy use of montage. Fifty of the 337 shots in the entire two-hour movie are in one four-minute section of the hunt. This sequence is central in relating the film to the war that was to follow and in signaling the change in civilization; thus a major shift in technique is quite appropriate. The identification of Octave, Jurieu, and the rabbits—anticipated in Octave's comment, "I feel like . . . disappearing down a hole," and confirmed by Jurieu's death—is underscored by Octave's remarking to Jurieu, "It's very dangerous, old boy. . . . They're going to mistake us for rabbits." There is a strong incongruity between the relaxed ease of the hunters—absorbed in their romantic intrigues, wandering off in pairs and then reuniting with the larger group—and the desperate movements of the rabbits fleeing for their lives, their bodies quivering with fear and twitching in death. People walk leisurely before the fixed camera and move off in different directions, but the camera actively pursues the fleeing birds and rabbits through movement, special lenses, and editing. Renoir edits to underscore the contrast between these two kinds of movement, and we experience the incongruity more intensely through the rapid shift in perspective. Yet this powerful sequence does not make us hate the people killing the rabbits and birds. All the major characters are included, and our

The Rules of the Game

sympathies with them have already been firmly established. But it does demonstrate how such people, with their "good reasons," can be destructive to others, and helps us to understand the "deplorable accident" of Jurieu's death and on a larger scale, World War II, which followed.

After the hunt, the pace continues to accelerate; the effect is no longer made by editing but by the increased hysteria and movement of the people running through the house (preparing for the entertainment that anticipates the war by its allusions to death and military glory) and by the increased mobility of the camera. During the entertainment, Schumacher's attempts at murder are interpreted by the guests as part of the pantomime and farce, since the stray bullets reach only Robert's mechanical birds. The culmination of the show is the mechanical organ, the finest acquisition in Robert's collection of mechanical toys, which he presents with a mixture of humility and pride. It is the ultimate sign of the decadence of this society; when combined with the farcical chases and screams, its sound reminds us of a carnival madhouse.

Everyone seems to be racing around (like the rabbits in the hunt sequence) with a sense of desperation, frequently participating in slapstick violence and carelessly breaking the rules of society. At a slower pace, but with equal absurdity, Octave moves about the house in a bear costume, asking first one, then another person he meets to help him get out of it. The costume does not disguise him but traps him in the role he plays in life: a bumbling, gentle clown. He has pursued the maid, but the costume now isolates him from the sexual play going on all over the household, ensuring that he will remain an observer, a confidant. His shambling slowness emphasizes the frenzy of movement all around him. Renoir's timing is always precise and brilliant, as in the scene where Corneille, the impeccably genteel servant, snaps his fingers to ensure that another servant will catch Jackie at the exact moment that she faints. It is the pace of farce, but ultimately leads to the tragic death of Jurieu.

One of the most brilliant achievements of *The Rules of the Game* is the modulation of tone; Truffaut pays homage to this quality in *Jules et Jim* (1962) and *Shoot the Piano Player* (1960). The combination of aristocratic comedy of manners, bedroom farce, slapstick burlesque, romantic tragedy, and satiric irony is essential to Renoir's conception of experience. Life is too complicated to express in single tone, mode, genre, or perspective. The mixture or meeting of these various aspects is at the center of experience. Life must be treated in depth. To accept all of life's contradictions is to be loving and humane.

CITIZEN KANE (1941)

Although Welles shares Renoir's emphasis on the complexity and ambiguity of experience, in *Citizen Kane* he focuses on the individual: how it is possible to understand him, to estimate his value as a human being and as a member of society (hence "Citizen" in the title), and to reveal the motives of his behavior. Welles seems to imply by his selection of techniques that there is no single answer, that the truth can never be fully known because it is made up of many contradictory perspectives. He reminds us that we are watching a film that is attempting to discover this truth, and by doing so he mocks the naive view that cinema is a medium capable of presenting an objective vision.

74

depth focus

The opening shots of *Citizen Kane* establish important themes and images, which are developed throughout the film: the "No Trespassing" sign on the gates of Xanadu; the entrapment imagery of fence, grillwork, and cages; the house, which looks as if it is out of a gothic novel; the contrasting light and sound values as the bedroom window darkens and the music stops when Kane dies; the snow scene in the paperweight that Kane drops as he says "Rosebud," his dying word. Ironically, the "No Trespassing" sign and the entrapment imagery are presented in a series of dissolves, a technique that denies boundaries and introduces the film's goal, which is, indeed, to trespass as thoroughly as possible. The first event of the film, Kane's death, is already a contradiction of the conventional chronological structure of biography. The plot moves freely back and forth in time just as the camera has free mobility in space. The style of the opening sequence, culminating in Kane's death, is highly poetic and evocative, the antithesis of reportage.

From the mysterious opening, the film cuts abruptly to a loud, bright *March of Time* type of newsreel on Charles Foster Kane, the public man. This documentary, with its (synthetic) grainy surface, pretends to give an objective view, but it merely catalogues some incidents in Kane's life that are a matter of public record and are usually considered to be most significant. The newsreel uses all the standard documentary conventions: a narrator with the voice of authority, overly dramatized music, emphasis on quantitative data, the organization of the dead man's life into significant "categories" (the building of Xanadu, the extravagant funeral, his career as a newspaper tycoon, his early life, his politics, his two unsuccessful marriages, his unsuccessful campaign for governor, the decline of his newspaper empire, his old age, and his death). The newsreel works in two ways. It exposes the limitations of the conventional "objective" newsreel or documentary, which tells nothing of what the man was like as an individual —his motives, his passions. This limitation is acknowledged within the film itself when the chief reporter says, "Seventy years of a man's life . . . it's hard to get in a newsreel." Another reporter agrees: "All we saw on that screen was a big American." But the newsreel is necessary, though not sufficient, for Welles's purposes. It allows him to establish economically the basic events of Kane's life and serves as a kind of prologue for the investigation in depth that follows; it frees Welles from chronology and the conventional plot.

The scene in the room where the newsreel is being screened

is dramatically lit by bright reflection from the screen, back-lighting the characters and transforming them into dark silhouettes. Light itself plays a dominant role in this scene; the camera offers a horizontal view of light beams from the projector as they move across the room. At one point, Rawlston, the editor who is leading the discussion, puts his head in the path of the projector beam, splitting it and making him the focus of our visual attention as well as emphasizing the importance of his words as they emerge from the general conversation, in which the reporters all speak at once.

This significant scene is essential to an understanding of the rest of the film. The conversation establishes the narrative structure. Rawlston observes, "When Mr. Charles Foster Kane died he said just one word—Rosebud!" He decides to hold up the release of his documentary for a week or two so that his staff can find out who or what Rosebud was:

> Find out about Rosebud! Go after everybody that knew him. That manager of his—Bernstein. His second wife—she's still living. . . . See 'em all. All the people who worked for him, who loved him, who hated his guts. . . . Rosebud, dead or alive! It'll probably turn out to be a very simple thing.

Rawlston assumes there must be a key to Kane's character, and since "Rosebud" was his last word, this must be it. This assumption is as simplistic as the structure of his newsreel, but the structure that Welles follows, skipping around in time and perspective, is expressive of a far more complex view of experience.

The scene also shows Welles's ability to solve one of the toughest problems of the "dramatic" film: how to render cinematically a scene with lots of dialogue, especially when the conversation gives dramatic exposition essential to the plot but not really inherently interesting. One might add flashy visual effects, but the problem is to relate them intimately to the content. Welles brilliantly solves the problem by making the visuals remind his audience that they, like the reporters, are watching a movie. The silhouetting and the use of light beams as a component of the scene emphasize the illusory aspect of the film medium and remind us that film is the projection of light images on a screen—a fact that applies not only to documentary but to all films. This logical connection between the visuals and the concept succeeds because of boldness and compositional elegance. Welles arranges large stark forms and highly directive lines into balanced but dynamic frames.

This sequence creates a double view of the ending. Although the entire film stresses the value of multiple perspectives, at the end the camera allows the audience (but none of the characters) to see that Rosebud was the sled Kane lost as a child. Suddenly we recall the flashbacks to his childhood and the brief, idealized snow scene contained in the glass paperweight that fell from the hand of the dying Kane as he said "Rosebud" at the beginning of the film. We want to see the film again to attend to more of these details. Perhaps Rosebud *is* the key to his character; perhaps all the information *can* be organized into a new pattern. Motivated by the desire for his mother's love and feeling rejected by his parents, Kane is simultaneously insecure and stubborn, bound never to find satisfaction. Perhaps this pattern can reconcile the contradictory details and views. But then again maybe it cannot. Perhaps it is just as partial and distorted as the others. The sequence in the projection room helps to underscore such doubts, for it implies that finding out the meaning of Rosebud is merely a gimmick used by Rawlston to write a newspaper story and make a documentary film that will sell. He says Rosebud is probably insignificant, but it is the little quirk about human behavior that fascinates us all. Perhaps, then, in this ending Welles is also consciously using a gimmick to give an artificial sense of closure.

To accept the implication that Rosebud is the key to Kane is to assume that omniscience is possible in the point of view of a film and in understanding human character. Yet practically everything in *Citizen Kane* (especially the projection room sequence) works against this assumption. Most of the visual techniques—lighting, transition through dissolve and montage, and the combination of depth focus and camera movement—emphasize the complexity of experience. They imply that an individual must be understood in relation to a particular context, which is never simple or static and which usually offers a variety of perplexing choices, making it difficult to relate successfully to a world of equally complex individuals. These implications provide an alternative to the simplistic vision of the newsreel and emphasize its inadequacy as a vehicle for biography.

Lighting is used to show that perception itself is complex. In the sequence where the reporter is allowed to read Thatcher's journals, a great shaft of light falling across the table transforms the library into a parody of a cathedral and the journal itself into a parody of scripture. The shrine exists because its author has the omnipotence not of a god but of wealth. In the scene where Kane writes the "Declaration of Principles" for the *Inquirer* and asserts,

"I've got to make the *Inquirer* as important to New York as the gas in that light," Kane's face is in darkness while Bernstein and Leland are in light, ironically casting a shadow of doubt on Kane's professed goals. The scene where the reporter talks with Leland in the old-age home is back-lit with cold, thin brightness from the open porch behind him, on which several indistinct figures are huddled in chairs. The abstract quality is enhanced by the light coming in from the high windows along the corridor. The barren, almost surrealistic effect of the lighting makes us distrust Leland because he speaks in a context so far removed from the rich complexity of visual detail in which the events he describes actually took place.

The two most characteristic ways in which Welles moves back and forth in time are through the dissolve, which frequently introduces the flashbacks, and montage, which economically telescopes a number of events. These visual techniques imply that everything is interrelated, that events reflect each other, perhaps even visually, and cannot always be easily distinguished. This merging effect is particularly striking in the montage sequences that cover the passage of a number of years. While these effects are usually praised for their economy, that in itself does not make them effective cinema. Most of Welles's montages of time, unlike the conventional riffling of the calendar in so many movies of that period, are based upon the repetition of events that make a strong statement about the emotional lives of the characters. The series of dissolves from one of Susan's jig-saw puzzles to another develops the passage of time conventionally through the seasonal images on the puzzle pictures but also expresses the mindless repetition of trivia that comprises Susan's life during that period.

The best example of montage is the breakfast room account of Kane's marriage to Emily. It opens with a shot of the entire room, bright and sunny; then the camera moves in for a two-shot of the newly-weds across the table from each other. The source of potential conflict, Kane's dedication to the newspaper, is raised in the first conversation, though at this point he is willing to "play hookey" and spend the morning with Emily. As the montage develops, through fast pans, each successive conversation shows greater resentment and hostility, moving on to include political differences in their attitudes toward the President of the United States (Emily Kane's uncle) and toward Bernstein, the Jew. The dialogue moves from spirited overlapping conversation through colder and flatter tones to a sullen and hostile silence between

Citizen Kane

them, while she reads the rival *Chronicle* and Kane reads the *Inquirer.* Then the camera pulls back, framing the sequence with a second shot of the whole room, now in shadow and darkness. The changing light values emphasize the changing emotional tone of their lives, which is further emphasized through extremely effective changes in make-up in this sequence and throughout the film.

Dissolves, used effectively in the opening sequence, continue to provide transitions throughout the film. As the reporter reads Thatcher's description of his first meeting with little Charlie Kane, the white ▓▓▓ of the journal becomes the even whiter snow of the y▓▓▓▓ of Charlie's home. The dissolve en▓▓▓ us to be ▓▓▓▓▓ reporter can experience it ▓

the page. The dissolve is also used to establish the relationship between private experience and public image. As Emily Kane and Boss Gettys leave Susan Alexander's apartment, the camera holds on them as they stand in the doorway and then slowly dissolves into a newspaper photograph of the same doorway under the caption "Love Nest." The visual dissolve is given depth by a sound effect; as Kane screams at them from above, "Don't worry about me, I'm Charles Foster Kane," his voice merges into the honking horn of a car on the street below. This combination of visual and auditory dissolve also occurs in the butler's account of Susan's departure from Xanadu, where the flashback begins with a cross-dissolve of a cockatoo ruffling and screaming over the image of Susan leaving. The shriek of the bird not only echoes Susan's irritating whine but also gives voice to Kane's impotent rage.

The dissolve is also frequently used effectively with depth focus to create a striking visual composition that illuminates the relationship between people and events. When Kane, in the left foreground, is finishing Leland's bad review of Susan's debut as an opera singer, Leland is seen at medium distance in the right background. Then the image dissolves to Leland in the old-age home but momentarily juxtaposes equal-sized close-ups of young Kane on the left and old Leland on the right, creating a split-screen effect. The two shots being juxtaposed contrast in time and also contest the physical proportion and position of Leland in relation to Kane, increasing his importance by increasing his size, perhaps making us suspect Leland of distortion. The splitting of the screen also underscores visually the break in their relationship and is another reason we should be cautious of Leland's judgments.

Welles uses space itself to show the difficulty of evaluating complex human experience. The characters live their lives in a variety of spaces. The awe-inspiring and lonely reaches of the great rooms at Xanadu and the echoing vault of Thatcher Memorial Library are in contrast to the confined, low-ceilinged newspaper office crammed with furniture and detail, where people collide as they pursue their various ends. At times we are shocked by the perspective. For example, when Kane walks into the fireplace at Xanadu, he is dwarfed by its enormous size. The important sequence where Susan decides to leave Kane takes place in her small but elaborate bedro___ __th its decorated, ____med ceilings and bewildering numb___ ___l objects. Just ___ne begins to destroy these ob____ ___m through a lens that creates an artificial sense of depth and makes him look almost like an abandoned child left far behind in space. Immediately after the destruction, he walks by the servants and guests, past a series of infinitely reflecting mirrors and into a series of arches and doorways, giving the sense of frightening, endless space. When the reporter goes to see Susan Alexander, the camera focuses on a huge poster of her face, moves upward to the marquee of the night club in which she is working, moves over the skylight with a single broken pane, and looks down on the drunken Susan in the room below. The contrast in size and perspective effectively portrays Susan's decline. This crane shot gives an omniscience to Welles, which is not shared by Thompson, the reporter, who is rudely dismissed by Susan. He retreats

Citizen Kane

into a dark phone booth, which frames the right half of the screen. Thompson's figure is a silhouette in the right foreground; the insignificant waiter is dramatically lit and is framed by the door of the phone booth in mid-screen and mid-depth; Susan sits in the harsh light of the night club far in the left background. This composition implies that all these characters are limited and enclosed, in direct contrast to the free mobility and omniscience of Welles's camera.

Depth focus, combined with camera movement, also makes of space an important element in developing the relationship between characters. In the sequence where Boss Gettys, Kane, and Emily confront each other in Susan Alexander's apartment, the arrangement of the characters in space implies the alternative values from which Kane must choose at this time. Emily stands in the left foreground, Kane in the center back, Gettys in the right middleground, and as the scene develops, Susan enters the left middleground. The camera constantly moves its point of view, recombining the people for each implicit choice. Kane rejects the combination of danger from Gettys and conventional security from Emily and chooses Susan, who represents for him the love of "the people," which he seeks throughout the film.

In the flashback to Thatcher's first encounter with little Charlie Kane, depth focus and camera movement are used very economically to develop a highly complex set of emotional interactions and establish visually the theme of Charlie's isolation. The scene opens with a shot of Charlie playing in the snow, but as the camera moves back, we realize the scene is being shot from within the house, isolating him from the other characters and the audience as we look at him through the window. As the mother moves toward the table where Thatcher waits for her to sign the papers, the camera precedes her and takes its place behind the table. The mother and Thatcher occupy the right foreground, the father (who opposes the move) is in the left foreground, and Charlie, the subject of the controversy, seen in extreme depth focus through the window, divides them visually. After the mother goes toward the window to call Charlie, the camera makes its first cut, moving outside and facing the mother, ready to follow the group as they come out of the house into the snow. Charlie's isolation, which has been expressed through his position in space, is now developed through the action, and the sequence ends with a close-up of Charlie's angry face, followed by a shot of his sled (Rosebud) abandoned in the snow.

The visual treatment of the final sequence again questions the validity of making Rosebud the key to Kane's character. True, the identification of Rosebud comes at the end, the usual position for significant revelation in conventional narrative. But Welles began his movie with the end of Kane's life and scrambled chronology throughout; therefore we cannot assume a simple, conventional use of the end position. Instead, the final sequence suggests a double perspective on the Rosebud revelation. It asserts Rosebud's value in understanding Kane's character by singling it out and undermines its simplistic quality by putting it into a context of bizarre complexity. The butler and the reporter move among the crated objects while others move around in the background. Certain items are recognizable: the cup with which the *Inquirer* staff welcomed Kane back from Europe, some of Susan's jig-saw puzzles. The camera moves along, including everything nonselectively, but the audience has the choice of focusing on the known objects. This double possibility is also offered by the dialogue:

> Put these things together and what do they spell? Charles Foster Kane or Rosebud. . . . Maybe Rosebud was something he couldn't get or lost. . . . If you could have found out what Rosebud means, I bet that would have explained everything. . . . I don't think any word can explain a man's life. No—It's just a piece of a jig-saw puzzle.

The camera dissolves to an overhead shot of the acres of crated objects, implying an omniscience in which it is impossible to identify any particular item, though all can be seen clearly. Then, as the camera moves in for closer tracking, we again begin to recognize certain objects, such as the bed Bernstein had brought to the *Inquirer* office. Finally, the camera rests on the sled just as someone picks it up to throw it into the fire. As it burns, we see for the first time the word "Rosebud," being blistered by the flames. The camera has selected the single significant item among all the riches in the world, but ironically this "truth" is not revealed to the reporters.

It has been shown throughout the film that all positions of the camera, all perspectives, are of equal potential importance in determining meaning. Why should we assume that the close-up is truer than the long shot? Although it may give emphasis and finer discrimination of details, it also sacrifices everything that exists in the background. It is a partial view and denies the complexity that the camera has just panned with such loving slowness.

Yet we need to organize, to see patterns, to gain closure and satisfaction. We select certain things and make art of them, fit them into patterns, and then claim that these patterns represent the true nature of experience. Kane futilely attempts to control the people in his life, especially Susan, whom he sees as representing the American public. Though Kane inevitably fails, Welles recognizes the strength of this need and expresses it through his own highly controlled style. This aspect of the double perspective is supported by the final sequence of images, beginning with a dissolve to the smoke coming out of the Xanadu chimney, followed by the gate, the "No Trespassing" sign, and the house itself, with the "K" of the gate in the foreground, bringing the film full circle as it repeats these images from the opening. The fact that the film offers both perspectives (significant detail and the nonselective overview) without endorsing either one is a sign of its final acceptance of the complexity and ambiguity of experience.

One of the reasons *Citizen Kane* is such a brilliant film is that Welles was able to marshal the techniques at his disposal—many of which were made possible by recent refinements of film stock and lenses and the optical printer [16]—to express this special conception that a man's experience is made up of a combination of fragmentary impressions, memories, and images, reflecting each other in time and space. This view is expressed in the dissolves, the fragmentary overlapping dialogue, the shifting camera angles, the mobility of the camera in space, the mobility of the plot in time, and the expressive use of contrasts between foreground and background in depth focus, creating an extraordinarily effective blend of realism and expressionism.

advanced technology

The movement from imitation to artful interpretation of reality that emerged from the new possibilities of sound and depth focus can be discovered in other technical innovations. While color made it possible for films to approximate more closely what we actually see in real life, it led to the kind of artificial coordination that is so beautifully parodied in Demy's *Umbrellas of Cherbourg*. Panavision offered the capacity to approximate more nearly our

---

[16] Linwood Dunn, who worked on the special effects for *Citizen Kane,* claims that approximately fifty percent of the film had special-effects work done on an optical printer. He made this assertion in a speech delivered at the American Film Institute Leadership Seminar, Santa Barbara, California, Summer 1968.

human stereoscopic vision, but it also increased cinema's tendency to be larger than life and led to the production of highly stylized musicals like *The Sound of Music.* It took imaginative directors like Fellini and Antonioni to break through these conventional uses and exploit color to express a uniquely subjective vision, as in *Red Desert* (1965) and *Juliet of the Spirits* (1965), or to play with the spatial possibilities of panavision, as Antonioni did in *Zabriskie Point* (1970). One of the best examples of a film that uses technology creatively to break down past conventions and explore new expressive possibilities is Stanley Kubrick's *2001: A Space Odyssey.*

2001: A SPACE ODYSSEY (1968)

Space Odyssey is a brilliant film that deals with man's progress in facing the unknown and creating new tools for the development of the species and the exploration of outer and inner space. Ultimately the film seems to posit two contradictory views: that man has progressed very far and that he is still basically the same. In treating this theme, Stanley Kubrick extends the boundaries of the technological resources of cinema; his own process of creating the film and solving its technical problems is the ultimate expression of the film's theme. He fully exploits the knowledge of the past and present in order to create a masterful illusion of the future, which has a striking authenticity. On the one hand, he is creating a new world of cinema; yet he is following the pattern established by Méliès, who was the first to exploit the technical capacities of film to create illusions and to express fantasies about the future and outer space.

The idea that man is basically unchanged is reinforced by the formal three-part structure of the film. It is a static form, externally imposed, based on established narrative conventions. Yet, by paying very little attention to time, which at first seems rather strange in a film dealing with progress, Kubrick rejects the traditional plot. There is a gigantic leap in time between the first and second parts—from four million years ago to 2001—and a relatively brief but indeterminate time lapse between parts two and three. The film is obviously concerned more with exploring space than time, perhaps implying that cinema is primarily a visual rather than a narrative medium. But this emphasis also has implications about the concept of progress. Time is not a singular linear development but a recurring cyclical pattern, a concept

that can combine both a static pattern and progressive development. In the final sequence, one of the spacemen watches
various images of himself going through the life cycle—growing
old, dying, and ultimately being reborn (a pattern underscored
by two previous references to birthdays in phone calls from
space to earth). We have witnessed this same cycle in the three-
part structure of the film—starting with the dawn of man, which
is marked by his creating a weapon out of the bone of another
animal; then moving to man in the space age and his sophisticated
technology, which is the marvelous creation of his highly developed brain; and finally culminating in the HAL 900 computer, a
tool based on the pattern not of man's bones but of his brain,
which can still function as a weapon against him and can lead
to death. Despite all the progress, there is still conflict and fear;
man is still curious and fearful of the black monolith, which appears in all three parts of the film. Though the new child at the
end of the film may be capable of finding harmony with the
culture that created the black monolith, the cyclical pattern
remains the same. Visually and spatially, the structural pattern
harmonizes with the circular images of the planets and satellites,
of the giant centrifuge, of the wheel-like Space Station 5, of the
various globular space vehicles, and finally of the embryonic
child.

Although the marvelous ingenuity of space technology and of
Kubrick's cinematic technique constantly suggests progress,
there is a recurring combination of the strange and the familiar,
of the new and the old, expressing the film's paradoxical view of
man's development. In the "Dawn of Man" prologue, the cinematic
technique seems to parallel the subject. The sequence opens with
a series of still shots of the primitive landscape, which are presented in marvelous visual compositions with a subtle use of
color, just as still photography represents the dawn of cinema.
(Interestingly, Kubrick began his career in still photography before going into moving pictures.) As we move into the live action
sequence with the apes, it is as if we have entered the era of
silent cinema, emphasizing the physicality of movement with
exaggerated gestures to communicate underlying feelings. There
is no language—only grunts and music. This is the appearance
and the illusion, but the underlying reality is quite different.
Actually, this is one of the most technically innovative sequences
in the film. Kubrick selected the southwest African setting as the
perfect primitive terrain, yet to film such a sequence on location
would have presented tremendous financial and technical prob-

lems. Instead he used front-projection of 8 x 10 transparencies to create the background. Since it is basically a desert scene, nothing had to move; thus one is not likely to realize that the sequence is shot on a sound stage against a background composed of stills, like the still photographs in the opening. Front-projection had, of course, been used before, but never on this scale. In fact, Kubrick had to build a special projector to accommodate the 8 x 10 transparencies. He selected this process instead of the conventional solutions of blue-screen matting and rear-projection because they probably would not have created so realistic an illusion when applied to such a vast image. This technique also enabled him to manipulate time. In an interview he explained that he and his crew

> were able to wait for just the right moment and shoot a scene in light that would remain exactly that way for perhaps only five minutes out of a whole day. But on the stage we could shoot the sequence at our own pace in constant light of the type you could never maintain on location, no matter how much money you might spend.[17]

These still shots taken in daylight were also transformed into night scenes "by using basically the same techniques that are routinely employed for shooting day-for-night exteriors in the true outdoors —namely, a couple of stops of under-exposure and printing through a light blue filter." [18]

The combination of the old and the new, the familiar and the strange, also recurs in parts two and three. The transition between parts one and two, for example, is a flat cut from the bone to an orbiting bomb. The visual similarity between the two images probably strikes our consciousness before we realize the narrative link —both weapons are products of man's technology, the most primitive and the most advanced—again implying that cinema is primarily a visual medium. As we move into the future and into outer space while listening to the familiar strains of the "Blue Danube Waltz," the incongruity is striking; yet the strange mixture works. The melodious waltz seems perfectly appropriate to the experience of gliding weightlessly through space. The interpretation of the visual image is obviously affected by the music; it encourages us to experience peace, regularity, beauty, and joy, but the imaginative range of the music is also expanded by its juxtaposition with this visual image.

[17] Stanley Kubrick, quoted in Herb Lightman, "Front Projection for *2001: A Space Odyssey.*" *American Cinematographer*, Vol. 49 (June 1968), p. 441.
[18] *Ibid.*, p. 445.

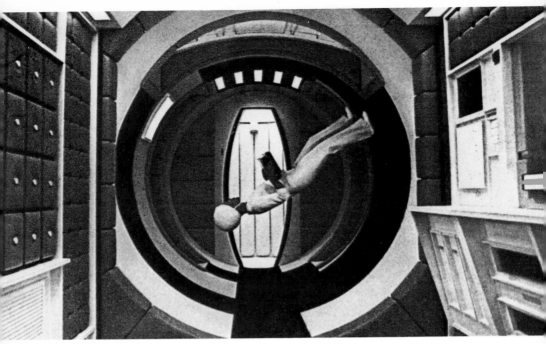

2001: A Space Odyssey

The spaceship clearly belongs to the same genre as the commercial airline that is part of our common experience—the arrangement of the seats, the manner of the stewardess, her relationship with the pilots, the dozing passenger. But mixed with these familiar cues are the incongruous touches of a pen floating in the nongravitational air and the stewardess who appears to walk upside down into the space kitchen. The latter sequence is visually fascinating; it intrigues us with its composition of conflicting surfaces and shapes. The spaceship is full of inner recesses, constantly intersected by new angles. Kubrick invites us to explore its space and understand its motion. The illusion is that the stewardess is walking upside down in a weightless chamber. But, in reality, the scene was shot by fastening the camera to the front part of the set, which rotated 180 degrees while the girl walked upright on a treadmill in the rear part of the set. Like the "Dawn of Man" prologue, this technically sophisticated sequence creates an illusion of considerable authenticity, which grows out of and alludes to the basic illusion of cinema—motion from a series of still images.

The concept of a space station is futuristic, yet Kubrick's rendering of its concrete form has many familiar touches—the names

Hilton and Howard Johnson, the attractive yet sterile modern furniture, the conventional clothes, the interactions of the people. When the American scientist makes a telephone call back to earth, the great distance of space and the video aspects are strange; yet the presentation of the instructions, the physical quality of the instruments, the behavior of his daughter back on earth, and the content of their conversation are all mundane and familiar.

Once we are in the space station, we have moved from the silent cinema into the talkies, but the conversations are trivial and uninteresting. The film begins to sound like a corny science fiction movie. What is happening on that distant planet? Does the American scientist *really* know what is going on? What engages our curiosity is not the conventional plot developed through dialogue but the conception of space developed visually and the intriguing black monolith, which is purposely never fully explained by the plot.

Questions about space dominate parts two and three. Some of the shots in the spaceship overwhelm the viewer with many different modes of reality. There is the interior of the spacecraft with the astronauts; the multiple dials and screens on the instrument panels, which look amazingly authentic, each projecting a separate moving picture on a different scale; the view, through the windows, of the stars and planets in the distance. To create an illusion of such complexity, Kubrick had to combine many separate images on one negative, probably the dominant technique of the film. Never before in the history of movies has a film employed so many of these complex special-effects shots while using the huge

2001: A Space Odyssey

scale of 70mm and achieving such marvelous clarity of image. Kubrick has attributed this accomplishment to the fact that:

> We purposely did all our duping with black and white, three-color separation masters. There were no color inter-positives used for combining the shots, and I think this is principally responsible for the lack of grain and the high degree of photographic quality we were able to maintain. More than half of the shots in the picture are dupes, but I don't think the average viewer would know it.[19]

Douglas Trumbull, a special-effects supervisor on the film, has described the complex procedures that were necessary in shooting some of these scenes:

> Each scene of the Discovery spacecraft required a different angle and speed of star movement, and a different positioning and action of the miniature rear-projected image in the cockpit. All moving images in the windows of the various spacecraft were rear projected either at the time of photography of the model, although as a separate exposure, or later after the model image had been duped using Technicolor Yellow-Cyan-Magenta Masters, or "YCM's." A few scenes show a miniature rear-projected image in the window of a spacecraft as the spacecraft is matted over an image of the moon.[20]

In order to make the miniature spacecraft models look real, it was necessary to keep both foreground and background in focus and to make the motion look smooth. As Kubrick explains, the answer was to use an extremely slow camera speed:

> We shot most of these scenes using slow exposures of 4 seconds per frame, and if you were standing on the stage you would not see anything moving. Even the giant space station that rotated at a good rate on the screen seemed to be standing still during the actual photography of its scenes. For some shots, such as those in which doors opened and closed on the space ships, a door would move only about four inches during the course of the scene, but it would take five hours to shoot that movement.[21]

While we are watching *Space Odyssey,* we are never really sure whether the scale is accurate, whether the moon is a meticulous model or a photograph, whether the action is live or animated, whether the setting is an actual landscape or a front-projected

---

[19] *Ibid.,* p. 442.

[20] Douglas Trumbull, "Creating Special Effects for *2001: A Space Odyssey,*" *ibid.,* p. 416.

[21] Kubrick quoted by Lightman, "Front Projection for *2001,*" p. 444.

transparency, whether an object is moving or stationary, or whether time is distorted. But do we really care? What matters is that these disparate elements are masterfully combined into a single image that creates the illusion of reality. It was a gargantuan task for the technicians to coordinate so many complicated processes in order to create this illusion. As Kubrick explains:

> We figured that there would be 205 effects scenes in the picture and that each of these would require an average of 10 major steps to complete. I define a "major step" as one in which the scene is handled by another technician or department. We found that it was so complicated to keep track of all of these scenes and the separate steps involved in each that we wound up with a three-man sort of "operations room" in which every wall was covered with swing-out charts including a shot history for each scene. Every separate element and step was recorded on this history—information as to shooting dates, exposures, mechanical processes, special requirements and the technicians and departments involved. Figuring 10 steps for 200 scenes equals 2,000 steps—but when you realize that most of these steps had to be done over eight or nine times to make sure they were perfect, the true total is more like 16,000 separate steps. It took an incredible number of diagrams, flow-charts and other data to keep everything organized and to be able to retrieve information that somebody might need about something someone else had done seven months earlier. We had to be able to tell which stage each scene was in at any given moment—and the system worked.[22]

Each one of those special effects was taken to completion and combined so that the resulting film could then be edited like normal footage. The successful design and operation of this technical system in making the film is almost as impressive an accomplishment as the Jupiter project. It is the strongest argument in favor of man's progress, yet we cannot ignore the narrative elements of the film.

The narrative links between parts two and three at first are not entirely clear. As we turn to the Jupiter project, we meet a new set of characters: the two astronauts and Hal, the computer that has never made a mistake. The fact that Hal is the most emotional and sympathetic character in the film is, of course, ironic, since he is a product of technology. Yet he is subject to pride, madness, and disintegration. Only he has advance knowledge of the goals of the Jupiter project and its connection with the black monolith, and,

[22] *Ibid.,* p. 442.

presumably, this knowledge is one of the factors leading to his breakdown. He is as frightened by the unknown and unexpected as the primitive apes. As in the "Dawn of Man" sequence, the conflict between the astronauts and Hal leads to irrationality and death.

In contrast to part two, part three explores not only outer space but inner space. The astronaut gets inside Hal and starts to disconnect his wiring. When the astronaut later confronts the black monolith soaring through outer space, he enters the Stargate Corridor and experiences an onrush of visual images that are difficult to identify. Do these images exist in outer or inner space? At first they are abstract—flashing columns of light, optical warpings created by the computerized slit-scan device created by Trumbull especially for this sequence. But then we begin to recognize negative shots of landscapes reminiscent of the muted-tone stills in the opening sequence but now transformed into wildly colored flashing kaleidoscopic images. We have moved from the dawn of cinema to the outer edge of visual experimentation usually found in underground films using the optical printer. The recurring shots of the multitinted, semiabstract human eye stress the primacy of perception, which fuses outer and inner space. We are reminded that the basic illusion of moving pictures is dependent not only on the projection of a series of still photographs at a certain rate of speed but also on persistence of vision. Cinema itself is a medium that combines inner and outer space.

When the astronaut is transported into the strange new environment of the green-tinted room with its traditional Louis XVI furniture and its futuristic luminescent floor, we are puzzled about its location. How did he get there? Where does the room exist—in outer space, on a strange new planet, inside his own mind? As he watches images of himself aging and dying and ultimately being reborn, we wonder whether this is the rebirth of one particular man or the beginning of a new species superior to the astronaut. In either case, the circular image of the embryonic child suggests that he is a world unto himself, a microcosm ready to continue the exploration of the macrocosm. In this final powerful image there is a mystical fusion between the individual and the universe, between inner and outer space, between verisimilitude and fantasy, between familiar images of the past and strange discoveries of the future, between linear progress and a cyclical pattern of repetition. These are the basic paradoxes that Kubrick explores so brilliantly in *2001: A Space Odyssey.*

four underground films

One of the questions frequently raised about art and technology is whether the combination results in a loss of humanism, whether the artist renounces his control to the machine. Kubrick's use of high-level technology in *Space Odyssey* demonstrates that the artist need not lose control and that such a film can still be concerned with humanistic issues. But this question is raised more frequently in the context of underground nonobjective films that employ computer-generated abstract imagery (like those of the Whitneys) or optical printers (like those of Pat O'Neill). Many of these films demonstrate a concern with humanistic values and a masterful artistic control.

Lapis (1967), by James Whitney, is comprised of animated, abstract computer-generated imagery accompanied by Indian sitar music. There is a constant motion of spots of color, forming a mandala, which is always moving, growing larger or smaller, changing shape and color. The camera slowly approaches the pattern and then backs away from it, providing another dimension of movement and suggesting a changing point of view as the subtle variations draw the viewer into the experience and then surprise him with sudden changes in the basic pattern. One is almost hypno-

Lapis

tized by the color and rhythm. At one moment of the film, a circle seems to evolve from a convex to a concave form through a subtle shift of perspective. In one series of changes, the center of the mandala slowly opens into blackness, suggesting to the eye and mind the infinitely empty center of the universe into which all movement ultimately disappears. The richness of tiny variation demands unusually alert perception, suggesting that if we look at a relatively simple form long enough and with intense concentration, it will lead into more complicated insights into the nature of the universe—insights about the relationship between the one and the many, between stasis and flow—which must be experienced visually and emotionally. Like the avant-garde films of the 1920's, *Lapis* uses the unique potentiality of cinema to expand our vision both perceptually and metaphysically.

In order to see how techniques shape what is being expressed, it is interesting to compare two films that treat the same subject but with different technical effects. *Dream of the Wild Horses* (1960), by Denys Colomb de Daunant, and *The Tempest* (1968), by Frank Olvey and Robert Brown, are short films that exploit technology to portray the abstract beauty of horses in motion and use classical music as a sound track. Daunant relies primarily on slow-motion photography and telephoto lenses to capture the grace, beauty, and symbolic power implicit in the horses. He enables us to see what we ordinarily ignore—the natural majesty of this creature, running freely, frolicking, confronting elemental fire and water. Slow motion and telephoto lenses create expressive images of leaping, plunging creatures that evoke powerful responses experienced as in the world of dreams. The dreamlike quality is enhanced not only by the basic elements of fire, water, and air (made mysterious by rolling mist) but by an effective use of repetition. Filmed with several cameras, *Dream* offers many shots of the same moment or the same animal from slightly different angles, subtly creating the discontinuous and rearranged quality of a dream. Yet this expressive power is dependent upon qualities inherent in the subject; the form, color, and movement of the horses are shown to have a power and beauty capable of evoking the deepest kind of visionary experience.

In contrast, Olvey and Brown in *The Tempest* take ordinary black and white footage of a few domesticated horses in a corral and transform it, through the use of the optical printer, into a dazzling display of abstract color and form. The images of the horses are multiplied in a variety of intense colors. Unlike *Dream of the Wild Horses,* this film's beauty and expressive power are not de-

The Tempest

pendent upon the natural subject but are totally the product of artistic manipulation of the optical printer. The film opens with shots of a beautiful glass plate bearing the stylized form of a horse, suggesting the power of art to transform this subject in yet another way. The choice of domesticated horses, creatures tamed and controlled by man, is an appropriate objective correlative for the artist's relationship to his subject. The emphasis on control and discipline is also enhanced by the selection of the piano étude as a sound track.

Although the directors of these films deal with a similar subject, their choice and handling of technical devices help them to express quite different conceptions of horses, of art, and of cinema. While Daunant relies at least partially on the camera's ability to record external reality (and uses it to create an emotional dimension not present in the more abstract film), Olvey and Brown emphasize cinema's magical distorting power. Yet both films show an awareness of the double potentiality of cinema as a representational and expressive medium. They both choose a subject, the running of horses, which was the subject of the first moving picture, Muybridge's photographs. While Daunant expands on Muybridge to prove a great deal more about the extraordinary nature of horses, Olvey and Brown demonstrate that one cannot rely on cinema to prove anything about external reality but that it can be used as a powerful means of expressing the abstract beauty that is the product of the artist's imagination.

Runs Good (1970), by Pat O'Neill, combines many of the techniques and effects dominant in the films just described but coordinates them for a unique, many-layered effect that, as in Léger's *Ballet Mécanique,* requires and trains the eye to perceive great complexity and richness.

O'Neill uses the optical printer to superimpose several layers of stock footage—which he buys by the pound—negative footage in black and white and color, footage filmed directly from television, rectangular insets of still more action placed within frames containing all these other layers, and blocks and bars of ever changing color placed on top of these other visual components. An early sequence shows a series of layered images including a huge, pulsating heartlike form superimposed upon an amusement

Runs Good

park, a home movie of a pair of middle-aged couples dressed for a double wedding in veiled hats and other finery, black and white negative footage of a flock of birds rising and flying, a football game, a city scene, and a rectangular color inset of someone doing sleight-of-hand tricks. The fast cutting among these images includes the number countdown from a strip of leader, which relates to the countdown meter with red numbers that appears throughout the film, as if keeping track of its pace. At first this layering seems overwhelming; we can never distinguish action and image. But soon we are challenged by the puzzle quality and are drawn into closer and closer attention as the eye strives to perceive both selectively and in combination the imagery created by O'Neill's sleight-of-hand.

Like *Tempest,* this film frequently depends upon commonplace footage transformed through imagination into compelling visual art. However, O'Neill goes beyond simple visual abstraction to combine visual wizardry with wit, developing the continuing theme of expanded perception. At one point, a single layer of film shows a man being taken into court with his hands hiding his face in shame. As we are teased by the unknown content (who is this man? what has he done?), there appear superimposed on the image two rectangles of color. Puzzled at first, we soon realize that the rectangles are slowly going through all the color changes of the spectrum, until at one point their original colors are reversed. We are urged out of our narrative expectations into further realization that this film is for and about our sensory perception.

The theme of training perception is presented with explicit wit in another sequence. As the narrator from some kind of educational film (who has been speaking about the young of a species who learn to avoid pain and danger) tells us, "The long, slow process of training has begun," lines of marching soldiers appear among the layers of images behind a bar of changing color. Wrong kinds of training, this implies (as does a sequence of an overgroomed dog at a show), make it impossible to perceive fluid variety and complexity.

Implicit in the film's range of images and techniques is an exploration of the great variety in movement, time, and space, suggesting the many ways in which experience and techniques for expressing it "run good." Extreme slow motion is used to enhance the grotesquery of some footage where a woman, smiling with huge teeth, brings an obscenely ripe and glistening strawberry jewel to her ear. At other times motion is speeded in loops and other kinds of repetition to enhance its abstractness and for comic effects. Sequences are shown with frames removed, creating a disturbing discontinuity in motion. In contrast, several series of numbers count off time with ironic regularity. Objects walk, run, fly, sail, roll, bounce, pulsate, and explode; and they perform these actions, moving in every possible direction, within a space that simultaneously represents the air, the sea, and the land. This joyful variety in experience is also developed through Bob Curtis' excellent sound track, which includes narration, overlapping conversations, music of all kinds including electronic and Dixieland jazz, feedback, echoes, and other mechanical effects, screams, bumps, lurches, and other unidentifiable but fascinating noise, usually presented, like the visuals, in several complementary layers, which demand careful attention from the ear.

Influencing others with his use of the optical printer and negative images, as in his earlier film *7362,* O'Neill's interest in the complexity of the single frame has been paralleled by others, who work with completely different techniques. Stan Brakhage, for example, paints individual frames, scratches them, exposes them, grows mold on them, and physically treats them in a variety of other ways. But the uniqueness of *Runs Good* is its development of the humanistic value of cinema's potential for wit, theme, and sound, as well as the transforming power of the optical printer to create abstract works of visual imagination.

The Future

We have explored some technical innovations used to create new filmic attitudes toward real experience and its imaginative reorganization. A few technological steps on the horizon could completely transform the way film relates to reality and imagination or mind. One that is upon us is the video cassette.[23] A relatively low-cost attachment can be installed in any television set to play back a prerecorded video tape of material presently screened on television, including films. This process will undoubtedly have enormous impact on both television and cinema, for it will mean that people will be able to purchase a copy of a film as they now purchase a record album and to record whatever they want from television programming. Although this change will primarily affect marketing and distribution, it will have an enormous impact on film production, probably creating new opportunities

[23] For further information see Peter Guber, "The New Ballgame, the Cartridge Revolution," *Cinema,* Vol. 6, No. 1, p. 21; Axel Madsen, "The Third Revolution," *Sight and Sound* (Winter 1970–1971).

for independent filmmakers and encouraging experimentation. Seeing a film on a small screen in the home is a very different experience from seeing it in a movie theater, as McLuhan has argued so convincingly. This change is bound to affect the relationship of the image to reality. Moreover, the nature of the image may differ depending on which of the available processes dominates the market: magnetic tape, super 8 film, CBS's Electronic Video Recording (EVR), or RCA's vinyl tape (SelectaVision), which creates a holographic image.

Holography, whether viewed on television or in a movie theater, could completely transform the way film relates to reality and imagination. An advance over photography, holography creates a perfect three-dimensional image without using camera or lenses. The primary tools are a laser, mirrors, and a piece of film or a photographic plate. An object is set before a laser, which emits a beam of coherent light. A portion of the light is separated off and allowed to fall directly on the film without striking the object. Both the light beam from the object and the other (reference) beam combine to form a complex interference pattern, which is recorded on the film or photographic plate. Later when the object is removed and the film or plate is placed before the laser beam, a perfect three-dimensional image of the object appears in space. Alex Jacobson, a physicist at the Hughes Research Labs, has developed real-time holographic movies, using 70mm film instead of sheet film.[24] Although there are several problems, like the limited size of the image and the lack of research funds, the implications of holography for the future of movies are extraordinary. The screen would be eliminated entirely. The three-dimensional image would be projected in space. The audience might sit in the round, with the images in the center, or might even mingle with them. In addition to its role in RCA's SelectaVision, holography has begun to be introduced into the context of art, with coherent light as a new medium for an expanded conception of sculpture and environmental art.

Many people claim that the ultimate extension of movies would be a "dream machine"—perhaps a machine to be "plugged into" one's head at night before going to sleep. Then in the morning, after awaking, one could flip a switch and see movies of one's dreams. An extension of this idea is an environment in which the ideas of anyone who entered would be projected on the walls in visual form. These ideas are still in the imagination rather than in

[24] For further information see Gene Youngblood, *Expanded Cinema* (New York: Dutton, 1970).

the lab. To be realized, they would require a number of technological advancements, but they are certainly not beyond the realm of possibility, and many scientists and artists are now working on them. For example, Tom Fresh, a Los Angeles artist, has created an environment totally controlled by his brain-wave patterns. Feeding his EEG patterns into an amplifier, he transforms them into laser-generated light patterns that cover the walls of a room and through photo-oscillators create electronic music. The light and sound patterns in the environment are controlled by the electricity of the mind. Even on the margins of the future, there is still a fusion between cinema as the ultimate recorder of sensory data and as the expression of subjective fantasy. Perhaps Bazin was prophetic when he said, "Every new development added to the cinema must, paradoxically, take it nearer and nearer to its origins. In short, cinema has not yet been invented." [25]

[25] Bazin, p. 21.

4

the
expressive
documentary

Beginning with the Lumières' *actualités,* the documentary tradition has been linked with the mimetic view of art. Conventionally,
the documentary is seen as a film that uses the camera to record
external reality objectively rather than to express a subjective
vision of experience. But, as Welles demonstrated in *Citizen Kane,*
and as Godard's hero points out in *La Chinoise* (1968), this is a
naive view. A documentary can be as expressive and subjective
as any other film because it too is controlled primarily by one
man's vision of human experience. Furthermore, the peculiar aim
of documentary is not only to offer the filmmaker's interpretation,
but to focus explicitly on the perception of experience offered
by the culture the film is scrutinizing. These goals account in part
for the great range of what can be called documentary in intention and also raise special problems of the role of verisimilitude
and objectivity in this particular use of film.

Documentary filmmakers, dealing with similar subject matter,
develop the expressive possibilities of the documentary, in different ways. Robert Flaherty's *Nanook of the North,* Luís Buñuel's
Land Without Bread, and Chick Strand's *Mosori Monika* are
ethnographic films exploring primitive cultures. Three documentary films linked to World War II are Leni Riefenstahl's *Triumph
of the Will,* Humphrey Jennings and Stewart McAllister's *Listen*

to *Britain* and Alain Resnais's *Night and Fog.* D. A. Pennebaker's *Monterey Pop,* Michael Waldeigh's *Woodstock,* and the Maysles brothers and Charlotte Zwerin's *Gimme Shelter* document contemporary rock festivals.

three ethnographic films on primitive cultures

A film that explores the way of life of a primitive culture usually focuses on survival and the quality of life. It explores the culture's organization and values. But the filmmaker almost inevitably passes judgment on the culture because his selection and arrangement of the time and space he films reveal his own view of human experience. A contrast is always operating between the culture as subject and the culture that produces the film. *Nanook, Land Without Bread,* and *Mosori Monika* reveal particular awareness of this contrast and the manipulation of the medium to make the evaluation of the cultures quite clear. Each film implies a different attitude not only toward the subject culture and its survival and values but also toward the culture of the filmmaker, his assumptions about experience, and his conception of ethnographic documentary film.

NANOOK OF THE NORTH (1922)

In *Nanook of the North,* Robert Flaherty explores the Eskimo culture by focusing on the constant struggle for survival waged by one man. Unlike that of western man, the Eskimo's solution to this problem does not lead to security and leisure time that might enable him to explore and make a film about another culture, as Flaherty has done. For the Eskimo the solution is always temporary. The battle for survival is constant and is at once the source of Nanook's limitation and the basis of the heroism Flaherty celebrates. Flaherty's focus on one individual is important. If Nanook should fail or die, then his family will perish. An individual in his culture is not an insignificant cog; his actions are crucial to the lives of others. The simplicity of the life and death struggle and its dependence upon an individual's resources are the necessary requisites for heroism. If one "primitive" man is capable of such resourcefulness, he implies the great potentiality of man in general. The film, in which Nanook becomes a romantic and symbolic figure, offers an optimistic view of man.

Flaherty increases our respect for Nanook and touches him with romantic heroism through a variety of cinematic choices and techniques. The film's structure follows the seasons, implying that Nanook's fate is inextricably fused with nature. Nanook must adapt to each season, which tests his resourcefulness and flexibility. The film begins in the spring, when nature is most fertile and living is easiest, and it ends with winter, the most difficult time. Our respect for Nanook grows as we see him cope with each increasingly difficult season, and at the end of the film, we know that spring is coming once again and that Nanook will continue his cyclical battle. The structural emphasis on the seasons implies that time is significant to Nanook. It is one of his most valuable resources, and he knows how to use it efficiently. We see this demonstrated in a sequence where he races against time to straighten the dog lines so that he will have enough light to build an igloo.

Flaherty also creates growing admiration for Nanook by first establishing in the audience a sense of superiority and then forcing us to relinquish it through the development of the film. One of the early springtime shots takes place in a market, where we see

Nanook of the North

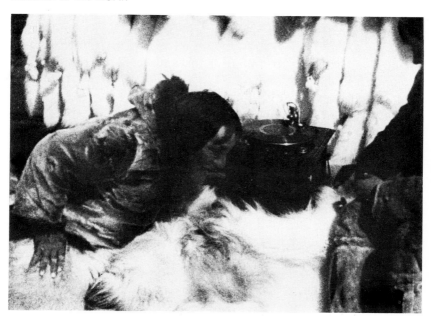

Nanook's first encounter with a phonograph and laugh at his ignorance. However, the ethnocentrism of our attitude becomes apparent when we see this man apply knowledge that we and our culture do not have, as he faces the difficult seasons.

Another important technique by which Flaherty increases our sense of Nanook's heroism and introduces a certain romanticism in our attitude toward him is by setting up a fixed camera and having it record sequences in uninterrupted takes, utilizing real time rather than editing for effect. The use of this technique implies that Nanook's actions are interesting and appealing and that every detail is significant. We see that however difficult the task, however much endurance may be required, there is a certain simplicity in the demands of Nanook's life. He is free from the complexities of priority and variety of choice. Instead, there is inevitability in his tasks. He must do what he must do, in a certain way. This is best seen in an otter-hunting sequence. We really do not know what is happening except that Nanook is hunting. The camera seems nailed down as we watch him locate a little hole in the ice and settle down to wait. He can do nothing else. Flaherty's reliance on the passing of real time emphasizes, to an audience made up of busy and fragmented modern citizens, Nanook's admirable patience. We, the sophisticated audience, do not know what Nanook is waiting for, nor do we know what he will do when something happens. By now we have developed enough confidence in Nanook so that when he begins the great struggle with the animal, we feel certain that our curiosity will be satisfied and that Nanook will prevail. Thus we are moved to respect Nanook's patience and strength, to imbue them with romantic heroism, as we wonder about the presence of those skills in our own culture, which is not conducive to their development.

The long uncut take also builds our trust in Nanook by creating a high degree of belief in what is before our eyes. It allows us to see for ourselves in a reliable way, without commentary, which could be full of lies; in other words, it allows us to judge Nanook for ourselves. Through this technique, Flaherty consciously "proves" Nanook's value and constantly justifies our growing trust in him. We see that the huge otter is pulled through the small hole and that a kayak actually holds many people—phenomena we might ordinarily question.

The intention and effect of the fixed long take raise disturbing questions about the sequence in which Nanook builds the igloo. It seems to be true, though seldom stated, that Nanook and his family lived in wooden structures, not in igloos. Flaherty had to urge Nanook to exercise his old skill, one no longer a part of his life, in order to shoot this impressive sequence. Is there justification for such a manipulation of reality in a film like this? Flaherty's goal is not simple verisimilitude but a celebration of Nanook's powers, which are dependent upon a combination of great prowess and a freedom paradoxically resulting from necessity. Despite his permanent wooden dwelling, it is clear from the incredible speed and efficiency with which Nanook uses his limited time to build the igloo that this is an art he commands, whether he uses it often or only occasionally. The sequence is essential and powerful. In order to establish Nanook as a culture hero, the full range of his abilities must be revealed; he must be the master of all the skills required by his environment. When he makes an opening in the igloo and begins to prepare a block of ice, Flaherty's technique of neutral observation forces the audience to try to guess the purpose of these preparations. Suspense is created, and we are delighted when we learn that there is to be a window. The delight comes from our respect for Nanook's problem-solving ability. The window is a tremendous accomplishment under the circumstances, and we realize that Nanook, like Flaherty and ourselves, places great emphasis on seeing and can accomplish this goal by means outside our command.

Flaherty leaves many things in Nanook's hands—both the quality of his footage and his own survival as he becomes one of Nanook's family, totally dependent upon him. Thus, in a way, Flaherty is as heroic as Nanook. To survive as a filmmaker, he had to go out of his culture and explore new worlds. Like Nanook, he is able to make use of his limited technical resources to accomplish an impressive feat. His film technique is as economical as Nanook's survival techniques. He never wastes a shot. He makes them all contribute to the theme, arranging them in a structure as purposeful as Nanook's igloo, in a style that emphasizes patience, skill, and the value of time. The audience is forced to relinquish its ethnocentricity and to share Flaherty's admiration for Nanook.

This shift in attitude toward Nanook is essential to understanding Flaherty's treatment of the contrast between cultures. Although he celebrates Nanook and the Eskimos, he is not necessarily saying that their culture is superior to our own. The particular strengths and powers of Nanook become symbolic of the potentialities of man in general. The film implies, through the heroic success of one man in one culture, that when man sets himself wholeheartedly to any task, he can prevail. Both Nanook and Flaherty demonstrate the validity of this heroic vision.

LAND WITHOUT BREAD (1932)

Buñuel's *Land Without Bread* is a documentary about the Hurdanos, a group of villagers in Spain who live in a remote area in terrible poverty. Along with *Un Chien Andalou* and *L'Age d'Or* (1930), Buñuel considers it to be one of his three early surrealistic films. It presents in a conventional, low-keyed documentary style grotesque and nightmarish images: a donkey being stung to death by thousands of bees, the body of a dead child with flies buzzing around her face, prancing idiots with broken teeth. The dramatic music, the flat monotone of the narrator's voice, and the rather conventional camera work suggest that the film might be treating the village as an object of study to which the narrator has come with an expedition. The techniques seem to show little awareness of the bizarre nature of what is being portrayed. The incongruity between style and content is striking and is the source of the film's strange power, linking it to the esthetic assumptions of surrealism in painting as well as in film.

The narrative commentary (by David Shephard) is essential, a sign that Buñuel (like Hitchcock and Lang) was able to exploit the potential of sound quite early and quite effectively. Rather than focus solely on the action and allow it to speak for itself, as Flaherty did in *Nanook,* Buñuel implies that interpretation is equally important. The narration is almost as shocking as the visual images, and the juxtaposition of the two heightens the impact of both.

The commentary is crucial in establishing the basic contrast between the culture of the poor villagers and that of the educated narrator. As the product of a dehumanized society, the narrator tries to observe without passion or sympathy the misery of villagers controlled by impersonal institutions like the church and the state. He remains detached and rational like a scientific observer. His primary goal seems to be recording interesting phenomena and satisfying the curiosity of his audience, even if at the expense of the "almost wild" idiots who had to be "calmed and amused" by a Hurdano "friend" before they could be photographed, and at the expense of a goat that conveniently falls down a mountain to its death, illustrating a common occurrence.

In a sense, the narrator's objective stance conceals an underlying cruelty, to which Buñuel sacrifices a goat. In a couple of instances the narrator displays emotion. He sarcastically asks of the "unexpected and shocking" picture on the schoolroom wall, "Why is this absurd picture here?" He refers to the "miserable little stream" that, with its "disgusting filth," is both the source of drinking water and a cesspool. His anger and contempt seem to be aimed at least partially at the villagers. Why does he respond emotionally to some things and treat other horrifying phenomena (like the dying child, the idiots, and the frequency of goiters in the village) with cool detachment? His behavior is almost as absurd and inexplicable as that of the villagers. He may have superior knowledge, but it does no one any good. There is further irony in the fact that even if he had been sympathetic and had tried to help the villagers, their condition is so hopeless that the attempt would have been futile. Thus, his detachment is a cover for his impotence. After all, what can one do about people who know neither bread nor chimneys? At the end of the film we discover that immediately after leaving the Hurdanos, the narrator left the country. He escapes from these unpleasant conditions just as he blocks his emotional responses. Despite the obvious differences between his culture and the Hurdanos', the film ultimately demonstrates that both are inadequate, both are unable to cope with reality, both must deny the truth in order to survive. The only alternative is Buñuel's brutal honesty, which leads to cynicism, anarchy, and a questioning of the value of survival.

Buñuel effectively develops an ironic perspective on the ethnographic film by causing his narrator to expect all its conventional elements. His "essay in human geography" contains the appropriate statistics: "Fifty-two towns with a population of eight thousand"; "we can catalogue two hundred species of trees." To give scientific depth to his statement that "malaria is everywhere; all of the Hurdanos carry the disease," he cuts to a page from a textbook with pictures of harmless and dangerous species of mosquito and then clinically illustrates with a shot of a man shaking with fever. His pride in his candid objectivity is emphasized as the camera moves in for a close-up of a woman nearly unconscious with illness, and the narrator says, "This woman, lying on her balcony, does not even realize our presence." With condescending ethnocentrism, he sees signs of "progress" in resemblances to his own culture ("The cut paper and the pot covers on the wall show a certain flair for interior design."), and he classifies the differences as primitive. In looking at the ornaments worn by a child attending a "strange and barbaric ceremony," he acknowledges that they are Christian but says "we cannot but compare them to the ornaments of African tribes." He even expresses a petulant disappointment that his film will be lacking a conventional element when he says that in all the time his team was there, they "never heard a single song." The conventional ethnocentrism of the narrator is, however, but one aspect of the film's double message. Its internal structure emphasizes the plight of the Hurdanos.

One critic has pointed out that the structure is based on the phrase "yes, but." [1] Yes, the conditions are bad and the villagers have come up with a way of surviving. But the solution is sometimes as bad as the original situation. This pattern is repeatedly pointed out by the narrator. For example, the villagers practically starve during the winter so they eat wild cherries before they ripen. But the fruit gives them dysentery. A group of men set out to work in the harvest. But they soon meet "another group coming back as they went—without money or bread." We see a man who has been bitten by a snake. The narrator tells us, "The serum is not deadly, but the Hurdanos, trying to cure it, infect themselves and die." Their principal crop is honey, but the Hurdanos do not own the hives. Each spring, as they return the hives to the owners, men and animals are stung to death. Furthermore, the honey is "very bitter." After arduous labor, their first year's harvest may be plentiful—unless floods destroy it. Even if they do not, the humus becomes dry and sterile the following year.

This "yes, but" structure is developed in one of the film's best visual sequences. We see rich fertile lands and are told they belong to the monks of the Carmelite monastery. The camera focuses on a tower against the sky and a fountain playing delicate streams of water, emphasizing their beauty. But the narrator tells us the lands are now preserved by the order's last surviving monk. Now, as the camera shows, "toads, adders, and lizards are the only actual inhabitants." These people go through the motions of trying to cope with their situation, but all their attempts are meaningless and futile.

Part of Buñuel's surrealism is an iconoclastic attack on social institutions. We are struck by the absurdity of hearing school children reciting the maxim "respect the property of others" and seeing the Hurdanos' luxury only in the churches. In the narrator's stupid objectivity, he is pleased to observe that "despite the

[1] Raymond Durgnat, *Luis Buñuel* (Berkeley: University of California Press, 1968).

misery of the Hurdanos, their moral and religious ideas are the same as in other parts of the world." These poor villagers share the values of Spanish civilization, though these values actually impede and mock their survival.

The question that Buñuel is raising is whether survival is really of value. Why do these people go on? Why do they continue to believe in the church? Why don't they commit suicide or destroy their civilization? Their survival arouses our curiosity but, unlike Nanook's, not our admiration. Rather, it convinces us of the absurdity of human existence. If we consider this view of life in relation to Buñuel films such as *Viridiana* (1961), *The Exterminating Angel* (1962), and *Diary of a Chambermaid* (1964), we see that Buñuel's vision has remained fairly constant.

This conception of experience perhaps becomes even clearer when we compare *Land Without Bread* to *Nanook*. Whereas *Nanook* focuses on the individual man, *Land Without Bread* deals with anonymous groups. We never learn anyone's name. When the camera does move in for a close-up of an individual, he is usually a freak of some kind—like the midgets, the cretins, and the dying girl. The narrator has no emotional involvement with these individuals, who are used merely as examples of human misery. The narrator too remains an anonymous representative of his culture. Buñuel is concerned much more with condemning society and making a general statement about the human condition than with focusing on an individual.

The attitude toward time is also different. The structure of the film seems rather repetitive and haphazard, as though it merely flows along with the journey. There is no clear structural principle like *Nanook*'s seasonal pattern. In *Land Without Bread* all seasons are equally bad; each has its own horror. We never see these villagers in good times. Their only celebrations are the annual "strange and barbaric ceremony" in which newly married men must tear off the head of a living rooster and the funeral procession for a dead child. Death is not seasonal, nor is it confined to old age. Every time of life is equally miserable and equally close to death. The repetitive structure effectively heightens this sense of unrelieved misery. The film closes with an old woman's chanting through the streets at night. The narrator tells us, "Here is what this woman says, 'There is nothing better to keep you awake than to think always of death, to say an Ave Maria for the sake of your soul.' "

Unlike the world of *Nanook*, this world does not consider time an important resource. Time is another cruel joke played on the people—the irony of having to eat the cherries before they ripen, of the thirty-one-year-old woman who looks seventy, the twenty-eight-year-old idiot who looks twelve, the men who search for bread knowing they are wasting their time. Time intensifies the misery by prolonging it. So why survive? Appropriately, then, the film ends with the abrupt announcement by the narrator that "after a stay of two weeks in Los Hurdes, we left the country." The film ends abruptly for us, but where do we go? We go back to a culture that suffers from similar absurdities. The development of this film is almost like the pattern of *The Exterminating Angel:* When the guests finally escape from the house in which they have been trapped, they soon discover that the outer world is merely the same trap on a larger scale.

MOSORI MONIKA (1970)

Made under the auspices of the UCLA Ethnographic Film Program and emerging from an anthropological film tradition that did not exist when Flaherty and Buñuel were making *Nanook* and *Land Without Bread, Mosori Monika* consciously redefines the ethnographic film. Conceived as a scientific adjunct to the study of anthropology, the ethnographic film attempts to document a culture objectively by giving the appearance of a nonselective recording. The camera tends to remain apart like a detached spectator; it must not heighten dramatic effect by close-up or interpretative editing. This tradition, respecting and indeed growing out of Flaherty's early work, attempts to avoid the romantic dimension of *Nanook.* However, the affirmation of primitive life present in *Nanook* justifies the fixed camera and the development through real time, techniques giving to *Nanook* the appearance, though not the reality, of nonselective recording. In *Mosori Monika* director Chick Strand is questioning the assumption that this objectivity is either valuable or possible. Just as Buñuel questioned these same assumptions through surrealistic contrast and ironic evaluation and through the introduction into the documentary of values from the avant-garde film movement, Strand expands the ethnographic film by introducing techniques from the contemporary underground.

The film explores a tribe of Warao Indians in Venezuela whose culture has been altered by the arrival, twenty years earlier, of a group of Spanish Franciscan missionaries. Strand accepts the subjectivity of perspective by focusing on three women from three different cultures: Carmelita, a Warao Indian who lives on the Orinoco River delta; a Franciscan nun living with the Indians; and Chick Strand herself, an American underground filmmaker who has done graduate work in anthropology. Strand uses three perspectives not to make a simple contrast or judgment but to establish the ambiguity of the different values expressed and to raise the question of how, if at all, they can be integrated with each other.

The controlling characteristic of the film is contrast. The most obvious example is the contrast between the main narrators, Carmelita and the nun, who tell their own stories (translated into English by other voices for the film). Their differing narrative styles imply different conceptions of time and nature.

The nun speaks first, briefly referring to her life in Spain, selecting only the detail that she did not want children and was therefore willing to accept the revelation that she should become the bride of Christ and begin her work in the jungle. As she organizes her own story in terms of before and after, so does she conceive of the life of the Indians before and after the coming of the missionaries. Carmelita, on the other hand, in a long, non-selective narration of the details of her life, manifests no need to distinguish between life before and after the coming of the Spaniards or to consider the relationship between the two periods. She does not perceive a contrast but sees all events as the continuous flow of her life. In fact, she makes little distinction between her life and that of her ancestors. Her story begins with an account of her mother's pregnancy, which soon merges into an account of her own ten children, seriatim. For her, childbearing was not an individual decision, as it was for the nun, but a component of the lives of all women, and all manifestations of it merge into each other.

Strand comments on these attitudes toward time and their different implications about the nature of life itself through her filmic development of the first two sections. In the first, Strand's technique both supports and undermines the nun's narration. The film opens with still shots of the nun in muted colors and stark composition, supporting her simplistic values. We are first aware of movement when we watch the nun lighting ceremonial candles. We are looking at events as the nun might look at them: Time and motion are restricted and controlled; the only action, the lighting of candles, is ritualistic. This presents a sharp contrast to the fast and spontaneous camera movement that follows when the film cuts to the natural environment. As the nun says, in her ethnocentricity, "This was pure jungle, and the Indians lived like animals, just like them," Strand ironically celebrates the beauty and freedom of the river, trees, and birds. As the nun continues to condemn the Indians' culture with remarks like, "They didn't work! The Indians didn't work . . . They were always sleeping in the hammocks," Strand shows a boy learning to use a bow and arrow, women busily cooking, and the peaceful image of men sleeping in swaying hammocks. Thus the visual treatment of the sequence suggests that a proper appraisal of life demands far more complexity than is implicit in the nun's before-and-after, primitive-progress, black-white dualistic view of experience.

In the second section, Strand's camera work affirms Carmelita's conception of time as an ongoing flow and cycle in which there are no sharp distinctions among past, present, and future. The shots of the sparkling water celebrate the archetypal beauty of the story, which is relevant to one generation after another. In these shots Strand successfully integrates her underground filmmaker's interest in abstract visual effects. When Carmelita describes the details of her childbearing and preparing food, Strand illustrates the sequence with images of Indians doing similar things in the present, supporting the cyclical view. The sequence ends with a dramatic contrast between the two conceptions of time. When Carmelita says that time passed, the camera swiftly pans by a number of trees out of focus, suggesting that time is natural motion. But then the film cuts to a shot of a friar ringing a bell as part of a church service, a ritualistic action implying that time is something to be portioned out and controlled, an image that prepares for the following sequence.

The next major section, a marriage ceremony and celebration, brings together the two cultures and allows Strand to emphasize her own perspective by raising the question of how or whether the cultures can integrate. The section explores the possibility and value of this integration through contrasts in narration, camera movement, and images.

The beginning is clearly marked in the narration by a shift to the voice of the priest who is performing the Christian wedding ceremony before an Indian congregation. His reading of the ceremony stands in contrast to Carmelita's earlier description of her own courtship and wedding, which stressed the freedom and spontaneity of those events in her life. How will this new ceremony affect those values in the lives of the younger Indians?

The handling of time in this sequence is very revealing. The earlier sections had been marked by a freedom and rapid pace in camera movement and editing, linked more closely to Carmelita's conception of time than to the nun's. Now that the perspective has altered, the camera shows us that the ceremony, for those directly involved in it, prevents any spontaneous change in the use of time until its conclusion. Strand, however, linked to the producing culture, is freer to break up time and use it as she sees fit. Her camera work implies a desire to communicate both attitudes. First of all, the sequence is marked by considerable reduction in the pace and range of camera movement. Shots and sequences approximate real time more closely as the ceremony goes on and on. The camera, as it moves within its newly confined space, reveals shuttered windows and a slatted fence, which increase the sense of restriction and control.

But the section also includes fast cuts, though far fewer than before. When the camera does move, it frequently offers close-ups of hands and faces, a technique used throughout the earlier sections, especially with the nun in the opening sequence, and in exploring closely the bodies of the working Indians. Now the camera closely examines the people at the wedding. It is as if Strand is using these close-ups to ask: Who are you? What is your special quality? These questions, having been prepared for with the earlier close-ups, become more poignant as, from the cultural perspective of the camera, the answers grow increasingly ambiguous.

After the ceremony, itself the introduction of an alien or at least a new symbolic ritual, the double cultural quality of this section is emphasized at a banquet. The wedding feast is washed down with soda pop, and the music comes from a phonograph. It is interesting to compare the effect of the phonograph here with its role in *Nanook.* In this film, the phonograph evokes not a false ethnocentrism in the audience but a heightened awareness of its double nature. It seems at once appropriate to the mixed cultural quality of the party and detestable because it is perhaps the most alien of elements from the new culture. It makes a strong statement about cultural interference. It suggests what these people may have lost by raising the question: How did they make music before they were given the phonograph? It embodies in its small, mechanical self the larger substitution of cultural expression in the Catholic wedding that has just taken place among Indians in Western clothing, presided over by a Spanish priest.

Yet the camera also reveals the obvious joy of the participants, and, as the nun tells us later, "Women don't die giving birth any more." The plastic milk bottle next to the brown breast in an

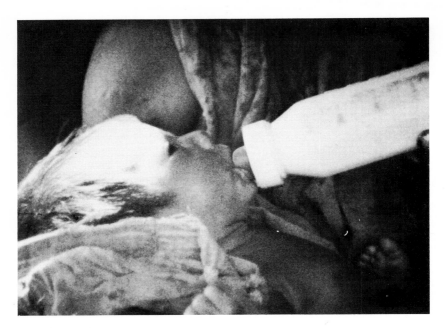

Mosori Monika

earlier shot may indeed be a valuable help to the mother of many small children. Besides, the missionaries have been there for twenty years, and inevitability must be considered as we evaluate from the perspective of our membership (and the filmmaker's) in an "advanced" Western culture.

After the wedding celebration, the film cuts to a simple shot of an Indian paddling a canoe with swift ease and then resumes its strategy of offering a series of contrasts: Carmelita's description of dividing the food among her family contrasts with the nun's account of how the sisters feed "their seventy children"; the intricate weaving of hammocks is juxtaposed with the nuns' teaching Indian women how to use a sewing machine; the local healing methods, which are illustrated through many brief cuts, ending with children laughing and playing in the river, is followed by a long close-up of a child's arm being probed by a hypodermic needle, which results in tears.

The film ends as Carmelita finishes her narrative with an account of her husband's sickness, death, and burial. Unlike the nun, who insists that the husband will go to the Christian heaven like a Spaniard (another version of the before-and-after view of time), Carmelita sees death as part of a natural ongoing process, a view reinforced by the visual montage of water images. We see many transformations of rain: in clouds, on leaves, on the river, in long shots, in close-ups. It is also linked by association to Carmelita's description of the many tears she has shed. This imagery supports the view that death is merely another transformation that takes place in nature rather than in some remote heaven. Carmelita tells us that her husband asked her never to leave this place, and she is careful to bury him on a nearby island and then wait to join him. The film ends by freezing on the words to an Indian love song, which also accepts death as natural transformation:

> Like a waterlily,
> I'll go floating
> with the outgoing tide.

Lilies form little islands by clinging together, in much the same way that individuals cluster together to form a culture. Perhaps this elegy can also be applied to the way of life of the Warao tribe. Since encountering European civilization, it has undergone a transformation and is being carried along with the outgoing tide.

three documentaries related to war

Triumph of the Will, Listen to Britain, and *Night and Fog* use many of the techniques and conventions of the documentary but reject its basic assumption of objective recording and instead select and organize material in order to offer a didactic message. Like the ethnographic films, these documentaries manipulate time, space, and tone to express interpretative and propaganda goals that are part of the filmmakers' intention and are explicitly stated in the first two films. All three are particularly interested in the problems of relationships between events in time and space, between individuals and groups, and between visual images and the responses they evoke.

TRIUMPH OF THE WILL (1934–1936)

When the Nazis came to power in 1933, they immediately took over the film industry. Goebbels foresaw that films could do for Germany what *Battleship Potemkin* had done for the Soviet Union. In *Mein Kampf* Hitler recounts how he "experienced a mass demonstration of the Marxists," with "a sea of red flags, red scarves, and red flowers," which gave to the demonstration "an aspect that was gigantic from the purely external point of view." He concludes, "I myself could feel and understand how easily the man of the people succumbs to the suggestive magic of a spectacle so grandiose in effect." [2] *Triumph of the Will* tries to achieve this "suggestive magic." Ironically, though it supposedly documents the Nazi party congress at Nuremberg, the huge extravaganza was actually staged for the film.

The goal of the film is to unify the German people. The congress is a massive public relations event, as Hitler observes, "a demonstration of political power for millions." Many of director Leni Riefenstahl's techniques are designed to reveal the variety of groups and national elements participating in this gigantic effort.

During the first parade, the camera reveals soldiers saluting Hitler, women and children offering him flowers, office workers cheering from windows, old people watching him more quietly, and even a cat, under a Nazi flag, silently observing. During the rallies, Hitler addresses groups of men and boys whom we see cleaning, eating, dressing, competing in games, playing in bands, marching. Women and children dance, cheer, and parade in national costumes. He addresses a variety of official groups like the SA, the SS, the Labor Servicemen, and the Hitler Youth. Occasionally a dissolve juxtaposes two contrasting images to show their contribution to the unified purpose. For example, the picturesque towers of the old city buildings dissolve into the orderly rows of tents erected to house all the participants in the congress, uniting the old and the new, the permanent and the temporary.

The emphasis on review of troops, both marching and standing in formation, exposes the great range of subtle variations between the kinds of people and activities that will contribute to the unified effort. The Labor Servicemen shoulder their spades like weapons. Marchers carry band instruments, flags, swords, packs, and guns; they wear helmets, officer's hats, and caps. They march in a variety of styles including, of course, the famous goose-step; they offer various military salutes, including the "Heil" with arm extended.

Although the film shows this variety, its emphasis is on unity as it focuses always on groups rather than on individuals, with the single exception of Hitler, who is seen as the living symbol of the entire German nation. His person is frequently intercut with other

[2] Adolf Hitler, *Mein Kampf,* trans. Ralph Manheim (Boston: Houghton Mifflin, 1943), p. 492.

visual symbols such as the swastika, the eagle, and the iron cross. Speakers underscore his symbolic role with statements like, "You are Germany. When you act, the people act; when you judge, the people judge." "The party is Hitler and Hitler is the party. Germany is Hitler, and Hitler is Germany." Hitler has a variety of functions. He is performer and audience, creator and judge, all-perceiving and perceived by all. The opening titles announce that this film was produced "by order of the Führer" and immediately direct attention to his action: "Adolf Hitler flew again to Nuremberg to review his faithful followers." To strains of music, a plane moves silently across lightly clouded skies. God's airplane does not need engines. We get an aerial view of the town from Hitler's omniscient perspective, which is continued in the parade as the camera shoots over his left shoulder. It is slow to give us a shot of Hitler's face, as if reluctant to offer his full glory too quickly. Later, however, the camera shows not Hitler's perspective but a view of him as the symbolic center of attention. It shoots his face from upward-angle close-ups against fluffy clouds or with other people out of focus. His double role as performer and audience is perhaps best seen in the review of the "52,000 Labor Servicemen." The men put on a stunning performance for Hitler—huge masses chanting, singing, and moving in unison, alternating with occasional soloists, who, when asked by the group, "Where are you from?" tell their points of origin. The camera pans their ranks, reviewing them as Hitler is doing. They dramatically lower their flags as the battlefields of past German defeats are named and then on cue suddenly thrust them upward to show that Germany is alive and powerful. This mass ritual is preparation for Hitler's solo number, a powerful speech that stresses that "work will bind us together." The sequence ends with a cross-dissolve of the troops singing and marching in unison across a gigantic close-up of Hitler's face. This shot anticipates the final image of the film: a close-up of a swastika dissolving to an upward-angle shot of the troops marching, with puffy clouds in the background. When we recall the opening sequence, these visuals equate Hitler with God, with the swastika, and with the German nation. It is not that God is on the German side, or that he is German, but that God is Germany.

The film's handling of time supports this view of the transcendental sources and potentialities of the new state. Events are followed chronologically through morning, afternoon, and evening. In one sequence, we watch the passage of time as the light changes from late afternoon through evening. This handling of time gives to the film the illusion of documenting the congress in an objective way: All time is accounted for; nothing is left out. The huge numbers of people and great sweeps of space require a lot of slow panning intercut with close-ups and demand that the camera remain focused for an extended period on single events in order to get their full effect, creating slow-paced camera work that heightens the illusion of nonselective documentary-like recording.

However, the reliance on chronological development enhances another quite different quality: the film's mythic and religious dimension. The movement of the film through time implies that the energy and resources of the people participating in this great rally defy the limitations of time. The film can run on (in its original version) for the full three hours without exhausting the financial resources of the producer, the physical energy of the persons being photographed, or the patience and enthusiasm of its intended audience. The national fervor also transcends distinctions between night and day. The inclusion of night scenes allows for visual effects that further intensify the mythic quality. The evening rallies are dramatically heightened by the abstract beauty of flickering torches and bonfires, the explosive light of fireworks, and the mysterious effects of billowing smoke. In the second evening rally, this quality is strengthened by effective cutting carefully synchronized with the music, giving the impression that the nation is supported not only by the clear purpose and discipline of the daytime events but also by the dark sources of raw energy and symbolic allegiance revealed at night. Goebbels emphasizes the importance of the recurring smoke and fire imagery as he says, "May the flame and light of our enthusiasm never fail." The night sequences also permit visual effects that develop the analogy between national goal and religious belief. The final night rally takes on the appearance of a religious ceremony as the hall, darkened by shadows, becomes like a cathedral and the camera cuts to the twisted cross of the swastika as Hitler says of the party, "Its total image will be like a holy order."

The mythic dimension of the film is further enhanced by the Germans' own conception of time as an infinite commodity that can nevertheless be controlled, shaped, and absorbed into the national vision. The film's emphasis on youth, expressed in the crowd shots, the youth rallies, and the recurring theme of training and indoctrination, implies the desire to transcend mortality itself. Hitler suggests that the youth can unite past and present in flesh and spirit. He says, "We will pass away, but in you Germany will live." The state, too, must transcend time, as Hitler prophesies that it will "endure for thousands of years." Time itself is shown as pregnant with the possibilities of Germany's destiny as the very opening locates the congress in time's movement toward this destiny. We are told that it took place on September 5, 1934, twenty years after the First World War, sixteen years after Germany's "crucifixion," and nineteen months after its "renaissance." In the first morning sequence, time is presented as poised and waiting for Germany to make use of it. We see, in the early light, overhead shots of the quiet city, windows open, flags waving, streets empty as the day and the city awaken expectantly. In his closing speech at the final night rally, Hitler announces, "We are happy to *know* that the future belongs to us entirely."

Thus in this film the techniques of documentary are used to create the appearance of objective recording where the explicit purpose is to create a sense of group unity to which the individual is subjugated. In fact, these techniques help to create a mythic conception of national destiny.

LISTEN TO BRITAIN (1942)

Directed by Humphrey Jennings and Stewart McAllister, *Listen to Britain* celebrates the values of British civilization that are being threatened by World War II but will in turn be the source of Britain's triumph. The directors frankly abandon the conventional objectivity of the documentary and instead develop a structure that articulates these values. The British documentary movement, largely formed and influenced by John Grierson, developed principles for this kind of film that are most fully expressed by Paul Rotha.[3] First of all, the documentary must be interpretative, not merely a descriptive travelogue or film lecture; the filmmaker should reveal his attitude toward his subject by choosing and organizing according to his esthetic sense. The film must fulfill a social responsibility: It must focus on contemporary social problems; it must use real people instead of actors, living stories instead of fictional plots, and natural locations instead of studio sets; it must deal with the mass nature of society rather than with the individual; and finally, it must lead the audience to conclusions by changing their attitudes. This conception of the documentary is partly a reaction against certain aspects of the work

[3] Paul Rotha, *Documentary Film* (London: Faber & Faber, 1952).

119

of Robert Flaherty: the focus on the individual's powers, the setting in remote lands, and the reliance on the noninterpretative long take rather than on montage. Instead, like the German documentary, it looks to the Soviet expressive cinema, especially the work of Eisenstein, with its dialectical montage.

The basic structure of *Listen to Britain* is that of a symphony, which implies full possession and knowledge of all the parts and confidence in arranging them in this traditional structure. The opening sequence, which contains the exposition, centers upon a Canadian who introduces the themes of the film (the dancers, the clanking of machines, the trains, and the BBC) and offers the musical parallel as he refers to the film as "one great symphony," "the music of Britain at war," "the war song of a great people," and "the sure notes of a song of victory." The film can be construed as loosely following the traditional four-part structure of the symphony. The first sequence, beginning with the image of wheat waving in the wind and ending with the fade after the ballroom sequence, approximates the allegro or fast movement with its rapid cutting and development of two basic themes: the preparation for war and the ongoing work and play of national life. The second sequence, adagio or andante, beginning with workers approaching the tunnel and ending with the women in the ambulance station singing and knitting, is marked by long takes and a slower pace. It also offers variations on the two themes introduced in the first movement. The highly structured minuet or scherzo of the third movement is reflected in the next sequence's emphasis on physical motion (machines working, wheels turning, tanks rolling, men and horses walking, children playing circle games) and its incorporation of other forms of music in the public domain (Big Ben's chimes, radio music, vaudeville tunes, the lunchtime concert of Myra Hess at the pianoforte, and the martial strains of the military parade). The quick finale is heralded by a choral rendering of "Rule Britannia" as the camera returns to the wheat fields and other images of the first movement. The final signature shot, a violin crossed with a gun instead of a bow, again identifies the sound track as a "war song."

One of the functions of the symphonic structure is to develop a sense of harmonious community. People from all walks of British life are part of the war effort; they sing together, work together, play together. This sense of community is expressed through editing, recurring images, and the composition of individual shots. By juxtaposing through montage a great number of quick shots of many different kinds of activity, the editing emphasizes that the war effort will succeed because of the great variety of individual contributions to it.

One of the unique strengths of this film, its sound montage, also emphasizes this view of Britain's strength. In one sound sequence, we hear first "Home on the Range" sung and even yodeled by two soldiers. Blended with the singing is the conversation of other soldiers discussing women, and then superimposed on all this are the sounds of the train in which they are traveling. The sounds of the train are developed into the clanking of machinery as workers build airplanes in a factory.

The editing and sound montage show that the power of this community resides in cooperation among a great variety of individuals. This is quite different from the conception of unity in *Triumph of the Will,* in which masses of people are transformed into a single voice, mind, and action by the power or charisma of an individual leader who functions as the symbol of the entire culture. In *Listen to Britain,* the editing shows that no single person, event, or image can symbolize all Britain.

The sense of community is also enhanced through certain recurring images. The concept that life is an ongoing process or cycle is emphasized by various circular images such as the children's circle game, dancers moving around a ballroom floor, people walking through revolving doors, wheels turning, and the wheat images that encircle the whole film. Repeatedly we see a performer facing an audience. In the third movement, two concerts are juxtaposed: vaudeville singers in a canteen and a classical luncheon concert. Both are shot to emphasize the unity between the audience and the performers. In the canteen, the camera focuses first on the singing team and then moves back to include the audience, which whistles and sings along with the performers. The position of the camera reverses in the final shot and focuses only on the audience, shooting over the shoulders of the performers. In the luncheon concert, we are as much concerned with the audience's arriving and arranging itself, the fire equipment in the building, and the streets outside the window as we are with the performance. The people may be listening to this special event, but the sources of energy are circular, and these shots link performance and audience to the general life of the community. This is underscored by the classical music, which runs through the sound montage of this sequence, unifying the various images. When we cut away to the arriving train, the sounds of the train are blended with the music and become part of the symphony, which is finally drowned out by parade music. Another aspect of the unifying nature of the concert is emphasized when the camera shows us in passing that the Queen Mother is in the audience. Instead of symbolically assuming the dual role of performer and judge as Hitler does in *Triumph of the Will,* she merges inconspicuously with the other British individuals who form the community of the audience. This sense of community is further emphasized by the juxtaposition of these two performances, which implies that despite differences in musical and social style, the people share certain basic civilized values.

The composition of individual shots also contributes to the sense of community. The two best examples are the shot of a tank seen through the window of a quaint old inn and the image of a blimp flanked by the massive Greek columns of a public building. In both cases, war images are, in a sense, framed by the best values of normal life. The threatening nature of these implements of war is put into a new perspective. The blimp seems tiny in comparison to the columns, implying that the war threat is only a minor episode in the history of Western civilization. This perspective is antithetical to that in *Triumph of the Will,* where the architecture of the past is interpreted as merely the foundation of the current war effort.

Thus, in *Listen to Britain,* editing, recurring images, and composition of individual shots underscore the idea that Britain's national greatness depends on individuals who cooperate to maintain the values of a civilized community. The film's continual sense of motion—created by the movement of objects photographed, the movement of the camera, and the syncopated montage of sight and sound—implies a healthy vigor that is the source of Britain's strength in the war effort. All these elements and values create the "one great symphony" that is the "war song of a great people." The conception of community based on individuation may make the film's "message" more congenial to us, but this film, like *Triumph of the Will,* celebrates rather than records the national effort.

NIGHT AND FOG (1955)

Alain Resnais's *Night and Fog* is about the horrors of the German concentration camps during World War II. Although it has a great emotional impact on the viewer, the film is designed to show that it is impossible to document the horrors that took place in the camps. We have nothing but fragmented records, which only begin to hint at what it must have been like. The photographs are shocking, horrible, but what they cause us to imagine is far worse. The commentary states this explicitly:

> No description, no picture can restore their true dimension: endless, uninterrupted fear. We would need the very mattress where scraps of food were hidden, the blanket that was fought over, the shouts and curses, the orders repeated in every tongue, the sudden appearance of the SS, seized with a desire for a spot-check or for a practical joke. Of this brick dormitory, of these threatened sleepers, we can only show you the shell, the shadow.[4]

Thus the documentary becomes not a complete and accurate record but only an evocative shadow, a dim suggestion.

Resnais develops this perspective in a variety of ways. First, he separates quite vividly the past (when the atrocities took place) from the present (in which he is making his film). For the past he relies on black and white documentary film taken by the Germans and by the Allies when they liberated the camps. Footage of the present, shot in rich color, focuses on how the same location looks today: a peaceful ordinary landscape, quite lovely, with very few signs of the horror. This footage is reminiscent of travelogues and postcards, which show little of the truth. But one must suspect that the abundant, bright green grass owes its luxuriance to the unusually rich fertilizer it received in the past. Resnais heightens the contrast between the two time periods by continually cutting back and forth between them. While the shots of the past are frequently a montage of still photographs, with the camera panning the image to emphasize certain details, in the present the camera is continually moving. The past is frozen and dead; the present is fluid and unformed. Our knowledge of both is imperfect. When he shifts to the present, the narrator usually asks questions that illustrate how little we remember and how little we know today: "And who does know anything? Is it vain that we in our turn try to remember? What remains of the reality of these camps—despised by those who made them, incomprehensible to those who suffered here?"

The question seems to be one of the few acceptable verbal patterns, for it is open-ended. Otherwise, Resnais seems to distrust language because it implies a false certainty and creates false patterns. Words are used by the Nazis to hide and distort their

---

[4] Jean Cayrol, *"Night and Fog:* The Script for Alain Resnais' Film," in *Film: Book 2,* ed. Robert Hughes (New York: Grove Press, 1962), pp. 240–41. All additional quotations from the film are taken from this edition of the screenplay.

atrocities. They wave their banners in the rallies; their leaders give emotional speeches that allow no questions and demand a uniform response. Within the camp, the SS slogans are proudly and absurdly displayed: Cleanliness Is Health; Work Is Freedom; To Each His Due; A Louse Means Death (which ironically leads the narrator to ask the unpermitted question, "What about an SS man, then?"). The Nazis record all their efforts in huge ledgers and books, compulsively counting the living and the dead, just as they carefully documented these events on black and white film, the very footage we are watching. In order to make the recording process orderly, they label and categorize their victims with gold stars, tattoos, red and green triangles, or the letters NN for *Nacht und Nebel* (night and fog). Even the camp society is carefully organized into a clearly labeled hierarchy: At the bottom are the prisoners (who include many subdivisions, such as victims versus workers, medical guinea pigs versus prostitutes); then the Kapos; next the SS officers; and finally the commandant at the top. But this hierarchy so carefully described by the language is completely undermined later in the film when we see the mass of naked mutilated corpses, interwined, age and sex indistinguishable, and hear the uniform responses of those in charge within the hierarchy:

> "I am not responsible," says the Kapo.
> "I am not responsible," says the officer.
> "I am not responsible."

The narrator is the only one to offer a variation and significantly it is phrased in a question: "Then who is responsible?" The understated, cryptic style of the narration, made up of choppy sentences and fragments, catalogues and questions, creates a distance between the auditory and visual aspects of the film.

But at times asking unanswerable questions finds visual parallel in long tracking shots of the present that explore the location for signs of the past. For example, the film cuts from a black and white shot of a train on a foggy night, transporting the Jews to a camp, to a color tracking shot along the empty rails on a beautiful sunny day in the present, and the narrator asks:

> Go slowly along it, looking for what? For a trace of the corpses that fell out of the cars when the doors were opened? Or the footprints of those first arrivals, driven toward camp at gunpoint while dogs barked, searchlights wheeled, and the incinerator flamed in the distance?

The questions evoke images that are never actually shown in the film and have to be imagined.

Even the black and white footage from the past does not give a full account but only suggests the horror. For example, when the camera pans the huge mountain of hair taken from the women who were killed, we begin to consider just how many must have been murdered. When the narrator reluctantly points to the scrapings on the concrete ceiling of the gas chambers, we begin to imagine the kind of terror that would lead human beings to such futile acts of desperation.

The camera work catalogues the experience by cutting from item to item as the narration offers lists of phenomena. This itemizing, which restructures the experience through selective arrangement, creates a strong incongruity with the chaotic visual images stirring our imagination. We see photographs of Jews being rounded up like nameless cattle as the narrator lists their points of origin: "Deported from Lodz, from Prague, Brussels, Athens, from Zagreb, Odessa, or Rome." We watch hundreds of bewildered human beings standing naked in rows trying to cope with their humiliation, and then we cut to a montage of close-ups that illustrate the narrator's cryptic comment: "Shaved, Tattooed, Numbered, Dressed in blue striped uniforms, caught up in the game of a still incomprehensible hierarchy, sometimes classified as *Nacht und Nebel*—Night and Fog." This itemization reminds us of the Nazi compulsion for order, which is so effectively demonstrated in *Triumph of the Will* when the fifty-two thousand Labor Servicemen chant in unison, incorporating into their routine the point of origin of a few individuals. Perhaps Resnais is mocking this "pretended" interest in the individual, which is as ironic and hypocritical as the SS slogans posted in the camp. In one sequence Resnais cuts quickly from one exterior shot to another of different camps as the narrator observes: "Any style will do. It's left to the imagination. Swiss style; garage style; Japanese style; no style at all."

Both the cutting pace and the commentary emphasize the variations in architectural style. As a result, the barbed-wire barriers, also present in each shot, may be ignored. This ironic attention to variations in external style emphasizes Resnais' awareness of how easy it is to ignore the pervasive horror that went on inside these buildings. He underscores the point that the style of the film gives us a selected and distorted vision of reality. Any style of film is shaped by the imagination of the filmmaker and appeals to the imagination of the audience. We are always aware of gaps between what is seen and heard and between what is perceived and imagined. The main theme of this film is that we must never forget what happened in Germany. Yet there is a full awareness that this is an extremely difficult demand because, as the film itself suggests, it is almost impossible to retain or re-capture the reality of the past. This contrasts sharply with *Listen to Britain,* the structure of which implies that all aspects of experience are fully known and confidently arranged. Resnais's conception of documentary questions not only the possibility of objective presentation but also whether we can possess enough of the past even to approximate or interpret it.

the rock documentary

A new film genre has developed very rapidly within the last few years. Like the wartime propaganda film, it has grown out of a new social phenomenon—in this case, the rock festival, which results from the growing importance of alternative subcultures in American life, especially among youth, who comprise much of the movie audience. In common with the ethnographic documentary, rock films evaluate the cultures they portray. By exploring the subculture, they provide a contrast through which the main culture can be examined. Thus they raise a question pertaining to the filmmaker and the audience: Do they share the values of the subculture under scrutiny? Unlike the ethnographic films, which are usually noncommercial ventures, rock documentaries are aimed at a mass audience, which suggests the possibility of financial exploitation of the subject matter. Films are expensive to make, so a filmmaker's success in getting financing implies that he has strong ties with the establishment. The young audience wishes to identify with the youth culture under scrutiny and is therefore suspicious that the filmmaker is exploiting the rock festival and co-opting its values for money. Distortion for financial gain would seem to be a moral question, but we will explore it in relation to its effects on the esthetics of the films. Granting a filmmaker his subject, the significant question for us becomes: Does he make of it a work of art with its own integrity? Does the film confront the issues it raises?

Some of the special esthetic problems of the rock documentary are rooted in the fact that it must translate a live performance into the film medium. In the past, the attitude toward reduplication of events in different media—for example, the film recording of a play—has been negative. But the filmic rendering of live music performances and festivals offers possibilities that make the relationship fruitful, implying that one art can be the proper subject for another and that artful performances are an aspect of "life" to be recorded on film. The filming of a performance increases the distance from live action, but, paradoxically, it can actually increase the audience's intimacy with the performance. Film allows us to get closer to the rock stars and to the music than we ever could as members of a huge audience. The filmmaker's use of space and his variety of shots are extremely important in the successful translation. These films tend to be visually experimental, expanding cinematic possibilities, frequently through the split screen and fast cutting—techniques that strive for a heightened sense of life and simultaneity of multisensory input, which sometimes emerge as "cheap thrills." The film medium often allows far better reproduction of sound than the live performance. Rock music itself relies on high-powered technology both in live concerts and in recording studios. Film, a medium also based on high-level technology, can offer sound systems of extremely high quality; sometimes special equipment is installed in theaters where rock films are screened. However, some rock documentaries offer technology as a substitute for esthetic quality and turn out to be overequipped and underresourced.

Translation into film can also offer a broader perspective than could ever be achieved by a member of the live audience. Film can show preparations beforehand, effects on the outside community, and the relationships between different elements of the event. These films are concerned not only with understanding the subculture's conception of time (as in the ethnographic films), which celebrates spontaneity and focuses on the present moment, but also with restructuring time in order to evaluate the total phenomenon.

Monterey Pop, Woodstock, and *Gimme Shelter* are bound to stress different values in their translations to the film medium because they document festivals that represent such different stages in the growth of the rock subculture. At Monterey, musical excellence raised hopes for the future of the youth culture, based on psychedelic energy, peace, and love. At Woodstock, the dream of a liberated nation was temporarily realized; at Altamont, fragmentation and self-destructive forces shattered that dream. Since these films have different subjects and different goals, it is futile to expect them to have the same qualities. Though they share various personnel among performers, promoters, and technicians (for example, Albert Maysles, one of the directors of *Gimme Shelter,* was a cameraman for *Monterey Pop*), they necessarily present visions expressive of each film's unique focus.

MONTEREY POP (1968)

The first of several rock documentaries, D. A. Pennebaker's *Monterey Pop* indicated directions the others would take and focused on various aspects of the festival experience that would later diminish in importance. The film emphasizes the power of the music itself rather than the phenomenon of the festival or its social and cultural implications; it also makes very limited use of the medium's ability to translate the concert into film. This emphasis is closely linked to the film's strength and also to its limitations. Its subject, the Monterey Rock Festival, was one of the first rock events to attract national attention, and it took place at a time when hopes for rock music and the psychedelic revolution ran high. Thus the film documents a creative energy, which, through the variety of performers and the innovations they brought to rock, makes the music of this film better than that of *Woodstock* and *Gimme Shelter.* Many groups offered qualities that were exhilirating in their newness: the close relationship between members of the Mamas and Papas "family," singing their own California history; the destruction of instruments by the Who and Jimi Hendrix; Simon and Garfunkel's sweet poetic harmony; the mix of Afro-jazz and rock in Hugh Masakela; the acid rock of the Jefferson Airplane; soulful blues, black and white, from Otis Redding and Janis Joplin; the music of an entirely different culture in Ravi Shankar's classical sitar.

When we see this film only a few years later, it evokes nostalgia for that period's innocence and creative energy, particularly for the groups that have disbanded (like the Mamas and the Papas) and for the performers now dead (Redding, Joplin, and Hendrix). Thus part of its value lies in providing a permanent record of performances that can never be repeated, yet the film treats them visually with varying degrees of success. In recording Janis Joplin and Jimi Hendrix, the camera work, neither elaborate nor innovative, is effective because it respects the special qualities of each performer. Since much of Joplin's effect depended upon her facial expressions and the rhythmic tension of her body, the camera moves in frequently for close-ups of her distorted face and of her feet as they snap out the beat. Occasionally the camera moves back in the wings to give the total effect of her silver costume in pink light and her intimate use of the microphone. Hendrix, whose performance includes much more movement and variety (somersaults, playing the guitar over his head and behind his back, sexual play with guitar and amplifier, ritualistic burning and destruction of the guitar), is shot from a variety of positions and angles that let us appreciate his full range. The Otis Redding sequence, on the other hand, is frustrating. By shooting directly into the spotlight focused on Redding, the cameraman probably hoped to create a strobic effect as Redding moved in and out of the light. But it results in too bright flashes, held for too long, making it impossible to see what Redding is doing. Occasionally, his face, outlined thinly in bright light, is silhouetted against the dark background. Although this technique is not enough to save the Redding sequence, it is used very effectively with Gracie Slick, whose profile is enhanced by the lightning and camera perspective.

The innocence of this period of rock history is suggested by the fact that this film, unlike the later ones, concerns itself only in passing with social and cultural problems. Although there is no extended contrast between two cultures, there are verbal references and brief glimpses of the various events and problems that would require greater attention in *Woodstock* and *Gimme Shelter*. Like the later films, *Monterey Pop* shows us the groups arriving in airplanes, the setting up of the stage, and the size of the crowd. It also touches on problems like the eating and sleeping facilities. One policeman asks, "What if we get fifty or fifty-five thousand people?"—a small number seen from the perspective of *Woodstock*. He is worried also about the potential danger in the presence of "Hippies, Hell's Angels, and Black Panthers," dangers realized only too fully in *Gimme Shelter*. But these problems never materialize in Monterey, and the festival turns out to be a great party, as predicted by a girl interviewed in the opening scene. It is as if the energy that caused violence in later festivals found playful expression at Monterey. The demonic impulse emerges in the fireworks of the Who and the flames of Jimi Hendrix's guitar and in the "creative destruction" of their instruments (though stage hands are not so sanguine and occasionally rush out to save a microphone or a set of drums).

The prime value of the film is its focus on the music, which is achieved in a variety of ways. Many of the comments from the audience concern the music. The girl interviewed at the beginning is thrilled with the prospect of so much talent at one festival. Later, another girl expresses her confidence in the whole rock scene, saying that we only have to wait and new waves of music will be created. The camera focuses not so much on the interaction between performers and audience (which is handled with mixed success in *Woodstock* and *Gimme Shelter*) but confines itself mainly to the stage, as if it too is there for the music. In fact, the performances control the entire structure of the film, almost replacing cinematic sequence as an organizational unit. Within the performances, the value of the music is further emphasized by the omission of introductions, comments, and almost all other talk by the musicians. For example, just as Hugh Masakela is about to speak at the end of his performance, the film quickly cuts to an interview with a spectator. Shankar's sequence completely omits the long discussion about Indian music, and against drugs and cigarettes, with which he had introduced his performance. The only exception is the occasional comment by John Phillips, who is shown in his role as the producer of the festival. For the most part the film focuses on the interaction among performers onstage, stressing the value of the creative process. Frequently the camera offers us two performers side by side, seen in profile, often glancing at and responding to each other, as in the interaction of Hugh Masakela and his saxophonist and of Michelle and Mama Cass of the Mamas and Papas. This relationship is further developed as we frequently see a close-up of a performer in the audience watching appreciatively as others work onstage. The camera cuts twice to Mama Cass as she watches Janis Joplin do "Ball and Chain." She sits with her mouth open as if hypnotized and after the performance utters a silent "Wow!"

The close-up, mainly of faces, allows us to recognize the performers among the audience, providing some link between the two, and is one of the film's main visual techniques. It allows us to read the expressions of performers and audience, intensifying and making more intimate the concert experience translated into film. Movement is created almost entirely by panning and fast cutting rather than by different kinds of camera motion, not implying a great range of space or experience but directing our attention toward different aspects of a contained and intense event. The rapid pace of the cutting, along with many shots of the flashing light show (by Headlights) reproduce the total psychedelic effect that was characteristic of rock performances at that time and provide some of the film's most effective visuals.

Most of these elements are combined in the performance of Ravi Shankar, the most successful part of the film and one of the few sections that works as a cinematic sequence. As we hear the first strains of the sitar, the camera focuses on a close-up of a pair of shoes in the middle of the road. Then it pulls back to show the morning world of the festival, moving through the crowd of people beginning the new day and panning the stalls as if the camera, inspired by the new music, is full of energy for the final performance of the festival. Because we have seen so many joyful close-ups, when the camera finally reaches Alla Rakha's beaming face, we cannot tell whether he is onstage. But then, when the camera shows us Ravi Shankar for the first time, we realize that they are indeed performing, which is the source of Rakha's pleasure. The film's emphasis on interaction between performers is fully realized here as they smile and nod at each other, even making comments, and respond with approval and pleasure at each other's improvisations. Their reactions reflect their musical process because their improvisations work off each other in the same way. At one point, the camera cuts back and forth between them, as the tabla and sitar alternate in musical focus. The close-up frequently draws our attention to Shankar's intricate finger work and to Rakha's flying hands, sometimes moving so rapidly that they are out of focus. The rhythm is intensified by the close-up of Shankar's bare foot in the foreground, keeping time with Rakha's drum in the background of the shot. As if the heightened excitement of the music requires it, the film now offers more of the audience's reaction than at any other point. The close-ups of faces in the audience reflect the same joy that Rakha and Shankar are experiencing; this is further affirmed as we watch the enthusiastic reactions of other performers, like Jimi Hendrix and the late Brian Jones, in the audience. When the performance ends, the audience rises and begins shouting for more. In an overhead long shot, the camera pans the huge crowd, then comes in closer, panning the rows of cheering people, moving finally to a close-up of hands clapping, as if in joyful appreciation of the entire festival, until the screen goes black. The successful development of this sequence, beginning with a close-up, moving out to include the joy and excitement of the whole scene, and moving back into the final close-up, provides a satisfaction that expresses well the film's overall conception of the festival.

Woodstock

WOODSTOCK (1969)

Like the ethnographic film, *Woodstock* has as one of its primary goals the exploration of a subculture in relation to the larger American society it hopes to replace. The film itself can be seen as aiding that replacement because it has many characteristics of a propaganda documentary like *Triumph of the Will,* meant to authenticate the magical power of the huge spectacle in order to bring acceptance of new values. But the various intentions of the film are seriously undermined by the fact that it reflects an inadequate conception of the great event it records; in many cases the film is mechanical and oversimplified, failing to distinguish between what works and what does not, both at the festival and in the film.

In treating the larger American culture, often represented by the New York state locals, the film focuses on its relationship with the youth culture and with the media recording the event. Many sequences reveal a surprising harmony between the two cultures. For example, the film opens with a grainy shot of an old farmer. "The kids were wonderful," he says and is pleased to find certain traditional values still intact: "It was 'Sir this' and 'Sir that.'" He also understands that both the event and the film will have great impact on audiences all around the world. This cultural harmony is reinforced by the visual montage of preparation for the festival. The camera reveals artfully composed shots of an idyllic green landscape in which radiant blond hippies and locals are working to prepare the land; we see them with tractors, harvesters, cars, buses, horses, cows, motorcycles, and construction lifts. The first song of the film, "It's Been a Long Time Coming," underscores the traditional and religious roots of this activity, which are felt by the young spectator who says prophetically, "This is unbelievable. . . . It looks like some kind of Biblical epical scene." A local police chief says, "I think we should be proud of these kids. . . . Their clothes are their own business; as far as demeanor goes, they're good Americans." The youth culture too at times encourages this harmony as Hugh Romney urges the audience to help the man whose hamburger stand burned down, "If you can still dig capitalism." Other locals, while showing a humane sympathy, fail to understand that this culture poses an alternative. The Port-O-San maintenance man, while cheerfully cleaning the job johnnies, says he is "glad to do it for the kids. . . . My son's here too." Then he adds, unaware of the incongruity, that he also has a kid in Vietnam. The film tests the awareness of the movie audience by giving them shots of arriving musicians on both sides of the split screen. We look back and forth quickly as we identify Joe Cocker, Richie Havens. Gracie Slick, Janis Joplin, Pigpen, Jerry Garcia, and others, experiencing the same intensity of excitement that the Woodstock audience must have felt. The more we can recognize, the more we are in harmony with the subculture.

Other sequences illustrate the hostility and differences that exist between the two cultures. The fish-eye lens distorts the faces of locals who call the Woodstock people "freaks," "an invading army," and refer to the whole event as a "shitty mess." Their hostility is matched by that of a paranoid Woodstock youth who, after the rainfall, asks, "How come the fascist pigs been seeding the clouds, and why doesn't the media report that stuff, man!?" The gap between the cultures is also shown by the distance between interviewer and interviewee in several sequences. For example, one interviewer must deal with a local who screams, "They're all on pot! There are fifteen-year-old girls sleeping in the fields," but who declares it "irrelevant" when the interviewer suggests that Vietnam might be a more dangerous place for young people. However, when an ABC man interviews Mike Lang, one of the promoters, the interviewer himself is implicitly condemned. He begins with negative questions such as, "What's the worst part of one of these things?" He reveals his ignorance with "What is it that the musicians have that communicates so well to these young people?" Mike Lang can only answer "Music. I gotta split," to which the short-haired, sideburned, sport-shirted interviewer unfortunately replies,

"Groovy." Then he turns to his cameraman and says he would like to shoot Lang with natural sound when he gets "all tense and bugged." This sequence strongly implies that the outside media, not the Woodstock people or the filmmakers, are the exploiters. Another attitude toward outside interviewers is revealed in the effective sequence with a young couple arriving at the festival. The interviewer is discreetly boggled because he is not prepared for the genuine unconventionality of their responses. When they say that they live together with other people and "we ball and everything," he can only ask, "Are you two going together?" His clichéd "Can you communicate with your parents?" evokes from them a sensitive and complex statement implying that, while they are not hostile to their parents and understand their concern, they have chosen completely different alternatives in living.

While the film is willing to show the positive and negative elements of the outside culture, it tries to explain all the negative elements of the youth culture as inevitable results of the size of the gathering. Further, it is unwilling to admit that there are any exploitative elements within the Woodstock nation. We repeatedly hear people exclaim that this is the second largest city in New York. Hence the mud, illness, death, bad trips, garbage, food shortage, and long lines. In fact, these things are almost welcomed because they strengthen the community's ability to cooperate in the face of adversity.

One of the few "officials" whose comments reflect the real life of the community is Hugh Romney of the Hog Farm. We accept as authentic his membership in the community and his enthusiastic idealism for two reasons. His concern for the bad acid that is circulating shows a poised awareness of the real dangers of life at Woodstock, and his playful wit and comic energy, as he participates in many aspects of community life, make acceptable in him a joyful idealism suspect in others. He speaks to the tired crowd on the last day: "Good morning. What we have in mind is breakfast in bed for four hundred thousand. . . . We're all feeding each other. . . . We must be in heaven, man. . . . Remember, kissing builds up your mouth."

Yet the sense of community is expressed most effectively not through the verbal reiterations but through the visuals. The long shots of the huge crowd have an inspirational power, as they did in *Triumph of the Will*. The new freedom of this community embraces a great variety of human responses, which are well documented in the rain sequence, which tests the community's strength in coping with an unexpected crisis. The sequence opens as camera, equipment, and people are threatened by the high winds of a sudden storm. The camera, which follows the signs of crisis, moving quickly from the violently whipping canvas sheets to people scurrying around onstage to the audience scrambling to unfold bits of shelter, is vulnerable itself as we see raindrops on the lens. The fast pace of the camera work implies that all elements of the community are galvanized into harmonious action. Leaders encourage a sense of cooperation and confidence by making comments such as, "We'll ride this out together . . . Hang on to your neighbor . . . Please move away from the towers . . . Take it calm and easy," and by leading the group in a "no-rain" chant.

The variety of response to the storm is effectively expressed through the split screen. While on the left the camera moves through the crowd and shows people huddled together under plastic, the right shows a woman bathing by the road and several people walking nude, good-naturedly accepting the rain. After the storm, the camera on the left playfully participates in a mud slide, as the camera on the right focuses on a spontaneous jam session with bongos. Both activities are linked to the primitive no-rain and peace chants and to other archetypal communal practices such as dancing and the sharing of wine.

Unfortunately this effective sequence ends with one of the best examples of an aspect of the youth culture that the film would like to disguise—the hype and exploitation within Woodstock nation. As a couple is stripping to make love in an idyllic setting on the right, the left side reveals the two promoters, Lang and Kornfeld, being interviewed about the financial aspect of the festival. Because it was spontaneously transformed into a "free concert," Kornfeld confides, "Financially this is a disaster, but I am happy." Lang concurs: "People are communicating with each other. [The couple on the right continues to make love.] . . . It has nothing to do with money . . . [accompanied by flute music]." Unfortunately the audience is aware that the promoters have sold the exclusive film rights for more than two million dollars and that, in many places, tickets to see the film cost as much as five dollars. The focus of the hype shifts slightly as the owner of the land on which the festival is taking place addresses the crowd: "I'm a farmer. . . . I don't know how to speak to twenty people at one time," he begins. But he gets into the spirit of his oratory as he claims, "This is the largest group of people ever assembled in one place." He endorses those of whom we are already suspicious: "Your promoters have done a mammoth job. They deserve a vote of thanks." Our distrust of the promoters rubs off onto the filmmakers who are presenting them in this completely positive light, especially when we recall that a number of important stars, including Janis Joplin, the Jefferson Airplane, and the Grateful Dead refused to participate in the movie because, among other reasons, they were unable to reach financial agreement with the filmmakers. It seems filmmakers are willing to sacrifice the best music for money.

The music, the core of the film, cannot help but suffer from this lack of judgment. Although groups are carefully arranged by the symbolic values they represent in the youth culture and the narrative links between lyrics, there is no discrimination in the quality of the music. Some groups are successful both musically and filmically. The sequence of Country Joe's performance, one of the best in the film, relies on his interaction with the audience. We constantly see and hear the crowd as he leads them to spell out "fuck" and then draws them into the sing-along, where the camera participates by following the bouncing ball along the lyrics, inviting the participation of the film audience. When he says to the crowd, "There are about three hundred thousand of you fuckers out there," the audience spontaneously rises and the camera pulls back to show its huge size before cutting to a close-up of Country Joe's face. We see the happy faces of others onstage, and someone embraces Joe with pleasure at his performance. This sequence, perhaps more than any other, actually shows the spontaneous communication between audience and performer that is often mentioned but seldom seen. Country Joe's qualities as a performer encourage this authenticity: He is playful, helping the audience over its hesitation at singing along; he relies on the quality of his music and its value to his audience rather than on trying to create in himself an artificial intensity that, it is hoped, the audience will imitate.

The effectiveness of other performances, however, is undermined by the filmic treatment. Sly and the Family Stone can create audience excitement through their extravagant costumes, consciously sensual movements, and the intensity with which their music builds to crescendos. But the purple light obscures the colors of the costumes. The camera impedes the effect of their movement by frequently cutting them off at the knees and renders suspect their appeal and intensity by showing us the audience's reactions only once, at the very end of the sequence.

The oversimplified and mechanical quality of many of the visuals is clearly revealed in Joe Cocker's sequence, especially in the use of the split screen. The words of his song "I Get By with a Little

Help from My Friends'' dictate the first split image—Cocker on one side, his friends "helping" at the mike on the other. Another predictable juxtaposition is set up between Joe's famous guitar-playing hand gestures on the right and a guitar player doing the real thing on the left. When the singing begins to get wild, we see a double image of Cocker, with slight variations in size and angles, implying simply that if one Joe Cocker is good, two must be better. At the end of the performance when he thanks the audience, the final split screen shows Cocker on the left getting a little more help from his friends, this time the audience.

The weakness of the visual solutions to certain admittedly difficult problems can be shown by examining the film's treatment of three solo performers: Joan Baez, Arlo Guthrie, and John Sebastian. Although they vary in musical talent, none is really a magnetic performer. Hence the film focuses on a simplistic conception of the particular values each represents to the youth culture. Joan Baez, one of the biggest names in the film, is not singing with her usual precision; her timing and pitch are frequently off. The solution is to stress her symbolic role of purity. We see still shots of Joan and her husband David Harris, linking her narratively to draft resistance, a source of sympathetic approval in the subculture. During her performance, she is shown mainly in close-ups as if to reveal her sincerity. These close-ups, which vary in size and position, are always surrounded by the simplicity of basic black, insisting upon a visual equivalent for the purity of her a cappella singing. The use of soft dissolves and superimpositions rather than the sharp divisions of the double and triple screen also contributes to this effect. Her sequence is strategically placed immediately before the orgiastic Who, a juxtaposition that unfortunately underscores the dullness of Baez's performance.

In Arlo Guthrie's sequence, the filmmakers face the problem of a performer whose strength lies not in his extraordinary musical ability but in the wit and social comment of his appealing talking blues. Their solution is to develop the sequence largely through narrative, linking Guthrie to other parts of the film and to popular social positions. First, he is introduced by Country Joe (the only time a perfomer's sequence is introduced by another performer), who is supposed to represent the same iconoclastic and rebellious values, though anyone familiar with the rock scene can only greet this connection with amused tolerance. Someone shouts "marijuana," suggesting the main theme of the sequence, and Country Joe begins "Your love is like a rainbow," creating a narrative link back to the previous rain sequence, which stressed communal values. Then the sound offers a recording (assuring the musical quality) of Guthrie's "Coming into Los Angeles," introducing the visuals of Guthrie's arrival, the huge crowd, and a montage of people turning on. As in the Baez sequence, Guthrie's night performance (of the same song) is intercut with narrative shots of his arrival and interview. In stressing his banter with the audience ("Hey! The New York Thruway is closed!" "A million and a half people are here tonight!") rather than his musical performance, the film emphasizes his social role as messenger, bringing the news of this group's effect on the larger society outside.

With John Sebastian, the filmmakers face even greater problems. How will they render believable his innocent optimism, especially in relation to the limitations of his music and the sentimentality of the song he offers? The film attempts to convince us of his sincere enthusiasm by creating interaction between him and the crowd. In his introductory remarks, he offers sweet idealism, albeit sprinkled with words appropriate to the subculture: "It's looking like there ain't gonna be no fuckups. . . . Just love everybody around you and clean up a little garbage on the way out and everything's gonna be all right." He urges the audience to sing along (with little success) as his song about the generation gap, dedicated to the man whose wife has just had a child, becomes the narrative commentary for a montage of shots of beautiful children. Then, as if trying to insist on the power of his enthusiastic sincerity, the camera moves behind him and shows him together with the crowd, an awkward choice, since they are still unwilling to sing along. Like Baez's performance, Sebastian's is placed with obvious but ineffective strategy; he is followed by Country Joe, as if to group together performances eliciting audience participation. The strategy backfires because it only emphasizes the difference between genuine involvement with the audience and an attempt to fake it.

Woodstock is framed with the performances of Richie Havens and Jimi Hendrix, two black soloists whose positions at the beginning and end imply that they give equally valuable performances. In Havens' performance, the camera reflects a shallow and stereotyped conception of black simplicity and energy by shooting from Havens' knees up into his toothless gums and by focusing on the sweat staining his shirt and dripping off his nose—all designed to show the unselfconscious integrity of his personality and performance. Ironically, his singing of "Freedom" is presented with the most restricted guitar work and monotonous visuals of the film. The entire sequence is presented on the single screen, and the camera moves little, showing only his face, his banging foot, his jaw leaning on the guitar, the simple barring of his left hand, and repetitive downstroke of his strumming. While the simple camera work is intended to offer a visual equivalent to the "basic driving energy" of his musical style, it actually emphasizes its limitation, especially since this long sequence is one of the few in the film shot in real time. The symbolic values are presented with an equally heavy hand. As Havens sings "Marching to the Korean War," the camera cuts to a helicopter (demonstrating the song's political relevance) hovering over the unfinished construction (showing that the energy of the music demands that it begin even before the site is completed).

But as Jimi Hendrix's performance concludes the film, the creativity of his guitar work and the audience's demands for "More! More!" convince us that the energy of the audience, after three days at the festival (and ours, after three hours in the theater) can still be revived by excellence. His performance combines many of the values offered in earlier sequences: His choice of song, a parody of "The Star-Spangled Banner," evokes the comic energy of Sha Na Na; his discordant rendering is linked to the iconoclasm of Country Joe; his orgasmic delivery, with the red, white, and blue motif, reminds us of the Who and Ten Years After; he presents another views of the black appeal for freedom in contrast with that of Richie Havens.

The film focuses on the quality and power of his music rather than on the theatrics of his performance, as in *Monterey Pop.* We hear his music before we see him. Then the camera emphasizes the movement of his hands and his serious but immobile expression; as he opens his mouth, we hear the guitar scream. There is a minimum of hokum in the visuals; a close-up of Hendrix briefly superimposed against the cranes and poles creates a simple abstract design, one of the film's few artfully effective compositions. The red, white, and blue motif is not manufactured through lighting but is an authentic part of Hendrix's costume, inherently related to the song he is singing. As he plays, we see long shots of the nearly deserted fields covered with rubbish, relating well to the conception of America being expressed by Hendrix's music. For the first time, the connection between the music and the visuals is not dependent upon narrative or lyrics.

This sequence, as opposed to Havens', effectively departs from real time, for we next see an image of Hendrix superimposed on a long shot of people leaving; then a close-up of his fringed arm moving in slow motion is superimposed on an aerial shot of the full

Woodstock audience, moving jerkily in speeded-up motion, clapping and calling for more. The film ends with sudden silence. This manipulation of time allows a juxtaposition of the two cultures: decadent America, evoked through Hendrix's music and through the image of the rubbish-strewn wasteland, contrasted with the final image of the full strength and energy of the Woodstock nation.

GIMME SHELTER (1970)

Like *Woodstock, Gimme Shelter* has as one of its primary goals the exploration of the youth culture as manifested in a historic rock festival. However, the main contrasts lie not between the youth culture and the larger society around it but between various elements within the youth culture itself. The entire film is informed by a spirit of inquiry rather than by a propagandistic desire to celebrate the values of the youth. This inquiry, the need for which is created by the terrible murder at Altamont, can be seen in the general structure of the film and in the selection of the songs and the techniques by which they are presented. As a result of its inquiry, the film implies that everyone—the Stones, parts of the audience, the Angels, and the promoters from the outside culture —must share the guilt.

Again, like *Monterey Pop* and *Woodstock,* this film is faced with the special problems in handling time that result from the translation of live performances to film. *Gimme Shelter* is the most effective of the three in handling the relationship between the media. In fact it introduces a third element, the tape replay of the film itself (thus making *Gimme Shelter* three media deep) and handles simultaneously five time structures: the individual live performances, the concert tour, the Altamont festival, the TV replay, and the film as a whole. This is the special quality of *Gimme Shelter's* success. Whereas *Woodstock* and *Monterey Pop* constantly stress (with varying degrees of success) different aspects of the excitement we would feel if we were there, *Gimme Shelter* develops the potentiality of film to give a better understanding of the Stones and Altamont than we would have had if we had been there. Keith Richard, discussing Altamont, said:

> Most of this I've seen from the movie. Same as anyone else. Most of the people who've seen what went down at Altamont have caught it from the movie. When I was there,

I just heard a bit, I never actually saw anything flying till we went on.[5]

Despite the fact that the film includes several different time structures, its controlling pattern is chronological, proceeding from the beginning of the Stones's tour through the planning of Altamont to the festival itself, implying that one way to investigate a murder is to follow the causal development of events. But the movement forward and backward in time provided by the TV tape replay, the discontinuities of time in individual performances, and the parallel cutting of certain transitional sequences suggest that simple chronology is not enough. Complexity of time is present in the opening sequence. The screen is black as we hear an announcer say, "Everybody seems to be ready," and we anticipate the Stones's first performance. But the opening visual image is a rather ironic shot of Keith Richard astride a mule ambling down the highway, followed by Jagger and the other Stones with a cameraman filming their movements on the road. We cut to the visuals that match the audio of the Stones performing "Jumpin' Jack Flash" and then cut away (perhaps more quickly than the audience would like) to the TV studio with the Stones watching their own performance on the monitor. As the camera moves in for a close-up of each, their names are printed as we continue to hear the sounds from the concert with a voice saying, "Let's see how they look." The audio then switches to the TV studio, as Charlie Watts asks one of the filmmakers about how long it will take to put the film together. The answer is eight weeks. They are listening to a radio interviewer who reports on the deaths at Altamont and asks, "What was the Altamont free concert like?" In the studio, the Stones watch the tape unfold as we watch the film, implying an inquiry parallel to that of the audience. Though they were present at Altamont, they too need a broader perspective for an understanding of the events, and this the film medium alone can provide. Simultaneity in time not only presents two investigations; it also informs us about the Stones's reactions to Altamont, helping the film audience to evaluate the Stones. The fact that the studio replay takes place after Altamont is over allows the filmmakers to include a radio interview with Sonny Barger of the Hell's Angels, introducing an evaluation by still another involved group and offering that reaction, in turn, for judgment by the audience. Barger insists that all the world knew the Angels were hardly pacifists;

[5] Keith Richard, quoted by Robert Greenfield in *Rolling Stone* (August 19, 1971), 35.

they had been invited to come in free, drink all the beer they could, and sit and look impressive on the stage. He is annoyed at all the surprised horror and insists that the world should know that if you mess with an Angel, you can expect trouble. People messed with their bikes and trouble was, predictably, forthcoming. Barger complains, "Jagger put it all on the Angels. . . . We were the dupes of that idiot." The camera then moves in for the reaction of Watts, who says, "I think I remember him, do you? . . . A couple of them were really very nice. . . . That was really a shame." Then we cut to the titles. During this interview we are evaluating not only the professed innocence of the Angels but also the naivete of the Stones and others who expected the Angels to keep the peace at Altamont. Before the film audience sees the titles we have already been introduced to the investigative nature of *Gimme Shelter:* its central question about Altamont, its focus on the murder, and its three views of the Stones (on stage, on tour, and in the TV studio).

The film continues its investigation by surveying the various cultural groups participating at Altamont, particularly the rock performers. For example, in all three views of the Stones in the film, they are carefully costumed to give the proper image and are self-consciously aware of the camera. In many sequences on tour and in the studio, the camera moves in for an extreme close-up of one of the Stones. Unlike the close-ups in the Baez sequence in *Woodstock,* which present a stylized vision of sincerity, the close-ups here carefully scrutinize as if the key to the Stones lies in the details of their faces, bodies, and clothing. The camera dwells on Keith Richard's worn snakeskin boots. As Charlie Watts listens intently to the tape, the camera focuses on the strange shape of his mouth as if it is a significant clue to his feelings. Watts, however, remains largely impassive, as do the other Stones—possibly a sign that, despite their participation in the investigation, they are unwilling to reveal themselves in front of the inquiring camera. Perhaps the most revealing insight into the Stones comes from the juxtaposition of the three kinds of performances. For example, as Jagger sings, "I can't get no satisfaction," the words are ironically undercut by the music and visuals, and the implication is that of all people in the world, Mick Jagger surely can get satisfaction. When we cut to the TV studio, we see Jagger laughing at his own performance, as if he is also aware of the irony. Then the image on the TV monitor changes to a press conference where Jagger, colorfully costumed, is being asked whether he is now more satisfied. He flippantly replies, "Financially dissatisfied, sexually satisfied, philosophically trying." Then we cut back to the TV studio where Jagger, who is displeased with his flippant response, says, "Rubbish."

The selection and arrangement of the musical performances are most revelatory about Altamont. As we move through the film, the narrative message of the lyrics becomes increasingly important and the performances increasingly fragmented. Significantly, this shift transforms our view of the Stones as well as the basic tone of the film. The first two numbers performed by the Stones stress the joyous energy of both Jagger and the audience. The first song, "Jumpin' Jack Flash," is lit in red and lavender and characterized by zooms and fast cutting. The harmony with the audience is suggested by the girl's jumping up and down between Jagger and the camera, thereby creating a strobic effect that goes with the beat of the music. This visual treatment enhances Jagger's beauty, the audience's enthusiasm, and the exhilaration with which the tour and film begin, contrasting sharply with the low-keyed interview that opens *Woodstock* and the long monotony of Richie Havens, its first performer. The visual treatment of "Satisfaction," Jagger's second song, emphasizes his physical energy and grace. The camera catches him striking a dramatic pose as he leans his head back on his hand and twirls his long red scarf to mesmerize the crowd. In both songs the relationship between performers and audience, which the camera carefully authenticates, is harmonious, to say the least. The film's treatment of "Love in Vain," the next song by the Stones, offers not celebration and participation, as in the first two performances, but a closer examination, which is achieved in two ways. First, the camera explores both audience and Jagger in slow motion, giving the film audience the opportunity for a more detached scrutiny of Jagger's beauty and his power over the crowd. The film is now working for a separation rather than a merging of the two audiences. The second way in which this sequence invites scrutiny is by cutting suddenly from Jagger at the concert, filmed through soft red light with effective superimpositions, to a shot of him in the harsh, realistic light of the sound studio, stripped of the glamour of the concert.

The use of comparison to define Jagger's uniqueness is further developed in Tina Turner's performance of "I've Been Loving You Too Long." First of all, she is black and female, and secondly, she offers a kind of sexuality very different from that of Jagger's androgynous appeal. The camera does not cut to the audience but focuses on her style of explicit sexual desire. It moves up and down, following her caressing of the microphone, cutting away from Tina only to show Jagger backstage. Jagger acknowledges this contrast and her style as, watching the videotape, he comments, "It's nice to have a chick occasionally."

The performance of "Country Honk" elicits the first hint that an audience might offer something other than joyful enthusiasm. As one girl, and then others, must be removed from the stage, we see that the crowd can also interfere with a performance. This is further emphasized by the fact that the Stones are out of rhythm and harmony because they cannot hear themselves over the crowd noise. With the hindsight of Altamont, we in the film audience begin to realize the potential danger. Jagger, however, does not realize this, and his own excitement seems to feed on the crowd's. This is ironically underscored as he provocatively teases his already excited audience by saying, "I think I busted a button on my trousers . . . I hope they don't fall down. . . . You don't want my trousers to fall down, now do you?"

The threat of violence suggested earlier is first realized during the performance of the Flying Burrito Brothers. It follows a long sequence that shows the bad vibrations building in the crowd: Mick Taylor being hit; one of the promoters telling people to get off the scaffolding; someone on a trip laughing hysterically; the promoter refusing to announce that someone is freaking out because he does not want "to lay bum trips on the crowd," even when he is reminded that they made such announcements at Woodstock; a blond freckled woman collecting money for the Panther Defense Fund who says, "After all, they're just Negroes, you know"; a grotesque nude woman being led in a daze and a nude fat man moving through the crowd; a man with a wounded head going for help; the Angels driving up on their bikes; and a girl being dragged off the stage as she tries to reach Jagger. Despite these ominous signs, promoter Mike Lang (perhaps still thinking of Woodstock) naively remarks, "I think we're okay," and someone else (echoing the opening remark in *Monterey Pop*) says, "This is the greatest party of 1969 that we've had." As soon as the Burrito Brothers begin to sing "Six days on the road and I'm going to make it home tonight," the vibrations get better: People throw Frisbees and blow bubbles, a girl dances joyously, a young man experiences ecstacy as he is passed through the crowd. But then the first scuffle begins, and the Angels start beating people with sticks. We hear the first pleas from the stage for a doctor and for people to "stop hurting each other." Then we cut to close-ups of the audience: a girl playing a flute, another girl in white make-up with painted tears, and a bubble bursting. For the first time at Altamont, violence has stopped the music.

The pattern continues, and the violence escalates while the Jefferson Airplane is onstage. As the group begins to play, the camera cuts to more signs of mounting tension: Vito freaking out onstage, a man in the audience stripping, people drinking, Angels whispering conspiratorially onstage, Mike Lang frowning, a black man dancing in frenzy with crazed eyes. Meanwhile, the Airplane is singing "Hey that's the other side of this life" and "I don't know what I'm doing." When the scuffle breaks out and the Angels begin beating people in the audience and onstage, Gracie Slick at first responds with a naive chant of "easy, easy," intended to be soothing, and then she says, "That's really stupid . . . people get weird and you need people like the Angels to keep people in line, but the Angels get weird, too." In contrast, Paul Kantner boldly condemns the Angels after they hit Marty Balin: "It's a drag . . . you guys can't control yourselves anymore."

Monterey Pop, focusing almost exclusively on music, revealed

Gimme Shelter

little about performers' personalities. *Woodstock* created a one-dimensional image of the stars in which personality and performing ability were sincerely integrated, especially in the treatment of Joan Baez, Arlo Guthrie, and John Sebastian. *Gimme Shelter,* however, shows that their capabilities under stress are limited, despite their glamourous qualities as performers. Like Jagger, they can be naive and helpless.

The serious violence leading to the murder takes place during the Stones's performance of "Sympathy for the Devil" and "Under My Thumb." This sequence suggests that all present at the festival contributed to the violence. The contribution of the Stones has a double quality. First, the lyrics to both songs are demonic. After the first eruption of violence, during "Sympathy for the Devil," Jagger stops singing and jokingly comments, "Something very funny happens when we start that number." Then he starts the song again. Ironically, at the very point in "Under My Thumb" when Jagger sings "but it's all right," the Angels jump the black victim. It is here that we understand fully the danger, suggested in "Country Honk," of playing on a crowd to increase its frenzy. The screams we hear in the background are ambiguous; it is impossible to tell whether they are reactions to the music or to the violence. On the other hand, as the violence repeatedly interrupts the Stones's performance, Jagger plays the cool head, trying to soothe the audience, asking them to "cool out" and "why are we fighting." But his manner reveals his helplessness and uncertainty in the face of this situation, qualities also reflected in such comments as, "I can't see what's going on . . . It's just a scuffle . . . This could be the most beautiful evening . . . I can't do any more than just ask you to keep it together." Although Keith Richard gets more angry ("Either those cats cool it or we don't play. . . . We're splitting if those guys don't stop beatin' up everybody in sight."), his threats are as impotent as Jagger's pleas.

This double quality is also reflected in the audience. The camera shows a young man smiling, as if for the joys of what has been, next to a girl weeping, as if for the horror of what is coming. Although some people in the crowd are futilely making the peace sign, the view of the audience as a potential source of hostility and violence is clearly shown as the camera focuses on a man (probably on a bad trip) who is freaking out onstage, almost as if he were being transformed into a wild beast. The telephoto lens allows us to examine his distorted facial expressions, his clenched fists, the tearing of his hair. Because of his extreme hostility, we in the film audience are likely to think he is an Angel, especially since the telephoto lens earlier focused on the face of an Angel staring with hostile contempt across the stage at Jagger. Thus we are surprised when the Angels throw the man off the stage. The contribution of the Angels to the violence is apparent throughout the sequence.

The lyrics in the final sequences of the film speak directly to the events at Altamont. As the Stones perform "Street Fightin' Man" and the Angels toss flowers to the crowd, the violent message of the lyrics loses its appealing glamour. The film continues its comparative investigation by showing us several exits: the Stones and their promoters piling into the departing helicopter as if to make a fast getaway; the crowd beginning to leave at night, with the floodlights ironically creating rainbow effects; then, after a moment of silence, Jagger leaving the studio, held by a freeze shot so that we can examine his face for the effects of the Altamont experience; and finally, to the accompaniment of "Gimme Shelter," the young people leaving the festival. The final exit is the most significant. There is a quick cut to a sign that says "Reduced Speed Zone." As Jagger sings "it's just a shot away," we see a red flag waving in front of the camera. Although the clothes of the people are colorful, the land and sky are very pale. In the final shot, the camera shoots directly into the sun, creating a glaring overexposed image, which, when combined with the song lyrics, stresses the vulnerability of the youth culture from forces within and without.

The threatening external forces include not only the outlaw Angels but also Melvin Belli, the famed San Francisco lawyer who, along with other members of the straight culture, is willing to give Altamont to the youth for a considerable fee. He says to the owner of the land, "You take the publicity, and the Rolling Stones don't want any money, it's for charity, so I'll take the money." There are many shots of Belli's puffy cherubic face next to pink flowers and a crystal chandelier in soft focus, "talking for the Stones" on the "open phone" in his plush, stylized office; they reveal his confidence in his own ability to handle all the details of the festival. But his conventional conception of the smooth operation is shown to be pitifully limited. While Belli is talking to Mike Lang on the phone, an aide estimates that from five to twenty thousand kids are on their way to Altamont "like lemmings going to the sea." Belli responds, "Now? You got to be kidding." Once the festival gets under way and the trouble begins, we see only a brief glimpse of Belli walking anonymously through the crowd. That's the last we see or hear of him. Like Jagger and the other performers, Belli is incapable of dealing with the unpredictable, dark forces unleashed at the festival.

Gimme Shelter also tests the abilities of the Maysles brothers and Charlotte Zwerin, directors of the film, to deal with the unpredictable. Starting out to film the pleasures of the Stones concert tour, they find themselves making a movie about violence. Though they have been charged with exploiting the murder, they could not possibly have excluded it from the film. Many critics have particularly objected to their way of presenting the murder, calling it sensationalistic, but actually it can be seen as manifesting the inquiring quality that pervades the whole film. The first time we see the murder it looks like one of the other scuffles. Then we cut to the TV studio, and Jagger asks, "Can you roll back on that, Dave," as if he, too, is trying to determine what actually happened and who is responsible. They roll the film back to the point where Jagger is singing "it's all right," and we see the murder again in slow motion and stop action, with an arrow guiding the perception of the Stones and the film audience by pointing out the knife and the gun. This technique is similar to that in the "Love in Vain" sequence, where slow motion was used to examine Jagger and his audience. This investigative approach seems to reflect the filmmakers' responsible way of handling an incident that happened unexpectedly in front of their cameras and became the most important event at the festival and in their film. As Keith Richard observes: "Maybe what saves the whole thing is making a movie about it and showing what went down and maybe a little less belief in uniforms." [6] If they had given the murder less emphasis, they probably would have been charged with whitewashing the Stones and romanticizing the youth culture, as in *Woodstock*. As even Mike Lang admitted, Altamont was not Woodstock West. *Gimme Shelter* acknowledges the defeat of hope for harmony and joy implicit in the youth culture as it moves from the unqualified enthusiasm of its opening to the depressing horror of its conclusion, stunning the film audience with its emotional impact.

[6] *Ibid.*

5

three
cinema
movements
views of
realism

Italian neo-realism of the late 1940's, the French new wave of the late 1950's and early 1960's, and American humanistic realism of the late 1960's and early 1970's—each of these cinema movements was influenced by the social and economic milieu in which it developed. In discussing neo-realism, we focus on Roberto Rossellini and Luchino Visconti, both founders of the movement, and compare a classic neo-realistic film with a later work to illuminate their changing approaches to realism. In the French new wave, we follow the careers of François Truffaut, Alain Resnais, and Jean-Luc Godard, tracing the development of their different conceptions of reality and of the medium itself. Finally, we compare similar themes expressed through different conceptions of humane realism in the films of John Cassavetes, Andy Warhol, and Paul Morrissey.

neo-realism

Neo-realism is a film movement that arose in Italy after World War II, dominated the Italian cinema in the late 1940's, and influenced filmmakers all around the world. At a time when musicals and light comedies were allowing moviegoers to escape from the grim facts of war, the neo-realists presented an authentic treatment of the wartime experience and grappled with the social problems of postwar Italy. Mainly Marxists or liberal Catholics,[1] neo-realists advocated leftist ideas and were strongly influenced by the Soviet cinema.

Ironically, the development of neo-realism owes a great deal to the Fascists. Like the German Nazis and the Russian Communists, the Italian Fascists realized the power of cinema as a medium of propaganda, and when they came to power, they took over the film industry. Although this meant that those who opposed fascism could not make films and that foreign films were censored, the Fascists helped establish the essential requirements for a flourishing film industry. In 1935 they founded the Centro Sperimentale in Rome, a film school headed by Luigi Chiarini, which taught all aspects of film production. Many important neo-realist directors attended this school, including Rossellini, Antonioni, Zampa, Germi, and DeSantis; it also produced cameramen, editors, and technicians. Chiarini was allowed to publish *Bianco e Nero,* the film journal that later became the official voice of neo-realism. In 1937 the Fascists opened Cinecitta, the largest and best-equipped movie studio in all Europe. Once Mussolini fell from power, the stage was set for a strong left-wing cinema.

The neo-realists tried to make films that documented the external reality of their immediate local environment by exploring its society, politics, and economic activities. These filmmakers, dealing with current problems, were committed and involved. They followed in the documentary tradition of England and of Russian expressionist films by making social and moral commentaries in an effort to bring about social change. They developed a theory and a number of techniques to define their conception of realism and the film medium. The neo-realists focused on what is normal in experience rather than on what is exceptional. Their task was to draw significant implications out of ordinary events that usually pass unnoticed. Cesare Zavattini, screenwriter for many De Sica

[1] George A. Huaco, *The Sociology of Film Art* (New York: Basic Books, 1965), part 3.

films and leading theorist of the movement, described the task this way:

> A woman is going to buy a pair of shoes. Upon this ele-
> mentary situation it is possible to build a film. All we have
> to do is to discover and then show all the elements that
> go to create this adventure, in all their banal "dailiness,"
> and it will become worthy of attention, it will even become
> "spectacular." But it will become spectacular not through
> its exceptional but through its *normal* qualities; it will
> astonish us by showing so many things that happen every
> day under our eyes, things we have never noticed before.[2]

Drawing out the implications suggested the need for interpretation: In order to demonstrate that the subject was "something
worth watching," the filmmaker had to "disembowel it" or reveal
its interior value, and he did so through his manner of presentation, which frequently reveals a moral perspective. For example,
by focusing on the normal, these films frequently celebrate the
values of the common man who is exploited by corrupt institutions.
The search for a lost bicycle, for a place to live, or for a job becomes symbolic of a man's struggle to retain his dignity. The neo-
realists never tried to hide the moral basis of their movement; they
saw it as the controlling force for the all-important interpretive
process. Zavattini argued:

> Neo-realism, if it wants to be worthwhile, must sustain the
> moral impulse that characterised its beginnings, in an
> analytical documentary way. No other medium has the
> cinema's original and innate capacity for showing things,
> that we believe worth showing, as they happen day by day
> —in what we might call their "dailiness," their longest and
> truest duration. The cinema has everything in front of it,
> and no other medium has the same possibilities for get-
> ting it known quickly to the greatest number of people.[3]

Like the Soviet cinema of the 1920's and the British documentary of the 1930's and 1940's, neo-realism abandoned the traditional well-made plot, which was seen as an artificial contrivance
distorting normal life. Zavattini claimed:

> The most important characteristic, and the most important
> innovation, of what is called neo-realism, it seems to me,
> is to have realised that the necessity of the "story" was
> only an unconscious way of disguising a human defeat,
> and that the kind of imagination it involved was simply a

[2] Cesare Zavattini, "Some Ideas on the Cinema," in *Film: A Montage of Theories,* ed. Richard Dyer MacCann (New York: Dutton, 1966), p. 221.
   [3] *Ibid.,* p. 220.

technique of superimposing dead formulas over living social facts.[4]

Thus these films do not offer simple, neat solutions to the problems they raise. They almost never end happily, for that would falsify reality and minimize the need for prompt social action.

Striving for authenticity also led these filmmakers to shoot on location, rather than in studio sound stages, and to use ordinary people rather than professional actors for many of the roles. According to Zavattini, "To want one person to play another implies the calculated plot, the fable, and not 'things happening.' "[5] Partly because of the use of nonprofessional actors and partly for economic reasons, the films were shot without sound and the dialogue was synchronized back in the studio, a process that gave the director much greater freedom in capturing what was happening spontaneously in front of the camera. Neo-realism departed from the practices of Soviet cinema and the British documentary in tending to use real time rather than relying heavily on montage. If they were going to record daily events as they happened "in their longest and truest duration," then these filmmakers had to rely on long takes that captured the pace of normal life.

By 1949 neo-realism began to decline. Pressure against the leftist orientation was exerted by the government and the Catholic Church, making it difficult for neo-realist directors to get financing. Moreover, as some of the postwar problems lost their immediacy, the treatment of the characteristic themes began to be sentimentalized. Some directors, like Vittorio De Sica, tried to keep the old patterns alive, the result being a serious esthetic decline in their work. Others, like Fellini and Antonioni, who began as neo-realists, went in new directions. They realized that the movement's conception of realism was limiting, for it was confined to external conditions and common experience and was incapable of exploring the psychological reality of the individual. An often-quoted comment by Antonioni about De Sica's *Bicycle Thief* (1949), one of the best neo-realist films, is very revealing: He said that if he had directed the film, he would have told more about the people and less about the bicycle. Fellini's conception of realism also differed from that of neo-realist films: "For me, neo-realism means looking at reality with an honest eye—but any kind of reality: not just social reality, but also spiritual reality, metaphysical reality, anything man has inside him."[6]

[4] *Ibid.,* p. 217.

[5] *Ibid.,* p. 227.

[6] Federico Fellini, "The Road Beyond Neorealism," in *Film: A Montage of Theories,* p. 380.

In focusing on Roberto Rossellini and Luchino Visconti, the two filmmakers who were most significant to the early movement, we find that although their recent films reveal their growth as directors, their works are still clearly rooted in neo-realism. In many ways, Rossellini and Visconti can be called the founders of the movement. Visconti is the only filmmaker who managed to make a significant independent film during the Fascist regime. His *Ossessione* (1942), a realistic adaptation of James Cain's novel *The Postman Always Rings Twice* to a contemporary Italian setting, is the most important precursor of neo-realism,[7] and *La Terra Trema* (1948) is one of the best films to come out of the movement. Although Rossellini was working on propaganda films for Mussolini during the Fascist era, his *Open City* (1945), the first film made in liberated Italy, launched neo-realism. It was ignored at the 1946 Cannes Film Festival but soon won international praise in Paris and in New York, where it received the New York Film Critics Award of 1946 and was acclaimed as a masterpiece.

In order to identify their unique types of realism and to discover in what ways their visions have changed, we are going to discuss an early and a late film by each director: Rossellini's *Open City* and *The Rise to Power of Louis XIV* (1966) and Visconti's *La Terra Trema* and *The Damned* (1969). After the decline of neo-realism, both men were involved in opera, a stylized art form, which affected the structure and conception of realism in their later films. Both have made an important deviation from neo-realism by selecting subjects set in a foreign country and in the historical past (a trend that was also apparent in some of Eisenstein's later films, such as *Ivan the Terrible* and *¡Que Viva México!*). Instead of documenting the here and now, they are concerned with reconstructing the past and interpreting it in a way that makes it relevant to the present. Yet their recent films do continue to focus on external reality and to explore similar themes of knowledge and power.

Roberto Rossellini

OPEN CITY (1945)

The concept of realism in *Open City* was to get as close as possible to contemporary events with minimum artifice. The film was

[7] This film has never been released in the United States because M-G-M, the producers of the 1946 American version of Cain's story, had (unlike Visconti) purchased the film rights to the novel and to protect their investment have not allowed Visconti's film to enter this country.

begun during the occupation, two weeks before the Allies reached Rome; as a result, there are many shots of German soldiers taken with hidden cameras. The events of the film were so recent that one of the staged shots of German soldiers making an arrest was interrupted by a passing streetcar conductor who thought the scene was the real thing. Rossellini worked with a screenplay, written by Sergio Amidei and Federico Fellini, based on the actual experience of Amidei, who, like the hero, Manfredi, was in the Resistance. The film uses few professional actors. For example, Maria Michi, who plays Marina (the girl who betrays Manfredi), was a friend of Amidei and was also active in the Resistance, having hid its leaders in her apartment. Rossellini used Maria's own furniture to add to the authenticity; he could not use her apartment because it was too small for the camera and lights. All the characters in the film were based on actual persons. Don Pietro, the Catholic priest, was a composite of two priests executed by the Germans. Manfredi was based on the Resistance leader Celeste Negarville; Pina (played by Anna Magnani), on a woman shot by the Germans as she threw stones at the soldiers taking away her husband. The Gestapo leader was a composite of Kapler (the head of Gestapo headquarters in the Via Tasso) and Dolman (the German commander of Rome).

Although Rossellini was dealing with the extraordinary situation of a world war, he nevertheless focused a great deal of attention on the ordinary activities of the people—eating, playing, quarreling, loving, and praying. We first see Pina in a scene where women are storming a bakery to get food for their families. Despite wartime conditions that make the bakers hoard food and cause the black-market prices of eggs and other commodities to soar beyond her reach, Pina is still generous enough to give bread to a friend. Despite the grim circumstances in this scene, elements of humor are provided by a sexton and an Italian police officer who also want bread. The first time we see Don Pietro, the Catholic priest who is active in the Resistance, he is playing soccer in the church courtyard with a bunch of young boys. When the game stops, the ball hits him on the head, a source of humor for both the children and us in the audience. This is not a conventional way of introducing a courageous hero. In the scene where Pina goes to see Don Pietro to confess before she marries Francesco, there is an excellent shot of her in the right background and the sexton in the left foreground waiting for Don Pietro in his living quarters. Our eyes, however, are drawn to the steaming pot of cabbage in the right foreground. When Don Pietro enters the room, he chides the sexton for cooking the cabbage, and the latter responds by chiding Don Pietro for buying books when they have no food. Although the subject of their quarrel is related to the war (the scarcity of food and the books that will be used to pass money for the Resistance), we can tell that this affectionate bickering between them is part of their ordinary interaction. In the scene when the Germans are rounding up all the Italian men in the area in order to catch Manfredi, the Italians use their daily activities to cover up their efforts to resist. One woman, hiding her men, insists that she will not leave her laundry unattended. When Don Pietro tries to prevent the Germans from finding Romoletti's bombs, he claims that he has come to comfort a dying man, one of his ordinary duties as a priest.

The children provide the best example of the combination of the ordinary activities of daily life within the extraordinary context of war. They have organized their own resistance cell, which uses the language and ideology of Communism and performs meaningful acts of sabotage such as blowing up a gas truck. At the same time that they can be seen as patriotic war heroes, they are also children enjoying the fun, excitement, and secrecy of playing war games. Their decisions to exclude girls, to avoid church, and to keep their activities a secret may be justified by Romoletti's ideology, but they are also typical of ordinary child's play. This double dimension is emphasized in a scene where they return home late after blowing up the gas truck. As they flee the explosion, they seem bold, courageous, and unified. Yet once they get on the stairs and begin going home one by one, these resistance heroes are comically transformed into little boys who fear a beating from their parents. At the end of the film, when they come to watch Don Pietro face the firing squad, whistling to let him know they are there supporting him, we are struck by their bravery. These children have been forced by the cruel circumstances of war into the inappropriate role of adults. Yet, ironically, most adults facing war are also like children, frightened and unprepared by previous experience. As in *Listen to Britain,* the continuation of the ordinary daily routine during wartime implies that the nation will have the strength to withstand the German aggression. A man's ordinary daily activities give him strength to face the extraordinary. This is the essence of Don Pietro's last words: "It is not difficult to die well. It is difficult to live well."

A mixture of the ordinary and the unusual, the comic and the tragic, is presented as a source of Italian strength. The Resistance involves a great variety of Italians, differing in age, sex, class, and ideology. Rossellini is aware of the possible tension between the Catholics and the atheistic Communists. The first sign of conflict occurs in a scene where Marcello tells Don Pietro that "these are not days for catechism." Although the potential for conflict is serious, we take it lightly in this scene because it is presented by a child (who is playing at being a Communist) in order to excuse his absence. Yet this sarcasm is later echoed by the director of Francesco's print shop, who tells Don Pietro, "We can't all hide in monasteries," and by Pina's ironic comment, "It's better to be married by a partisan priest than by a fascist official." The tension disappears once the serious crises begin. When Marcello fears that the Germans will discover Romoletti's bombs, he dresses as a choir boy and goes with Don Pietro to cope with the situation. When Pina is shot by the Germans, Don Pietro comforts Marcello, and even Francesco looks to the cross. Ironically, it is when Don Pietro tries to hide Manfredi in a monastery that they are captured and led to their deaths. And when he is being questioned at Gestapo headquarters, Don Pietro uses a style of catechism that gives him moral strength and humorously exposes the ignorance of his interrogator. Despite the fact that one is a Communist and the other a Catholic, Manfredi and Don Pietro both die bravely, respecting each other as brothers and comrades.

In contrast to the Italians, the Germans in the film are uniformly weak and sinister. *Open City* is clearly expressing a view that is as nationalistic as that of the Gestapo leader who is constantly making disparaging remarks about Italians, such as "dumb Italians!" and "Italians of all classes have a weakness for rhetoric." When asked what will happen if Manfredi refuses to talk, the German replies: "Then it would mean an Italian is as good as a German ... that there is no difference between a master race and a slave race ... and there is no reason for this war." But clearly the film is showing not that Italians are as good as Germans but that they are much better. Their capacity for humor, their rhetoric and emotional outbursts all demonstrate their humanity. When a deserter from the German army warns Manfredi and Don Pietro that the Germans "can make cowards of heroes," Manfredi responds, "We're not heroes, but we'll still not talk." One does not have to be a hero or superman to do brave deeds; one need only be an ordinary human being who knows how to live well. And the essence of living well, as we learn in a scene where Manfredi argues with Marina, is loving other human beings. Marina betrays him because, as she tells Ingrid, she loves no one. Manfredi and Don

Pietro cannot become informers because they love others, and this love helps them to die bravely.

One might argue that Rossellini's use of German stereotypes is melodramatic: the willful, effeminate Gestapo leader; the lesbian Ingrid, who maliciously exploits Marina's drug habit and coolly watches Manfredi being tortured; the cowardly deserter who hangs himself in his cell. Only Hartmann, the cynical German officer who realizes that Germany will lose the war and that the idea of a master race is absurd, does ont fit the usual stereotypes. Yet Rossellini insures that we see him as another example of German weakness, for he is drunk when he challenges the Gestapo leader and he is the one who shoots Don Pietro. Melodrama is reinforced by the music and by the symbolic scene of the lambs being "butchered" by the Germans. Yet the basic structure of the film certainly rejects melodrama and even departs from the conventional narrative pattern. It successfully combines a documentary-like realism with effective artistic control.

This combination is particularly apparent in the pacing of the film. Scenes and sequences vary in length; as if to imply that Rossellini is using as much "real" time as is needed for any particular event and that he is not cutting the film to fit a preconceived pattern. The sequence in which the Germans take away the Italian men in order to find Manfredi is very long because it includes so many important elements: Pina bringing the news that the Fascists are coming, people running and hiding, Germans organizing the search, children running to the church, women lining up outside, Don Pietro hiding Romoletti's weapons, and finally the shooting of Pina. If one charged Rossellini with contrived irony for having Pina killed on her wedding day, he could respond by pointing out that the heroines of melodrama never die halfway through the film. There is no doubt that Rossellini has exerted effective control in emphasizing the power of this sequence by foreshadowing it in the opening scene in which the Germans search Manfredi's house and by preceding it with three very brief scenes that build tension (Marina calling Manfredi's house, a Gestapo leader discovering Manfredi's identity, and Don Pietro calling the boys into the church). Realism and artistic control can also be seen in the torture sequence, which is extremely long (as if to express the victim's psychological experience of time) but in which Rossellini achieves great variety by cutting back and forth between the room where Manfredi is being tortured, the office where Don Pietro is being interrogated, and the richly decorated salon where the Germans are having a party. By cutting back and forth instead of dwelling on the torture, Rossellini is able to maintain the tension over a long period of time without seriously offending the audience's sensibilities. In a quick cut we see Manfredi's nails being ripped out, but for the most part the audience hears screams and sees bloody bruises and instruments rather than the torture itself; the rest is left to our imagination. Whenever the film cuts away, we keep wondering what is happening to Manfredi and how long he will be able to resist. The film ends not with the victory of the heroes, as in melodrama, but with their death and with the Germans still in power. The last shot is of children walking arm in arm along a hill with Rome in the background, and we recall the words Francesco used to comfort Pina: "The war will end by spring, we must believe it . . . there must be a better world, for our family, for Marcello . . . we mustn't be afraid." The ending implies that the struggle against tyranny is not over and that we should focus our hopes on the future.

Realism and artistic control are present also in the visuals. The realism is expressed by the grainy quality of the black and white photography and by variations in lighting. Because the film was being shot while the Germans were still in Rome, there were a number of technical difficulties. One camera and some of the sound equipment were captured from the Germans. The film was purchased on the black market and was at least five years old, and, since it was so hard to get, Rossellini had to use short pieces of various kinds of stock, giving the film a rough, uneven quality. To make things worse, there was a scarcity of electrical power; it frequently fluctuated from minute to minute, and this too was

Open City

bound to affect the film. The results of Ubaldo Arata, the cinematographer, under such conditions, are astounding.[8]

The visual power is enhanced by several overhead shots which invest the image of stairs with symbolic meaning. In the first sequence, we associate the stairs with the Germans' efforts to capture Manfredi. The barred railings support this association. The stairs are also the setting for important meetings between friends: Pina and Manfredi get acquainted on the landing; in a tender love scene Francesco and Pina reminisce about their first meeting, which took place on the stairs. When we see Marcello running up the stairs to join Romoletti on the roof, the railings and shadows suggest the drama and mystery that surround their daring exploits. Finally, the film builds intensity and suspense by dramatically cutting between overhead shots of the Germans going upstairs and upward-angle shots of Don Pietro and Marcello running downstairs to hide a gun.

Another highly effective scene is the one immediately preceding the sequence in which Pina is killed. The screen is totally black. Then as Don Pietro, with his back to the camera, opens the door to the church to let the boys in, we see the daylight outside. Marcello, the last to enter, is chided. Don Pietro closes the door, and the screen again goes totally black. It is hard to justify this scene in terms of the plot, but its visual power helps to evoke feelings in the audience that are appropriate to the death that is shortly to follow. Most frequently, Rossellini uses such control to achieve an extraordinary authenticity and an appearance of artlessness.

THE RISE TO POWER OF LOUIS XIV (1966)

In *Louis XIV,* a film originally made for French television, Rossellini's central problem is quite different from that in *Open City:* He is reconstructing history rather than documenting present events. Yet the two films have a similar mixture of historical authenticity and ironic humor and a similar focus on the external details of daily living. The film attends to subtleties of lighting that change the quality of space, to sounds of creaking doors and pacing footsteps, to realistic touches like chipped paint and scuffed shoes, to the elaborate furnishings with carving and intricate tap-

[8] Vernon Jarratt, *The Italian Cinema* (London: Falcon Press, 1951), ch. 6.

The Rise to Power of Louis XIV

estries, to the rich fabrics and extravagant styles of clothing. We focus on the mundane details of the lives of famous historical personages: how they ate, dressed, played, slept, made love, and died. Yet there are ironic contrasts between the visual splendor of the furnishings and the quite ordinary physical appearance and actions of the people, between the playful tone of the film and the somber mood of its characters. Louis's homely face and dwarfish body, particularly when garbed in rich velvet and surrounded by opulent halls, may strike the audience as slightly absurd. Yet Louis's strength as a king lies precisely in his understanding of the symbolic power of physical appearance, of the imagination's ability to interpret these appearances and to influence the interpretations of others. Throughout the film a pattern is established where events and effects dependent upon appearances are undercut by details of visual and thematic realism that follow. Rossellini had always agreed with Zavattini that interpretation was one of the most important elements of neo-realism, but only in *Louis XIV* does it become the main source of his power as a director.

Rossellini's controlled interpretation of his material is apparent in the film's three-part structure, which is as symmetrically balanced as the gardens of Versailles. The first section, the death of Cardinal Mazarin, provides the background for Louis's rise to power and the dramatic exposition of the film. The introduction of Mazarin is preceded by a shot of peasants, just as the introduction of Louis is preceded by a shot of his maid awakening. The dying Mazarin is attended by an audience of doctors who examine the contents of his chamber pot and smell his perspiration. The ceremonial costumes and behavior of the sick room are undercut by the realistic shots of the cardinal's pale, dangling legs and feet as he is carried to the chair to be bled. The awakening Louis is attended by members of the court who watch every movement he makes as he prays, eats, washes, and dresses, and who applaud (with four claps) the queen's symbolic announcement that last night the king performed his marital duty. In preparing for his death, Mazarin has parallel interviews with his priest and with Colbert, his financial adviser, both focusing on materialistic and political concerns. When he asks his priest, "What must I do to be able to face God?" the answer is very practical: Leave your worldly holdings to your godson, the king, rather than to your own family. Colbert warns him against Fouquet, his political enemy, advice that leads Mazarin to call a meeting with Louis. Louis also has two important interviews, both of which emphasize his awareness of his symbolic role as king of France. The first is with his

The Rise to Power of Louis XIV

godfather Mazarin; both men are very concerned with physical appearance and with what they represent. Although Mazarin is on his deathbed, he prepares for the meeting by rouging his pale cheeks. We see the empty halls of the stately palace, then hear someone call, "Le roi, le roi," and finally see the squat figure of Louis waddling forward with his hands behind his back. When Mazarin offers to leave Louis his money, Louis refuses it "not as a godson, but as the king" because of "my person and what it represents." Louis's interview with the queen mother focuses on the past rather than on the future. As Louis begins to consider his own possible rise to power, he reviews the history of the throne of France in one of several set speeches, characteristic of dramatized history. As he speaks deliberately, the camera moves in for a close-up of the queen's face as she begins to glimpse his intentions, though she quickly denies them to her friends. The first section culminates with the death of Mazarin. As soon as he dies, everyone outside awakens, and all begin the ritualistic funeral preparations, carefully dressing the dead cardinal and decorating the room with ornamental candles. The cardinal's death is transformed into a performance to be viewed by the courtly audience, as they earlier attended the king and queen's awakening. Louis stands in the outer hall but cannot enter the bedroom because "neither the sun nor death can be faced steadily." Though ritual forbids him to see a corpse, Mazarin's death engages his full attention and releases his latent powers. After announcing, "I shall return to Paris after my dinner," he immediately orders everyone into deep mourning and begins plans to take over the council meetings. He also drops an epigram, which becomes the main theme of the next section of the film: "We have lost a good lord, but don't fear, you have gained a good master." Significantly, he first demonstrates his mastery by attending to the ordinary external details of food and costume, which become extravagantly significant in section three.

The second section shows how Louis actually acquires power as the king of France and proves the truth of his epigram. At a meeting of the council, which opens the section, Louis repeats the epigram to his attending courtiers and tells them of his intention to govern. Fooled by the appearance of his former behavior, they unwisely predict (as his mother had done earlier) that he will soon grow weary of the role he wants to play and go back to his hunting, gaming, and wenching. Then in parallel interviews with Colbert and the queen mother, Louis demonstrates his ability to play several roles. He demands secrecy from Colbert, who tells him of Fouquet's frauds. His decision to keep his mother out of the council is tested in the next scene, where she scolds him for bathing in the nude at Fontainebleau and, in a shrewd attempt to regain her political power, threatens to enter a convent. Although Louis goes through outward signs of childish dependency, which his physical appearance renders convincing (he hides his tear-stained face on his mother's breast as he apologizes), he sticks to his decision to keep both her and his brother off the council and after his successful performance jauntily dons his hat.

Hunting and card-playing sequences demonstrate that Louis is able to continue his favorite pastimes while attending carefully to his political power. He is the central focus for the camera and the attending court, which is formally arranged like an audience to observe his every move. This tableau, suggesting a historical painting, contrasts sharply with shots of deer swimming with realistic, painful slowness to escape the dogs pursuing them. In the card-playing sequence, Fouquet is not so good as Louis at interpreting the reality behind appearances. As Louis leaves the drawing room firmly convinced it is time to crush Fouquet, Fouquet confidentially observes to his mistress, "I saw the King smile at you as he left." At the council at Nantes, Louis's strategy is to have D'Artagnan and the three musketeers move on Fouquet in utmost secrecy and then make the action widely known. Louis understands public relations and propaganda, and he acts with boldness and mastery.

The arrest of Fouquet is a remarkably economical scene that simultaneously demonstrates the skill of Louis as a politician and of Rossellini as a filmmaker. Like the death of Mazarin, it is the climax to a section and an important step in assuring Louis's rise to power. As Fouquet is detained in a meeting, Louis goes to the window to look out over the square. The film cuts to an overhead shot, as if from Louis's point of view, implying his control over what is happening below. The beautiful geometric composition of the men intersecting Fouquet's path on the square, carrying him away in a carriage with his mistress, who is dressed in bright red velvet, following in a chair, is all captured in one long take. The brilliant visual treatment accentuates the orderliness of Louis's plan.

The third section, the fruition of Louis's vision of France, is introduced by his discussion with Colbert of his plans for the future, a sequence that (like the earlier epigram) functions as a bridge between sections. Fouquet assumed he could rule others by appearances; Louis accepts this assumption but interprets it more broadly and applies it more effectively. He makes the court at Versailles a temple of the monarchy, employing every available artist to beautify it. Thus he realizes the inherently political nature of religion and art. He weakens the power of the nobles at home by demanding their constant presence at court, to attend which they must spend their money for elaborate clothing. Preparations with the tailor and the construction work on Versailles culminate in a court procession scene, where Louis appears in the new fashions, reminding us of the story of "The Emperor's New Clothes." Though we may laugh at his dwarfish body in his absurd outfit, we admire his shrewdness and audacity in making other members of his court feel inferior for not looking like him.

The banquet scene is an even more elaborate demonstration of Louis's effective use of appearance. As the camera moves through the kitchen, it is clear that the appearance of the food is at least as important as its taste. When the film cuts to a medium close-up of Louis seated alone at the table, we can see a few people around him. As the camera pulls back slowly, it reveals the entire court in attendance. An upward-angle shot revealing musicians playing "the King's music" is immediately followed by a shot from behind Louis, facing the whole crowd and emphasizing the huge scale of the entire scene. When the film cuts back to a close-up of Louis eating, we are reminded that all this pomp is a ritualistic elaboration of a common human activity. We watch the court attending to every trivial move that Louis makes, creating myths around him as if he were a god. When the king finishes his fourteenth dish, an announcement is heralded through the kitchen. The "king's meats" are brought out on a locked plate handled by several men before it reaches the king; after this elaborate preparation, he may not even taste the food. Both Louis and Rossellini know that power derives from interpretation, from the amount of time and attention devoted to something, rather than from the nature of the thing itself.

The final sequence offers striking tableaux of the court arranged in the formal gardens at Versailles. The camera follows Louis as he reads a book and leads the procession. When he goes inside to be alone, we suspect that we may at last discover what lies beneath his consciously controlled appearance. Slowly and laboriously Louis removes his elaborate apparel (wig, sword, vests, medals), but just when we think he is finally going to relax and be himself, he begins to put on new garments. The only sound we hear is his footsteps. Then he reads aloud from his book: "There is a loftiness that does not depend on fortune; it is a certain air of superiority. . . . This quality helps us usurp other men's deference [more than] birth, rank and merit itself." We realize that this idea is the basis of Louis's strategy. He maintains the external appearance even when he is alone, for his understanding of its symbolic power has become the essence of his nature, at least as interpreted by Rossellini.

Luchino Visconti

Points of similarity between Visconti's two films are more apparent than those between Rossellini's. *La Terra Trema* and *The Damned* are quite long ($2^3/_4$ and $2^1/_2$ hours respectively) and rather slowly paced; both show the influence of opera; both explore the disintegration of a single family and consider the family's relationship to the larger, self-enclosed culture of which it is a part. The house and the foundation of the family income (the fishing boat and the steel factory) are important symbols and central locations in each film. There are also parallels within the two families: a grandfather who is out of touch with the changes in society and who dies in the film; a heroic father who has been sacrificed before the picture begins; and the young grandsons whose rise to knowledge (Antonio) or power (Martin) is the main focus of the film.

Both films have a strong mythic quality: in the archetypal struggle between different generations within the family, in the use of fire and water imagery, in the incorporation of elements from the Faust and Oedipus stories, and in the substitution of historical inevitability for the Greek concept of destiny. Visconti is not a prolific filmmaker, but all his films are carefully controlled and consistent. Many of these qualities are also found in the films between *La Terra Trema* and *The Damned*—especially *Rocco and His Brothers* (1960), *The Leopard* (1963), and *Sandra* (*Vaghe Stelle dell' Orsa,* 1965).

LA TERRA TREMA (1948)

In 1947 Visconti went to Sicily with money advanced by the Communist Party to make a brief documentary on the plight of workers and their efforts to better their situation. There was the possibility that the documentary might help to mobilize the workers. But once Visconti arrived in Sicily, he enlarged his plans and decided to make a long film in three episodes: on the fishermen, the peasants, and the miners.[9] He made only the first episode, and it turned out to be one of the masterpieces of the neo-realist movement.

Thus from the beginning there were conflicting strains in *La Terra Trema.* The film was an ethnographic exploration of a strange culture in Sicily that speaks a dialect unfamiliar to most other Sicilians, propaganda trying to argue for a Communist revolution, and, perhaps strangest of all, a symbolic drama evocative of Greek tragedy. The third strain helps to reconcile the other two and establishes the prevailing tone.

Ethnographic realism was achieved primarily by using an authentic Sicilian location, the small village of Aci-Trezza, and actual fishermen (instead of actors) speaking their own dialect. Immediately following the titles, a long note stressing the film's authenticity explains this to the audience. The use of dialect made Visconti introduce an Italian narrator, who brings an outside view of this self-contained culture. Many of his comments, frequently expressed in the tone of an objective observer, call attention to the main dynamics of the society. Yet the realism is like no other in neo-realism, for instead of being rooted in the particularities of the here and now, it has a strong symbolic power that translates the story to the level of myth. For example, when we first see Mara Valastro walking into the street, the narrator begins to describe the old house in which she and her family live. The narrator calls it "a house like the others . . . with walls as old as the fisherman's trade." Later, as they are evicted, he emphasizes the symbolic importance of the family house as a source of identity and strength: "Now they must turn their backs on those walls, those stones worn smooth by so many steps." The black and white photography captures the stark contrast between the crumbling white walls and the dark, beamed ceiling and shutters, somehow emphasizing their simple strength. When a bank assessor later calls them weak, we are angry and do not believe him.

The written explanation that opens the film stresses its timeless, archetypal quality: "The story told in this film is the same story that has recurred over the centuries the world over, wherever men have exploited other men." This statement can also be interpreted politically. Here we have the model for any revolt of the workers against their capitalist oppressors, and many comments of the narrator support this interpretation. When Antonio is arguing with the other fishermen, trying to convince them that they should

[9] For more information about the background of this film see the screenplay of the original version published in *Bianco e Nero,* No. 2 (March 1951); and Geoffrey Nowell-Smith, *Visconti* (New York: Doubleday, 1968), ch. 2.

unite in order to cut out the wholesalers who are exploiting them, the narrator, who has just described their "arduous work" in the manner of an objective anthropologist, breaks out of this role and says, "If the old ones are content to be exploited, why should the young ones be? . . . Antonio should try to put an end to the exploitation by the wholesalers." Suddenly he is like a Marxist analyzing social and political dynamics and prescribing the proper course of action. This ideological approach, though clear in its political purpose, is transformed by the film's symbolic power into another dimension of man's eternal struggle with existence, occurring in different ways at any time and any place. The story is not merely a model of historical class struggle; it embodies many archetypal conflicts: man against nature and destiny, man against man (both conflict between classes and between generations within a family), and, especially, man against himself. When the Valastro boat is "wiped out in one night," the narrator comments, like a chorus in Greek tragedy, "Man wasn't their only enemy . . . nature was their enemy, too." And later when they are on the point of starvation and their family has almost completely disintegrated, he says ironically, as if comparing their fate with that of Oedipus, "All that is left of the Valastros are their eyes with which to cry." The neighboring women accuse Antonio of pride and think he is responsibile for his own fate: "God is punishing you for your arrogance, you're the worst family in Trezza." The Marxist interpretation that Antonio is being exploited by the wholesalers is only one among many that must be integrated into this story. The Valastros, like the Greeks, try to resign themselves to God's inscrutable will. As Mara parts from Nicola, the mason whom she has hoped to marry, she says, "We'll do God's will." The mason answers, "God's will is bitter."

Historical inevitability, not the classical concept of destiny or submission to God's will, is perhaps most important in the film's exploration of causality. The old people constantly stress the influence of the past, arguing that "one should listen to the elders." The narrator, though recognizing that this attitude toward tradition inhibits necessary change, sees it as a source of strength and satisfaction in life. As he describes the fishermen's rhythm of leaving each evening and returning each dawn, he says, "From grandfathers to fathers to sons, that's how it has always been." At the end of the film, tradition and inevitability give Antonio the strength to face the merchants (sitting under a wall showing the remnants of earlier slogans about Mussolini, linking them visually with fascism) and begin his life, and perhaps the political struggle, over again. As he prepares to go to sea once more, he returns to the ancient ritual as he says, "Bless me, Mother."

One scene that combines effectively the problems of family, political conflict, and tradition is an encounter between Antonio and Cola, his younger brother who is being lured away from the village by an American stranger, a faceless and nameless demonic figure. Cola's departure begins the disintegration of the Valastro family. Antonio argues that Cola will encounter meanness and injustice wherever he goes. He insists, "We were born in Trezza, we must die in Trezza." On one level, we can interpret this as a statement about the symbolic meaning of the story: Man will always face hardship and conflict, for they are part of his destiny. Yet, when we recall Antonio's arguments with his grandfather, who answered his pleas for change with "It's always been this way. . . . There's nothing we can do," it is possible to see Antonio assuming the role of the older generation within the family and Cola playing his former role of advocate for change. This view is supported by the fact that the grandfather's illness is brought on by the news of Cola's departure. Yet Antonio's final words to Cola set him apart from his grandfather: "Cola, remember, our struggle is here." He is ready to face the archetypal struggle in his own existential context: He does not escape into romantic fantasies like Cola and Lucia; he knows that others in his family are counting on him; for the good of the larger group, he comes to terms with his personal failure and succeeds in the struggle with self.

The significance of the encounter between Antonio and Cola is given considerable power by the visuals. The two brothers stand in a bare room. Cola is in front of a mirror. As they talk, the camera focuses on the mirror, which shows one brother's reflection and then the other's. The mirror is warped and distorts their faces but in different ways. Antonio's face is blurred, and we observe it from the perspective of Cola, who is unable to understand the truth of what Antonio is saying. Cola, however, is standing directly before the mirror, and we see his reflection with dramatic ominous shadows, as if the glass is reflecting his shadowy future.

The predominant characteristic of myths or archetypal situations is that they are simple and elemental, yet profound and complex. We find this combination in the visual style and structure of *La Terra Trema*. The high-contrast black and white photography, the formally arranged compositions, the effective depth focus shots, and the interaction of the movements of camera and subjects help to define Visconti's mythic style. The film opens and closes with

La Terra Trema

shots of fishing boats gliding to and from shore on the glassy sea, their lights beaming like stars, their formation framed by the two mountainous rocks that mark the limits of the harbor and of the photographic composition, just as the shots frame the film. In many of the carefully composed seascapes, the fishermen walk into the frame and become, along with the clustered boats and rocks, part of the natural environment. As the Valastro women wait on shore for the family boat to return in the morning, we see a long shot of their huddled figures in black shawls, and they resemble clusters of rocks or great birds that belong in the landscape. When Antonio first speaks to the other fishermen of his revolutionary ideas, he sits facing them and the camera; in the background between him and another fisherman, we see a lone boat and one of the rocks—single images foretelling that his ideas will isolate him from the others and bring about his martyrdom.

Although the ideology is Marxist, the visuals frequently develop religious implications. As Antonio returns to life and work, the family portrait is hung once more near the picture of Christ. As he throws the "Judas scales" into the sea, a huge cross appears in the right background. When Antonio experiences his short-lived happiness and has just made love to Nedda, the visuals of the final shot foretell their separation. The scene ends with a long shot of the lovers walking up a road. She walks in the shadows on the left, while he walks in the sunlight on the right, with a snow-covered mountain centered far in the distance between them. After the Valastros have been evicted, the film dissolves to a long shot of them walking in single file through the town at night, carrying their belongings; the shot is from a balcony, with the bars from the railing in the foreground suggesting the entrapment of their financial ruin.

Depth focus shots frequently expand the self-enclosed Valastro house and village spatially in order to give a sense of communion within the group that occupies the space. For example, in the first shot that combines the exterior world of men with the interior world of women, the camera is inside the dark house with the women but shoots through the doorway as the men carry their nets from the bright sunlight through the narrow passageways and through the subtle shadings of gray into the dark interior. Later, we see three Valastro men washing and carrying on a conversation in two rooms. Similarly, as the women cook, they carry on parallel activities in different rooms at different depths. When news about the mortgage comes, Cola is shaving in a room in the left foreground; Antonio moves into the next room beyond and finally joins his mother who is outside but clearly visible through the window. Despite the fact that the family is divided spatially, they have free mobility and communication with one another. This is perhaps best seen in a rooftop sequence, where the whole neighborhood participates in a conversation, each person standing, sitting, or reclining on a different level—in a window, on a rooftop, or on a balcony.

The interaction of the camera and subject is very effective. When the camera is shooting movement, it tends to be static. When the subjects are static, the camera moves. For example, as the men on the dock run in front of the camera, it remains stationary, but in the market, when the men stand in little circles haggling over prices, their voices creating a strong cadence, the camera moves around the group and pans from one face to another, as if participating in the action. In the scene where Antonio throws the scales into the sea and a fight develops, the camera is at first moving through the market. When the men begin to move, it stops. Then as the fighting erupts in one circle after another, the camera follows the action and eventually pulls back to an extreme long shot to observe the arrival of the police and the resulting arrests.

Such alternation of camera position results in a steady flow of motion.

The structure of the film is both progressive and cyclical. On the one hand, it traces the disintegration of the family and the enlightenment of Antonio. This development can be divided into five acts, with the reversal coming precisely in the middle of act three, as in Greek tragedy. Act one reveals the life situation of the fishermen and Antonio's basic goals of working for his own family and marrying Nedda. Its dominant image is one of the security that can become entrapment. The fishermen in general and the Valastro family in particular are both sustained and trapped by their daily routine. Antonio, who intends to break out of this pattern, is linked to entrapment in a scene with Nedda when the narrator compares him to the fish that are caught and she compares him to the caged rabbits. Act two deals with the struggle for change. Antonio throws the scales into the sea, an action that leads to his arrest and to the knowledge that the wholesalers need him—an awareness so powerful that, as he gains it, he cannot even eat. With the energy of his new understanding, he is able to convince his family to mortgage their house in order to buy their own boat, to risk what little security they have in order to win a better life. While this decision brings the family closer together, it begins to separate them from the rest of the villagers. Act three focuses on the brief success of Antonio and his family. As the narrator puts it, Antonio has everything he ever wanted (success in fishing, his own boat, which gives him independence from the wholesalers, and Nedda), and the family is most united. The unity is best expressed in the scene where they are salting anchovies. Everyone is working in one room, people of all ages laughing and joking and listening to music, as the camera pans from one beautiful face to another. However, they laugh so long and so loud that it becomes ominous. Act four documents their financial ruin, beginning with the loss of everything in the storm and ending with the thirty barrels of anchovies being taken away by the wholesalers for a measly eighty lire. Once the efforts of that unity have been destroyed, we are ready for the final stage of the family's disintegration and Antonio's loss of courage and strength. As Antonio puts it, "Now the devil's got us where he wants us and there isn't a hope." Simultaneously, strangers take away Cola and the Valastro house, and the grandfather becomes ill and Lucia dishonored. Antonio becomes a shiftless drunkard. In the scene where Antonio and other riffraff are loitering in the street, their gentle dancing is an expression of their civilized values and their powerful desire to be part of the community and to escape from the contemptible condition to which fortune has reduced them. Act five begins with an encounter with a young girl who is working by the sea on Antonio's abandoned boat. Antonio realizes that "we must learn to be good to each other and unite for the common good . . . only then can we move forward." He must sacrifice himself for his family (pawning his possessions, withstanding the cruel taunts of the wholesalers) in order to build a united strength with his two younger brothers. His own attempt at revolution and social change has failed, but he is contributing to the hope for the future. Once again he and his brothers go back to sea as the Valastros have always done.

In addition to the progressive development of the plot, many elements suggest a cyclical pattern. Each act contains the daily ritual of eating; each has an alternation between men and women, between exterior shots of the sea and land and interior shots of the house; each contains the family portrait. The movie opens and closes with similar shots of boats leaving or coming to the shore. Most important, each act begins with a shot of or by the sea, as if, in its combination of cruelty and benevolence, danger and calm, it is the source of energy and the symbol of life itself.

Like Eisenstein in *Battleship Potemkin,* Visconti was faced with the difficult problem of making a pro-Communist film about a rebellion that failed. In order to acknowledge and dignify the failure while presenting it as historically inevitable, he turned to classical drama, in which heroes who are important to their families or race are defeated by destiny but are heroic nevertheless. The fusion of the ethnographic, political, and mythic dimensions gives *La Terra Trema* a richness and complexity by which it transcends the particularity characteristic of the neo-realist movement.

THE DAMNED (1969)

In *The Damned* Visconti goes back to the period before World War II, treating the corrupt and perverting power of Nazi Germany. His manner of treating this theme is somewhat paradoxical, and this distinguishes it from the rather naive idealism in *Open City.* The conception of power in Rossellini's film is melodramatic though the style is realistic; in *The Damned* Visconti employs a highly melodramatic style to express a complex view of power that is sexual as well as political. In this film, power is based on the paradoxical combination of madness and control. We learn that

"Germany is the most orderly country in the world"; yet that order is rooted in irrationality and chaos. The struggle to gain power, to dominate, to impose a structure onto others, leads to constant warfare and disintegration. The rise to power is not rationally predictable as in *Louis XIV* but is full of surprises.

The film ends with Martin von Essenbeck—the character who was introduced as a weak transvestite and seemed the least qualified of all—in power. Martin succeeds not through masterfully transforming his limitations into strengths, as Louis XIV had done, but merely through a cyclical movement from one perverted extreme to another. He moves from a whining, hysterical femininity to an austere, cruel masculinity, but both manifestations are part of the same perverted identity, which is passive and aggressive and sado-masochistic. Since his strength and control are based on his madness, he is a perfect symbol for Germany. To express this paradox, Visconti portrays a world of chaos through a highly structured plot and a tightly controlled visual style.

Another unusual aspect of Visconti's treatment of the theme of corrupt power is his emphasis on the internal damage to Germany rather than on Germany's destructive effect on other countries (which was shown in *Open City*). There is a tendency in *The Damned,* as in *La Terra Trema,* to focus on a self-enclosed culture. Visconti explores the many internecine conflicts within the larger world war—between political parties, between the regular army and the SA, between the members of the Von Essenbeck family who are struggling for control of the steelworks, and ultimately between the conflicting impulses of an individual. The Von Essenbeck family becomes a microcosm of the entire German society, and Martin plays the role of Hitler.

At the same time, Visconti stresses the universality of his theme about the corruption of power by creating a strong mythic level. The recurring fire imagery and the dramatic amber and red lighting (as well as the title) evoke the inferno. Martin and his mother Sophie act out the classical Oedipus complex, while Frederick plays Faust to Jorgem's Mephistopheles. The plot, acting style, make-up, and music evoke the world of Wagnerian opera. Struggles move inward and outward, forming concentric circles that comprise an orderly vision of chaos (as in Dante's *Inferno*). The pervasive tension between chaos and order gives the film a cosmic scope.

One of Visconti's main techniques for developing this paradoxical conception of order is the incorporation of surprise into a highly controlled structure and visual style. The film is clearly divided into five long sections, which are more like acts in an opera or drama than cinematic sequences. Each act is, in turn, divided into clearly distinguishable scenes. Despite the fact that the struggle for the Von Essenbeck steelworks is so neatly organized, it is still full of surprises. Although act one leads us to think that Konstantin will gain control, Frederick succeeds in his place. Although act two seems to be consolidating Frederick's power, it ends with Konstantin's taking over. Martin's transvestism and homosexuality, presented as an eccentric deviation in act one, are revealed to be common traits of the SA in act three. Even with this revelation, we are still surprised by Martin's rise to power through incest in act four, by his transformation into an austere Nazi, and by Sophie's mental and physical deterioration into a grotesque mannequin in the final act. There is a pattern of dramatic irony: the baron's birthday, the SA's spring holiday, Frederick and Sophie's wedding—rituals ordinarily linked to renewal —all lead to death in the demonic universe of this film. Movement back and forth between union and disintegration contributes to the cyclical pattern of the film. Yet, instead of being associated with renewal and the natural process of growth, the cyclical pattern is ironically linked to eternal chaos, like endlessly walking in a circle or burning in the endless fires of damnation that open and close the film.

The first act is the longest and the most elaborate. It opens with a number of fragmented scenes, occurring simultaneously, of members of the Von Essenbeck family preparing for the dinner party that will temporarily unite them. In the banquet scene, the only one in which all the characters are together, Visconti deals with a single event, but it is also the setting for arguments concerning the burning of the Reichstag and the transfer of power within the Von Essenbeck steelworks, which lead to the disintegration of the family and the nation. Significantly, Visconti does not begin with this scene, as if to imply that divisive forces are already present and that unity is an abnormal condition. The order and manner of introducing the characters before the dinner party are extremely important. The first image is a close-up of a place card with the name Baron Von Essenbeck, as if the family name is the most important way of defining these characters. The camera pulls back to show the servants setting the long table that is now empty, efficiently executing the Von Essenbeck orders; a number of depth focus shots assure us that the house and the culture are still intact. The first Von Essenbeck we see is Konstantin, naked in his bath, being washed by a servant, talking about the guests and contributing to the dramatic exposition of the plot. At first there is some confusion about whether he is the baron, but, even when we learn he is not, the fact that he is introduced first leads us to suspect that he will be the baron's successor. This idea is reinforced by a parallel scene in which the baron is being attended by his servant.

After Konstantin, we meet all the characters who are to be victimized that night: Herbert, the impetuous but earnest left-winger who is to be accused of murder and chased into exile; Elizabeth, his fragilely beautiful young wife, who is to die in a concentration camp while trying to follow her husband into exile; Erika and Thilde, their two innocent young girls, dressed in blue organdy, one of whom is to be molested by Martin; Gunther, the sensitive son of Konstantin who is sympathetic with Herbert; and the old baron, who is to be murdered. The key characters in the struggle, who survive the longest, are introduced last: Frederick, the intelligent, ambitious outsider, and Jorgem, the cousin who is on the margins of the family and who is a dedicated Nazi, are appropriately on their way to the Von Essenbeck mansion. Through the rainy windshield of their car, the wipers moving back and forth as if to stress the tension, the camera examines their faces in close-up. Jorgem, who seeks not his own power but the strengthening of the Nazi Party, is the only one in the film who consistently succeeds in manipulating others to do his will; here he satanically plays on Frederick's ambition, encouraging him to propose to Sophie and subtly suggesting that he murder the baron, later assuring him that "we are in an elite society where everything is possible." The scenes with Frederick and Jorgem, the outsiders, are intercut with scenes of the drawing room where most of the family is assembled to hear the innocent performances of Gunther, Erika, and Thilde. As Gunther plays the cello, the camera pans around the room, as if composing a family portrait. After Frederick and Jorgem join the others, the camera zooms in on a servant bringing a message for Konstantin, who leaves the room while at the same time a spotlight is carried through the door. Suddenly the tone shifts as Martin, under multicolored lights, convincingly dressed as a woman, does an impersonation of Marlene Dietrich. During this performance, we cut to the first shot of Sophie, his mother. A huge close-up of her ironically smiling face on the left side of the screen is dramatically lit in red, while the right side of the screen is black, clearly suggesting her demonic power. Ironically these pairs are to be recombined for the final battle: Martin, with Jorgem's encouragement and support, must ultimately destroy Sophie and Frederick. But in this scene all four of them oppose Konstantin, who interrupts Martin's performance with the news of the burning of the Reichstag. Everyone except Martin leaves the room, and the camera zooms in for a close-up as he removes his wig. This is a very significant scene, for it shows all the strands being drawn together in complicated patterns, before the union of the entire group at the dinner table.

In the dinner scene, the camera pans around the table from face to face, shooting over crystal, flowers, and fruit, which are also sharply in focus. Yet when the discussion turns into a heated argument, the material objects slip out of focus as if the polite rules of civilized order are beginning to break down, and instead we see only the angry faces. Once Herbert leaves the room in anger when he realizes that the baron intends for Konstantin to take over the steelworks, the disintegration has begun. The cutting pace of the rest of the act as well as the process of disintegration are accelerated; again, we return to a number of simultaneous short scenes with two or three characters: Sophie and Frederick being joined sexually by their pursuit of political power, Martin molesting

The Damned

little Thilde under the piano, Konstantin arguing with Gunther about his future, Herbert and Elizabeth planning their departure from Germany, the old baron lying back in his bed. Then suddenly we hear a scream that fuses these incidents and their consequences: the discovery of Martin's perversion, the murder of the baron, the arrival of the Nazis who have come to arrest Herbert. When the remaining members of the family are once again assembled, this time in the drawing room to be questioned by the Nazis about the murder, Visconti arranges them symbolically as in an opera or tableau. In one shot they all are seated between two massive columns, except for Frederick (the murderer), who stands outside the group. When they meet again, in the scene where Martin reveals to Konstantin that he is making Frederick the president of the Von Essenbeck factory, ironically set in the same room where Martin's performance as Dietrich was earlier interrupted by Konstantin, there is a powerful shot, lit in red and amber, of Konstantin in the foreground with his back to the camera, Martin facing the camera from deep in the background, and Sophie walking seductively between them. Konstantin ends this elaborately complicated scene and act with a prophecy of things to come: "Don't have any illusions, this war has just begun."

The pattern of alternation between union and dispersal continues in act two, which begins with the baron's funeral, a scene in which the remaining members of the family are assembled. Then it moves toward disintegration through simultaneously developed strands: the first signs of alienation between Jorgem and Frederick and between Martin and Sophie, new alliances between Martin and Konstantin (which result from the suicide of a little Jewish girl whom Martin has molested) and between Sophie and Jorgem (as they plot Konstantin's destruction). The act ends with a bedroom scene between Sophie and Frederick, the only alliance in act one to survive, which exaggerates, almost to the point of grotesquery, the already explicit connection between sexual passion and political ambition. Sophie enters the room naked to find Frederick in bed reading *Mein Kampf*. She urges him to kill Konstantin and tries to bolster his confidence with such heavy lines as "You produce cannon!" her sexual excitement growing. Like Martin, Frederick collapses on her breast; he exclaims "God, the complicity grows. . . . I've accepted a ruthless logic."

The bloody spectacle of the SA massacre is portrayed in act three in a style strikingly different from that of the rest of the film. Most of it is shot in one setting in chronological order. The lan-

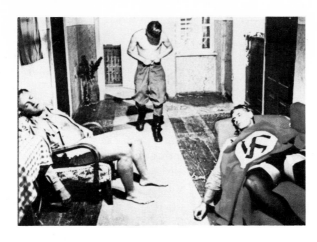

The Damned

guage suddenly shifts from English to German. There is less reliance on dialogue. The camera is constantly moving through the rooms of the inn and panning the various faces of the beautiful young SA men. The style is different because it is portraying a different kind of experience; the focus seems to shift from the Von Essenbecks to German history and to a harmonious group of people. The camera becomes a participant in their earnest patriotic singing, their dancing and drinking, and their orgiastic play. Yet there are several signs of disintegration, usually lit in red: the male couples (with one in drag) disappearing into bedrooms, Konstantin drunkenly singing out of tune, a group of young men trying to rape one of the bar girls—incidents bound to remind us of Martin's deviant behavior. In the beginning of the sequence, when the camera pans the portrait of Hitler, it seems perfectly appropriate; but by the time we return to it near the end of the sequence, we have learned about the SA's distrust of Hitler and their inflated confidence in their own power, and we react to the portrait ironically. But the disintegration is most dramatically expressed by the shift from panning to quick cutting, as the camera records the intrusion of the Nazi troops into the idyllic landscape, arriving from a variety of directions in a variety of vehicles and ultimately leading to the fragmented massacre. Konstantin is the last to die. The camera, reverting to the pan, reveals his murderers, Jorgem and Frederick, and thereby takes us back to the focus on the Von Essenbecks.

Acts four and five are full of ironic parallels with act one, completing the demonic cycle with Martin's rise to power. Act four begins with Jorgem satanically urging Martin to overthrow Frederick, just as he had urged Frederick to overthrow the baron in act one. The scene at the dinner table, which reunites the few remaining members of the family (even Herbert, whom we have not seem since the first banquet), only emphasizes how far the disintegration has gone. There is no longer any attempt to keep up the appearance of refined politeness; they are openly hostile to each other as they review the family casualties. Even Gunther, the one character who has remained innocent in the midst of all this complicity, is approached by the seductive Jorgem, who is attracted by his hatred. Just as the first dinner party was followed by a scene in which Sophie bragged to Frederick, "I'll take care of Martin ... I know Martin's desires ... he has no sense of values," the second is followed by a struggle between Martin and Sophie. The disintegration of their relationship is stressed by the incongruities between the visuals and the sound. First we see an overhead shot of them separated by a column. Though we hear Sophie ordering Martin to get "on his knees," we see *her* being forced to kneel before him. This time she is the one who is crying; their embrace is a mixture of hostility and lust, yet neither is in control. The scene ends with Martin sitting alone, pounding the table as he anticipates his victory.

The incest sequence, again like the massacre, is shot in a different style. The camera selects significant symbolic details, like Sophie's blood-red nails, Martin's cold blue eyes, and their clasped hands. The main device is to show her rapid disintegration by changes in the handling of time. The sequence is framed by shots of a hypodermic needle and drugs, as if in the physical fusion of incest Martin has parasitically drained her psychological strength and left her with his infirmities. As her mind retreats to the past, fixating on Martin's baby shoes and childhood drawings, Visconti makes it increasingly difficult for us to gauge the passing of time.

The final act covers the marriage of Frederick and Sophie, which (like the baron's birthday) leads to their deaths and the consolidation of Martin's power. It begins with a car driving up to the house, this time containing Martin dressed in a Nazi uniform, rather than Frederick and Jorgem, whose powers he has absorbed. As in the first act, we see the preparations for the party, but this time it is Frederick dressing before the mirror instead of his victims Konstantin and the baron. When Martin enters the room and stands in the background, we see his reflection in the mirror instead of Frederick's, visually expressing the transferral of power. Similarly, the first view of Sophie is an extreme long shot of her and her maids standing in front of a red-draped wall, as Martin enters the room from the foreground and walks toward her, another visual expression of their power relationship. As Martin arranges her pearls (which might remind us of Lisa) and the flowers at her breast (which perhaps recalls Jorgem's Hegelian quote about the crushing of flowers), Visconti does not permit us to see her face. When the film cuts back to the large drawing room, we recognize that the silver dress Martin's sluttish girl friend wears is exactly the same as the black dress Sophie wore in act one as she embraced Frederick, revealing the narrow glittering straps on her back, making her look like a black widow spider trying to lure Frederick into her political intrigues by means of her sexual power. The house, now full of Nazi flags, young soldiers, and whores, has also undergone a deterioration. But not until we see Sophie's deathly white face, with its blood-red lipstick, black-rimmed eyes, and yellowish teeth are we fully struck by the grotesque horror of the transformation. It is a dramatic shock, even though we have been watching the steady pattern of deterioration, and it reminds us of our first image of Sophie—the huge close-up with half of the screen lit in red and the other in black. In the last shot of Sophie and Frederick, the camera pans

The Damned

their dead, mannequin-like bodies, in a deep wine-colored light. His work complete, Martin clicks his heels and salutes like a good Nazi, and the camera zooms in for a close-up of his face, which dissolves to the abstract shots of the factory inferno that opened the film. Martin has become the demonic embodiment of the Von Essenbeck empire and the Nazi Third Reich.

the french new wave

The French new wave is not a film movement in the same way as Italian neo-realism. It is not made up of a group of filmmakers who share a theoretical approach to film and politics; nor does it consist of a body of films that express similar themes through similar techniques. Most simply, it is a brief period in the history of French cinema, from 1959 to 1963, when more than 170 directors made their first feature films. Essentially, then, it is the result of an economic condition that enabled new young directors to transform the French cinema temporarily, not in any one consistent direction but in a variety of ways.

The French film industry of the 1950's was not very hospitable to the young filmmaker. In order to get backing, one had to be a known director; in order to be a director one had to go through a long apprenticeship. Some brilliant films were being made, but by people who were well established like Bresson, Tati, and Clement. There was one important exception. In 1956, Roger Vadim, a twenty-eight-year-old apprentice within the commercial industry, was allowed to direct a relatively low-cost film. He used his own wife, an unknown starlet, as his leading lady. The film was *And God Created Woman,* the starlet was Brigitte Bardot, the result was a huge financial success. Producers, who were eager to repeat this success, figured out the winning formula: a young director and a low budget. They figured if they took the same amount of money and invested in three low-budget pictures, rather than in one expensive film, they would have a much better chance of getting their money back. Simple economics!

But the new wave never would have been launched if only Vadim and others like him were making these movies. There happened to be a number of young filmmakers waiting in the wings. Actually, they were doing more than just waiting. Some, like Alain Resnais, Agnes Varda, Chris Marker, Jean Rouch, and Henri Colpi, were making highly effective, noncommercial short subjects. Others were critics, associated with *Cahiers du Cinéma,* a journal founded in 1951 by the distinguished critic André Bazin and filmmaker-to-be Jacques Doniol-Valcroze; this group included most of the major new-wave directors except Resnais: Jean-Luc Godard, François Truffaut, Claude Chabrol, Eric Rohmer, and Jacques Rivette.

The *Cahiers* group attacked the established French cinema of Clément, Becker, Clouzot, Autant-Lara, Cayatte, and Allegret, and instead looked back to earlier French directors such as Abel Gance, Jean Vigo, and Jean Renoir. They also praised American action films, especially westerns and gangster movies, which they preferred because, unlike the slick products of the established French cinema, they showed the unmistakable stamp of the director. One could always recognize the personal quality of an *auteur* like Alfred Hitchcock, Howard Hawks, and Fritz Lang. Each of these critics was dying for the chance to become an *auteur* and to express his vision through his own personal style in cinema. Most of them experimented with 16mm short subjects. Chabrol had the first chance to make his own feature. His *Le Beau Serge* (1958) won international critical acclaim and was a modest financial success; this encouraged the others to follow and made it easier for them to get backing.

The big year for the new wave was 1959. Each of three major filmmakers to emerge from the movement screened his first feature: Godard's *Breathless,* Truffaut's *400 Blows,* and Resnais's *Hiroshima, Mon Amour.* Two films from the *Cahiers* group were huge financial successes: *Breathless* and Chabrol's *The Cousins.* The new wave also swept the Cannes Film Festival that year: *Hiroshima, Mon Amour* won the International Critics' Prize, *400 Blows* the prize for best direction, and Marcel Camus's *Black Orpheus* the grand prize.

By 1961 there had already been enough financial failures in the new wave to make the backers more cautious. By 1964 the money was almost as tight as it had been in the 1950's. The new wave was over. Most of the 170 directors who made their first film were never to make another, and probably that was a good thing. Some were absorbed within the commercial industry, but a few survived the movement and have continued to make personal films that have had a significant impact on cinema all over the world.[10] Truffaut, Resnais, and Godard are three filmmakers from this last group.

[10] For more information about this movement see Roy Armes, *French Cinema Since 1946,* 2 vols. (London: Zwemmer, 1966); Borde, Buache, and Curtelin, *Nouvelle Vague* (Paris: Serdoc, 1962); "Nouvelle Vague," *Cahiers du Cinéma,* No. 138 (1962); Jacques Sinclair, *Nouvelle Vague?* (Paris: Editions du Cerf, 1961); and Peter Graham, *The New Wave* (New York: Doubleday, 1968).

Francois Truffaut

THE 400 BLOWS (1959)

The 400 Blows is a partly autobiographical film about the interaction of a thirteen-year-old boy who is free, sensitive, and vulnerable, and a society of adults who are restrictive, insensitive, and selfish. Although he is mischievous and derives moral strength and pleasure from his rebelliousness, he is still a vulnerable child who earnestly needs the love and support of the adult world. Hence even his rebellion is bound to leave him lonely and dissatisfied. The prevailing tone is a poignant mixture of humor and pathos that successfully avoids sentimentality. Although the film is relatively simple, Truffaut effectively uses cinematic technique to express the conflict between a spontaneous individual and a restrictive society.

One of the most effective ways of presenting this conflict is the structural alternation between motion and stasis. It is pointless to discuss this film in terms of conventional sequences, which are highly irregular in length, or in terms of a narrative plot, which is extremely flimsy. Rather, the film is made up of many short scenes that flow into each other. There is a continual motion—the camera tracks or pans, the boys run, cars are driven, life flows down the streets of Paris—enhanced by a flow of lyrical music but also periodically interrupted by static scenes in confining places such as a school, a cramped apartment, a prison, a reform school. The opening images are shots (taken from a car driving down Paris streets) which capture the trees and the new and old buildings, accelerate in pace, and are accompanied by romantic music. Far away we see the impressive Eiffel Tower, approach it rapidly, observe it from various angles, and then, with the camera immediately beneath its grill-like structure, it looms like a giant cage; but then we quickly speed away out of its reach. These free-flowing images fade and are replaced by the classroom, where boys are made to suppress their natural energy and enthusiasm. They are forced to be still and orderly, to stand in the corner, to remain confined within the room during recess, to copy and recite on cue, to walk in lines and respond to bells and whistles. No wonder they break into a run as soon as they leave the classroom. No wonder they all rebel by running away from the gym teacher who mechanically leads them on a walk through Paris. The natural flow of the streets is too tempting for any of them to resist. But the free-spirited Antoine and René are almost constantly on the

183

run. In the scene where they are cutting school, the camera rapidly pans after them as they walk out of a movie theater. Then the camera races ahead of them, moving faster than they could possibly walk, but we find that they are already on the other side of the street ahead of the camera. This motion stresses the quick passing of time and the merging of one event into another when enjoyment is spontaneous; it is antithetical to the regularized time in the institutions.

Some of the most effective scenes in the film contain elements of both motion and stasis. When the boys are cutting school, Antoine goes for a ride in the rotor (a centrifugal machine) while René watches from above. In an overhead shot, we watch Antoine as the drum begins to spin and the floor drops out. At first it spins around so fast that even we in the audience are made dizzy by the motion, but some static elements enable us to keep our balance— the fulcrum in the center and Antoine held against the wall by the centrifugal motion. We admire his bravery as he pulls his arms and legs away from the wall and squirms around, altering his position and testing the limits of his mobility, yet he is literally up against the wall. This scene is a perfect visual metaphor for his entire experience in the film: Antoine is in constant motion that makes both him and his observers dizzy, but despite his bravery and ecstasy, his mobility is severely limited and he is only going in circles.

Another effective scene that combines both elements takes place in a police van that carries Antoine off to jail. He looks out of the barred windows as the Paris night whizzes by. The camera moves in for a close-up of his tear-stained face, with the other adult prisoners in the van out of focus; then the camera moves into the van, looking out at Paris in motion over Antoine's shoulder as if from his point of view. His solitary confinement is made all the worse by the visual reminder of the free life he must forgo.

In the final sequence, Antoine moves from the structured soccer game directly into a running escape from the reform school, the camera tracking along beside him in one continuous shot. This time both he and his surroundings—trees, hedges, road signs, farm buildings, fences, open fields—appear to be moving until he reaches the sea, which is the natural embodiment of perpetual motion. The camera reaches the beach first, makes a 180-degree pan to show Antoine running on a hill, then cuts to him running down the slope making footprints in the sand. He runs ahead of the camera until he walks into the water, then turns back to the shore and looks directly at the camera, which approaches him and

184

The 400 Blows

then freezes on a close-up of his face with the sea behind him. His quizzical expression seems to ask: Where do I go from here? As in the rotor sequence, although motion gives him a feeling of momentary freedom and exhiliration, he stands at bay, the sea at his back. He must ultimately return to the reform school like the other boy who had escaped.

The world of *400 Blows* is polarized. One group is the children, who have all the natural vitality and life, and the other is untrustworthy adults, who have all the power. In the puppet show sequence, the camera affectionately watches the beautifully expressive faces of children deeply engrossed in the story of Little Red Riding Hood. We in the audience are startled by the extraordinary range of expressions and realize that their reactions to the puppet show are probably more spontaneous and more deeply emotional than ours to Truffaut's film. Yet the adults who run the schools do everything they can to stifle this emotional spontaneity. They teach their students how to express themselves in writing by making them copy stories about freedom. The little boy who messes up his composition book with ink performs a marvelously funny act that escalates like a Laurel and Hardy comedy routine; yet he is legitimately terrified of the teacher's punishment, which is not funny at all. The reform school refuses to allow René to visit Antoine, despite the fact that he is his only friend and the only human being who understands him. When the boys are allowed to play outdoors, the guards lock up their own children in cages to protect them from the juvenile delinquents. These adults probably do not understand the kind of communication that takes place between children, or, if they do, they fear it. When Antoine is interviewed by the staff psychologist, he transforms a confining situation (the format of questions, the static camera) into a marvelous improvisational scene by the spontaneity of his responses.

In contrast to the children, the adults are selfish and insensitive. Antoine's mother is alternately seductive and neglectful. His stepfather is warm and likable, except that he weakly accepts his wife's adultery in order to avoid trouble and ultimately rejects Antoine for the same reason. The only time we see the family having a good time together is when the three of them go to the movies (an activity we already associate with Antoine and René), but on this occasion all three are acting playfully like children. René's parents do not argue; they merely avoid each other, and they also avoid René. The teachers, police, and guards are all authoritarian personalities who derive pleasure from exercising their power. For example, the watchman is happy he catches Antoine because no one will be able to give him a hard time for not watching the doors; he thinks only of himself. The fence tries to cheat Antoine and René out of the typewriter. The stranger on the street selfishly tells Antoine to scram so that he can make time with the woman who is trying to catch her dog. (Jean-Claude Brialy and Jeanne Moreau are playfully cast in these cameo parts.) When Antoine is in jail, he can feel no comradeship with his fellow prisoners because they are all adults. When he is taken to his own cell, his spirits are momentarily raised when he rolls a cigarette out of a scrap of newspaper and some loose tobacco in his pocket. He feels better because he is doing something on his own, something rebellious that would not ordinarily be tolerated in school or at home. Yet, ironically he is doing something that makes him look and feel more grown up at the same time that he is trying to rebel against the adult world. The same irony is seen in his farewell note to his parents when he runs away: "I want to prove I can become a man—then I'll return and explain everything." Antoine, as well as Truffaut himself, can never resolve this dilemma; at the root of his rebellion is a desire to be loved and accepted by the very world he rejects. This paradox makes him vulnerable, makes him run in circles and ultimately traps him.

After *400 Blows,* Truffaut's films moved in two different directions, but the roots of both movements were present in this first feature. One line developed the autobiographical element and traced the growing up of Antoine (who continued to be played by a maturing Jean-Pierre Leaud): the Antoine and Collette episode in *Love at Twenty* (1962), *Stolen Kisses* (1968), and *Bed and Board* (1970). These films develop the sad consequences of Antoine's dilemma. As he continues to adapt to society, he is changed. He retains his charm, energy, and humor, but he loses his rebelliousness as he eases into the comforts of the bourgeois life. In *Bed and Board,* a charming film in luxurious color, he marries a nice young girl who has a nice warm, accepting family, the very thing that Antoine had always lacked and wanted. Though he makes one last half-hearted effort to rebel (a boring affair with a Japanese girl), he ultimately chooses to return to his wife, baby, and in-laws.

Such a turn of events is reflected in Truffaut's career; he turned into an established filmmaker with his own production company (Les Films du Carrosse), making charming little films in which the humor gets stronger and the pathos weaker, in which the texture is richer and the ideas thinner.

The other line of Truffaut's development continued to explore the theme of freedom versus involvement in a restrictive society, but it did so in an impersonal and complex way. Although Truffaut retained the humor, the pathos deepened into tragedy, which gave the ironic tone more of an edge. This movement led directly out of *400 Blows* into Truffaut's two best films, *Shoot the Piano Player* and *Jules et Jim.*

SHOOT THE PIANO PLAYER (1960)

Shoot the Piano Player focuses on Charlie (Charles Aznavour), a timid, sensitive hero who is trying to withdraw from life in order to avoid harming others and experiencing pain. He has renounced a career as a concert pianist because it led to the suicide of his wife. Yet he is drawn back to the piano in a honky-tonk cafe and to love, which inevitably makes him vulnerable to pain. He is passively drawn into a love relationship with Lena, which leads to murder, and into involvement with his brothers, resulting in Lena's death. Involvement with other human beings is essential to being alive; it includes all the intense aspects of experience, both pain and joy, which are inextricably fused. To give up his involvement with people, he would also have to give up his art. The film ends with Charlie once again at the piano and with the line, "Music is what we need, man." One cannot escape the pain and responsibility of life and still be alive, so one might as well plunge into action.

Truffaut does precisely that. In contrast to his timid hero Charlie, Truffaut is extremely bold in his unconventional techniques that celebrate life. One of the dominant characteristics of this film is a blending of the incongruous tones of slapstick comedy, romantic melodrama, and American gangster thrillers. The range is much greater than in *400 Blows*, and it is used to express the conception that pain and joy are mutually inclusive and that the world is marked by incongruity. We cannot predict what will happen in life, just as we cannot predict what will happen next in this film; we may be laughing or crying. This is evident in the opening sequence, which makes us think the film is a comedy and does not prepare us for the three deaths that occur; yet the opening does suggest the unpredictability of experience.

The film begins with the accidental meeting of two strangers, whom we expect to be central characters but who turn out to be rather insignificant. Chico (Charlie's brother) runs into a pole, and a stranger carrying flowers comes along and helps him up. The latter talks about his marriage, his desire to escape his wife and gain his "freedom," and recounts how he fell in love with her. There are several incongruities in this encounter: The man's feelings about his wife are contradictory; he is revealing personal information to a stranger; after this scene he disappears from the film. The scene is even more odd when considered in relationship to the scene between Chico and Charlie that follows; in an encounter between two brothers who have not seen each other for four years, the conversation is confined to small talk. When Chico describes the two men who are chasing him, he says, "They're not brothers, but they look like it." Yet he and Charlie, who are brothers, look like strangers. The pattern of incongruity for the entire film is quickly established, and we should not be too surprised by anything, not even friendly chatter between kidnapers and victims; a conversation about the purity of women while the boss is choking Charlie to death; the iris inset of the gangster's mother keeling over as he swears, "If I'm lying may my mother drop dead!"; the absurd lyrics of many of the songs; a musical genius' being born into a family of beastly criminals;

the camera's following the girl with the violin, whom we never see again, as Charlie is auditioning for the impressario; and the beauty of Lena's death in the snow. Truffaut has written:

> I honestly believe that pleasing people is important, but I also believe that every film must contain some degree of "planned violence" upon its audience. In a good film, people must be made to see something that they don't want to see: they must be made to approve of someone of whom they had disapproved, they must be forced to look where they had refused to look.[11]

He succeeds with this "planned violence" in *Shoot the Piano Player* and in *Jules et Jim.*

JULES ET JIM (1961)

In *Jules et Jim* the techniques and the basic situation reflect Truffaut's continuing concern with the possibilities of freedom, but the theme is developed in a complicated way and with implications that broaden its scope. Truffaut is concerned not only with the personal situation of three individuals but with the issue of war and peace. The story centers on two young friends—Jules, an Austrian, and Jim, a Frenchman—living the bohemian life in Paris before World War I. Like Antoine and René, they have extraordinary rapport, but the freedom they pursue is embodied in Catherine (brilliantly played by Jeanne Moreau), whom they both love. She is completely unconventional; she refuses to be limited to any one nationality, social class, or sex. Her moods, desires, and roles are constantly fluctuating. She has great curiosity and is eager to experience everything in life. She rejects external codes and relies entirely on her instincts.

This free individual embodies an irresistible force that captures both Jules and Jim, and it can be seen from two perspectives. On the one hand, it can be an important source of creativity. Catherine is definitely linked to art: Her father was an artist; she is a source of creative inspiration for Jules and Jim; she reminds them of an ancient statue with a mysterious smile; she sings and writes songs; she creates playful games; she makes an art out of life. When she was a child and heard the line "Our Father art in heaven," she thought it meant that God was an artist, and she has been operating on that assumption ever since. In this sense,

[11] François Truffaut, "We Must Continue Making Progress," in *Film: A Montage of Theories,* p. 371.

Catherine is linked to the creative spirit that dominated Paris before World War I. In many scenes we catch glimpses of paintings by Picasso that demonstrate his constantly changing style. Because of her belief in art, Catherine insists on honesty at all costs (she burns letters that tell lies and keeps vitriol for lying eyes) and strongly prefers action to talk. After the trio has seen Strindberg's *Miss Julie,* Jules and Jim discuss the inferiority of women and attack the heroine for insisting on freedom, categorizing her in terms of psychology and metaphysics and complaining that they do not even know her social class or whether she is a virgin. Catherine dramatically contradicts their arguments and shows her disdain for their abstract discussion by jumping into a river, an action that diverts their attention from the play and proves her superior courage and freedom.

But Catherine's freedom is also negative and quite destructive. If one relies on the individual instead of on external codes of behavior, one must be certain that the individual's instincts are good. How do we know they are not evil and that the individual will not turn out to be a tyrant? That is precisely what Catherine becomes. She is like a queen, demanding constant adoration and obedience. If she cannot get her way, she will destroy everything and everyone around her. This is her Napoleonic side (she admittedly worships Napoleon), but it also links her to Hitler. The final meeting of Catherine, Jules, and Jim takes place in a theater in which we see newsreels of the Nazi book burnings in Germany before World War II, an image bound to remind us that Catherine also burned what she thought were lies. Her creative power can easily be transformed into destruction because she can never be satisfied, she can never possess and control everything. Jules and Jim both realize that she will never be happy, for life demands choices, compromise, and sacrifice and she is unwilling to cope with such demands. Ironically, while they are discussing the book burnings, she takes Jim in her car and tells Jules, "Watch us!" as she calmly drives off to their death. It is like her earlier action of jumping into the river, but this time she has forced someone else to come along for the ride.

The film contrasts friendship with love. Friendship is peaceful; it stresses brotherhood and tolerates differences. Love, on the other hand, is like war. Catherine tries to conquer her lovers and to abolish the differences between them. Both love and war are temporary states of high intensity, which are bound to pass and be replaced by peace and order. In the war sequences, we find that after the initial chaos, things begin to get organized and men adapt to life in the trenches. The same thing happens in the love affair between Jules and Catherine. The similarity is also shown in Jim's story about the soldier who won a woman in the war. He experienced love only through letters. The point is that this could happen only during wartime. Although war is destructive, like love it makes possible certain kinds of intense experiences that could not happen under other circumstances. But the price for these unique moments of ecstasy is extremely high.

One has the feeling that at the end of the film Jules is relieved to be alone. Catherine was a fascinating person whom he never ceased to pursue and whom he could not think of giving up; yet she was the disruptive force in his life. With her dead, he can retreat into a quiet life with his child and his insects and perhaps become comfortably bourgeois. He, like Antoine, is ready to give up freedom. The irony, of course, is that he has been enslaved by freedom and now at last is free to enjoy the security of conformity. Again Truffaut concludes that absolute freedom is impossible.

The film's style reinforces this idea of the elusiveness of freedom. Truffaut's constant modulations of tone are like the constant shifts in Catherine's moods; the film is never restricted to any single genre, tradition, or mode. The different kinds of reality inhabited by an individual in a lifetime are expressed through different visual textures. The romance and charm we have come to attribute to artistic life in Paris at the turn of the century (bequeathed to us largely through fiction and painting) are emphasized by the detailed authenticity—the narrow stairways, miniature courtyards, picturesque street scenes, cafe interiors, and costumes—of the early part of the film. As Catherine and Jules marry and move to the country, the romantic quality of their charmed vision and its unreality (to become more ironic as the war moves closer) is emphasized by the impressionistic visuals of their country house—the sunny setting; the long shots, overhead shots, and pans, which soften details, heighten the impressionism of blurred outlines, and give a dreamlike quality to that part of their lives. As in *400 Blows,* camera movement captures the exhilaration of free motion: The camera sweeping across landscapes, bicycle riding, and close-ups during a race on a bridge evoke the vitality and gaiety of the prewar period and of Catherine's gift for creative play. In almost surrealistic contrast to this subjective impressionism come the war scenes, given exaggerated realism by Truffaut's use of documentary footage from World War I, which force our recognition of the bizarre

Jules et Jim

contrasts life offers. In the reunion scene after the war, the camera pans rapidly from one character to another, implying the great distance that has grown between them. The use of the freeze shot is different from that in *400 Blows*. It captures fleeting moments, such as Catherine's expressions in various moods, implying that they will be lost too soon. It creates nostalgia for lost innocence. It captures an embrace between Jules and Jim after they have fought on opposite sides during the war, a union soon to be broken. This technique seems to imply that experience is fluid and can be pinned down only by artificial means; it exposes the futility of Catherine's attempt to capture and control everything around her.

Certain visual symbols, however, operate in an almost literary way, suggesting the permanence or inevitability of certain kinds of experience (like the rotor and the sea in *400 Blows* and the snow in *Shoot the Piano Player*). The sculpture that reminds Jules and Jim of Catherine is very old, suggesting that life has always included women with Catherine's qualities and that men have always been enchanted by them. Jules's role as naturalist (also a familiar symbolic occupation)—his passion for collecting and drawing insects—implies his obsessiveness and his desire to escape into the ordered small details of life and, finally, implies the fascinating variety of life itself. The truncated bridge of the death sequence suggests the fragmented unpredictability of life, providing dangers for those who demand too much of it. Yet, largely through these symbols in the fluid context of his style and through a series of relationships expressing the poignant variety of experiences, Truffaut is able to effectively capture the elusive quality of that period and of life itself.

THE WILD CHILD (1970)

Although most of Truffaut's films after *Jules et Jim* have been disappointments, one that is particularly interesting in light of the development we have been tracing is *The Wild Child*. While clearly in touch with *400 Blows, The Wild Child* also incorporates elements from the two directions in which Truffaut moved after his first feature. Like *400 Blows,* it deals with a vulnerable child, abandoned by his parents and unable to communicate with adult society. He has spent the first twelve years of his life completely cut off from other men (this was Charlie's fantasy in *Shoot the Piano Player*) and freely living by his instincts (Catherine's fantasy in *Jules et Jim*). Yet the film focuses not on these wild years but on his confrontation with society, embodied in a humane scientist, Dr. Itard, played by Truffaut himself.

This film polarizes more sharply than any of his others the two worlds of learned social behavior and primitive freedom. It applies the brute force, relentless authority, and moral assumptions that we do not question in dealing with a twelve-month-old child to the acculturation of a boy of twelve years. The true story, based on the *Memoire et Rapport sur Victor de l'Aveyron* (1806), by Jean Itard, provides an extraordinary perspective that forces us to re-examine the familiar, raising the conflict to the level of allegory, which speaks to the condition of all men.

Victor, the savage boy (played with almost mysterious power by Jean-Pierre Cargol), resembles both Antoine of *400 Blows* and Charlie of *Shoot the Piano Player,* as well as other Truffaut heroes. He is fierce in his own protection. In the opening scene he kills a hound with his bare hands and must be smoked out of a burrow. But he is terribly vulnerable. He tries, as did Antoine and Charlie, to protect himself from becoming involved with social life and other people because he senses that involvement will only increase his vulnerability; like Antoine and Charlie, Victor fails. Inevitably he is drawn into society as Dr. Itard forces him to abandon the qualities that preserved him in the forest and moves him toward membership in the race of civilized men. The changes in Victor's body and mind reflect each other and measure the changes in his social condition. When the hunters finally trap him, he is filthy and scarred from twelve years of animal-like survival, but he bears the scar of a great gash on his neck— probably a reminder of his last encounter with civilization, the parents who abandoned him. He moves on all fours (visually identifying him more with the hunting dogs than with the hunters) and slowly learns to walk upright. At first people think he is deaf because he does not respond to loud noises, but when a nut is cracked his head snaps around in response. Slowly through the film he loses his imperviousness to external conditions and is chilled by the wind; the acquisition of clothing has made a necessity of them. This concretization is developed with great economy throughout the film, which is only eighty-five minutes long. He must no longer look at the world with a kind of amorphous awareness, selecting only phenomena relating to his survival; he must now focus his attention on phenomena selected by Dr. Itard as necessary to his education. In short, his perception must be not expanded but trained. As his body becomes more vulnerable, so does his spirit. Having come to expect a certain kind of treatment from Itard, he is wounded and angry when, to expose him to injustice (inescapable in social living), Itard locks him in a closet for no apparent reason. By the time the film is over, having experienced the pains of acculturation, Victor is afraid of the dark and afraid to be alone in the woods. However, he has expressed the human quality that we demand from each other, that invariably touches us because we think it binds us together; he has shown his need for his fellow humans by contriving to touch Itard as they work with a drum. His expression of need is complete when, after his attempt to run away to his old life, he voluntarily returns to Itard's house, acknowledging either his basic human need (which Itard has released) or succumbing to the circular effect of need created by acculturation.

Every element of the film subtly questions the value of the civilizing process and shows the pain and loss it brings. Every lesson between Itard and Victor demonstrates the difficulty, frustration, and uncertainty of the process, as in a scene where Victor hides in a tree to avoid another excruciating lesson. The sound track offers little dialogue and is dominated by a voice-over narration of Itard's journal, read calmly and with no ironic stressing of its goals or concepts. However, the sounds of the forest (bird songs, running water, rustling leaves and brush) provide a kind of relief as they interrupt the rational discourse and develop further the contrast between the two worlds. The visuals emphasize the dominance of civilization over our perceptions, yet this is questioned. The plastic qualities of the setting—the simple beauty of an important writing desk, the bizarre clarity of the anatomical diagram of the head— suggest the esthetic potentiality of order and craft. Cameraman Nestor Almandros uses black and white with extraordinary effectiveness, giving us clear, bright contrasts in the interiors and more gray and shadow in the forest scenes, suggesting a valuable (because beautiful) lucidity and order in Itard's world. The long shots give a kind of rational distance to the film's examination of the process before it, and a minimum of camera movement enhances our illusion of calm stability. But the iris shots force us to focus on the phenomena selected by Truffaut, to confront again and again the deeply disturbing mystery and intensity of Victor's face, which expresses the fear and confusion that we, as members of Itard's culture, are willing to induce in every child born among us. The film ends as the last iris shot freezes on Victor's face after he

The Wild Child

The Wild Child

"willingly" returns to Itard's world; then the circle of the iris closes, leaving us with blackness.

The fact that Truffaut himself plays Dr. Itard also links *The Wild Child* to his other films; it adds another autobiographical dimension to the conflict between freedom and socialization, individual and society, order and unpredictability, which is central to all his films. The autobiographical connection is made strong and more complex by the fact that the film is dedicated to Jean-Pierre Leaud, star of the autobiographical series. But the view of society's demands is enriched in this film because its spokesman is not the weak and selfish couple of *400 Blows,* the killers of *Shoot the Piano Player,* or the warmakers of *Jules et Jim.* Instead, the restricter of freedom, the imposer of punishment is the gentle and unselfish Dr. Itard. As played by Truffaut, his motives—to save the boy from an insane asylum and to acquire knowledge—are pure, and he has a dimension of great tenderness that he cannot express but that seems to emanate from him, implying his acute awareness of the pain he is inflicting and his desire to make loving contact with

Victor. It is left for the housekeeper (the mother figure of this allegorical family) to provide physical warmth. Perhaps Itard's desire for "knowledge" is not so pure a motive, but one that inhibits and dehumanizes him. Freed from the easily recognizable evils of Truffaut's earlier films, the value of the socializing process, upon which Itard insists, however benignly, becomes harder to assess. As in any conflict, the price for giving up each alternative seems too hard to bear, no matter what the value of the other choice. But despite the terrible lesson the teacher must continually learn about the price he extracts from his pupil, Truffaut ends the film with Itard's affirmation, born of hope: "Soon we'll start our lessons again."

Alain Resnais

HIROSHIMA, MON AMOUR (1959)

Unlike Truffaut and Godard, the development of Resnais as a director has been in a straight line, beginning with pre–new wave short subjects and moving directly through *Hiroshima, Mon Amour,* to his later features. He has undergone no conversions or regressions but has continued to explore a vision of reality that is neither commercial nor revolutionary but private. As a result, he is finding it increasingly difficult to get financial backing.

For Resnais, reality is located mainly inside the mind rather than in external action or details. Reality to him is not what happens or how it affects one (Truffaut's view) or how behavior interacts with art (Godard's view), but what the mind does with what happens. Resnais is concerned with the way a mind perceives experience while it is happening, how it holds the fragments and rearranges them into patterns, and how it distorts or forgets them. Since each person perceives differently, point of view is very significant in his films. Since consciousness is a combination of various tenses (past, present, future, and conditional), his treatment of time is innovative.

Hiroshima, Mon Amour, opens with two pairs of bare shoulders in an embrace; the arms and hands are so intertwined that it is difficult to tell them apart, suggesting the closeness of the two lovers. The lovers (a French woman and a Japanese man whose names we never learn) are actually two strangers in a casual sexual adventure who have found that they are deeply in love.

Constantly stressed in the film is their knowledge that the close-ness they are experiencing must inevitably be lost; it is an impossible love, bound to be forgotten.

One strange thing about the opening scene is that the bodies are covered with a glistening substance that could be ashes or dew. It may be perspiration produced by their lovemaking, but, since the scene is set in Hiroshima, it could be radioactive dust. At first the audience is not sure whether the bodies are dying or making love. The two experiences merge just as the two lovers merge. The union of death and love is important to the film's meaning.

While embracing, the lovers are talking about Hiroshima. He tells her, "You saw nothing in Hiroshima, nothing!" And she replies, "I saw everything, everything." The shots of the embracing bodies are intercut with shots of what she actually saw in Hiroshima. There is a shocking contrast between the beauty of the bodies and photographs of ghastly mutilations. The museums, the photographs, and the newsreels try to make the memory of the bomb permanent, but the point that the Japanese lover keeps making is that the truth of the experience has been lost and cannot be recaptured. These are merely recreations that have altered the actual experience; they are fragments and illusions. The fragmentation of the record is also suggested in the way she describes what she saw:

Hiroshima, Mon Amour

The reconstructions have been made as authentically as possible. The films have been made as authentically as possible. The illusion, it's quite simple, the illusion is so perfect that tourists cry.

One can always scoff, but what else can a tourist do, really, but cry? I've always wept over the fate of Hiroshima. Always. I saw the newsreels.

On the second day, History tells—I'm not making it up— on the second day certain species of animals rose again from the depths of the earth and from the ashes. Dogs were photographed. For all eternity. I saw them. I *saw* the newsreels. I *saw* them.

On the first day. On the second day. On the third day. On the fifteenth day too. Hiroshima was blanketed with flowers. Here were cornflowers and gladiolas everywhere, and morning glories and day lilies that rose again from the ashes with an extraordinary vigor, quite unheard of for flowers 'til then. I didn't make anything up. Nothing. Just as in love this illusion exists, this illusion of being able never to forget, so I was under the illusion that I would never forget Hiroshima. Just as in love.[12]

Many of her sentences are separable fragments. Her language is very repetitious, and certain phrases ("I saw them," and "I didn't make anything up") almost become a refrain, as if repeating the words will make them true. She also uses itemized lists in a futile attempt to capture the reality of the experience. But finally she admits that never forgetting is an illusion about Hiroshima as it is about love.

This opening sequence establishes the central theme, which is the horror of forgetting. The horrors of war and the joys of love have in common the fact that they are experiences of the greatest intensity and have the greatest emotional impact on men's lives, yet even they are doomed to be forgotten. Just as he has tried not to forget Hiroshima and its horror, she had an experience in Nevers (her birthplace in France) that she has unsuccessfully tried to preserve. The Japanese lover reminds her of the experience with her first love, a German soldier killed by her fellow Frenchmen just before the two of them were going to elope. They shaved her head, her parents hid her in the cellar, and she went mad. But the true horror is that she did not die of this love; her life went on, she got over it, and she began to forget him.

Thus in this opening sequence between the two lovers, Resnais

[12] *Hiroshima, Mon Amour: Text by Marguerite Duras for the Film by Alain Res-nais* (New York: Grove Press, 1961), pp. 18–19.

is expressing a complex attitude toward the relationship between the past and the present. He was shaped by what happened in Hiroshima when the bomb was dropped, she by what happened in Nevers. Yet only in the present is there a total merging of the past with the present, of love and death, of the two lovers, of Hiroshima and Nevers.

This scene also reminds us of Resnais's short film *Night and Fog* (1955)—the horror of forgetting, the impossibility of reconstructing from tangible fragments what it was like to have experienced concentration camps or the bomb at Hiroshima, the cutting back and forth between the present and the past. *Hiroshima* also has an ironic relationship to the tradition of documentary cinema. The heroine is in Japan to make a film about peace. At one point she says, "What else do you expect them to make in Hiroshima except a picture about peace?" But Resnais's film, made in Hiroshima, is not about peace. Marguerite Duras, the screenwriter, has called it, "A sort of false documentary that will probe the lesson of Hiroshima more deeply than a made-to-order documentary." [13] *Hiroshima* is fiction and consciously reminds the audience that they are seeing a film because Resnais distrusts the idea that cinema, even a documentary or newsreel, can record the truth. The reason this is impossible is that reality exists not in external action but in the subjective mind and experience of the individual. This conviction leads Resnais to a highly unconventional, highly intellectual style of filmmaking:

> Let us say that I am concerned to address the spectator in a critical state of mind. For that I need to make films that are not natural. The realist cinema, the reconstruction of daily life, the reproduction of gestures, all that does not interest me at all. . . . I want the spectator to identify himself not with the hero but only, from time to time, with the feelings of the hero. [14]

The relationship between the past and present is much more complicated in *Hiroshima* than the simple alternate cutting between the present (in color) and the past (in black and white) in *Night and Fog,* for in the more recent film Resnais is trying to suggest the merging of different time dimensions within the consciousness of an individual mind. In the first sequence, the selective images of the sensuous present are intercut with illustrative shots of what she has experienced since she has been in Hiro-

[13] *Ibid.,* p. 10.
[14] Alain Resnais, in Armes, vol. 2, p. 99.

shima; her own memories of the recent past are merged with the official public memories that have been recorded on film and placed in public museums. In the second sequence that takes place the morning after, as she looks at her Japanese lover, there is a quick cut back to her German lover, baffling to the audience because we do not yet know the story of Nevers. Later, when we finally hear her tell the story, her words evoke the image Resnais has already planted in our memory, and we too have a sense of *déjà vu* and can identify more powerfully with her feelings and mental process. When the lovers meet in Peace Square, the juxtaposition between past and present and between the public issues of war and their personal love story is achieved not through cutting but by the inclusion in the scene of Japanese extras from the "peace" movie parading with posters that give factual information about the bomb. We realize that this scenery is now becoming part of her present experience and will become sensuous fragments that she will recall in the future when she thinks back to her "impossible" love in Hiroshima. When they make love later that day in his home and she begins to tell the story of her first love in Nevers, fragmentary images from her memory are intercut with their embracing bodies. Changes in lighting make the present scene seem as fluid and elusive as the images from the past. As she continues the story later that night when they are in a bar, she begins to relive it, addressing the Japanese as though he were her German lover and reexperiencing the madness; he recalls her to the present by slapping her. Her story is told not in chronological order but in fragmentary visual and verbal images as they come to mind. The sense of linear or rational time is also absent from the present scene between the lovers. Since this is their last night together, we would probably expect it to go rapidly, but instead it goes at a very slow pace, as they move restlessly from place to place, the camera alternating among long tracking shots, long static takes, and fast cutting. We have no way of knowing how much time elapses between the shifts in setting, and we cannot even be completely sure of the order of events. As she is walking the streets, speaking to her Japanese lover in an interior monologue, the camera cuts back and forth between the empty streets of Hiroshima and Nevers; the present experience in her consciousness is a total blending of the past and present, and her words apply equally well to both lovers:

> I meet you, I remember you. This city was made to the size of love. You were made to the size of my body. Who are you? You destroy me. . . . A time will come. When we'll

> no more know what thing it is that binds us. By slow de-
> grees the word will fade from our memory. Then it will
> disappear altogether.[15]

Both the form (interior monologue) and content (memory) of her
words draw our attention to what is going on inside her head, and
we begin to realize that this aimless walking through the streets is
a visual metaphor for her mental process. Yet Resnais repeatedly
reminds us that the external sensory details are part of the present
experience. Like the crowds of extras in Peace Square, the old
woman in the railroad station and the young man in the bar intrude
upon their personal scene and are registered upon her consciousness. In the final encounter between the two lovers, her mind succeeds in "drowning him in universal oblivion" and transforming
their experiences into symbolic verbal abstractions. As they say
their last words, they already do not see each other:

> She: Hi-ro-shi-ma. Hi-ro-shi-ma. That's your name.
> He: That's my name. Yes. Your name is Nevers. Ne-vers-in-
> France.

We are reminded of some of her lines from the opening scene:
"Just as in love this illusion exists, this illusion of being able to
forget, so I was under the illusion that I would never forget Hiroshima. Just as in love." The ending combines the individual and
the city, love and death. It blends not only her past and present
experience but also the beginning and ending of the film, thereby
enabling us in the audience to experience the merging of the past
and the present in our own consciousness.

Despite the fact that Resnais has collaborated with many distinguished writers (Marguerite Duras, Alain Robbe-Grillet, Jean
Cayrol, Jorge Semprun) who have undoubtedly exerted a great
influence over his films, he has continued to deal with similar
themes in a similar style to express a consistent view of reality.
His later films—*Last Year at Marienbad* (1961), *Muriel, or the Time
of a Return* (1963), *La Guerre Est Finie* (1966), and *Je T'aime, Je
T'aime* (1968)—are also concerned with the way the mind works:
Experience is presented as fragmented sensory perceptions;
various time dimensions are combined; the characters try desperately to hold on to the past; love and death are juxtaposed as
the two most intense experiences in life. In order to express this
vision, he continues to reject the conventional plot with a beginning, middle, and end; to experiment with the incongruity be-

---

[15] *Hiroshima, Mon Amour*, p. 77.

tween the aural and visual aspects of the film; and to achieve a highly varied cutting rhythm. These qualities are developed with even greater complexity in *Muriel*.

MURIEL, OR THE TIME OF A RETURN (1963)

Man's use of the past as a means of defining experience is Resnais's concern in *Muriel, or the Time of a Return*. The plot is fairly simple, but the treatment is complicated. Hélène, an attractive widow in her forties, lives in Bologne with her stepson Bernard, who has just returned from the war in Algeria. Hélène writes a letter to Alphonse, her lover of twenty years ago, asking him to visit her. He brings with him his young mistress Françoise, whom he passes off as his niece. The film deals with the present relationship among these characters during the visit and the past that each brings to it. Resnais has thus expanded the web of complications, focusing on two major characters in *Hiroshima*, three in *Marienbad*, and four in *Muriel*.

The return mentioned in the title refers to many things: the return of Alphonse to Hélène, the return of Bernard from Algeria, the threatened return of Alphonse and Françoise to Paris (which never takes place). It refers also to each character's attempt to return to the past.

Each has a different relationship to the past, but all are involved in deception or distortion. Of all the characters, Françoise is least concerned with the past and most absorbed in the present. She has a bad memory and recognizes that her relationship with all these characters is temporary. She adopts roles in the present (she is in fact an actress); her current role is that of Alphonse's niece. But she is willing to face the unpleasantness that goes along with this deception. In contrast, Hélène, an antique dealer, tries to escape into a romanticized version of the past that omits all unpleasantness. She wants the past as well as the present to be fluid (she is afraid of taking photographs because they freeze experience), always open to new possibilities and new interpretations. This grasping at new possibilities is also reflected in her compulsive gambling. She is unable to control her unconscious distortion of experience just as she is unable to control her gambling. She seeks comfort in the past but is never satisfied. Like Hélène, Alphonse is unable to face reality. Yet his distortion of the past and the present is conscious. Not only does he lie, but he steals the memories and feelings of others. In contrast to Alphonse, Bernard is trying desperately to retain the past, to make sure that he does not forget a traumatic experience, his participation in the torture and murder of an Algerian girl named Muriel. He carries around a camera and tape recorder not to create art but to collect evidence. Like the woman in *Hiroshima,* in trying to hold on to the past, he seriously distorts the present, pretending that Muriel is his fiancée.

Through the unconventional style of this film Resnais defines his conception of experience: Life is divided into a series of separate moments, perceptions, and objects. This fragmentary quality is suggested mainly by the editing and by the relationship between sound and visuals. The film is comprised of many short scenes that never really develop. We learn about incidents in a piecemeal fashion. The opening montage, for example, immediately communicates a sense of fragmentation: a hand on a doorknob, a teakettle, someone's face shot from several different angles. This quality is also expressed in the dialogue; conversations never develop, characters rarely finish sentences; talk is full of non sequiturs and seemingly trivial statements. Moreover, the visual and auditory rhythms do not move at the same speed. For example, the film cuts from a scene with Alphonse, Hélène, and Françoise talking in Hélène's apartment to an exterior shot of Bernard alone on his bicycle, but the conversation from the previous scene continues. Sometimes the shift in the audio comes before the visual cut.

One of the most important scenes makes particularly effective use of this discrepancy. While we watch a home movie of French soldiers in Algeria laughing and playing and acting quite normally, we listen to Bernard describing the atrocities these men committed. There is no sign of this horror in the film. The point is similar to the one Resnais made in *Night and Fog* and in *Hiroshima;* the significant record of the (Algerian) experience exists only in one's mind.

More generally, the auditory and visual portions of the film represent different conceptions of time. The screenplay (which Resnais considers part of the audio portion) is in perfect chronological order, divided into five acts covering the period from September 29 to October 14, 1962. But the visuals contradict this linear pattern. For example, when Hélène, Alphonse, and Françoise are walking home from the train station in the evening, Resnais intercuts several quick daytime shots. Resnais's own statements about this technique are very revealing:

> For me, the film is an attempt, still very crude and primitive, to approach the complexity of thought, its mechanism. . . . I believe that, in life, we do not think chronologically, that our decisions never correspond to an ordered logic. . . . I think that mental life is something that forms a part of life, that our night life is in complete intimacy with our daytime life: realism does not consist solely in filming our conversation, for example, but also in showing the images that I have in my head at this moment.[16]

He inserts shots of places when the main characters are not there, suggesting that the places have an existence apart from the characters' mental image of them. He also focuses on characters who are insignificant to the plot. For example, Hélène has a casual encounter in a casino with an employee who tells her that he and his wife work on the Riviera every summer. Later we see a shot of them departing, but not a word is spoken about this image. Thus, in contrast to the neat, logical chronology of the screenplay, the visual portion of the film is kaleidoscopic; it presents a fluid array of sensory perceptions from various perspectives and time dimensions.

The structural treatment of the relationship among the four main characters emphasizes this fragmented view of experience. We would expect the relationships to become more intertwined and complex, but they do not. In their first meeting, Alphonse and Françoise come to visit Hélène and Bernard, and the four are united at the dinner table. After dinner they form new patterns: Bernard and Françoise, the two young people, go out together and leave Hélène and Alphonse to deal with their past. But then unexpectedly Hélène goes off to gamble and leaves Alphonse home alone, and Bernard goes off on his own and leaves Françoise alone in the street. They all spend the evening apart. Moreover, the film follows the separate path of each character, showing each one performing trivial actions like reading the paper, going to the store, talking to strangers on the street. Each lives in his own time scheme and his own consciousness; their paths and experience intersect only temporarily.

Experience is also marked by uncertainty. People are subjective filters, distorting experience either consciously or unconsciously. Their language is contradictory. They are constantly moving—walking in and out of rooms, opening and closing doors, going somewhere or returning. Their moods are always changing, frequently alternating between laughter and tears. In the midst of

[16] Resnais, quoted in Armes, vol. 2, pp. 96–97.

profound grief, Hélène strikes up a trivial conversation with a stranger on a bench. She observes, "One can't control one's own feelings." This fluidity also characterizes the environment: Old buildings are being torn down and new structures built; the furnishings in Hélène's house keep changing. There are constant reminders that time is passing and that past, present, and future are all uncertain.

The most profound experiences are frequently linked with the banal. When Hélène and Alphonse try to think back on their past love affair, they remember seemingly trivial sensory details like a day in the woods, a fire, staying at a particular hotel because of a certain mirror. This implies that past memories are comprised largely of sensory impressions, precisely the kinds of images that Resnais focuses on in the present. From the very first image, of a doorknob, *Muriel* bombards us with objects: merchandise in the store windows; antiques in Hélène's house; junk bought and sold; crystal, china, and silver on the table; bread, wine, chicken, and cake at the meals. The minds of all the characters are focused on objects. Even Bernard says his trade is "to look at things."

The significance of apparently trivial events is developed most fully through the banquet scenes that recur throughout the film. Eating is the one activity that unites everyone, yet it is a temporary union as in a love affair. Roland observes that a love affair is like a banquet: Some people behave well and others badly. The banquet or meal becomes a metaphor for their existence, and it has an important structural role in the film. The first dinner is the setting for the first union between the four major characters. Significantly, the climax of the film, when all the strands finally come together, also takes place during a banquet scene. Alphonse's story reaches its climax as his brother-in-law arrives unexpectedly; his past marriage to Simone, which he has been so frantically trying to escape, intrudes upon the present and exposes his web of lies. Realizing what is happening, Bernard runs to get his camera and tape recorder in order to document the present exposure of Alphonse's guilt. When Françoise turns on the tape recorder, we hear laughter and moans, probably from the experience with Muriel. In trying to record the present, Bernard must give up the past; one erases the other, which is precisely what he has been so desperately trying to avoid. His own guilt is exposed, and he too reaches the climax in his story as he runs out to murder one of his accomplices, thus ensuring that the murder of Muriel will not be forgotten. Parallels between Alphonse and Bernard suddenly become clear. Both have important early memories with Hélène. Both have a woman in their past whom they met after Hélène and whom they have wronged in some way. Before the banquet, both confronted a man who had been involved in their relationships with Muriel and Simone—confrontations that took place simultaneously in the same cafe. Their reactions are exactly the opposite: Alphonse tries to forget Simone and pretend their relationship never occurred; Bernard tries to freeze the memory of what he has done to Muriel. Both attempts are bound to fail. After the double climax at the banquet, everyone leaves and pursues his own path, the camera following one at a time. The film ends with the camera's tracking through the now deserted dining room, observing the dirty dishes and the left-over food.

In *Muriel,* as in his other films, Resnais confronts us with a world of fluid being that we perceive through our senses and that

Muriel

resists our attempts to mold it into a static order. Although he recognizes man's desire to hold onto experience and record it permanently in memory, he suggests that this is impossible. The fluidity of experience enables man to go on living despite the traumas he encounters. Yet, without permanent memory, there can be no absolute values, no absolute truth, and this awareness undermines belief in ideology, in love, and in tragedy. The only tragedy is man's inability to remember.

Jean-Luc Godard

BREATHLESS (1959)

Starting as a critic, Godard has never lost his powers of intellectual analysis and his practice of self-criticism. He is the most radically experimental of all the new-wave directors and is continually breaking existing conventions and exploring new territory. His intellectual powers are combined with a playful sense of humor and an extraordinary inventiveness that frequently make viewing his films, even those that present a rather grim vision of life, an exhilarating experience.

In *Breathless* the sense of reality is immediate, active, and mythic. Godard deals not with the past but with the present moment—with what the actors are doing and what the audience is experiencing. He always sets his films precisely at the time that they are being shot. The hero, Michel Poiccard (played by Jean-Paul Belmondo), always lives in the present without worrying about the past or future, a quality that distinguishes him from Patricia (Jean Seberg), the girl who betrays him. He loves her without having to ask why or to consider the effects. Thus even when the police are on their way to arrest him, he cannot leave because he is too much in the present. She, on the other hand, turns him in because she does not want to love him because her freedom may be restricted if she does. Yet she returns to see whether in fact she really loves him. Her actions are controlled by her thoughts rather than by her feelings; frequently they are designed to test theoretical ideas. She is so worried about future consequences that she is totally out of touch with her present feelings. In an interview with the writer, she asks him not about love and sex, as the others do, but about ambition, which is future oriented. In the love scene in her bedroom, she says she is afraid of getting old, and she quotes the end of Faulkner's *Wild Palms:* "Between grief and nothing, I will take grief." Michel responds, "Grief's a waste of time—I'd choose nothing." He rejects grief because it focuses on past regrets instead of on present risks. After he makes his first date with Patricia, he runs past an advertising poster that could be taken as the motto for his existential attitude toward experience: "To Live Dangerously to the End." Yet this motto could also be seen as one of many omens foreshadowing her betrayal and his death.

Why should there be so many anticipations of the future in a film that celebrates the present moment? The reality in *Breathless* is also mythic; the foreshadowings are one way of showing that the unique action in the present is related to more general patterns in art and life. In this film the particular mythos is derived from the popular media of movies and newspapers, but in his later films Godard also includes many other art forms. The plot of *Breathless* is based on the conventions of the American gangster movie. It opens with the gangster-hero committing a murder, is complicated by his falling in love with and being betrayed by a woman, and ends with his death in the street in a gun battle with the police. Yet this summary of the plot communicates almost

Breathless

nothing about the unique quality of this film, for Godard plays down these actions, which are conventional events in the gangster myth. They are not really central, for the film stresses neither plot nor causality. The murder at the opening is casual and spontaneous, and Michel's death at the end is almost an absurd accident. The major attention, instead, is on Michel's attitude toward experience: his playful mood, his fast pace, his external gestures, his spontaneity. These are the qualities expressed by the style of the film: the jump cuts, the rapid pace, the hand-held camera, the natural lighting.

Yet, ironically, Michel's attitude toward experience also has mythic roots. He patterns himself after Humphrey Bogart, whose face is prominently displayed in movie posters. The last thing Michel does before dying is rub his lower lip in the Bogart manner, a gesture imitated by Patricia. The Bogart myth in American gangster movies had a historical basis, but it became a model for the behavior and thinking of its audience. (Ironically, Godard's treatment of the genre influenced *Bonnie and Clyde*.) Myth and reality go on endlessly influencing each other. There are many allusions to other movies throughout the film: Michel's pseudonym Laszlo Kovaks is the name of a well-known cinematographer; Michel and Patricia go to a theater where *Westbound* is playing; their dialogue alludes to film titles such as *A Certain Smile* (which starred Jean Seberg) and *Aimez-vouz Brahms?*

The best film allusion also involves the newspaper, another important source of myth in *Breathless*. A man on the street looks at Michel's picture in the paper, recognizes him as the murderer, and calls the police. This stock situation from gangster films is transformed into a joke by the fact that Godard plays the role of the informer. Thus, while he is pretending to recognize Michel, the audience should be recognizing Godard. Further, film buffs will recognize that appearing in his own movie is a practice Godard borrowed from Alfred Hitchcock, one of his heroes at the time. Thus this little scene makes the audience think of other films and of real life, for they are constantly fused in the world of Godard's movies.

Godard links the newspaper with the documentary function of film. *Breathless* opens with a shot of Michel reading the comics. He continually buys newspapers to keep up with the latest news about his exploits and frequently uses them to hide his face. When he reads a story in the paper about a thief and the woman who loved him, he tries to transform it into a myth that he and Patricia will reenact. But she has other fantasies that come from the press.

Although she sells the *Tribune* on the street, her ambition is to become a journalist. She is eager to retain her freedom in order to pursue her career, a goal that conflicts with Michel's fantasy. To prove her journalistic ability, she attends an interview with a writer, a characteristic feature of most Godard films, which simultaneously mocks the interviewing process and yet authentically records its inanity. While she relates to the mythic possibilities of the press in terms of future ambition, we actually see the press being used to broadcast Michel's current mythic actions. The lights atop buildings even announce that "a dragnet is being drawn around Michel Poiccard," as if to imply that he is taking part in a great chase scene that all Paris is eagerly watching.

Probably the most important quality about Michel as a hero and the film as a whole is their mobility and speed. Emphasis on free motion links the film to *400 Blows.* Michel is constantly running down the street or speeding in a car. The automobile usually had an important role in the American gangster movie, but its transient usefulness and rapid interchangeability are unique to *Breathless.* Michel changes stolen cars as easily as he changes handkerchiefs, demonstrating his mobility and willingness to take new risks.

His playful spontaneity is probably best demonstrated in a scene where he is driving down the boulevard and impulsively stops to lift up the full skirt of a girl strolling by. He does it because he had the impulse. And this is precisely the feeling that one has about Godard's style of making a movie. The tone abruptly shifts from comedy to unexpected violence. The camera cuts abruptly from one scene to another. In one of the most unconventional scenes in the film, Godard cuts rapidly from one shot to another of the back of a cab driver's head—all taken of the same subject from the same angle. The entire film seems to be shot at a breathless speed; there is no time to worry about the jiggling of the hand-held camera and the variations in the natural lighting. In fact, these qualities define Godard's pace and vision. This was Godard's first film, and he seemed to have as much speed and energy as Michel: "When I began I was very fast. I made *Breathless* at a ratio of about three to one. But *La Chinoise* was ten to one. I'm getting old." [17]

Actually, Godard has continued to make movies at an extraordinarily rapid pace. By getting his own financing outside of the commercial industry, by keeping the cost of his films to an amaz-

[17] Michael Goodwin, Tom Luddy, and Naomi Wise, "The Dziga Vertov Film Group in America: An Interview with Jean-Luc Godard and Jean-Pierre Gorin," in *Take One,* Vol. 2, No. 10, p. 9.

ingly low figure (sometimes as little as $100,000), and by cutting his shooting schedule to about three weeks, he has developed a style of filmmaking that has given him unusual freedom and has enabled him to become one of the most prolific filmmakers in the history of cinema. He followed *Breathless* with *Le Petit Soldat* in 1960 and *Une Femme Est une Femme* in 1961 and then began averaging about three films per year—in 1962, the "La Paresse" episode in *Les Sept Péchés Capitaux, Vivre Sa Vie,* the "Il Nuovo Mondo" episode in *Rogopag;* in 1963, *Les Carabiniers,* the "Le Grand Escroc" episode in *Les Plus Belles Escroqueries du Monde, Contempt;* in 1964, the "Montparnasse Levallois" episode in *Paris Vu par . . . , Bande à Part, A Married Woman;* in 1965, *Alphaville, Pierrot le Fou;* in 1966, *Masculine-Feminine, Made in USA, Two or Three Things I Know About Her;* in 1967, *La Chinoise, Weekend, Le Gai Savoir,* an episode in *Far from Vietnam,* an episode in *Vangelo 70;* in 1968, *A Film Like All the Others, One Plus One (Sympathy for the Devil), British Sounds (See You at Mao), Communication;* in 1969, *Wind from the East, Struggle in Italy, Pravda, One American Movie;* in 1970, *Vladimir and Rosa, Til Victory (Palestine Will Win).*

Godard has taken advantage of his freedom by continuing to experiment and continuing to transform his style. His films after *Breathless* are much more experimental, challenging conventions and expanding the conception of what is cinematic, drawing upon cinema's expressive and documentary powers, and increasing the number of art forms that it can incorporate. Some of these qualities are apparent in *A Married Woman.*

A MARRIED WOMAN:
FRAGMENTS OF A FILM MADE IN 1964

The title of this film suggests its emphasis on the present moment (1964) and its thematic focus on the fragmentation of French bourgeois life. Yet ironically, although its subject matter is sterile, Godard's inventiveness and originality are extraordinarily fertile. Charlotte (played by Macha Meril), the central character, is a shallow housewife, incapable of loving either her husband or her lover. The ideas and images that make up her reality are shaped by commercial art: movies and advertising on billboards and in magazines. Yet she interacts with others who are affected by more traditional literature. As in *Breathless,* there is a conflict in mythologies, but in this film Godard develops the conflict more fully by techniques that define life as fragments in conflict and cinema as a dialectical mixed medium: the frequent incongruity between the visual and the audio, exhibiting both the visual and verbal powers of cinema; the constant mixture of the subjective distortion of the characters (frequently expressed by interior monologues and obtrusive films techniques) with a realism that documents the external images of 1964; an emphasis on high contrast in the black and white photography; and a frequent alternation between positive and negative photographic images.

A Married Woman goes beyond *Breathless* in proving the cinematic importance of language. Several playful shots demonstrate the visual power of words, which is fully exploited by advertising but is also the basis of concrete poetry. There are close-ups of words. The camera zooms back to reveal the *Eve* in *rêves* (dreams) as Charlotte stumbles, thereby making a double visual pun, to *anger* in *danger,* and to the compound nature of *pass-age.* He reminds us that words are not merely signs that refer to objects in the extensional world; they are also arbitrary visual designs and sounds that have their own self-reflexive value. He exploits the power of words as an artistic medium by having Robert and Charlotte read the parting scene from Racine's *Berenice* as they are about to experience their first separation. Godard uses allusions as T. S. Eliot did in *The Waste Land* to incorporate the entire context and mythology of the author into his own work of art, which becomes denser in meaning as the two situations are compared. This allusiveness, not only to literature but to other media, is a major characteristic of his work. The excerpt from Dreyer's *Passion of Joan of Arc* and the reading of Poe's story in *Vivre Sa Vie,* the reenactment of Leroi Jones's *The Dutchman* and the parody of Bergman's *The Silence* in *Masculine-Feminine* are particularly effective examples. In *A Married Woman,* Godard also develops the potentialities of the spoken narrative, particularly in the sequence where Charlotte's maid gives a hilarious account of her sexual adventures entitled "The Java," and the audio portion of the film dominates the visual, a device Godard employed very effectively in *Weekend,* where an account of a sexual orgy is accompanied by a visual image that is almost completely static.

Closely related is his expanded use of the interview. Like the interview with Antoine in *400 Blows,* those in *A Married Woman* capture the spontaneity of the characters, but they are used in more complicated ways to comment on the relationship between art and reality. When Robert (played by Bernard Noel) is interviewed by Charlotte about acting, we are unsure whether he is speaking about Robert or Bernard:

Charlotte: And right now are you playing a part?
Robert: Right now I'm trying to ... to combine the actor and the man. It's not so easy.
Charlotte: How can you tell what's real and what's stage?
Robert: Well, in life I don't play act. At least I don't think I do. Some men seem to be acting all the time ... you can tell. I don't think I do. I may be wrong ... The theater's quite different. There's a script, you interpret something that's not you. Whereas right now you're asking me questions and I'm answering. But here the script is mine. That's the difference.[18]

In this scene it is almost impossible to sort out illusion and reality, impossible to determine who is making up the script and whom these characters represent, an ambiguity that is increased by the reading from Racine that follows.

The interview is a documentary convention, yet its format calls attention to it as an artistic contrivance. In breaking down dramatic illusion and reminding us in the audience that we are watching a film rather than life, it achieves the ultimate in realism (ironically, the antithesis of verisimilitude). Godard learned this technique from Brecht and he effectively adapts it to cinema. The characters often express themselves in monologues. Charlotte's poetic interior monologues combine fragmented associations, frequently of advertising slogans, abstractions, and sensory perceptions:

To find bliss ...
Like in the movies ...
The sky is blue.
The past is wiped out.
With lipstick on.
What are you thinking?
I hesitate.
The next morning.
He didn't know.
In the clouds.
To get undressed.

Other characters make set speeches, sometimes titled and numbered and delivered while the speaker is standing against a wall

[18] *The Married Woman* (New York: Berkeley, 1965).

and directly facing the camera. Godard flattens out space and reminds his audience that they are watching a two-dimensional screen rather than three-dimensional reality. Again, as in his use of concrete poetry, he shows that words are words, film is film, and art is art.

In this film, as in *Breathless,* Godard makes many, but more complicated, allusions to film. Several of the most obvious are to new-wave heroes such as Hitchcock, Cocteau, and Dietrich, and to the new wave itself, in a question about the slow-motion sequence between Frankie and Cecile in Jacques Demy's *Lola* and in the excerpt from Resnais's *Night and Fog.* Yet sometimes they are subtle, as in the opening sequence of the film, which is almost like a parody of the opening of *Hiroshima, Mon Amour.* The point is not to make fun of Resnais's film but to bring the entire context of that film to bear on the issue of fragmentation in *A Married Woman.*

Both films open with two naked lovers in bed, but the subject is treated in extremely different ways. In *A Married Woman* a love scene between Charlotte and her lover Robert is shot against the background of a white sheet. Her arm slides across the sheet, then his arm intersects hers at a sharp angle. There is a fade-out. Next we see her leg on the sheet, then his, then a fade-out. Then her thigh, his thigh, fade-out. The parts of the body are shot separately. There is no intertwining as in *Hiroshima;* the audience can always tell quite clearly whether it is her arm or his.

Most unusual in this scene is the use of fade-outs, which conventionally signify the passing of time. Two lovers embrace in bed; there is a fade-out; and the audience assumes the next scene will take place in the morning. But Godard breaks this convention, rejecting its narrative function and using it as a visual marker to separate the parts of the body. The fade-outs also suggest that one day in bed is just like any other, a suggestion that is reinforced by the fact that later in the film the entire love scene is repeated, with only minor variations, by Charlotte and her husband Pierre. In contrast to *Hiroshima,* one intense experience with a lover in the present does not recall fragments of another from the past, for in Charlotte's world no experiences are intense. The present is merely made up of interchangeable parts that can be shuffled at random. When Charlotte is making love to her husband and saying the same things to him that she said to her lover, she shows no awareness that she is repeating herself. She makes no attempt to regain the past, as the woman in *Hiroshima* tried to do.

While Charlotte and Robert make love, they disagree not about serious things such as what was perceived in Hiroshima but about parts of their bodies and other banal subjects:

Robert:	Why not be like the women in Italian films; not shave under your arms?
Charlotte:	I like American films better. It looks much nicer.
Robert:	But it's less exciting.
Charlotte:	You've nice eyebrows.
Robert:	Do I?
Charlotte:	That's what counts most in Japan.

The focus on the body stresses people's separateness. At one point Robert observes about their lovemaking, "You kiss, caress, but you're still outside. It's like a house you can't enter." This is antithetical to the physical and mental fusion that takes place between the lovers in *Hiroshima*.

The opening sequence in bed is followed by a shot of a radio with an announcer predicting how many auto fatalities will occur during the coming holiday. Here, as in *Hiroshima,* death and love are juxtaposed, but with different implications. The allusion to death has no apparent relationship to what preceded, except as an example of the fragmentation of the present. Life is made up of a series of disjointed parts, hence the series of disjointed shots, unlike the merging of love and death that occurred in *Hiroshima*.

The result of this sequence is to emphasize the fragmented quality of the present, rather than of the past as in Resnais's film. Godard's characters cut themselves off from one another; they divide their experience into parts having no meaningful relation with each other and thus cannot understand the present. This idea provides the theme of the four separate "speeches" made by Pierre, who speaks for the values of memory; Charlotte, who speaks for the present; Leenhardt, an old intellectual who speaks for intelligence and understanding; and little Nicholas, Pierre's son, who speaks for childhood. This "conversation" occurs not while the characters are engaged in an important action (as it did in *Hiroshima,* while they were making love); it is set apart from the action. Each person faces the camera and in a monologue explains his attitude. Charlotte says she loves the present because she can neither control nor understand it. As soon as she tries to understand, she alters and distorts it and it becomes part of the past. The characters in *Hiroshima* also realize this, but they try to retain the past because they consider understanding all important. Charlotte no longer values understanding and thus willingly accepts the loss of memory.

In *A Married Woman,* as in all Godard films, form and subject are consciously coordinated to express anti-establishment content; the film simultaneously mocks conventions of film and of bourgeois culture. Yet it is not as explicitly political as Godard's later work became. A film crucial for an understanding of his political development is *La Chinoise.*

LA CHINOISE (1967)

In *La Chinoise* Godard first went beyond social criticism to focus primarily on political ideology. He proved his documentary ability as a political analyst, for his film predated the student riots that took place in Paris in May and June 1968. Radical students reacted unfavorably to the film since it was not clearly committed to their cause and, in fact, made revolutionaries seem foolish.

In 1968 Godard began making films with the Dziga Vertov Film Group, which included Jean-Pierre Gorin, his close friend. Their first work was *A Film Like All the Others,* which deals with the May-June events from Godard's new militant perspective. Godard had renounced the egotistical notion of making his own films, the *auteur* theory of filmmaking, his role as hero of the cineastes, and the example set by Truffaut, who became part of the bourgeois establishment. He did so at quite a price—the renunciation of his previous films, including, of course, much of their humor, complexity, and inventiveness.

These three qualities are still present in *La Chinoise,* which is probably one of the reasons Godard has renounced it as a bourgeois film. When recently asked in an interview, "If you're serious about Marxism and revolution, why do you make the revolutionaries in your movies do such absurd, silly things? Like *La Chinoise,* where they kill the wrong person," Godard responded, "Yeah, but that was three or four years ago, when I was still making bourgeois pictures even if I thought I wasn't. In a bourgeois picture a revolutionary looks silly." [19] Yet Godard still seems to believe in *La Chinoise*'s ability to evoke political action. When the same interviewer observed that *La Chinoise* opened in New York a day or two before the student take-over at Columbia and that he had "always felt that there was a very clear cause-and-effect relationship," Godard and Gorin replied:

Godard: I know, I know.
Gorin: Don't tell him that. He has been noting—putting

[19] Goodwin, Luddy, and Wise, p. 22.

in a notebook—every student insurrection just
after a showing of La Chinoise, and coming to
me and saying, "Look! You see, it works!" [20]

The political strategy Godard used in La Chinoise was to pose a
number of theoretical questions and imply a number of contradictory attitudes, in order to force the audience into an intellectual
and critical examination of the film. When we leave the theater,
we can either reject the film entirely or try to figure out what it is
expressing. The fascinating visuals almost force us to do the latter.
And once we try to figure it out, we must deal with the political
issues it raises. It presents no neat, melodramatic solutions to
political questions as Z does, for example, enabling us to go
home pleased for having followed all the twists in the plot and
thankful we do not live in Greece. Nor does it beat us over the
head with boring propaganda, as Godard's own Wind from the
East unfortunately does. More in the tradition of Brecht or of
Weiss's Marat/Sade, it deals simultaneously with esthetics and
politics, raising ideological questions but leaving the work open-
ended.

The film treats five young people in a Communist cell who
share an apartment that is lent to one of them by a friend whose
parents are away for the summer. They lecture to each other, have
ideological arguments, and finally botch up an assassination.
Then, when the summer is over, they return to school. They are
playing at revolution. In terms of the fictional reality of the film,
when we consider them as Veronique, Guillaume, Henri, Kirilov,
and Yvonne, we condemn their behavior, for they are performing
bad theater and bad politics. But when we consider them as Anne
Wiazemski (the second Mrs. Godard), Jean-Pierre Léaud, Michel
Semeniake, Lex de Bruijn, and Juliet Berto, five actors performing
in Godard's Brechtian theater, we judge both their art and their
politics more favorably. Supposedly, Godard wanted the credits to
read, "A film acted and filmed by the actors and technicians of
the Rosa Luxemburg cell."

This double dimension of reality is emphasized in a variety of
ways: by showing the filmmaking process (the shots of cinematographer Raoul Coutard); by having Léaud play an actor who frequently lectures on acting, theater, and cinema; by having Léaud
point to the need for a new interpretation of the Lumières as the
creators of expressive cinema and Méliès as the father of documentary film—perhaps implying that films normally considered

[20] Ibid., p. 12.

expressive may be more political than documentaries. The interviews and reading of texts practically dominate the entire film, stressing their dual associations with cinema vérité and with artifice. The walls of the apartment are painted with bold primary colors, giving the setting a pop art feeling and frequently emphasizing the flatness of the two-dimensional movie screen; at times the imagery resembles the comic books that appear in occasional quick cuts. In a sequence on a train, as Veronique argues the radical cause with a liberal philosophy professor who opposes burning down the university without a positive alternative, our eyes are drawn away from this futile conversation to the window that visually separates the two figures. We see outside life moving by very rapidly, looking like a movie screen framed by a static theater piece.

Several things in the film make us question the values of the young revolutionaries. They not only assassinate the wrong man; they treat each other very badly. They unfeelingly reject Henri over a point of ideology. They exploit Yvonne, the very person whom they ironically cast in the role of the Vietnamese peasant, to do their housework. In a scene where Veronique tells Guillaume that she no longer loves him, she is as callous and insensitive as Patricia in *Breathless*, Charlotte in *A Married Woman*, Marianne in *Pierrot le Fou,* and Madeleine in *Masculine-Feminine*. Instead of

La Chinoise

making any direct contact, the cell members read and preach to each other, practicing their skills at arguing and speechmaking. In this film, Godard was still in touch with feelings, exploring the effect of their absence:

> In *La Chinoise* it was done only with feelings, and the feelings ended when I was doing *One A.M.* Maybe the feelings were good, but at a certain point they stop being good. You have to analyze, to distance yourself from feelings, and to know where the feelings are coming from.[21]

Yet *La Chinoise* also demands analysis. Despite the limitations of the militant students, there are no clearly positive alternatives. The liberal professor has no suggestions of how to change society, and the film clearly rejects the present system. The audience is left with the need to make critical discriminations, to separate the value from the limitations within the political cell, to engage in a process that is analogous to Godard's self-criticism.

Godard himself seems to be going through an experience parallel to that of the young actors. Right after the filming of *La Chinoise,* he moved into that apartment. Subsequently, he too has become part of a militant group making revolutionary films for revolutionary audiences, films that could have direct political effects—for example, helping Al-Fatah of the Palestinian liberation movement to make the propaganda film *Til Victory (Palestine Will Win).* He now believes that "during the showing of a militant film, the screen is simply a blackboard or the wall in a classroom that presents the concrete analysis of a concrete situation."[22] He too has renounced earlier good friends, such as Truffaut, Demy, Belmondo, and Coutard, for political reasons. He also has had to face the same problem of making art that is good both politically and esthetically. In a 1968 interview, Godard quotes Mao as saying, "A piece of art which is politically just, but which fails from an artistic point of view, is bad. But the contrary is bad too. Bad politics and good art is bad too."[23] Guillaume quotes the same statement in *La Chinoise.*

While Godard has renounced his pre-Vertov films on the basis of their politics, we would renounce the more recent ones on the basis of their esthetics. They no longer have the intellectual toughness, the visual and verbal complexity, the free inventiveness and ironic wit that characterized Godard's style. Perhaps Godard needed a dramatic transformation in order to ensure that he would

[21] *Ibid.*, p. 13.
[22] "Jean-Luc Godard," *Kinopraxis*, No. 0 (Berkeley: Jack Flash, 1970).
[23] *Ibid.*

never get into a rut, that he would not follow the traditional pattern of the young rebel metamorphosed into a middle-aged, bourgeois conservative like Truffaut, that he was not too old to be in touch with the militant students. Ironically, he was rejected by Berkeley students for his rigid, doctrinaire brand of intellectual radicalism, which is so out of touch with feelings. On this basis he criticized *One Plus One* (*Sympathy for the Devil*). He, like Marat, wants a revolution of the mind and is mistrustful of forces like the Marquis de Sade, the Stones, and the American cultural revolution, which also emphasizes the importance of the body. As in *Breathless, A Married Woman,* and *La Chinoise,* this situation implies a conflict between different mythologies, and in the world of Godard, that is the same as a conflict between ideologies. It is hard to believe that Godard will continue making films of this kind or that he will ever get locked into a single style or conception of cinema. His greatest strength is his ability to keep growing and changing.

the new american humanistic realism

During the 1960's in the United States, a group of films emerged that commanded a great deal of attention and seemed (with a little help from sophisticated advertising) to announce themselves as the most significant cinema of the time. Films like *The Graduate, Midnight Cowboy, Easy Rider,* and *Five Easy Pieces* had certain characteristics in common. Many were interested in the "lower classes," often sentimentalized as in *Midnight Cowboy* or used exploitatively as the alternative or foil to complex sensitivity as in *Five Easy Pieces.* They focused on characters who were, to some extent, social deviants, outside the cultural mainstream. But the films, particularly *The Graduate,* render suspect their own "revolutionary" perspectives by easing back into the values they appear to be questioning. The central characters share the qualities of an anti-hero whose failure or helplessness can be taken to measure with almost mathematical precision the beauty and independence of his quest for self. Effective and authentic as such characters can be, their value is often undermined in these films by extreme sentimentality, by inconsistent and unimaginative development, as in *The Graduate;* by slick and exploitative values, as in *Easy Rider;* and by pretentious and unrealized complexity, as in *Five Easy Pieces.* Cast with little-known actors, rising young stars, or actors with quasi-underground reputations, these films often contain performances stronger than the characters and concepts that lie behind them; in fact, the value of several of them depends largely upon performances, such as Dustin Hoffman's in *Midnight Cowboy,* Jack Nicholson's and Dennis Hopper's in *Easy Rider,* and, to some extent, Nicholson's in *Five Easy Pieces.*

These films and others like them to some degree reject highly subjective, expressionistic techniques and turn instead to a kind of realism or naturalism of setting, characterization, and visual techniques. *Easy Rider's* best scenes offer with chilling realism the hostility of the locals encountered along the road. Much of *Midnight Cowboy's* limited effectiveness comes from realistic details of setting and location. *The Graduate* tries to generate uniqueness by emphasizing the banality of middle-class America; the film, however, is trapped in its own banality, unable to transcend it with the hero's sudden flight into heavily symbolic but impish freedom.

While these films are usually considered America's important contribution to contemporary cinema, several filmmakers working at the same time were making far better films and offering more valuable statements about similar themes and problems. Furthermore, each one was developing a conception of realism that could express with great power his unique vision of experience. John Cassavetes' *Faces* (1968), Andy Warhol's *Nude Restaurant* (1967), and Paul Morrissey's *Trash* (1970) are representative of this group, which also includes Cassavetes' *Shadows* and *Husbands,* Warhol's *Chelsea Girls, Lonesome Cowboys,* and *Bike Boy,* and Morrissey's *Flesh.*

As in the French new wave, it is misleading to talk of these filmmakers as a school. Warhol and Morrissey work together. Although Cassavetes may have seen their films, he did not share their ideas or reflect any of their influence, and his work seems to have had no influence on theirs. Rather than relating to each other self-consciously in some way, these directors have developed a kind of creative community through certain qualities common to their films and to the process of making them. Like Godard, each director sought complete control over his films by getting money from sources outside the commercial film industry. Cassavetes, after several years of a double career (one in industry films and television, the other beginning with his own film *Shadows,* 1957–1960), decided to do another film entirely on his own. Without enough money to finish but with friends who contributed equipment, props, locations, money, and time, he began *Faces* in 1965. Warhol's and Morrissey's films, too, were made within a kind of creative family based at Warhol's Factory, the silk-screen studio that he converted to a film studio starting about 1964. Privately financed, these movies completely ignored the formulas of commercial film, questioning even its very definition.

All three directors are interested in the details of various kinds of modern decadence: Warhol and Morrissey in the drug culture of freaks, addicts, and homosexuals; Cassavetes in the booze culture of businessmen, whores, housewives, and hustlers. All three create a unique relationship between performer and the role he develops, and all depend largely for their effect on the camera's recording rather than its reshaping potentiality. Through their use of extreme cinema vérité techniques, together with emphasis on the close-up, they sometimes give to the films a grotesqueness bordering on the surreal. This mixed effect is enhanced by the fact that the films include or even focus on details of life that are usually ignored or disguised—pimples, masturbation, vomiting, impotence. However, all the films approach such aspects of life and the broader social extremes in which they occur, with a sympathetic acceptance manifested in their structure, visual techniques, and approach to performance. These shared qualities create a fascinating mixture of spontaneity and artifice, which each director develops differently and which gives to each film its unique, humanistic realism.

FACES (1968)

The realism of *Faces* reflects the intimacy and spontaneity with which it was created, in careful balance with artful control; this balance is reflected in the film's overall structure, in its themes, sound track, and visual effects.

Faces begins with a strange prologue, which seems to refer satirically to the making of the film itself and to Cassavetes' attitude toward it. Richard Forst (played by John Marley) hurries down a stairway (the first of many stairway shots throughout the film) to a business meeting, where, as manager of a savings and loan firm, he is to be shown a film for his approval. Forst represents the type of person from whom Cassavetes had to try to get money to finance his own film. Forst reminds the others of his power as he says, "It had better be better than the last one,

Harry." [24] The public relations men who have brought the film argue that it is good because it is like successful foreign films:

Kazmier: Actually, it's a very good film.
Judd: We call it the *Dolce Vita* of the commercial field. [25]

They continue to hustle the film, using embarrassing clichés:

Jim: We were talking facts and figures till we practically went out of our minds. Losses, gains, ratings, schmatings ... You know, you can lose your mind if you keep analyzing things like ...
Kazmier: Then we came up with an impressionistic document that shocks.
Forst: Is that so?
Jim: I don't think it so much shocks as it's honest.
Kazmier: It's honest, but it's a good piece in itself.
Jim: So you see, we're a little nervous about hitting you with this. [26]

When the room darkens and the film is projected, *Faces* appears on the screen. This surprise prologue immediately suggests several implications. Perhaps in Forst's comments about *La Dolce Vita,* Cassavetes means to suggest, through ironic inversion, that, with its glamorous visuals and controlled development, Fellini's film (also dealing with modern, urban decadence) is far more commercial than this one. Perhaps the media hustlers parody the language with which Cassavetes had to (or refused to) hustle his film's particular kind of honesty to those who might put money in it.

While these realistic, even topical, suggestions relate the prologue closely to life outside the film, the very technique of projecting the film within a film reinforces our awareness that we are watching not "life" (no matter how "realistically" rendered) but a controlled piece of work—an artifice, a movie. The prologue, which seems to have little influence on our experience of the rest of the film, does suggest intellectually the special blending of "art" and "life" that gives *Faces* its particular kind of realism.

The relatively simple plot structure, like that of *Husbands* (1970), Cassavetes' third film, also encourages a mixture of spontaneity and control. Richard and his wife Maria (played by Lynn Carlin) are locked into a grim domestic situation. In only ten sequences, covering less than twenty-four hours, the film carefully compares their parallel escapes into night-long binges of liquor, sex, fear,

[24] John Cassavetes, *Faces* (New York: Signet Books, 1970), p. 90.
[25] *Ibid.,* p. 42.
[26] *Ibid.,* p. 46.

and anger. Their adventure "lets them discover themselves sensually in the arms of youth, releases them from the conformity of their existence and forces them into a different context, that of the new morality: the classy whores, the hip and the hypes, the inside thoughts and reactions of their friends when all barriers are down." [27] In the morning, having experienced a kind of ironic modern version of death and rebirth (indeed, the wife tries to commit suicide in the hours before dawn), they come together again, faced with the problem of how to reassemble their lives after the shattering intensity of their separate experiences. The simple structure allows each sequence to be quite long, giving the impression that events take place in real time, creating a sense of spontaneous unfolding.

The combination of control and spontaneity produces a kind of hysterical violence held tightly in check. The sound track moves from long silent stretches to bursts of hysterical laughter. In a sequence where Richard competes with two other businessmen for the favors of Jeannie (a prostitute) everyone seizes any opportunity to break the tension with outbursts of laughter. Such outbursts are often linked to sexuality in some way. When Maria tells Richard a story about oral sex, she screams with nervous laughter and Richard joins her. Later in the film, when she walks into her darkened living room and finds Chet (played by Seymour Cassel), the young man with whom she is about to commit adultery, she responds immediately with shrieks of laughter. The characters themselves recognize their extreme tension and the various kinds of release they find. The young hustler, Chet, admits that he uses dancing in this way and, when Richard asks Maria for a divorce, she begins to laugh. After he repeats his request, he asks her cruelly, "Well, why don'tcha laugh?"

The film's whole concept of "fun," with its extraordinary number of jokes and song and dance routines, its constant flow of liquor, and its hidden agenda of painful competition, develops double qualities linked to control and spontaneity. The characters seek freedom and spontaneity with a desperation born of their rigid, frozen lives but unpredictable violence and terror constantly surface through the thin veneer of civilized control: Freddie (Richard's friend) and Richard slap each other; Jackson (one of the businessmen) slaps Stella (Jeannie's friend); McCarthy (the other businessman) and Forst have a fist fight; Maria slaps Chet; Chet slaps Maria; Maria slaps Richard—middle-class America at play.

Despite the candor with which *Faces* reveals the ugliness and

[27] *Ibid.,* pp. 8–9.

pain of this world, we sympathize with the characters because they are presented, in the tradition of *Rules of the Game,* with sympathy and wit. However, Cassavetes insists that this sympathy be based on full recognition of ugliness and pain. His use of "natural" lighting, relentless close-ups, and nonselective camera angles, his fascination with faces distorted by emotion, the realism of make-up, costume, and setting—all these present human experience unalleviated by the artful beauty found in Renoir's film.

Cassavetes is always interested in breaking down the distinction between an actor and the role he plays, but he achieves balance by choosing highly accomplished professionals. He values mastery of timing and delivery, the traditional skills of the actor:

> A big passage of dialogue in a nervous actor's hands is a traumatic experience and will end up . . . deleted when the film is edited. A big passage in John Marley's hands, or Gena Rowlands', or Lynn Carlin's, or Seymour Cassel's . . . is like no words at all; you're not even conscious of the number of words being used, or the time that is passing.[28]

Yet, at the same time, he creates working conditions in which the actors can define the roles through their personal experience. The brilliant ending of the film took shape in this way:

> And so during the earlier shooting no one, including the actors playing the characters, had any idea how it would end. I recall Cassavetes asking John Marley how he thought it should be. He didn't quite put it in those words. He asked Marley what he thought he would do, what his reaction would be, having gone through this man's life up to the point at which his wife tells him that she doesn't love him any longer, that she hates her life, and even physically strikes him. I remember Marley answering that he felt he would just walk down the stairs and leave the house, since he wouldn't put up with that crap for more than a minute. John didn't agree with him, but instead of fighting Marley's idea, he said, "O.K., let's try it, let's see if it works. Let's do a rehearsal right now." Sure enough, after Lynn struck Marley across the face, he walked down the stairs and got as far as the kitchen door and found he couldn't leave. Thus the staging revealed itself. That was the truth for Richard Forst and that's how *Faces* ended, with John Marley coming back to the staircase and both husband and wife sitting there for that unbearable stretch of time.[29]

Perhaps this approach to creating a role, closely related to the techniques of psychodrama, gives to the performances a kind of

[28] *Ibid.*
[29] *Ibid.,* p. 23.

realism so effective that audiences have sometimes found them painful to watch.

Lighting, timing, and composition help develop with great power the ending arrived at by Cassavetes and Marley. Throughout the film, we have seen the stairway lit with bright, grainy light from the window at the top; modulated from pale light to gray in the early morning; bright and dark with contrasting light from the hallway, kitchen, and bedroom. We have seen it empty and full of traffic; we have looked up and down it. Richard has run up, down, and up again as he returns to see Chet fleeing out the bedroom window; he has run up to be slapped and rejected, gone down again through the dark hallway into the sudden brightness of the kitchen, and returned to the bottom of the stairway. At the end the characters are poised upon it as if at the center of their lives. Richard sits at the bottom, with Maria halfway down from the top, visually suggesting their isolation yet implying a closeness greater than at other moments in the sequence, when the entire stairway separates them. Their business also suggests a habitual yet comforting intimacy: She asks for a cigarette and light; he gives a pack to her and then, with childish belligerence, demands his lighter back. As at Jeannie's, he is childlike in intense moments. In the thin, bright light that diffuses down the stairs, Maria coughs and Richard coughs as if in response. For several seconds, they can neither act nor speak, framed in narrow space. Unexpectedly, Richard moves to the other side of his stair; she follows. But the confines of the composition emphasize the poignant futility of their imitative movements. They are both separate and together, intimate and strangers, trapped and moving. Though they finally leave the stairway in opposite directions, Richard picks up his cigarettes as he goes, the mundane gesture undercutting the dramatic finality of their exits. Nothing has been resolved, and the stairway is empty. The camera holds on it, looking up to the top, drawing us in as titles appear to tell who has brought us to this empty center. This sequence demonstrates, perhaps most effectively, the successful combination of spontaneity in characterization, plot development, and performance with careful control in lighting, timing, camera position, and composition, preserving the sympathetic realism unique to the film.

Throughout *Faces*, lighting displays realistic fluidity, which results in part because the technicians did not try to create artificial light values but used what little equipment they had to develop natural light until it was adequate. As Maria and her friend Florence stand on either side of the open door through which Chet

Faces

has just walked out, the darkness in the doorway becomes a great gulf between them, ominous also for anyone planning to leave the safer brightness of the foyer. As Maria walks around the house to lock up, the dramatic light changes (as she moves from darkened to fully lit rooms; as she abruptly turns off bright lights, plunging rooms into darkness; as she walks down long hallways to distant light) reflect the erratic and unpredictable quality of her emotional state and of the night's events.

Al Ruban, director of photography, and George Sims, camera operator, developed a variety of visual techniques that express the film's balanced realism with extraordinary success. The camera is often placed in a relatively stable position where its lens may be completely blocked by a back or shoulder passing close in front of it as the characters move about freely, creating the impression that events have a life of their own, uncontrolled by script or director, as in a newsreel or even a home movie. Our sense of overlooking is enhanced by the fact that the camera often watches people through doorways, as they move along halls, and as they go up and down stairways. As Chet revives Maria after her suicide attempt, we watch through the partly open bathroom door as he drags her limp body out of the bathtub. The effectiveness of the shot is enhanced as the door frame narrows the image, and the light values of hallway and bathroom contrast sharply. The camera is often placed behind the ear or the shoulder of various characters, giving fluid expression to the variety of points of view observing the action. A great deal of the panning appears to be nonselective but actually develops some significant detail as it reveals, for example, the speed with which Florence is downing her Margarita in the scene at the discothèque.

The excellent use of depth focus provides a kind of balance for the fluidity of point of view and camera movement. From time to time the camera stops its apparently nonselective movement and locks in on one of several characteristic kinds of images in depth. Many shots include part of a character's body in the extreme foreground though the central action is taking place further back in space. Early in the film, as we watch Richard and Freddie getting ready to show off for Jeannie by doing their old college song and dance routine, we see her crossed knees in the left extreme foreground; depth focus shows that her presence is the cause of their behavior. Later, the camera focuses on McCarthy and Forst from shoulders to knees only, as they stand face to face, the middle of their business suits confronting each other with comic aggression. Appropriately, quite far back in the picture but in sharp focus, Jeannie, the blond and seductive cause of this comic confrontation, can be seen through the inverted parentheses of their stomachs. Depth focus is also employed effectively to include in a single frame several people whose reactions are of interest so that they can be viewed simultaneously. In a scene where Freddie and Richard are competing for Jeannie, a large candlestick divides the screen as it becomes clear that Freddie, on one side of the screen, is the unwanted third party. Depth focus helps to develop for the whole film a point of view not linked to a single perceiver but with an omniscience that turns away from nothing, that reminds us of Renoir's films as it unites all the characters in common humanity and accepts them with sympathy as they try to relate to each other.

The editing also reflects spontaneity and control. It is used primarily in two ways. Quick cutting from face to face gives the impression of capturing spontaneous reactions to the events that are unfolding. In a scene in Jeannie's apartment, where Forst and McCarthy fight, the film jumps from face to face, often in distorting close-ups, as the characters register the extreme tension of the situation. Later, as the four women party with Chet at the Forst home, the camera surprises their faces as they try to cope with this extraordinary disruption of their regular lives. Cutting is also used interpretatively and for controlled effect. Later in the evening at the Forst home, when only Florence and Maria are left with Chet, Maria sits on the sofa and Florence and Chet stand in the entrance hallway. Florence asks Chet if he will kiss her. As they begin the embrace, the camera cuts to Maria (whom Chet has already chosen for his partner), her mouth and chin quivering slightly as she lights a cigarette. The cut emphasizes her controlled terror, made even more intense by the sexual play in the hallway, which reminds her that she will soon have to confront her own fearful sexuality. At the end of the sequence where Maria, just revived from her attempted suicide, sits sloppy and exhausted, the film cuts abruptly to a radiant Jeannie, bringing breakfast to Forst as he dresses, emphasizing the differences in each one's reactions to the recent sexual adventures.

This last cut illustrates the fluid shifting of tones that characterizes the film. In the first sequence at Jeannie's apartment with Freddie and Richard, the tone moves slowly and subtly from one of childlike play to the dark and threatening disharmony that finally causes Richard to leave, though he has successfully competed with Fred for Jeannie's favor. When the four women and Chet party at the Forst home, the sequence moves quickly and unpredictably through joy, fear, anger, sensuality, playfulness, jealousy, and grief. This fluidity is expressed with particular poignance as Jeannie, singing and cheerful, removes Richard's breakfast tray; as she moves from bedroom to kitchen, her humming becomes softer and finally changes to tears as she throws away the uneaten breakfast.

Such fluidity is reflective of the unpredictable changes of mood in *Rules of the Game* and links Cassavetes' realism to the mixture of tones in Warhol's and Morrissey's films. The organic quality of the performances, the shifting light values, the camera movement, the cutting, and the use of depth focus—all contribute to the combination of spontaneity and control that characterizes *Faces'* humane realism.

NUDE RESTAURANT (1967)

Andy Warhol offers cinema a realism that succeeds in breaking down the visual and dramatic conventions of both documentary and fiction films, primarily through his conception of the actor's function and his attitude toward experience, which values uninterrupted duration and requires neither selective organization nor dramatic climax. Yet like a work in any medium, *Nude Restaurant* raises basic questions about the relationship between art and reality, between actor and individual, between perception and interpretation, between spontaneity and artifice. Indeed, Warhol's special conception of cinema requires that such questions be carefully confronted before the innovative experience of his films can be fully realized.

Warhol explores the life of a particular subculture—the underground world of drugs, freaks, whores, and other "social cripples." But he does not simplify the underground; instead, he explores its complexity and range. Hippies, usually stereotyped as the basic population of the underground, are represented only by the painted Sierra Bandit, who claims his father is a Chickasaw Indian; the others are strangely naive about hippies, as if unwilling to be identified in any way with this stereotype. Viva tells us that her mother says hippies are dead. Taylor Mead thinks perhaps they still flourish because he saw a picture of a demonstration with thousands of people in costume who were probably hippies. This rejection of the stereotype emphasizes the film's implication that individuality must be acknowledged, the first step in breaking down conventional, usually hostile, reaction.

The next step in creating sympathetic awareness is developed through Warhol's passion for the long, uninterrupted take, in which the camera moves very little, if at all, to heighten intensity or interpret events. Instead, his assumption seems to be that if he points the camera at a human individual, he will eventually reveal himself and prove interesting. This contradicts several conventional ideas—that dramatic interest depends on artfully constructed situations, that esthetic value is linked to traditional moral value, that deviance is repulsive.

Most directors assume that too much talk is dangerous in cinema; *Nude Restaurant* is extraordinarily verbal. Characters ask questions, exchange anecdotes, tell tall stories, trade witty lines, complain, sing, and give long monologues about their personal history. Nudity itself is largely asexual and seems to function as a metaphor for literalness and self-revelation through language, somehow casually taking care of the visuals behind the real business of interactions. (Viva reports that Warhol, emphasizing the playful, metaphoric quality of the nudity, thought of the black G-strings as parodies of the black patches that cover genitals in film advertisements.) Though composition is often extremely effective, it is largely controlled by the physical requirements of conversation. In one sequence, Viva, behind the bar, is framed by the Sierra Bandit on the left and Taylor Mead on the right, as they consider the authenticity of the Bandit's claims to Indian heritage. The opening sequence of Viva and friend in the bathtub provides the first conversation and establishes several themes that will dominate the film. Viva attacks her friend for talking about sculpture all the time but never doing anything: "It gets me angry that you pretend." She is highly aggressive, in both talk and sexual play. Her friend tries to respond with wit, but his responses are weak in comparison with Viva's verbal prowess. Yet, ironically, she denies him sexually, demanding that he overpower her if he really wants her. She introduces recent scholarship denying the existence of the vaginal orgasm, claiming that this news is as good as the birth of Christ and announcing that "the female is capable of self-reproduction. They've discovered that." However, as she grandly claims that women really do not need men, it becomes clear that she is often frustrated and suffers from the fact that she is more powerful than most men around her. She reveals her power, too, by controlling the entire situation as well as the conversation. She acts like the director, telling her friend to talk louder: "This is no time to become camera shy. All this film is very expensive." She also reveals a highly developed sense of life as art when she says that the bathtub is the place for precoital play as this sequence is foreplay for the film itself, revealing an awareness of behavior as performance, an important source of her effectiveness before the relentless camera.

The only discernible structural movement follows verbal interaction. Even the ending is thrown away as the film stops abruptly in the middle of a story. This development implies an acceptance of unpredictability and transience in human experience, since we are given no impressive imagery, no interpretive center, no thematic integration that might invite us to remember the film's enduring statement about life. Had the speakers been different people, had their moods been different, we would have had a different, equally valid, movie whose power would also have been entirely dependent on the flow of things at the time of filming.

Warhol's films as artifacts have come to echo this view in an interesting way. Prints of them are extremely hard to find, are often in very bad condition, and have often been rearranged and pirated. The titles are frequently changed, and certain films are sometimes shown on split screen or superimposed upon each other, requiring each projectionist to participate esthetically. *Nude Restaurant,* like a home movie, has no titles of any kind at beginning or end, and the few extant prints are reported to be quite different from each other. Warhol, of course, emphasizes his view of the transience of experience and artifacts through his own casual stance: He cannot remember names, dates, situations concerning the making of his films; he cannot or will not clarify questions of proper arrangement or completeness of mutilated prints. Some films have never reached the stage of commercial prints, existing only in their original footage. Thus his attitudes and his films (as well as his work in other media) effectively break down the reverence with which works of art are conventionally viewed.

Warhol's focus on the moment of filming succeeds largely through his effective use of the close-up, which sees human anatomy as an inexhaustible source of interest and sympathetic identification. He dwells on Taylor Mead, as the activist tries to encourage him politically, proudly claiming, "The FBI is after me." His face at once registering childish pride, sympathy, and contempt, Mead answers, "About fifteen corner boys are after me!" During one of Viva's long monologues, the camera continuously includes Mead in the picture because he can successfully compete with Viva through the expressive power of his mobile face. In the opening sequence, Warhol contradicts the competition and tension of the verbal interplay by offering extreme close-ups that celebrate the beauty of the human body. Textures are contrasted by filling the screen with the boy's hairy arm and hand against the smooth whiteness of Viva's breast. Especially appealing is the close-up of the boy's shoulder and arm curving gently down along armpit and chest. The beauty is heightened by the sheen of the water. Later, as Viva dances with a nameless black man, the camera moves in for a close-up of their bodies, focusing finally on their hips and thighs, which seem most expressive of movement and sexuality. But the primary subject of the close-up is Viva's face. Carefully made up to heighten her classical bone structure, she maintains a glamour-girl deadpan, which provides an excellent background for the life and energy that constantly break loose from this control. She draws attention to her face by talking about various reactions to her mouth, her neck, and especially her nose. She puts on make-up several times, arches her neck, arranges her hair, and obviously prefers the exclusive attention of the camera, which Warhol is wise enough to give her a great deal of the time.

The entire film exhibits a unique interplay of art and reality, artifice and spontaneity, truth and fiction. Characters frequently refer to the fact that a film is being shot. In the opening sequence, Viva tells her friend how to act in relation to the camera; she tells Ingrid to speak louder and condescendingly advises her on how to perform before the camera. Ingrid later admits her crush on Warren Beatty and then says, "I hope he never sees this movie." Warhol parodies editing through a strobe effect (which actually comes from stopping and starting the camera) that calls attention to itself and creates a high degree of discontinuity, heightening awareness of the filming process. The camera suddenly abandons its fixed position and moves around for a fast pan or a zoom as in the first sequence, reestablishing the presence of a controlling artist. In the second sequence, Viva has told the wonderful story of her visit to Bishop Sheen's office ("He knew backlighting was important!"). The camera, which has been fixed on her face, suddenly zooms back and we encounter the fictional situation for the first time. Viva (a waitress) is leaning over a counter in a restaurant; three naked men are listening to her. The characters maintain this fiction throughout, their references to it ranging from casual to mocking. Someone asks Viva for a drink of water. She brings root beer. Taylor Mead orders some No-Doz; Viva suggests marigold seeds, and Mead orders three. Later Mead asks Viva if she works there. She says, "Of course I work here. I wouldn't be standing here if I didn't work here." Later Viva tries to seduce Alan Midgette as he tries to order "a ready-made sandwich ... ham and cheese." The primary role of this "situation" is to undercut conventional plots by offering this comic anti-plot, which director, players, and audience all know is a game. However, it also provides the actors with a source of stylized play-acting that would not exist if Warhol were recording the raw data of behavior untouched by artifice.

Other important aspects of the film stress the objective potentiality of the camera as it records the players as individuals reacting to their mutual situation. Of the extraordinarily long takes that characterize his movies, Warhol says:

> With film, you just turn on the camera and photograph something. I leave the camera running until it runs out of film because that way I can catch people being themselves. It's better to act naturally than to set up a scene and act like someone else. You get a better picture of people being themselves instead of trying to act like they're themselves.[30]

[30] Jonas Mekas, "Notes After Reseeing the Movies of Andy Warhol," in *Andy Warhol,* ed. John Coplans (New York: Graphic Society, n.d.), p. 141.

Viva constantly hides her breasts with the menu and finally with a vest as she exclaims, "That's the trouble with being around homosexuals. You always feel like covering up because you know you're not being appreciated." Ingrid Superstar puts a blanket in front of her to hide the folds of skin that form as she is seated. But perhaps the most interesting spontaneous development is the competition that arises among them all. Taylor Mead and the activist try to top each other's lines. Mead competes with Viva for the camera's attention as he puts on a hat, mugs Stan Laurel faces, yawns, and does other business while Viva speaks.

This competition is most clear in a sequence that focuses mainly on Viva and Ingrid. Ingrid is seated, wearing a beaded necklace as if to call attention to her beautiful breasts. Viva seats herself on the bar, above Ingrid, and tells her to speak louder. As Ingrid tries to tell a story, Viva corrects her, and soon Ingrid urges Viva to speak, admitting, "You can say it better." Viva then announces that she sees lipstick on Ingrid's nipples, a comment designed to expose Ingrid's vanity and make her more self-conscious. Meanwhile, Ingrid's breasts get considerable attention from Mead, and Viva resorts to bizarre statistics: "I should have brought my breast book. There are 412,000 varieties. Ingrid's are the most womanly. I'm immature and childish. It tells you what kind of personality you have." Viva translates everyone's pleasure in Ingrid's body to an intellectual exercise where she herself can excel. Later she corrects Ingrid's pronunciation of "narcissist." The attention of Taylor Mead and the camera seems to be the object of this complex competition. Ingrid wins physically as camera and Mead focus on her breasts, but Viva achieves a kind of victory through verbal play (which switches the camera's attention) and by disconcerting Ingrid, who is reduced to uncomfortable silence.

Some of the film's qualities, then, seem to suggest its controlled artistry, while others emphasize the spontaneous unfolding of events before the recording camera. But still others heighten the ambiguity of the relationship between "thing made" and "thing happening" in *Nude Restaurant.* Warhol has said:

> All my films are artificial, but then everything is sort of artificial. I don't know where the artificial stops and the real begins. I've been thinking about it. I'm trying to decide whether I should pretend to be real or fake it. I had always thought everyone was kidding. But now I know they're not. I'm not sure if I should pretend that things are real or that they're fake. You see, to pretend something

real, I'd have to fake it. Then people would think I'm doing
it real.[31]

There is a great range of credibility in the stories people tell. Viva
is a truth-teller, but she also loves a good story, which she tells
with full command of inflection, timing, and other aspects of delivery. When she tells about her early encounters with priests, we
are astonished; and it hardly helps when she repeats, "I swear I'm
telling you the truth!" Her sexual aggressiveness makes us wonder
when she presents herself as the constant victim of attempted
rape and other sexual violence and complains that men are always following her. When Taylor Mead says that he has been in
the hospital twice and in jail nine times, his quick delivery seems
to assure us that he is reporting real experience. But then he describes a wound in his head so hideous he could not possibly have
survived. Later, he and Viva swap sexual tall stories: Mead claims
to have "made it" with Castro, and Viva counters by claiming the
same achievement with Batista. Thus we constantly experience
shifts in the kind of truth that is being told—biographical or
esthetic.

This ambiguity is further developed in the relationship between
individual and actor, personality and role. This is especially evident in the activist, who, unlike all the others, never seems to
offer a line or thought of his own. All his remarks echo the clichés
of political meetings and pamphlets, which apparently have provided him alone with a kind of script for this movie, an artificiality
very out of place here where fantasy is delivered realistically and
significant truth very casually. The activist is testing Mead's commitment in the most stereotyped ways; Mead constantly undercuts
him with caustic realism. The activist asks Mead if he would shelter a draft runaway.

> Mead: I won't take anyone. I want someone beautiful.
> Activist: Everyone who opposes the war is beautiful.
> Mead: Not necessarily.
>   I've been in jail nine times.
> Activist: Civil rights activity?
> Mead: No. Personal rights activity.

It is impossible to tell whether Warhol has found this political robot
and has convinced him to exhibit himself by letting him make his
pitch or whether the actor, with an effective deadpan, is mocking
the character he creates.

The most interesting mix of individual and actor, of person and

---

[31] *Ibid.,* p. 142.

persona is, of course, to be found in Viva. She makes up, poses, develops, and arranges (if not creates) her stories, exhibits constant awareness of the camera. Yet she tells many things that hold together and reveal a great deal about her, as in the story of the one-legged millionaire, whom her father invited to choose between his daughters. The details may be artifice, but the anger is real as she asks, "And who's doing the pimping?" She then associates into a diatribe against "this Freudian super-heterosexuality bag. It's sado-masochistic. Forget it! I'd rather be a lesbian!"; she is rejecting the sexual role into which her father forced her. Thus, though Viva may interpret reality through artifice, she ultimately uses it to make true statements about herself and about life. She is an actress, an elaborator, sensitive to timing and effect in her own personality and life (where she has been, among other things, that most artful of posers, a high-fashion model). All her masks are "real" in that they reveal aspects of her personality. All her fantasies are "true" because they reveal the nature of her fantasy life. Everything reveals personality, even the catalogue of 412,000 breast types. Because of the energy, wit, beauty, imagination, and performing ability that Viva as person brings to Viva as persona, she can, better than anyone else, bear the camera's lengthy scrutiny as she moves, unsupervised, through an afternoon at the Mad Hatter. She is the perfect vehicle through which to express the fascination with personality and acceptance of human behavior which characterize the film's view of experience.

TRASH (1970)

Trash, Paul Morrissey's second film (the first was Flesh), for a variety of reasons lends itself to exploration, at least initially, through comparison with other films. The film suggests such relationships in a variety of ways. It is framed by excerpts from the music of Josef von Sternberg's Blue Angel (1930), perhaps implying, as the film develops, a link with Von Sternberg's classic affirmation of the beauty and pathos of human degradation. The titles appear in the bright light bulbs of old theater marquees, linking the film to the American tradition of the 1930's and 1940's and perhaps implying a playful rejection of much self-conscious sophistication that has developed since then.

The opening sequence suggests yet another comparison—with the pornographic, stag, or "skin" movie. It begins with a close-up of Joe Dallesandro's pimpled ass being caressed by a hand wearing a fur ring. The camera pulls back and we see that a girl is trying to arouse Dallesandro, whose impotence is the central fact of the film. She turns out to be the topless dancer from *Flesh* (this time with silicone-injected breasts) trying to repeat her performance on Joe in an elaborate studio set up to make films, probably pornographic. Although her body and her dancing have improved, she fails to arouse him at all; rather, the sexuality is pathetic. This sequence attacks sexual conventions in both films and "life." Contrary to expectations, the girl is aroused and wants sex more than the man, who ironically is the physical image of the muscular, well-equipped stud. The sequence shocks by the explicitness of the oral sex in a film that, we hasten to assure ourselves, is really "not just" pornographic (and, of course, it is not, but Morrissey insists on the connection). We must acknowledge the inadequacy of the conventional stag film to provide sexual stimulus. Though a film may present nudity and explicit sexuality, it does not follow that it will be sexually arousing, as indeed *Trash* is not.

Like the films of Warhol, Cassavetes, and Renoir, *Trash* is marked by effective, fluid movement among a variety of tones and emotions. In a sequence where Joe, in search of money to buy heroin, breaks into the apartment of a pair of young married "swingers," the tone moves from tragi-comic stealth and desperation to hilarious ironic comedy as he fails to oblige the "housewife" (played by Jane Forth), who wants him to rape her. There then develops between them a kind of camaraderie; she is willing to lie about Joe to her husband, saying he is an old friend. The tone gets more heavily sexual as it becomes clear that both people desire him and that they also harbor secret homosexual yens (the husband poses with his belt drooping; the wife confesses to being a little bit of a "lezzie"). But there is also an underlying hostility toward Joe, which is revealed first in a bath sequence, where Jane alternates between admiring his body and making nasty cracks about his odor and bad complexion. This is developed much further when Joe shoots heroin before them. At first the couple watch with fascination. But Jane's narcissism does not allow her to focus on anyone else for very long, and soon she is rattling on about her favorite subject, herself. Bruce launches into a vicious attack against Jane and her irritating voice. Meanwhile, the camera remains fixed on a close-up of the needle probing for the vein in Joe's arm, a shot that is almost unbearable to watch. Yet, as we in the audience are tempted to close our eyes or look away, we hear Bruce saying, "Jane, will you shut up and look." Jane replies, "I don't want to look . . . I'm not interested . . . I just want to have fun, a gay time." If we look away, then we are identified with the odious Jane. Thus, when Joe finally shoots up, he gives a sigh of relief as he is able to escape from the cruel hostility of Bruce and Jane, and we can sigh along with him, relieved that we are at last able to escape from the close-up of the needle. The camera cuts to a powerful overhead shot of Joe lying helpless across a beautiful Persian rug, in a position reminiscent of a Pietà, with Bruce and Jane leaning over him. Afraid that he might die of an overdose in their apartment, Bruce goes into an uncontrollable rage, screaming to Jane to get him "out of the fucking door." They brutally throw him out, naked. All the humor has disappeared from the scene. Again, like the work of Warhol and Cassavetes, Morrissey's film embraces elements that the culture normally rejects—"perverts" of all kinds, behavior that is "disgusting"—and explores them for the richness of their humanity.

Because of their common focus on this subculture and because

Trash

of Morrissey's years of association as Warhol's business manager, Morrissey's work invites particular comparison with Warhol's. Though there are several important similarities, *Trash* offers, in general, a more controlled, somewhat more "artful" conception of cinematic realism. As in the earlier film, the basic dramatic situation is a long encounter of two or three people. But in *Trash* the episodes are linked more closely in a line of fictional development and tend to move toward a cumulative, interpretative view of the experiences they record. In Warhol's film the encounters are less distinguished from each other; their setting changes infrequently. Morrissey's sequences are shorter, and the camera has greater mobility.

Like Warhol, Morrissey relies primarily on close-ups, which frequently slip in and out of sharp focus and are sometimes very artful. In a scene where Joe encounters an acid freak on the street, their profiles are silhouetted against red, green, and yellow lights, which are out of focus, creating an abstract effect. The typical function of the close-up is to capture the gestures that reveal the characters and their feelings. In the hilarious encounter with the high school student, Holly presses her face to his as, in her blatant attempts at seduction, she tries to find out what kind of sex he likes. When he says pretty much every kind, she replies, "That covers a lot of territory," and the camera captures her lasciviously curling her tongue, before cutting away to capture Joe's deadpan expression. Sometimes these two functions are effectively combined, as in a scene when Holly discovers Joe with her sister and bursts into an angry tirade. The camera focuses on her face, filled with pain and anger, her wild hair capturing the backlighting in a way that makes it look electric. The camera cuts back and forth between close-ups of Holly and Joe against a blank wall, and then finally as she calms down and they begin to make up, there is a close-up of both of them.

Warhol likes to obscure the distinction between actor and character. Morrissey (like Cassavetes) accepts it to a greater extent, for his characters have more clearly defined fictional identities, which are quite distinct from their own. For example, it is said that Joe Dallesandro has never touched hard drugs. On the other hand, there is fascinating play between "art" and "life" in Holly Woodlawn. In "reality" a male transvestite whose real name is shrouded in mystery, Holly plays Joe's girl friend so successfully that, during a scene in which she masturbates with a bottle neck, this illusion is maintained and strengthened. Thus Morrissey uses fictionality to ask what is real. Indeed, biology may not be enough to attack the illusions created by Holly the transvestite and Holly the actress.

The episodic structure, more controlled than in Warhol's films, is still quite loose in relation to conventional narrative and helps to develop Morrissey's attitude toward his material, breaking down stereotypes about life in this subculture and revealing slowly the humanity of these characters. Dallesandro moves through a series of encounters unified loosely by his need for drugs and his impotence in the face of everybody's desire. Through these episodes Morrissey can extend the universe of his film to include a broad range of society, all of which might be seen as "trash" from somebody's point of view. Joe meets a go-go dancer and stag-film actress; a young acid freak who has run away from her family; a high school boy, clad in a blazer, who smokes pot and goes to the Fillmore; a pair of "swinging young marrieds" with homosexual hankerings; a young, unmarried mother-to-be (Holly's sister); and a welfare worker with a shoe fetish or a taste for 1940's fashions. As their eccentricities (to put it mildly) are slowly revealed, we see Joe and Holly in a new perspective. Not only are others equally bizarre; they do not even have honesty or affection. Unreliable, helpless, inadequate, and generally dirty as Joe and Holly may be, they do not have the sudden cruelty born of fear displayed by the married couple, or a taste for power, which makes the welfare worker's perversion ugly in comparison to Holly's.

The order of the episodes at first seems random, but it actually builds in a variety of ways. In the first scene between Joe and Holly, we think theirs is merely one more shallow relationship because it is placed between the encounters with the go-go dancer and the acid freak. Yet five of the eight sequences are devoted to the relationship between Joe and Holly. The film moves slowly from an early impression that in this freaky world all relationships are shallow, toward a realization of the strong ties between Joe and Holly, which must obviously be based on things other than sex, at which they are never successful. The sequences also become more complicated—including three characters rather than two and frequently more than one scene. In fact, sequences six through eight (beginning with the conversation between Holly and her pregnant sister) could be interpreted as the development of a single narrative line—Holly's plan to get welfare and improve the quality of her life with Joe. Certain episodes within this half of the film are particularly strong in destroying stereotypes and revealing subtly the tenderness, loyalty, and complexity of their relationship. When Holly returns home to find that her sister's pregnancy has finally aroused Joe to sexual action, she is more outraged than the most traditional lady betrayed. She orders her sister out and be-rates Joe. But other, more loving and fruitful values weaken her anger. After her sister leaves, Holly says, "There's her mattress, now she's never gonna use it. And her kid's bassinet—so what if it's only a drawer." She relents, of course. Childbearing, family ties, affection—all these are more important than sexual jealousy. The fact that Joe also values the relationship is revealed in his at-tempts to calm her and to justify his own behavior ("Don't I keep trying? . . . I was just practicing . . . I didn't think I was doing any-thing wrong"). Once she is calm, he pleads, "What if we just tried one more time."

In the scene with the welfare worker (weakened somewhat by Bruce Pecheur's exaggerated performance), it becomes clear that Joe will place loyalty high on his list of priorities. Holly, sensing sado-masochism behind the welfare worker's desire to have the silver shoes she rescued from a trash barrel (he thinks they will make a wonderful lamp), refuses to give him her shoes, though it means he will spitefully wield his power and deny them welfare, which they certainly need. Joe tries to soothe her, gently coaxing her to give in. But it becomes willy-nilly a matter of principle for Holly, who will not allow the welfare worker to have control. Slowly Joe becomes aware of Holly's commitment to her position, and he becomes her ally, helping her to resist the welfare worker's pres-sure and ultimately throwing him out, though ruefully, because Joe and his habit could use the money.

The closeness between them is developed with greatest icono-clasm in a sequence where Holly, perpetually unsatisfied because of Joe's impotence, masturbates while he holds her hand in sym-pathetic encouragement. A scene like this, most difficult for many in the audience to take, attacks with poignant satire the American myth of total love in spotless surroundings, of clean togetherness in cineramic omnipotence. Instead, *Trash* urges us to accept as valuable the limited, the tawdry, the vulnerable, and the sordid because they are the common qualities of the human condition.

From the perspective of the entire film, the opening sequence with the go-go dancer takes on rich implications. Besides setting the pattern of Joe's encounters with a series of women with irritat-ing voices demanding from him a sexual performance that he is unable to deliver, it has many parallels with the final scene be-tween Holly and Joe after the social worker has departed. These are the only two scenes in the film between people who have no hostility toward each other. When the dancing fails to arouse Joe, he is quick to point out "it would if I wasn't so down," as if he wants to avoid hurting her feelings and to assume full responsibility for the sexual failure. When she decides they cannot see each other anymore because she cannot see someone without sex, she gives him her fur ring, "her favorite thing." There is the same kindness between Holly and Joe in the final scene. She asks quietly, "What'll we do now," almost the same question that the go-go dancer asked after Joe's sexual failure. He replies, "We'll just do what we always did." Then she says, "Joe, let me suck your cock." As the camera moves in for a close-up of Joe rubbing his eye, we know he is going to fail again just as he did in the first sequence. But we also know that Holly, unlike the go-go dancer, will be willing to go on trying.

The view of experience offered by Morrissey is given unique expression through a special explicitness, which renders literally behavior and ideas that are usually treated symbolically. Compare, for example, the symbolic impotence of the character played by Mastroianni in *La Dolce Vita* and *La Notte* with the futile grinding and limp penis of Dallesandro. The film's central concept of "trash" is made concrete in various ways. Holly and Joe are trash sexually and in every other way. They are the dregs, the failures who reject and are rejected by a society disgusted by them. Yet the camera finds them infinitely fascinating, and their development and the narrative structure involve us, slowly forcing us to re-examine our ideas of "trash," to stop rejecting and move toward acceptance.

The film also uses movie trash. Even the conventions of hard-core pornography can be valuable when used without preconception and with imagination and wit. Perhaps the concept and its concretization come together most successfully in Holly's passion for collecting things out of the city's trash. She gathers things no one else would want (furniture, shoes, and Joe himself), and through the rejuvenating power of her imagination, she transforms them into objects whose value can be recognized by others. When she discovers Joe with her sister, she is doubly angry because she has reclaimed a mattress and crib for her sister and her baby. She calls them both garbage and says, "Now I'm going to feel like a piece of garbage . . . now welfare won't take me." But then her assertion that she needs and deserves welfare is the first sign that she is beginning to calm down and that she is ultimately going to forgive Joe. In the scene where they throw out the social worker, his departing angry words echo Holly's earlier tirade: "You don't deserve it, you're garbage, you're low life." Yet his words are undercut by his desire for Holly's shoes. She cannot give him the shoes because to do that would be to acknowledge that they were still trash and that both she and Joe, because of their need for welfare, were merely garbage to be mistreated condescendingly by respectable society. In this way, of course, Holly's passion becomes the metaphor for Morrissey's intention in the film. Like Holly, Morrissey has a special passion for the reject; he values it for its history of involvement with humanity, for its soiled quality, its lack of pretentions to the sterile fantasies he attacks. Like Holly, Morrissey has a transforming imagination that can see and reveal to others the limits of their conventional vision if they reject what indeed has value. But before the tone of our praise exceeds the careful lack of romanticizing in the film itself, it should be tempered by Holly's statement, with which the film ends. She has lost the welfare money, her sister's baby is on the way, and Joe has his habit. However, things must be accepted; there is value in the world. Holly announces, as might Morrissey himself, "I saw some nice garbage up on 24th Street."

6

five
views of
filmmaking in
the 1960's

The dual nature of cinema—an objective recording of sensory data and a subjective expression of the filmmaker's personal vision—was an important issue in many films in the 1960's. Practically every major director made one or more films that dealt with it, selecting as their central character an artist who is sometimes a filmmaker (and who may have autobiographical associations) and making a statement about art in general and cinema in particular.

Fellini's *8½* (1963), Antonioni's *Blow-Up* (1967), Godard's *Contempt* (1963), Welles's *The Immortal Story* (1968), and Bergman's *Hour of the Wolf* (1968) are five such films. They show great diversity in treating this issue, and they all seem to reject the idea that an "objective" truth is possible, for the experience presented is ambiguous, contradictory, and open-ended. But in each the double capacity of the camera is fully exploited to express a complex vision of reality.

five views of filmmaking in the 1960's

8¹/₂ (1963)

Of the five films, 8¹/₂ is the most obviously autobiographical and deals most explicitly with the question of whether distinguishing between reality and fantasy is possible. This film marked an important step in Fellini's development. Beginning as a writer on neo-realist films such as Rossellini's *Open City* (1945) and *Paisan* (1946), Fellini made films in the 1950's—*I Vitelloni* (1954), *La Strada* (1954), *Il Bidone* (1955), *Nights of Cabiria* (1957)—that were strongly rooted in this movement. The neo-realists believe that objective reality exists and that they can capture it on film. Before making *La Dolce Vita* (1960), Fellini said that all his work was "definitely in the neo-realist style"; he defined neo-realism as "a way of seeing reality without prejudice, without the interference of conventions—just parking yourself in front of reality without any preconceived ideas."[1] On one level, even *La Dolce Vita* can be seen as a chronicle of Roman decadence in 1960, but it was obviously experimental, a trend that Fellini followed in 8¹/₂, clearly moving into the realm of fantasy and subjective experience. Although touches of the grotesque and the fantastic had been present in his earlier films, they become central for the first time in 8¹/₂ and continue to dominate *Juliet of the Spirits* (1965) and *Satyricon* (1970).

Like the other neo-realists, Fellini rejected the conventional plot and used some nonprofessional actors, but with quite different effects. In neo-realism these techniques were ways of rejecting the very limited conventions of stylized art and getting close to objective reality; Fellini uses them to express his own fantasy and subjective experience. Rejection of chronological time and a linear plot is a way to get at the chaotic manner in which the mind works, the way it blends present experience with fantasy and memory. The neo-realist knows his theme and setting and then tries to find people who can be themselves and therefore help make his treatment "authentic." Fellini uses nonprofessionals in an opposite way: He begins with an imaginative conception of what he calls "fantasy characters"—faces that have occurred to him in dreams or memories—then he examines hundreds of photos, looking for faces that will fit his fantasy, a process dramatized in 8¹/₂. The face may belong to an actor or a plumber; it does not matter. He tells the "actors" only what he wants to tell them and then tries to evoke from them spontaneous reactions that will coincide with

[1] Federico Fellini, "The Road Beyond Neorealism," in *Film: A Montage of Theories,* ed. Richard Dyer MacCann (New York: Dutton, 1966), p. 380.

246

his fantasy. Fellini's vision is being expressed, not the authentic being of the actor.

$8^1/2$ is about Guido, a filmmaker (a fictional version of Fellini played by Marcello Mastroianni) who is having trouble making a film about his own life. $8^1/2$ is solely from Guido's point of view and thus combines his various kinds of experience: his participation in his present surroundings (a nervous breakdown; a trip to a fashionable spa; his interactions with his wife, mistress, and people associated with his film—the producer, the writer, the actors), his memories (particularly of his childhood experiences, which have been reworked by his own creative imagination), and his fantasies (cast with characters from his present, past, and imagination). These three realms of experience become increasingly difficult to distinguish. In the present, Guido makes his vulgar mistress pretend she is a whore, a game to heighten their sexual excitement but also a cooperative acting out of fantasy. Although memories are filtered through the adult Guido's point of view, they retain the emotional content of his childish impression: the mysterious evocative power of the magical words *asa nisi masa,* large shadows looming on white walls, the joyful but frightening bath in wine, the large white towel in which his mother wraps him before carrying him upstairs and tucking him in his warm bed and whispering, "My sweetheart . . . the sweetest boy in the whole world." As Guido is talking to the cardinal, the glimpse of a barefoot woman evokes a memory of Saraghina and his first encounter with demonic sensuality. As little Guido, dressed in a black uniform with cape and hat, decides whether to go with the other boys to visit Saraghina in her lonely dwelling by the sea, an overhead shot reveals the huge cold marble statue of a pope with finger raised, as if to warn the boy against the adventure. We see a huge close-up of Saraghina's swaying body before she suddenly spins around and faces the camera, which moves in for a close-up of her sneering face, eyes circled in black and disheveled hair flying. Her rhumba is hypnotic, and she draws Guido into the dance before he is caught by effeminate clergymen (actually played by women) who skitter after him in their long black robes and warn him against women and the devil. As they chase him by the sea, the action is speeded up as in a silent comedy and Guido knocks over a priest; later he is punished and humiliated before his schoolmates, mother, and priests. In the mysterious dark confessional, a disembodied voice says, "Don't you know, Saraghina's the devil!" A tearful, contrite Guido replies, "I didn't know, I didn't know." The film then cuts to a statue of the Virgin, which dissolves into Saraghina's hut, empha-

$8^1/_2$

sizing that the church has indelibly implanted in Guido's young mind the image of woman as saint and whore. After his punishment, Guido returns to Saraghina and finds her singing alone by the sea like a siren.

The adult Guido retains the essences of those experiences, exaggerates some aspects, eliminates the least significant details, shaping the material for his fantasies and his art. The process is not rational and controlled but spontaneous and chaotic like the entire structure of $8^1/_2$. If we attempt to impose a pattern onto experience, we are bound to cut off possibilities and distort its richness. Such an attempt is a denial of life and ultimately leads to sterility and death. An art that seriously attempts to reflect reality must be open and nonrational; it must reject narrow dichotomies such as subjective and objective, right and wrong, left and right, past and present, fantasy and reality.

This attitude toward experience is particularly well expressed in three key sequences of 8¹/₂: the opening, the harem fantasy, and the ending. The opening is particularly powerful in combining various modes of time, space, and reality. It begins in absolute silence with a shot of the back of Guido's head as he sits in his car, which is stopped in a low-ceilinged tunnel in the middle of a nightmarish traffic jam. The camera pans out of the darkness over the tops of the cars into overexposed brightness, as if looking for some kind of escape, then moves in front of Guido's car and shows him looking at drivers in other cars. Soon the silence is broken by Guido's panicky breathing as the car fills with steam; the people in the other cars look like dead bodies. Guido's feeling of suffocation is a visual equivalent of what he must be experiencing emotionally. But we are unsure whether this scene is happening in the present, where Guido is having a nervous breakdown, whether it is a hallucination that he experiences under the break, or whether it is a fantasy related to the break in feeling and tone but not in time. As he begins to pound desperately on the car windows, he looks over to another car where a man is stroking the bare breasts of a woman, whom we later recognize as Carla, Guido's mistress. Guido climbs out of his car and escapes the traffic jam by flying through the air out of the tunnel and above the sea. The experience is clearly in the realm of fantasy. We later learn that the men waiting on the beach to bring him down to earth like a kite are members of his film production crew. (They are similar to the priests from his childhood memory who forcibly draw little Guido away from Saraghina.) When someone pulls on the rope tied to his ankle, Guido plunges into the sea and awakens in a room where he is examined by doctors and nurses and confronted by an intellectual writer who does not like his script—characters who, like the priests and crew, are restraining forces throughout the film. Because of this complex interweaving of various characters and events, we realize that a simple linear interpretation of any part of the film will have to be rejected.

The harem sequence illustrates the process by which Guido reworks his experience in order to create a fantasy or work of art. The event that triggers the fantasy is an accidental meeting between Guido's wife Luisa and mistress Carla in an outdoor cafe. As Guido falsely assures his wife that he is no longer having an affair with Carla ("Would I go with a woman who dresses like that? It was all over three years ago."), Luisa replies, "It could drive you mad. He talks just as if he were telling the truth. . . . Is it possible that you can't tell the difference?" He obviously cannot, for he sits back and fantasizes a comic scene in which Luisa goes over to

$8^1/_2$

Carla's table to embrace and flatter her, as Guido applauds. This
encounter is the kernel for the elaborate harem fantasy, which
immediately follows.

The harem fantasy incorporates many elements from Guido's
childhood memories that we have already seen. The environment
is very similar to the one in his memory of the wine bath, including
the looming dark shadows on the white walls. The two most important female figures in his early life—his mother and the demonic
Saraghina—are both present in the harem fantasy. He also incorporates highly sensuous memories we have not seen: Jacqueline,
an aging stripper, the first "artist" in Guido's life; a stewardess
from Copenhagen with a low husky voice; and a black girl whom
he has mentioned many times to Luisa and whom she (in the fantasy) brings him as a surprise. We suspect that some of these
women did not play an important role in his life but, like the mysterious woman on the phone, intrigued his imagination and earned a
place among his fantasy figures. He also includes most of the
women in his immediate environment whom he is unable to satisfy.
Gloria, his friend's young fiancée, who has enormous ambitions, is
transformed into a masochist; the paranoid actress (who is to play
his mother) and his hostile sister-in-law both become docile; Ro-
sella, his wife's mystical friend, plays the role of "Pinocchio's nag-
ging conscience"; Carla's vulgarity vanishes in her saintly harp
playing; and Luisa cheerfully accepts her role as servant and
asexual surrogate mother. Only Claudia is absent, for she represents the fantasy of the ideal woman, who would be completely

250

satisfying and to whom he would be completely committed, a role his wife can never fulfill. When Guido, as master of the harem, begins to feel guilty and finds that the evening is not so amusing as he expected, Luisa selflessly defends him: "My husband can do everything as he pleases; it's the house rules." The final image is of Luisa scrubbing the floor and saying with a smile, "It took twenty years to understand that this is the way it should be." Guido's fantasy has failed to cope with his emotional conflicts, for he still must reject some women and make them unhappy: "Happiness consists of being able to tell the truth without hurting anyone." He cannot find peaceful harmony even in fantasy because his desires are contradictory; he cannot decide whether he wants to crack his whip to the strains of Wagner or be treated like a helpless infant to the soothing sounds of a lullaby. Fellini's attitude toward Guido is symphathetically ironic.

The final sequence incorporates all the previous contradictions in the film—the characters, the problems, the musical themes, and the visual images. It begins, like the opening, with cars, this time driving up to a tower by the sea; circus music and the sound of wind are in the background. Guido tries to run away, but he is restrained by two men who lead him forward to a mass of people waiting with hostile questions, hoping to witness his failure. Included in the crowd are people he has hurt—the tearful old director Conocchio, Luisa in her wedding dress. Unable to meet the conflicting demands of the crowd, he hides under a table, crawling on his hands and knees as the crowd pushes forward, an image that evokes the same kind of entrapment he experienced in the traffic jam. His mock suicide, which represents his decision not to make the picture, becomes his escape. As Guido sits in his car watching the men dismantle the tower and listening to the writer's suffocating words ("You did the right thing . . . we must remain lucid . . . it's better to destroy than to create what's inessential"), he sees the magician from the spa, who tells him, "We're ready to begin." Suddenly all the significant figures from his memories, present experience, and fantasy appear in white against the background of the sea. In that moment he experiences an epiphany: "What is this sudden joy . . . I do accept you, I do love you, how simple it is . . . I do not know, I seek but have not found, accept me as I am, that's the way we'll discover each other." Luisa responds, "I'm not sure that's true, but if you'll help me, I'll try." Suddenly a line of clowns, led by little Guido in white, enters, and the adult Guido runs off to direct. As the curtains open, the entire cast of the

$8^1/_2$

film descends from the tower and forms a huge circus parade, which Guido and Luisa join. Gradually it becomes night, and the parade is reduced to the line of clowns, and finally to little Guido, alone in the spotlight, who then walks off into the blackness. Thus in the finale Guido accepts all the contradictory aspects of his experience, even the alternatives he had rejected.

Fellini expresses his view of art and life by incorporating material from his earlier films, raising the question of whether we can see $8^1/_2$ as an autonomous structure.[2] The title suggests the film is part of a series and stresses its connections with earlier films through the repetition of musical themes and visual images: an isolated beach, a meeting late at night in a deserted square, a line of people on a pilgrimage seeking spiritual rejuvenation, and the circus, which suggests the joyous acceptance of confusion.

[2] For a fuller treatment of this process see the discussion of *The Clowns* in Chapter 7.

We recognize Fellini's fantasy characters, especially from *La Dolce Vita*. Sometimes we recognize a face and sometimes a character. The writer reminds us of Steiner from *La Dolce Vita,* the intellectual who committed suicide when he discovered a crack in his tightly structured world. Guido ultimately rejects the writer's advice, for it would lead to sterile art, which denies the richness of life, or to nothing at all. In one of his fantasies he hangs the writer just as Fellini had killed off his prototype in the earlier film. There are other familiar characters, such as the pathetic father figures, but the most important is Claudia (played by Claudia Cardinale), for in many ways she represents a central problem in many Fellini films.

Claudia represents the ideal reconciliation of two contradictory images of woman, a product of Guido's Catholic upbringing, the madonna and the whore. Claudia represents the muse who will enable Guido to unify the various contradictory elements in his next film. In many ways Claudia represents Fellini's attempt to integrate the female figure in his life and in all his work. In Fellini's earlier films the major female role was played by his wife Giulietta Masina. In *La Strada* she is an innocent, childlike creature full of vitality but lacking sensuality, and the man's insensitivity prevents him from realizing and expressing his love for her. While retaining the innocent, childlike vitality, Masina in *Nights of Cabiria* is transformed into a whore, but potentiality for reconciling the two images is not realized. She is valued not for her sensuality but for her inner purity and her capacity to accept life's misfortunes. Since being a whore is one of her burdens, this character does not reconcile two contradictory sets of positive values.

The women in *La Dolce Vita* are much more complicated. Instead of the cold wife in *8½*, there is Emma, the hungry mistress trying to get Marcello to marry her. Her love is smothering, overprotective, and selfish. She attempts suicide to manipulate him. He cannot possibly meet her demands because he is curious and wants to know as much about experience as possible, and he is also selfish and emotionally shallow. Emma's opposite is Maddelena (played by Anouk Aimée, who plays Luisa in *8½*), cold, distant, and selfish in a different way. She wants neither to possess nor to dominate Marcello; she wants to use him to alleviate her own boredom. Afraid of human contact, she lives out the fantasy of being a whore, which is merely an escape from herself. The basic problems of both these characters are dormant in Guido's wife in *8½*: the coldness and boredom that frustrate Luisa and the desire to possess Guido and limit his experience. Yet she is treated much more sympathetically than either character in the earlier film.

Claudia also represents a synthesis of two opposite characters from *La Dolce Vita:* Paola, the beautiful young girl who looks like an angel; and Sylvia, the sex symbol (played by Anita Ekberg) who is like a Roman earth goddess leading the revels. Although they are opposites of purity and sensuality, they share a vitality and enthusiasm missing in the rest of the characters.

In *Juliet of the Spirits,* Fellini focuses on the wife (played by Giulietta Masina), who combines the qualities present in the women in *La Strada, Cabiria, La Dolce Vita,* and *8½.* The various aspects of woman are part of her fantasy life, which she must learn to accept. Ironically, the dominant female symbol of sensuality whom she would like to incorporate into her own identity is Sandra Milo, who in *8½* played Carla, Guido's mistress. At the end, Giulietta accepts her spirits and her own center; she need no longer be dependent on her husband, as are Emma and the wife in *8½.* But we do not see her integrate these various figures into her personality. Perhaps Fellini doubts whether it is possible for any woman to make this integration and have her own core of being.

This is the conclusion he reaches in *8½,* for Guido ultimately decides that there is no role in his movie for Claudia. She is the only figure in the film who is purely ideal; unlike the actress being selected to play a fictional version of Guido's wife (just as Anouk Aimée was selected to play a fictional version of Giulietta Masina), she always remains Claudia Cardinale, an actress temporarily embodying an ideal figure, a role she plays in Guido's fantasy, in Guido's movie, and in Fellini's *8½.* While Guido agonizes over the casting of all the other roles, he is sure that Claudia is right for her part, for she is the only character in the film who has no authentic basis in his present or past experience. But, if Guido and his movie are really going to accept life, he must ultimately reject Claudia just as he rejected the rocket tower and the rational superstructure recommended by the intellectual writer. Yet Fellini must include all three in *8½* because they represent impulses central to his emotional life and to his art.

8½'s focus on the creative process, its subtle mix of past and present, reality, memory and fantasy, and its allusions to his other films—all contribute to Fellini's success in using the medium to express a subjective and autobiographical vision. His techniques show how imagination, allowed to move freely, can arrive at the loving acceptance and intuitive selectivity necessary for creativity both in art and in private experience.

BLOW-UP (1967)

Blow-Up has an artist as central character and is concerned with the relationship between reality and illusion in art but treats them in ways remarkably different from those of $8^{1}/_{2}$. Antonioni's film is not autobiographical; it is abstract and impersonal. Antonioni has much greater distance from Thomas (David Hemmings) than Fellini had from Guido; in fact, there is no reason to suppose that he shares Thomas' conception of art or life. In $8^{1}/_{2}$ the main conflict is between a chaotic, spontaneous art and a highly controlled one. *Blow-Up* focuses on a slightly different question: Is the camera an objective instrument that randomly records what is happening spontaneously in front of it, or is art the expression of a subjective illusion cooperatively controlled by the creator, the performers, and the audience? Guido is concerned with writing a script, choosing the characters and actors for the roles, deciding which scenes to include—almost as if he were a writer. The fact that Thomas is a photographer immediately suggests a concern with the technical aspect of the camera. Yet *Blow-Up* raises the question of the relationship between the human and the technological aspects of the art, between the subjective and the objective.

At times Thomas seems to confuse his identity with that of his camera. In one scene, shooting Verushka with a camera becomes a substitute for sex; another time he contradicts himself by saying he "saw" a murder when what he really means is that his camera saw it. This confusion is generalized beyond Thomas and photography as the guitars and amplifiers of the Yardbirds receive as much adulation as the human performers. To what extent does the contemporary artist depend on technology? To what extent does it lessen or increase his control? If a dismantled propeller from an airplane can be considered an art piece, then who is the artist and what is art?

Out of this conflict between the subjective and the objective, *Blow-Up* develops several important issues crucial to most contemporary art: the degree and significance of the artist's control over his material, the role of interpretation in the creative process, and the importance of context.

Is control by the artist essential to a work of art, or is there value in randomness and spontaneity? In shooting Verushka, Thomas tries to excite her with his own body and with his camera, in order to evoke a spontaneous response that he will capture on film. He always takes many shots very hurriedly, hoping to see what he has after they have been developed. When he photographs the murder, he thinks that he is taking candid love shots that will contrast with the violence of the other photographs in his book. He accidentally captures murder on film. The real excitement comes in the process of interpreting what he has shot. The larger he blows up the pictures and the more distorted and ambiguous they become, the greater is the variety of interpretation they allow, which leads him to the discovery of the murder. Thus, interpreting ambiguous art is like solving a mystery, which is almost precisely what Thomas' friend Bill had said about his own abstract painting. He admits that the creative process is marked by confusion. He is not sure what he is doing while he is painting. But after the painting is done, he exercises control in the act of interpretation by finding one little area that works. Patricia (Sarah Miles) comments that the photograph of the body looks like one of Bill's paintings. The value of spontaneity and accident is also

Blow-Up

Blow-Up

apparent in the scene where the Yardbirds are performing before a passive audience, which is suddenly transformed into a screaming mob when one of the singers "spontaneously" smashes his guitar. Whether the whole thing was planned and merely "appeared" spontaneous is ambiguous, but in either case, spontaneity and loss of control are clearly valued. Hence, it does not really matter who created the propeller or for what purpose. Thomas' discovering it in the odd context of the antique store and recognizing it as an art piece is the significant creative act. This attitude justifies Warhol's soup cans and the supermarket or freeway as great works of art. It implies that potentially anything can be perceived as art; what is art is determined by interpretation and perception, which are bound to be subjective.

All these examples also demonstrate the importance of context in determining the value of any object. The propeller is the one item among all those antiques that is linked with technology and dynamic motion. Once it is transported to Thomas' studio, his excitement is considerably abated, not only because he is involved with the girl from the park but also because the context has been altered. Similarly, the piece of the Yardbirds' smashed guitar, so valuable in the rock scene, is merely a worthless piece of junk once Thomas goes outside on the street. In each case,

257

value does not lie in the object itself but is determined by sub-jective interpretation within a specific context. This is one of the basic justifications of pop art, which takes familiar objects like beer cans and toilet seats, puts them into the new context of the museum and gallery, and reinterprets them as art.

The two sequences where Thomas is obviously excited by the creative process link these issues to the specific medium of cin-ema. In one he talks to Jane (Vanessa Redgrave), considering her possibilities as a model and actress. Unlike Guido, he is not particularly interested in her face or in how close she is to one of the figures in his dreams; rather, he is concerned with the way she interacts in a particular context. He evaluates the way she moves, and he makes her smoke against the rhythm of the music as if he were filming the scene in slow motion; he places her in front of different colored backdrops. He is interested in her not as a human being but as a visual experience.

The connection with filmmaking is more obvious in the brilliant sequence where he is blowing up the photographs taken in the park. Here we actually watch the creative process, with no ex-planatory dialogue; we make discoveries at the same time Thomas is making them. What do we see? Still photographs that record a limited space as it appeared from a determined angle or point of view in a particular moment of time. But the meaning of any individual photo can be manipulated by the photographer. Blowing up an image (like going in for a close-up) may make it easier to recognize the gun or the body, but it increases the blurriness and distortions of the image. It simultaneously facilitates and hampers perception. Thomas also affects the meaning of an individual photo by juxtaposing it with others. By arranging them in a se-quence, he creates chronology, a pattern of cause and effect, a narative plot. In essence, this is the editing process, the illusion of creative montage, in which the meaning of the whole is greater than the sum of the individual shots; in this case, the whole is murder. In an even more general sense, this process captures the essence of moving pictures, the juxtaposition of individual still shots, which, together with persistence of vision, creates the il-lusion of motion.

In contrast to Fellini in 8½, Antonioni in *Blow-Up* is concerned more with perception than with cognition; he is concerned more with film as a visual medium than as a means of expressing feel-ings or incidents. The difference in emphasis can be seen in many of the formal elements. There is little dialogue in *Blow-Up.* What is there is always significantly related to the issues, but many of the most important sequences are practically nonverbal. Other sounds—wind in the trees in the park, the click of the camera and gun when Thomas is looking for the body, the imaginary tennis game—are much more important. They must be experienced like the visual images; they are never explained by dialogue.

Blow-Up is not solely about art, but art is its main focus. As in *8½* and Antonioni's earlier films, art and human relationships are closely linked, but it is not at all clear which imitates which. For example, the valuing of the moment or particular context is also reflected in the conspicuous absence of any long-term relationships. This impersonal detachment is characteristic not only of Thomas but of everyone attending the rock concert and the pot party. It is also implied in the love triangle of Bill, Patricia, and Thomas, which significantly never develops. Patricia wants to leave Bill and apparently is attracted to Thomas. But when she comes to ask him for help, she realizes it is useless. There is a simultaneous conversation about her situation and the murder he has discovered. If he was not interested in finding out who was killed and why, how can she possibly expect him to help her? Ambiguity is also pervasive. We see it in the dress of the people on the street: Distinguishing the boys from the girls is difficult. We see it in Patricia's fishnet dress: Is she naked underneath it? We experience ambiguity in the antique shop, where a man's face is hidden behind a screen, and in a scene where Thomas picks Jane, or someone he thinks is Jane, out of a crowd, and in the behavior of the teenyboppers, a baffling combination of extreme shyness and boldness. Perhaps it is most blatant in the neon sign over the park, which Antonioni had constructed to be intentionally ambiguous and which is only momentarily in focus. As in his earlier films, Antonioni suggests that there is a new style of behavior in marked contrast to traditional values, but in *Blow-Up* his emphasis is on changes in art rather than in human relationships.

The pace and structure of the film effectively express this new style. Thomas constantly moves from one context to another and is incapable of focusing his attention on any subject for very long. This is partially expressed by the rapid succession of visual images. Not one episode in the film is completed; there are always interruptions. For example, in the scene between Jane and Thomas at his studio, their attention constantly leaves their respective goals of getting back the film and finding out why she wants it and is attracted by things such as the telephone, the music, smoking, and her posture. Finally, when they are about to make love—a distraction for Jane, who carelessly throws aside the film she has been so desperately seeking—they are interrupted by the delivery of the propeller. Even the blow-up sequence is interrupted by a telephone call and the humorous encounter with the two teenagers.

The rejection of the conventional dramatic plot helps to reveal Thomas' conception of art. If an artist values spontaneity, randomness, and ambiguity, then he is unlikely to have a tightly controlled plot with a neat resolution, for such a structure would imply that the artist has carefully planned everything. He would avoid the conventional mystery plot. But there is an ironic duality in the structure of *Blow-Up*. Although at first it seems to be episodic, it has a rather artificially imposed order. Many of Thomas' encounters in the first half of the film (before he meets Jane) are repeated in reverse order in the second half, creating a neat circular pattern characteristic of Antonioni's earlier films.

For example, *Blow-Up* begins and ends in the morning, when Thomas encounters a mime troupe. His second episode is with Verushka, whom he later meets at a party before going to the park to look for the body the following morning. Next, he shoots the grotesque models, whom he calls "birds" and whom he sneaks out on, leaving them waiting with their eyes closed; there is a parallel scene right before the party when he sees the Yardbirds and their glassy-eyed audience and manages to sneak out with the piece of the smashed guitar. After leaving the models, he goes next door to see Bill and Patricia, a visit he repeats just before the scene with the Yardbirds. Returning from his first visit, he runs into the two teenage girls, who show up later while he is developing the photos before making his second visit to Bill. The two central episodes are his encounters with Jane. The first meeting, in the park, is framed by two visits to the antique shop; the second encounter, in his studio, is preceded by the restaurant scene and terminated by the arrival of the propeller, which links it to the first meeting. The structure, then, is not so haphazard as it at first appears, perhaps implying a distance between Thomas' and Antonioni's view of art. Perhaps this distinction can be clarified by a closer examination of the mime troupe, which frames the film.

The art of the mime troupe in the final scene provides an important contrast with the other examples of art in *Blow-Up*. It is not temporary. Pantomime is a traditional form with many conventions. The imaginary tennis game is a sustained creation requiring engagement not only from the performers but also from the audience, which helps create the illusion, and from the camera, which follows the path of the imaginary ball. The game succeeds in winning the active participation of Thomas, who, though usually detached, retrieves the imaginary ball for the players. This action recalls their first interaction in the opening scene, when, after posing as a wino to take photos in a flop house, Thomas runs into the troupe and contributes to their cause. In that sequence, the audience does not participate in the illusion. Just as Thomas fools his audience of winos into thinking he is one of them, Antonioni fools the audience of *Blow-Up* by giving them ambiguous cues. A man dressed like a bum steps into a Rolls. He contributes money to a car full of actors. Is his wearing a costume any different from the costume-wearing of the mime troupe or of the nuns and the beefeaters he passes in the street? In fact most characters wear costumes to baffle their audience, but not the mime troupe. The traditional mime costume and make-up frankly acknowledge the troupe's theatricality, linking it with the established traditions of the theater. The mimes are willing to admit that they are controlling the illusions they create; the supposedly spontaneous accident of the ball's going over the fence is obviously contrived. The ambiguity between illusion and reality is controlled by a willful act of imagination. They need no instruments, no camera, no guitars, no amplifiers. Only themselves. Thomas has to lay down his camera to participate in their act. This is the kind of art that is being replaced in the contemporary world, and its position at the end of the film helps to stress its significance. The film offers it as an alternative to Thomas' view. In the final scene, we see a long shot of Thomas on the grass in the park, and then, magically, as in a film by Méliès, he vanishes. By the end of the film, the view of the camera as an objective machine that randomly records what is happening spontaneously in front of it is balanced by the view that cinema expresses a subjective illusion, cooperatively controlled by the creator, the performers, and the audience.

The blow-up sequence can be interpreted from both perspectives and so can the entire film, a possibility that is emphasized by the dual nature of its structure. *Blow-Up* can be seen as Thomas' vision of art and reality and also as Antonioni's, but the visions are certainly not identical. The film can be seen in terms of centripetal and centrifugal meanings. Centripetally, *Blow-Up* is a separate world that creates its own context, that has its own time and space. From this perspective, the blow-up sequence evokes a powerful esthetic response—the joy of discovery and creation—

emphasizing the focus on art. The film can be treated as an art object complete in itself, like the propeller, with autonomous beauty. Centrifugally, *Blow-Up* is a film about London in 1967 or, more generally, about Western civilization undergoing changes in its conception of human relationships. If we approach the blow-up sequence in this way, we are struck by the strangeness of Thomas' response. Why isn't he concerned with finding out more about the murder: Who did it? what was the motive? who was the victim? Why doesn't he call the police and help solve the mystery? The film can be treated as a reflection or imitation of outside reality; like the propeller, its meaning is altered by its context, and it evokes images and associations that do not actually appear in the film. Although the centripetal side is dominant, both meanings work in *Blow-Up*. The various possibilities for interpretation offered by the film as a whole, the continuing focus on ambiguity, especially in the central episodes, the importance of context in identifying and valuing objects, and the structurally significant role of the mime troupe all seem to emphasize Antonioni's view, which incorporates different ways of experiencing the film. Its nature or meaning, always subjective, will be created by two acts of imagination—that of the filmmaker who wields the camera and that of the viewer, who responds to the moving pictures before his eyes.

CONTEMPT (1963)

On at least one level, Godard's films are all about art in general and cinema in particular, and most of them have a strong auto-biographical element. All his movies remind us that we are watching a film by Godard. We have chosen *Contempt* because movie making is one of its central actions and because the film defines Godard's view of filmmaking (as of 1963) in a complex and fascinating way.

On first glance, *Contempt* has a rather simple plot, which, as in *8½* and *Blow-Up,* relates art to human relationships. From one perspective, it is the story of the break-up of a relationship between a writer, Paul Javal (Michel Piccoli) and his wife Camille (Brigitte Bardot). From another perspective, it is a story about the making of a movie of Homer's *Odyssey.* The two lines are obviously connected: Getting involved in the movie helps to bring about the destruction of the writer's marriage, and the writer and his wife are treated as modern versions of Ulysses and Penelope.

Jeremy Prokosch (Jack Palance), the crass American producer who acts like a tyrannical god, is a destructive force to both the marriage and the film.

This simple narrative is complicated by the concern with the esthetic issue of adaptation. Godard has adapted Alberto Moravia's psychological novel *A Ghost at Noon*, which is, in turn, about a screenwriter who is collaborating with a German director on an adaptation of Homer's *Odyssey*. In both the novel and the film, the producer wants to exploit a classic by transforming it into a marketable Hollywood spectacular. In the novel, the director is a caricature of Max Reinhardt (Moravia calls him Rheingold), "a German director who, in the pre-Nazi film era had directed . . . various films of the 'collossal' type," but who "was certainly not in the same class as the Pabsts and Langs,"[3] and who argues for a "debased" psychological interpretation of the *Odyssey*. Godard transforms the character into Fritz Lang (played by Fritz Lang) who insists on retaining the autonomous reality of Homer's poem (the conception of adaptation that is held by the writer in Moravia's novel). In contrast, the writer in the film claims that Homer's story must be reinterpreted from a modern perspective to create a new kind of reality.

This view is actually endorsed by both the novel and the film, for Moravia and Godard express realities of their own that are quite distinct from the source material and from each other. *Contempt* implies that it is impossible to make a film that is faithful either to Homer's simplicity or to Moravia's psychological complexity because the time and media are different, and cinema is particularly sensitive to the time in which it is used. Practically all of Godard's films are consciously dated. As one critic has pointed out, *Contempt* can be seen on one level as a documentary on Italian filmmaking in 1963. In treating Paul and Camille as ironic modern parallels to Ulysses and Penelope, in shifting the final murder to an absurd auto accident in which both the wife and her suitor are killed, in leaving the question of the husband's intentions and the wife's faithfulness ambiguous, and in emphasizing the filmmaking process, Godard is practicing Paul's view of adaptation—reinterpreting the material from a modern perspective to create a new reality. Godard is adapting not his own memories and fantasies like Guido in *8½,* but material from other works of art: Moravia's novel, Homer's epic, the various stories told by the characters, the lines from Dante and other writers quoted by Lang, and the absurd homilies quoted by Prokosch from his little

[3] Alberto Moravia, *A Ghost at Noon* (New York: Ace Books, 1955), p. 71.

book of practical wisdom. There is also material adapted from other films: the bathroom scene imitating Dean Martin in *Some Came Running,* the allusions to *Rio Bravo,* and the posters from *Psycho* and *Hatari.* These allusions emphasize Godard's rejection of the condescending attitude toward film that pervades Moravia's novel.

Another way in which Godard adapts material to his own reality is by making autobiographical statements about himself as husband and filmmaker. The writer and his wife suggest a parallel not only with Ulysses and Penelope, but also with Godard and Anna Karina. Picolli wears Godard's hat (when we actually see Godard in the final sequence, he is wearing a similar hat), and Bardot imitates Karina's gestures and movements; she even wears a black wig. The view of the marriage is obviously subjective; both characters are treated sympathetically and yet both are potentially responsible for what happens.

Godard ironically presents himself as an artist worthy of contempt. In one sense this is a film about Godard's selling out. *Contempt* is the only film he ever made which he did not control; he worked as a director and was subject to the whims of Carlo Ponti and Joseph E. Levine, the producers. When the Italian version was entirely dubbed in one language, Godard withdrew his name from the film in disgust. Within the story, Paul mocks exploitation films that focus unnecessarily on women's backsides and the film ridicules the crass American producer's lecherous response to the nude swimming scene; yet, in ironic contrast, Godard as director of *Contempt* exploits Brigitte Bardot (as Anna Karina) in precisely the same way—by spending several minutes contemplating her bare behind and showing her swimming in the nude. Just as Paul represents Godard, Prokosch is explicitly linked to Levine, one of the producers with whom Godard had so much trouble. At one point in the film Levine calls and leaves a message for Prokosch. Godard sees Levine and the species "American producer" as part of a fascist system that destroys the freedom and autonomy of the artist. Godard and the writer are not the only victims; Lang, who came to the United States after fleeing Germany, links this kind of tyrannical economic pressure to the Nazi domination of the German film industry during the Second World War.

Godard's relationship to Lang is significant. Although he later renounced him as an idol, in 1963 he was paying homage to Lang. In the film Godard plays Lang's assistant director, a disciple following directions. He is particularly noticeable in the last scene, dashing about the set, shouting orders. But the film implies that Godard is rebelling against the disciple role. Particularly relevant is a little story about the young disciple who invents a new way of walking on water, which is rejected by the older and wiser guru, who calls him an ass. Similarly, Godard invents a new kind of adaptation, which Lang rejects. Perhaps we are reminded of the famous statement by Lumière that is seen on the wall of the projection room in Cinecitta: "Cinema is an invention without a future." If one slavishly accepted the vision and conventions of earlier filmmakers, artists, and gurus without experimenting to find one's own way of "walking on water," this statement would be true. But Godard's bold experimentation and brilliant originality constantly expand the potentialities of cinema and shape its future. He is the total *auteur,* combining the roles and concerns of writer and cameraman, a combination that is very apparent in his style of filmmaking.

The structure of *Contempt* is neatly divided into three acts, with a prologue and epilogue. A highly controlled linear plot is unusual for Godard, but it is appropriate for an adaptation of a classical narrative. The prologue is divided into two sections: first, shots of the camera crew dollying down a narrow street, immediately reminding the audience that they are watching a film—one, moreover, about filmmaking; second, the bedroom sequence of the writer and his wife while they are still in love, shot through various colored filters. The first act presents the meeting of the three main characters in the love triangle and the writer's initial involvement in the film. It also contains the action that first elicits the wife's feeling of contempt for her husband. The very first shot of all three characters shows Prokosch cutting between them in his Alfa Romeo and is a foreshadowing, as in Greek tragedy, of the ending.

The second act focuses on the relationship between Paul and Camille and takes place in their apartment, with a flashback to the earlier bedroom scene and a flash forward to Capri. Though its content apparently concentrates on the love relationship, the style in which it is shot is more relevant to the issue of filmmaking. Godard never lets the audience forget the presence of the camera, whether it is pacing through the rooms like the husband and wife or whether it is stationary before three different rooms through which the characters freely move, thereby creating a marvelous sense of the space beyond. Its presence is most obvious in a playful scene where Paul and Camille, with a lamp between them, are talking. Although their conversation is serious and significant, we suddenly find ourselves more interested in watching the movement of the camera and seeing whether the lamp is switched off or on than in listening to what they are saying. This technique is repeated later, in the movie theater. They are sitting on either side of the aisle, and a photographer's flash bulbs replace the lamp, and again we are forced to think of the technical aspects of film, its reliance on the camera, light, and persistence of vision.

The third act deals with the trip to the location in Capri, the setting for the crisis in both the film we are watching and the one being shot within it. Paul understands why Camille has contempt for him—because of the way he passes her off onto the producer and because he is willing to sell out as an artist. The accidental death of Camille and of Prokosch finishes the writer's story, but the filmmaking process, directed by both Lang and Godard, goes on and becomes an epilogue. The last word we hear is spoken by Godard as we see the vast ocean: "silence." It is a word appropriate both to human tragedy (recalling the line from *Hamlet,* "the rest is silence," and the recurring silence imagery in Moravia's novel) and to an art medium that is primarily visual.

However we should not minimize the importance of language. Like so many Godard films, *Contempt* is highly verbal, underscoring the filmmaker's dual role as writer and cameraman. The verbal emphasis is expressed most effectively through constant translation from one language to another—French, Italian, German,

Contempt

English—usually performed by Francesca (Georgia Mall), a character who does not exist in Moravia's novel. Like the adaptation of stories and literary quotations, translation emphasizes the importance of interpretation. As we listen to Francesca translate, we see how she alters the meaning of what is being said and realize that language is as ambiguous as visual imagery. Throughout the film (particularly in the apartment sequence) we are presented with many visual images that could evoke a great variety of responses but are never explained by the dialogue. The translations of phrases into a variety of languages imply that speech has a similar open-ended quality. As he does in other films, Godard tries, here with partial success, to transform language into visual imagery. After Camille's death, the camera focuses in a close-up on her farewell letter to her husband, filling the screen with lines of writing that suggest an abstract design.

The fluidity of meaning is also expressed nonverbally, in shifts of color between the inner and outer film and the various colored filters, and in the music, which elicits melodramatic emotions or suggests parody (as in a scene when the writer takes out his gun). When combined with the self-conscious camera work, these techniques create a constant modulation of tone, ranging from the comic to the tragic, and help to suggest the multifaceted nature of Godard's reality. Like $8\frac{1}{2}$, *Contempt* combines many contradictions; as in *Blow-Up*, the ambiguities are never resolved.

THE IMMORTAL STORY (1968)

In *The Immortal Story* (which was made for television), Welles, like Fellini in $8\frac{1}{2}$, is concerned with the artist as writer or storyteller, as the title implies. The narrative is more important than it is in any of the other films we have discussed in this chapter. Like Godard in *Contempt*, Welles begins with an apparently simple linear plot, complicated by esthetic issues, suggesting that his conception of the filmmaker is considerably more complex than we at first suspect.

An old man living alone in China, where he has made a vast fortune, asks his "bookkeeper" to read from something other than the account book. He wants to hear a story, but one that is true rather than fictional. When the bookkeeper responds by reading a prophecy from Isaiah, the old man says, "People should only record things which have already happened . . . I don't like prophecies. I like facts." To give an example of what he means, the old man begins to tell a story that he believes actually happened to a sailor who was paid by a rich old man to sleep with his young, beautiful wife. But the bookkeeper interrupts him and finishes the story, which he claims is told on every ship at sea. It is an immortal myth based on dreams and fantasy rather than on actual events. The bookkeeper understands that stories express unfulfilled hopes (which are dead in the old man, though greed remains). He tries to explain: "The story they told never happened. That's why it's told, Mr. Clay. It never will happen." But the old man in his stubborn desire for truth decides that he will make the story come true for one sailor. He commissions the bookkeeper to find a woman to play the young wife, and he himself finds a young sailor and watches the enactment of the story. The following morning the old man dies.

This story raises two important esthetic issues: the artist's desire for complete control and his desire to express objective truth. The old man (played by Orson Welles) is adapting a story, casting the roles, manipulating the actors, providing the financial backing for the production, bringing the story to life, making objective truth out of subjective fiction. And he himself is the audience for the performance. Like the crass American producer in *Contempt,* he is trying to play God and be omnipotent, but he too is mortal and is ultimately outlived by the story.

These issues are developed by the highly controlled visual style characteristic of all films by Welles. The composition of practically every shot is carefully designed. The brilliant use of light and volume hypnotically holds the eye. In the final sequence on the porch, the old man is in the foreground, mostly hidden by the back of a huge wicker chair in which he sits. Far down the otherwise empty space, the bookkeeper sits on a small stool. The camera shifts position, its new height emphasizing the lonely space enclosed by the white railings. When Virginie (played by Jeanne Moreau) later joins them, she stands against the rail, her presence hardly disturbing the hollow depth of the porch. Color and composition invite us to examine shots as if they were impressionist paintings. In one scene, Virginie sits under a beautiful old tree with the bookkeeper opposite her. The camera moves slowly back as the scene is softened by misty gray smoke rising around them. When the camera gains distance, her costume and pose suggest the female figures in the works of Degas. The large forms and clean contrasts of contemporary paintings are suggested by a shot in the bedroom when Virginie and the sailor are making love. An extreme close-up fills the screen with the curved gold of his back

The Immortal Story

against pure white as he moves slowly over her. The cutting rhythm is always carefully controlled; In the dining sequence it almost transforms the movements into dance. There are recurring images of bars and gates, which evoke a feeling of control and confinement as if everything in the film is locked into patterns. This imagery is related to the scene of the bookkeeper in his solitary room, where he closes the window to shut out the rest of the world, including the camera. An even better example is a depth focus shot where the camera sits motionless before two rooms; the bookkeeper stands in the foreground beside a door that is slightly ajar, while Virginie moves toward him from the bedroom, carefully framed by the narrow crack in the open door. This shot reminds one of the apartment scene in *Contempt* where the camera is poised before three rooms, but the effect is entirely different. Whereas Godard evokes a sense of free and spontaneous movement within a large space beyond the camera's reach, Welles creates the feeling of controlled movement within carefully designed paths. Every tiny detail is considered, even Welles's theatrical make-up, which harmonizes with the colors of the background. The colors throughout tend to be muted, revealing the sensuous texture of objects in space. When the color shifts in the scene in Virginie's bedroom, the effect is jarring. The obviousness

269

of this flaw emphasizes the control over visual elements in the rest of the film.

This high degree of control is also present in the handling of the narrative. The movie is short (one hour), the tone consistent, the characters few, and the narrative line economically drawn, all contributing to an intensity that holds the audience enthralled. One senses that everything in the film is essential. The shift in tones of *Contempt* or the nonlinear plots of *8½* and *Blow-Up* would destroy this effect. The use of an omniscient narrator (Welles) contributes to the effect, for he determines what facts will be related and the order and pace in which they are told. At times his voice merges into the dialogue of the characters, another sign of his omnipotence.

As the old man tries to make the story come to life, elements emerge over which he has no control. Each of the characters cast in the old man's drama has his own story, which is as mythic as the tale he is trying to enact. Virginie turns out to be the daughter of the partner the old man had ruined many years earlier. She was once rich and full of hopes. She had dreams of being like the Empress Eugenia, wearing beautiful white shoes that she would give away to little girls after wearing them once. Now no longer young or wealthy, the mistress of a clerk, she brings her own motives to the old man's story. If his plan succeeds, it will be her final humiliation. If, as his bookkeeper predicts, it proves too much for the old man, it will be her revenge.

The sailor is a young Robinson Crusoe who has spent a year alone on a desert island and has brought back priceless seashells. On the island he had created his own fantasy woman, who is now embodied in Virginie. Thus he too shapes the role she is playing in this drama. As he looks at her through gauze curtains (which suggest the transforming power of the mythic story), he tells her, "You're the most beautiful girl in the world." But with little details his autonomy is ironically established. While the old man eavesdrops, the sailor tells her he is still a virgin, a fact that is inconsistent with his role in the story. As he leaves, he asks the old man to give her one of his shells. This request has no place in the old man's scenario, so he drops the shell onto the floor. Because the sailor has fallen in love with Virginie (another autonomous event), he vows never to tell the story and thus defeats the old man's goal of ensuring that at least one sailor will tell it as a truthful account of what actually happened.

These two characters are like actors who bring to a film their own sense of reality, over which the director has little control.

While Moreau is playing a woman in her late thirties (this is be-lievable) who is pretending to the boy that she is only seventeen (this is unbelievable), the actor playing the seventeen-year-old sailor is obviously much older. Yet we accept this implausibility without a second thought while laughing at the acknowledged im-probability of Moreau's being taken for seventeen.

The bookkeeper, the old man's assistant in producing the drama, has his mythic past. Having left Poland after his family was killed in a pogrom, he is a wandering Jew who carefully guards his solitude. He knows the contradictions of Virginie's identity, and he correctly prophesies that the old man will not outlive the en-actment of the story.

The important point is that the old man, who thinks he is in complete control, dies unaware of all these complications, which are implicit in his adaptation of the story. His attempt to manip-ulate the story was a substitute for the human relationships he had avoided ("Love and friendship . . . these things dissolve a man's bones!"). He cannot accept the fact that stories come from

The Immortal Story

the imagination and will always defy translation into objective reality. To deny their organic, changing nature is to deny the humanity of those who made them up and live them out, as the old man denies his own. As the bookkeeper says, "No man in the world can take a story which people have invented and make it happen. Mr. Clay's total will come out wrong and be worth nothing." Though they may be accessible to those who survive him, no artist can completely control or even understand all the meanings implicit in his creation—not even an *auteur* like Welles, who adapts, casts, directs, narrates, and acts in the central role, working to please himself, not the audience. When the autobiographical elements of the film are considered, the old man suggests the kind of producer against whom Welles fought all his early life. Concerned exclusively with money and hostile to the imagination, the old man would control an event for his own profit as such people tried to control Welles. The actors he selects, his collaborators, his audience, all bring another reality to the film and, as a result, see different meanings. These meanings may have patterns —archetypal images or myths—that may be perceived by anyone, but the vision of any individual is bound to be partial. This view of reality and art is implicit in *Citizen Kane.* It is also similar to the view in *Blow-Up.* The meaning of any work of art or any man's life is always open-ended, subject to transformation. As if to emphasize the value of this unpredictability, in the final sequence Welles returns to Isaiah, who prophesied such transformations: "In the wilderness shall waters break out . . . the parched ground shall become a pool. Then shall the lame man leap like a hart, and the eyes of the blind man shall be opened." The old man cannot bear such dreams; whatever he wants, he must have at once and exclusively for himself. But the bookkeeper understands that these dreams belong to everyone, even though in the misery of his life he has turned away from them. As the film ends, he holds a seashell to his ear and says, "I have heard this song, long ago, but where?"

Welles's view of adaptation may be compared with Godard's. Godard takes the immortal myth of the *Odyssey* and adapts it to a specific time and space (Italy in 1963). In a sense, the old man is trying to take an immortal story and make it come true for a particular individual within a specific context, but the story becomes even more mythic and universal. Godard takes a myth and transforms it into documentary; Welles usually takes material appropriate to a documentary (the story of Hearst in *Citizen Kane,* the rise of the automobile industry in *The Magnificent Ambersons*), and transforms it into myth. Both solutions imply that the artist can never reach objective truth.

HOUR OF THE WOLF (1968)

Most of Bergman's work, on one level, is about art, particularly *Persona, Hour of the Wolf, Shame,* and *The Passion of Anna,* which together form a series of variations on the same basic themes and situations: two people (usually played by Liv Ullman and Max Von Sydow, sometimes joined by others) living on an isolated island and dealing with the problems of merging identities, madness, violence, and despair. Bergman says of the recurrent central male character at the end of *The Passions,* "This time his name was Andreas." Bergman's self-conscious exploration of the same basic issues in a series of films is an exciting artistic experiment reminiscent of Fellini's allusions to his earlier films in *8¹/₂.* In Bergman's work it reminds his audience that one of the recurring areas of exploration is the theme of artistic creation. In each of these films, one of the major characters is an artist working in a medium that is in some way connected with cinema: the actress in *Persona,* the painter in *Hour of the Wolf,* the musician in *Shame,* the architect who takes photographs of faces as a hobby in *The Passion.* We have rather arbitrarily decided to focus on *Hour of the Wolf* because it is one of our favorites and because it was while he was making this film that he first realized all his films were dreams.[4]

In *Hour of the Wolf* the issues of merging identities, sanity and madness, love and violence, and artistic creation are woven into the central question: What is reality? Bergman immediately draws our attention to this question by experimenting with point of view. During the titles, we hear in the background the noises and voices of the film crew as they are getting ready to shoot a scene, which (like the opening of *Contempt*) immediately lets us know that we are to remain conscious of our role as a film audience. A printed message (presumably from the filmmaker) explains the basic situation: An artist has mysteriously disappeared and is survived by his pregnant wife. In the opening scene we see Alma the wife (Liv Ullman) emerge from the cottage and prepare for an interview, which is shot in an extremely long take. She talks directly to the camera, thereby making us in the audience identify with the invisible interviewer, camera, and filmmaker. She tells her story in

[4] Ingmar Bergman in an interview for National Educational Television, April 12, 1971.

flashback. Presumably the images are from her point of view, but the question of point of view becomes ambiguous when she begins to read from the diary of her husband Johann (Max von Sydow). Is the camera presenting the visual images as they actually occurred; are they Johann's version of what happened, which is also the basis for the verbal descriptions in the diary; or are they Alma's interpretation of Johann's images? Any of these alternatives has the added dimension of being Bergman's version of that particular point of view, and our final understanding of these images is, of course, affected by the reality we bring to the film.

These ambiguities eventually lead to the question, explicitly asked by Alma, of whether it is possible for one person to adopt another's point of view, to experience another person's experience. If so, does this lead to a merging of identities? Does it lead to insanity? Does Alma, out of love for Johann, eventually adopt his delusional system and go mad? These questions can also be raised fithin the context of art. We must remember that Johann is an artist, and in some ways Alma is his audience. She does not see (or at least we have no evidence of her seeing) any of the other people on the island (Johann's demons) until she has seen them represented in two different artistic creations by her husband, the drawings in his sketchbook (which we do not see) and the verbal descriptions in his diary (which we hear and see visualized through an ambiguous point of view). Art is a process by which one person adopts another's point of view or experiences another's experience. Media such as drama and film depend, in Bergman's words, on an actor's ability to "unconditionally identify himself with his part." [5] This ability to identify with characters in a story is also required of the audience. We identify with Alma and Johann, adopting their point of view and experience as our own. And behind these fictional personae is Bergman; we adopt and experience the dream or "delusional system" he presents to us in his film *Hour of the Wolf* both visually and verbally.

Perhaps this analogy will be more clear if we examine the way Bergman treats the characters who are demons. In one sense, they are creations of the actors playing the roles and thus are no less real than any of the other characters in the film. They are also creations of Johann's sado-masochistic paranoia. Most of them can be seen as projections of aspects of Johann's personality that he fears or rejects: the leering jealous lover; the maudlin, self-abasing guilt-ridden homosexual; the authoritarian teacher

[5] Ingmar Bergman, *Each Film Is My Last* (New York: Janus Films, n.d.), p. 6.

wielding a stick; the coldly rational manipulative puppeteer; sexually devouring and capricious Veronica Vogler, with whom he merges his flesh; the old woman who hides her nothingness behind a mask; and the sado-masochistic wife desperately seeking erotic titillation to make her empty life seem meaningful. All are capable of violence and cruelty. Ultimately they are projections of Bergman's imagination; like all fictional characters, they are the artist's subjective experience. But their ambiguous nature in this film is brilliantly controlled, particularly in the dinner party sequence.

The camera first identifies with Johann's point of view as the characters step forward to greet him, their faces grotesquely distorted by the wide-angle lens. We in the audience experience their overbearing nature, their eagerness to devour Johann, and we sympathize with his fears. As the camera tracks completely around the dinner table and goes outside of Johann's point of view, we hear snatches of conversation, and the camera pans swiftly from one extreme close-up of a face to another, a technique that enables us to experience the evil emotionally. We recognize that they are also being used to satirize the decadent, corrupt rich who patronize the artist whom they actually envy and loathe and want to destroy. Later, as their behavior becomes more grotesque, they begin to remind us of villains from horror movies. The bird man bears a particularly strong resemblance to Bela Lugosi. Throughout the film they undergo many transformations as they shift from one mode of reality to another, but so subtly that it is almost impossible to perceive the boundaries.

Two of the most powerful sequences in the film are particularly effective in subtly integrating various modes of reality. The first is the sequence in which Johann murders a young boy. It is preceded by a conversation in which Johann tells Alma about a childhood experience that helps account for his sado-masochistic paranoia. His parents punished him by locking him in a dark closet and telling him that it contained an evil little man who bit off toes. After hours of terror, he was finally freed and then had his bare buttocks whipped by his father. When asked how many strokes he thought he deserved, he replied as many as possible. After the beating, he asked for his mother's forgiveness and kissed her hand. After telling this story to Alma, Johann begins to confess an action he believes actually occurred but which we interpret as a fantasy or dream, because the overexposed photography, heavy use of symbolism, and dislocations in image and sound distinguish this sequence from the rest of the film and because this

nightmarish fantasy incorporates important elements from the traumatic childhood experience. Johann is alone, fishing on a high bluff overlooking the ocean. Suddenly a demonic child appears. The music arouses tension until we in the audience are filled with fear that the boy will push Johann off the cliff. But this never happens. As the boy reclines seductively on the rocks, he seems aware of his appeal to Johann's repressed homosexuality, which was latent in the story of the whipping. The boy tries to bite him, suggesting the little man in the closet who bites off toes. Just as in his earlier attack on the authoritarian teacher with the stick, Johann now turns on the boy, repeatedly crushing his head with a rock. The boy, like the other demons, is clearly a projection—a combination of the frightened child in the closet and the demon who threatens to bite off his toes; Johann is both the authoritarian father with the whip and the child receiving the beating. Throughout the film, events of the past, present, or conditional—whether presented verbally or visually—are interwoven to blend various modes of reality.

The second powerful sequence is also a dream or fantasy connected by many strands of imagery to the murder of the boy. It occurs right after Johann shoots Alma. There is an abrupt shift in setting as in a dream. Johann wanders through the castle along frightening corridors filled with agitated birds, his shadow intersecting patterns of light in a large room. He is seeking Veronica Vogler, but he must first encounter some of the other demons. The lecherous old woman makes him kiss her feet, and as his mouth touches her toes we are reminded of the demon in the closet and the little boy on the cliff. The host, Veronica's current lover, tells Johann he will be watching jealously; he then walks up the walls and hangs from the ceiling like a grotesque bat in a horror movie. The bird man, who formerly acted as manipulative puppeteer, prepares Johann for the dramatic scene with make-up and costume

276

as if he is the director and Johann the actor. When he finally encounters Veronica, lying naked on a table like a corpse in a
mortuary, her posture evokes the image of the young boy lying
seductively on the rocks; later there is a brief cut to his head
floating underwater. When her hysterical laughter finally interrupts the lovemaking, Johann turns around to see the demons,
one hanging like a bat from the ceiling, an appropriate image
of a contemptuous audience created by a paranoid artist. The
close-up of Johann's face is remarkable, for his make-up has
smeared during the lovemaking and he looks like a grotesque
demonic clown. The symbolic psychological reality of humiliation,
hostility, and violence transforming him into a demon has a literal
basis in the physical details of the scene (the smeared make-up);
yet both the symbolic and the literal realities are part of Johann's
fantasy, which is in turn part of Bergman's.

The extreme close-up of the face is used very powerfully in
Hour of the Wolf, not only in this scene and in the dinner party but
also in the opening and closing shots of Alma looking directly into
the camera. Bergman, like Fellini, believes the human face is one
of the filmmaker's most important resources:

> Our work in films begins with the human face. . . . The ap-
> proach to the human face is without doubt the hall-mark
> and the distinguishing quality of the film. . . . We should
> realize that the best means of expression the actor has at
> his command is his *look.* The close-up, if objectively com-
> posed, perfectly directed and played, is the most forcible
> means at the disposal of the film director, while at the

Hour of the Wolf

> same time being the most certain proof of his competence
> or incompetence. The lack of abundance of close-ups
> shows in an uncompromising way the nature of the film
> director and the extent of his interest in people.[6]

The human face, as Bergman uses it, is a wonderful medium for expressing nonverbally a complicated combination of emotions in constant flux. Unlike Fellini's "fantasy faces," Bergman's facial images are based in objective reality. We perceive physical change in the expression of the eyes, the movement of the lips, the tightening of the muscles around the mouth, and we interpret these subtle modulations emotionally. Because they are nonverbal, they are hard to pin down and categorize; the interpretations they evoke are multiple and open ended. This is particularly evident in the final close-up of Alma, who, puzzled by her own unanswered questions about her sanity and her relationship with Johann, is cut off in mid-sentence and mid-gesture by the ending of the film.

Like Antonioni and Fellini, Bergman seems consciously to cultivate ambiguity. As in *8½,* it is difficult for the audience to distinguish between fantasy and reality and to organize experience into chronological order; but here the implications are not optimistic, for Bergman links this breakdown of distinctions not with a joyous acceptance of life's energy and diversity but with insanity and the total disintegration of personality. The artist's struggle for control is a struggle for his sanity, but the creation of fantasy and delusional worlds, the projection of himself into myriad personae, the adoption of artificial masks, are also essential to his art. Thus the artist is always confronted with a paradox; he must always struggle to maintain a precarious balance between genius and madness, between passion and reason, between spontaneity and control.

The supreme example of a work of art that successfully maintains this balance is Mozart's opera *The Magic Flute,* which is central to the film. Mozart's extreme poverty ensured that he understood the horror of life; yet his self-disciplined genuis enabled him to create works of perfect order and beauty. The conflict between order and chaos, reason and passion, is central to the plot of *The Magic Flute.* Bergman draws explicit parallels to it with his characters: Johann is identified with Tamino, the artist whose rational harmony is upset by his passionate pursuit of the elusive Pamina (Veronica Vogler). In this conflict he is advised by the rational Papageno, the bird man who acts as the controlling puppeteer in the performance of *The Magic Flute* at the dinner

[6] *Ibid.,* p. 5.

party and who directs Johann in his final encounter with Veronica. By presenting *The Magic Flute* as a puppet show, Bergman stresses the issue of artistic control, for it is the one form of drama or spectacle in which the actors or personae are completely manipulated by the artist. When Bergman subtly shifts the scale from the miniature puppet stage to the full-size stage in grand opera, and from tiny puppets to living actors, he is demonstrating his own masterful control as a filmmaker, exploiting his medium to create illusions, and demonstrating its connections with other art forms. Just as Johann expressed his world of demons both visually in his sketches and verbally in his diary, Bergman is master of the visual and literary aspects of film. Cinema, like opera, combines many art forms—music, spectacle, drama, poetry, dance. Only a genius can master them all and maintain the delicate balance among them. Mozart succeeded; Johann failed; and in film after film Bergman continues to struggle with this conflict. Yet there is no doubt that Bergman's powerful dreamlike films succeed in evoking strong emotions. Bergman has said that music and cinema are the only art forms that penetrate the individual in the audience and go right to his emotions without having to pass through the intellect.[7] Yet only in cinema can we recognize our own dream images in the dreams of others, and for Bergman this is the most intense and profound kind of communication that is possible in art.

five visions

All five films—*8¹/₂, Blow-Up, Contempt, The Immortal Story,* and *Hour of the Wolf*—present a reality that is multifaceted contradictory, ambiguous, and open-ended, one that cannot possibly be explained solely in rational, linear, or verbal terms. Art that expresses this reality must reflect these qualities.

All five directors seem to assume that it is impossible for an artist to control his creation completely. Fellini is most optimistic; he values spontaneity much more than he does control, which he conceives of as the imposition of an external rational pattern bound to distort and oversimplify experience. The control he wants to exercise is intuitive and unconscious. Godard's attitude is paradoxical. Although *Contempt* is about an artist who loses control by selling out, the boldly experimental style and the fact that he

[7] Bergman, NET interview.

successfully attacks the very people who are limiting his control seem to demonstrate that he is the *auteur* after all. Antonioni sees control as an issue that distinguishes contemporary from traditional art. Current art not only values spontaneity more highly than control, it transfers some of the control, formerly exercised by the artist, to the critic or audience. Welles, who like the old man in *The Immortal Story,* strives for maximum control, is forced to admit that he must share control with his audience, his collaborators, and his actors. Bergman sees the search for control as a struggle for sanity; the balance between control and spontaneity, passion and chaos, is absolutely essential.

Another assumption of these five films is the essential role of fantasy and illusion in art. Dreaming and fantasizing are seen as functions of the imagination, similar or identical to the creative process. In *8¹/₂* the flowering of fantasy is an important stage in Guido's creation of his film. *Blow-Up* shows the role of fantasy in traditional and contemporary art: In the former it functions consciously to create illusion, and in the latter it is a subjective interpretation elicited by the ambiguity of reality. In *Contempt,* fantasies arise out of earlier works of art, which must be absorbed and reinterpreted by the artist; through adaptation, they become part of his complicated subjective experience, which helps to account for Godard's allusiveness. In *The Immortal Story,* the need to create fantasies and tell them to others is shown to be innate in man, and this impulse is seen as the basis of the artist's creativity as well as the audience's response. *Hour of the Wolf,* like each of Bergman's films, is basically a dream combining many kinds of experience: memories, other works of art, present experience, projections of one's own personality.

In all five films the connection between artistic creation and human relationships is direct. In each, the artist is having trouble in both areas, one problem being symptomatic of the other. Most significantly, the way he relates to women clearly reveals his conception of art. In *8¹/₂,* Guido must reject the false dichotomy of the madonna and whore and the idealized figure of Claudia. Only then can he accept himself as a human being and accept the women who populate his life and who combine many contradictory qualities. When he makes this decision, he solves his creative problem; his film will reflect the chaotic nature of his experience without any attempt to organize it within a rational superstructure. In *Blow-Up,* Thomas' view of capturing the moment and valuing a particular context is reflected in his dispassionate turning from one woman to another. When he speaks to Jane of a woman who may or may not be his wife, with whom he may or may not have children, and whom he may or may not love, he is obviously concerned more with playful ambiguities than with the emotional reality of the relationship. In *Contempt*, Paul simultaneously sells out his wife and his art, an act that ultimately leads to the end of his marriage and his film. The old man in *The Immortal Story* uses art as a substitute for the human relationships he has avoided, but he fails to understand the limits of his control and the consequences of his actions in either area. This is particularly evident in his total ignorance of his relationship with Virginie. In *Hour of the Wolf,* Johann's insanity is destructive to Alma, to his art, and to himself. In pursuing his demonic Veronica Vogler, the femme fatale who is a projection of his own fragmented personality, he rejects Alma, the kind of person who is "made all in one piece." Alma also was his audience. He leaves her alone, pregnant, doubting her sanity, and coping with their child on her own. He abdicates all responsibility and control. The only record of his existence and of his creative power lies in Alma.

All five films see cinema as a medium particularly well suited to expressing a complicated and ambiguous vision of reality. Self-conscious techniques or the direct allusions to filmmaking constantly remind us that we are watching a film. We are also constantly reminded that cinema is both verbal and visual and that it combines qualities from many other art forms: literary genres such as epic, novel, short story, diary, and poetry; various forms of drama such as the play, the puppet show, the circus, opera, spectacle, pantomime, and dance; visual arts such as painting and sculpture; photography; television; and music. Each one uses the camera to record evocative sensory images that its audience is likely never to forget: the towering figure of Saraghina dancing in *8½;* the wind blowing through the trees in the park in *Blow-Up;* the shots from the rooftop sundeck of the Capri landscape in *Contempt;* the long shot of the woman and bookkeeper with smoke rising around them in *The Immortal Story;* and the drowning of the boy in *Hour of the Wolf.* They also use the camera to create illusion and evoke the world of dreams and fantasy. Every one of these films experiments with the medium, trying to push it a little farther, transforming it, questioning its capacity to record reality objectively, and finally subsuming this capacity as only one component of the medium's ability to express the filmmaker's particular vision of human experience.

7

myth
in
movies

Since their beginnings, movies have had the special qualities of
a mythic medium. Like the ballad, the circus, and other popular
art forms, they have drawn a mass audience. In images larger
than life, they both reflect and shape the popular myths. One of
their strongest powers lies in their ability to project dreams and
fantasies under quiet, darkened conditions, which enhance their
effectiveness. Certain filmmakers, like Godard, Buñuel, Bergman,
and Fellini, are especially aware of this power, exploring it as one
of their central themes and in this way influencing the vision of
other directors all over the world.

The mythic potentialities of cinema can be developed in a
variety of ways. Like literature, film can use myth as the basis of
its plots, displacing the abstract or fantastic with various degrees
of realism. It can tell simple stories that suggest profound depths
of feeling surrounding archetypal events like the journey, chase,
and quest, the exile of the outlaw, the descent into the pit. It can
deal with elemental themes like birth, survival, death, alienation,
freedom, and identity. Archetypal images—the sea, the desert,
the haunted house, the city, the plains, the circus—can be developed with unique power through this medium, which visually
shapes the experiential mode (comic, tragic, romantic, ironic) in
which the mythic events take place. Film's mythic texture can be

enriched by allusions to established mythologies like the ancient Greek and Roman and Judeo-Christian, developing universal visions like the loss of pastoral innocence and the coming of a savior.

Cinematic genres can also become the bases of self-perpetuating mythologies, each implying a comparison between worlds. Each genre is based on a set of conventions that act as signals, evoking a commonly held body of experience. In a western, the sophisticated audience enjoys the fantasy of the individual's being tested by a primitive environment that heightens his strengths and weaknesses and in which he discovers his identity and is forced to develop his powers of decisive action. In the gangster film the two worlds are not those of audience and hero; instead, the central figure must create an alternate society within the regular one, out of either defiance or necessity. Though the gun remains, it grows more sophisticated, and the automobile replaces the horse as this central figure must test his powers not in a primitive environment but within the complex mechanized world of the city. Usually darker in tone because the criminal threatens to destroy life and order rather than preserve them like the western hero, the gangster film must create sympathy with the outlaw figure, yet make us willing to accept his defeat. In the conventional horror film, the conflict lies between the human and supernatural worlds. Often darkly romantic like the Gothic novel, this genre gives free expression to a particular range of dream and fantasy. Although the supernatural may be populated with monsters—vampires, werewolves, witches, devils—that threaten ordinary, innocent life, the conflict between the worlds often points out limitations in the natural sphere, exposing failures of imagination or sympathy that harken back to the Frankenstein story, in which the instincts of the ''noble savage'' are perverted by man's cruelty as he rejects the freak. Finally, cinema is well suited to the development of a personal mythology, allowing a director like Fellini, Penn, Hellman, or Polanski to create his own universe composed of recurring images and situations.

This chapter is divided into three sections, each dealing with one use of myth in film. *Woman in the Dunes* shows the ability of cinema, like literature, to develop allegorical meaning around a simple story. *The Shooting, Bonnie and Clyde,* and *Rosemary's Baby* are films from three mythic genres. *Satyricon, La Dolce Vita,* and *The Clowns* are three films that express Fellini's personal mythology.

WOMAN IN THE DUNES (1964)

Based on the well-known novel by Kobo Abe, *Woman in the Dunes* presents a simple story as an allegory about the nature of human freedom. Its mythic quality is largely dependent on the original story, which is both simple and profound. Yet in bringing the story to the screen, Hiroshi Teshigahara enriches the mythic treatment by his brilliant visuals, particularly through his exploration of cinematic space. Although the use of allegory makes the story rather abstract (the characters are unnamed, the precise location of the dunes is unknown), the film is highly specific and concrete, mainly because of its sensuous visual imagery. It presents a world at once autonomous and universal. This doubleness of vision can be found in every aspect of the film and is the primary means of defining its paradoxical view of experience in general and of freedom in particular.

The film's basic situation is this: A man, in an attempt to give his life meaning, is trying to capture rare insects in the dunes, hoping that they will bring him fame. Instead, he is captured by locals who force him to live and work with a widow who lives alone at the bottom of a sandpit. This situation and its development suggest a number of comparisons and conflicts. First, there is an analogy between the man and the insects: Both are captured and imprisoned; both are exploited to achieve the goals of others who inhabit a different world. Thus, depending on one's perspective, the man is either the pursuer or the pursued, the master or the slave, an ambiguity that is intensified when he binds and gags the woman in a futile attempt to gain his freedom. There is a conflict between the man and the woman. Since he focuses primarily on the future, his basic fear is that things will not change. His conception of freedom is one of constant flux; he is afraid of making a total commitment either to his wife in Tokyo (whom we see in one of his hallucinations at the beginning of the film) or to the woman in the dunes. In contrast, the woman focuses primarily on the present and the past; her basic fear is that things will change. She sees stability as freedom, adapting herself to existing conditions. She loves her native place, her lost husband and child, and now the man who has been forced into her life; she is committed to whatever she experiences. When he falls into her pit, he is like a fly being trapped by a spider. On one level, the event symbolizes man's entrapment by woman, who draws him into the family, society, and the present, primarily through the allure of sex. It is also a retreat into the past, a crawling back into the womb, in which he must learn about his dependence on others. Yet, from another perspective, the entrapment liberates him from his focus on the trivialities of the external world and enables him to discover the inner world of spirit. Going down into the pit is like a journey into internal experience, where he discovers himself and accomplishes his original goal of finding meaning in his life.

The film's primary conflict is between an external and internal view of experience and freedom. The man's imprisonment has forced him to abandon only the externals: wife, job, city, and the written documents that certify his existence. At the beginning of the film, he believes only in these externals. He seeks meaning by trying to get his name printed in an encyclopedia and naively protests to his captors, "You can't imprison me . . . I'm decent, with a job that's registered . . . it's a crime." His entrapment is also external; he is forced to move within a prescribed space, to enter a physical relationship with a woman, and to become part of a community defined primarily by territorial proximity. But this physical entrapment leads him to realize that freedom and meaningfulness are concepts determined internally by his own emotional and spiritual attitudes.

An important step toward this realization comes in a scene where drunken villagers offer to grant the man's request to visit the sea if he and the woman will have sex outdoors so they all can watch. The primitive expressionistic masks that the villagers wear and the rhythmical beating of drums help to express the panic and desperation that the man and woman experience as they struggle in this situation. As the camera cuts from a close-up of one grotesque mask to another, with fiery torches flickering in the background, the villagers are depersonalized and transformed into wild beasts by their sadistic desires. The masks, drums, and fire make the scene highly symbolic, and they also have a powerful effect on the emotions of the man and woman and of the audience. The man tries to convince the woman to do it or at least to pretend. But she calls him a fool, for she realizes such an act would reduce them to beasts. His reply is, "You're a pig anyway."

He is willing to undergo degradation in order to gain his freedom. But how can he be free if he gives into such a demand? His behavior implies that freedom is an external quality that can be granted by others, but she realizes it is an internal state of mind controlled only by the individual. Sex also can be considered from this double perspective. In itself, it is not degrading, but it can be made so. We see sex being used to entertain others, to entice the man into staying in the pit, and to tire the woman so that he can escape more easily. In all these instances, sex is used as a means of gaining freedom and, ironically, is thereby transformed into a kind of entrapment. Since this double perspective could be applied to any kind of human behavior, the film implies that a meaningful life is dependent not on what one does but on one's attitude toward it.

A summary of the plot and of some of its philosophical implications cannot account for the film's tremendous emotional power. The audience experiences the feeling of entrapment with great intensity largely because of Teshigahara's masterful use of the cinematic medium, which convincingly expresses the supremacy of subjective experience primarily through the manipulation of space and visual perspective, and the central imagery of the sand.

Teshigahara's use of space implies relativity and paradox. He does several things to intensify the contrast between the expansiveness of the exterior shots of the sand and the narrow encapsulation of the woman's hut, and he effectively links this

Woman in the Dunes

Woman in the Dunes

contrast to the inner and outer views of reality. There are several shots of the open expanse of sand, sometimes marked with footprints, creating horizontal or vertical patterns. The artfully designed visual compositions perhaps remind us of abstract paintings, but, more significant, they stress the external actuality of the screen's flat two-dimensional plane. And the frequent cross-dissolves to similar shots at slightly different angles remind us that cinematic space is discontinuous. In contrast, the shots inside the narrow hut are frequently in depth focus (which contributes to the illusion of three-dimensional space and the depth of inner vision); the room is broken up by lines that divide it into smaller, more confining units. For example, in one shot the man sits in the background under an umbrella and in front of a straw matting; the woman's naked legs are far into the foreground, with one bent knee accentuating the boundary between the matting and the left side of the room; the room is further narrowed by the vertical beam that stands at the extreme right side of the frame. The effect is to encircle the seated figure of the man with the objects in the room that impinge upon him. This focus on extreme contrasts of space makes us in the audience forget that we are in a different space entirely (that of the theater), and hence we identify more closely with the man's physical entrapment and experience his struggle for freedom in a sensory way.

Powerful magnifying lenses also accentuate the similarity between men and insects and support the relativistic view that one's evaluation of anything depends upon one's own peculiar perspective. The image of the bug trying to crawl up the walls of the glass

287

jar in which the man has imprisoned it reminds us of the man's own futile attempts to climb the walls of the sandpit. When we first see a highly magnified image of the woman's hair and skin, it looks like an abstract design difficult to identify but similar to the desert landscape and to the magnified shots of the insects. We are able to identify objects only when we are aware of their scale or when we can relate them to other familiar objects—a sign that even our perception is relative and subjective.

The central image of the sand also helps to establish the film's mythic power, for like the most profound artistic symbols, its meaning is dense and ambiguous and can never be limited to a single interpretation. The complexity of the sand is suggested by the plot, dialogue, and visuals. The sand is one of the primary sources of conflict between the man and the woman. She has learned from experience about the paradoxical nature of the sand and tells him that it can attract moisture, but he refuses to believe this because it is illogical. Yet the visuals support her view, for the sand is frequently filmed in ways that stress its similarity to the nearby ocean, with wavelike patterns or rippling movement; when the sand begins to shift in the wind, it even suggests the fluid movement of a waterfall. It contains both stasis and motion; its highly patterned, grill-like surface seems to deny the fact that it can shift unpredictably at any moment. The link between sand and water can be both destructive (water rots wood and buildings made with ocean sand) and constructive (sand can function like a pump to bring life-giving water, a discovery that the man makes accidentally, which begins to give his life meaning).

Similarly, the sand both separates people (it swallowed her husband and child) and unites them. The woman observes, "If there were no sand, no one would give me heed." The sand brings the man and woman together, a fact that is concretely acted out in their first love scene. The grains of sand on their bare skin emphasize the sensuous texture and help to make the scene highly erotic. During the night her naked body is covered by sand falling through the ceiling, making her look like a sand sculpture, transforming the curves of her body into gently sloping dunes, a similarity stressed by exterior shots of the sandscape. The second love scene begins with the woman becoming aroused while she soaps the man's body as he bathes; the pattern of soap on his back looks very much like the patterned surface of the sand, an association that intensifies the eroticism of the scene. Despite its connection with their sexual relationship, the sand continues to be a source of disagreement between them. At the peak of his frustration, he asks the woman sarcastically, "Do you live to shovel sand or shovel sand to live?" Yet this question implies that sand, with its many levels of ambiguity, is closely related to the central questions of existence; from an existential perspective, how one spends one's time (which is traditionally measured by grains of sand), whether it be shoveling sand or collecting bugs, shapes the meaning of one's life. The ultimate value of the action is not predetermined but is created by one's attitude in the process of performing it. He finally learns some of these answers about existence when he discovers through his own experience what she had implied: Sand can function as a water pump. Ironically, he makes this discovery while he is trying to trap a bird in order to gain his own freedom. He builds a pit (like the one in which he is trapped) and leaves food as bait (like the rations of food, sake, and sex provided by his captors). As in the parallel with the insects, his attempts to trap natural creatures do succeed in fulfilling his goals—of finding meaning and freedom—but in ways he did not expect. After the villagers take away the woman, who is suffering from an extra-uterine pregnancy, he is alone in the pit. He looks in the bucket and sees his own reflection in the water and also that of a child who is standing on the rim of the pit. This shot visually communicates that the freedom he seeks is to be found in himself and in contact with other people—with the woman, possibly with a future child, and certainly with the villagers. For the first time he is free to escape but instead he says to himself:

> There's no need to run away yet. My return ticket is good to get back when I wish. In addition, my heart is about to burst with the desire to tell somebody about the reservoir equipment. If I tell about it, there might be none who can listen to me better than the people in this village. If not today, maybe tomorrow I'll have told about it to somebody. I may as well think of the means to escape the day after.[1]

He is beginning to realize that freedom is an inner thing, and this enables him to tolerate his physical confinement, to escape the pressure of time, and also to understand his relationship with other people. The final contrasting image is the official document that certifies the adjudication of his disappearance. Presented on a gridlike pattern, it gives all the external facts that the man no longer considers important—his name, the date of his birth

[1] Hiroshi Teshigahara, *Woman in the Dunes* (New York: Phaedra Publishers, 1966), p. 85.

(March 7, 1926), the date that his wife reported him missing (August 18, 1956), the date of the document (October 5, 1963), and the text of the judgment: "Junpei Niki is adjudged to be a missing person." From the perspective we have experienced in the film, we judge Niki to be a person who has found himself.

films from three mythic genres

The Shooting, Bonnie and Clyde, and *Rosemary's Baby* play with the conventions of established genres in order to explore the nature of myth. They belong to genres that have their own well-defined mythologies—the western, the gangster thriller, and the horror film. The films self-consciously comment on their genre and its conventions almost to the point of parody, while at the same time using the conventions to make a serious statement about the relationship between myth and reality that far transcends the typical films in that genre. They simultaneously mock the genre and expand its expressive possibilities.

THE SHOOTING (1965)

Monte Hellman's *The Shooting* lifts the conventions of the western out of their usual complexities of plot, motive, and sentiment to emphasize their archetypal simplicity. It accomplishes this by exaggerated attention to the conventions themselves—the suspenseful plot, the final showdown, the chase, the expansive barren landscape, the archetypal characters, and the symbolic role of the horse. The emphasis on the conventions has a double effect. The exaggeration creates a comic tone as well as an extraordinary sparseness and economy that suggest that man's existential dilemma can be evoked by conventions of the western. The latter effect is partly the result of highly unusual shooting conditions. Made in the Utah desert for a mere $75,000, the film was shot in three weeks by a crew of ten people:

> The equipment consisted of two cameras, two reflectors, one beat-up station wagon, and a small utility truck. Neither of the trucks could go off the road, so all the equipment had to be carried to the locations by foot or on horseback. To make matters worse, the crust on the desert surface broke easily, making it necessary to change the set-up slightly after each take. The actors, friends of Hellman

and Nicholson, had joined the project in a spirit of adventure which soon began to wear thin. The days were long and hot; nobody got much money.[2]

Focusing around the traditional plot of pursuit based on a desire for revenge, the script by Adrien Joyce (loosely taken from a story by Jack London) rejects all clarification and develops only the basic events. Willet Gashade (brilliantly played by Warren Oates) returns home to find his friend Leland Drum murdered, his brother Coigne fled, and his friend Coley (Will Hutchins) panicked by what has happened. He learns that Coigne had somehow been involved in the killing of "a small person." Suddenly on a nearby hill appears a woman in black (Millie Perkins) who wants to hire Gashade to lead her to a faraway town for reasons never stated. Later, they are joined by Billy Spear (Jack Nicholson), the woman's hired gunman, who kills Coley. When they finally overtake the man they seem to be pursuing, Will smashes Billy's gun hand and runs into the showdown gun battle between the woman and the man pursued. Conventionally, suspense would grow out of the question of who is the man being pursued. This question is answered in the slow-motion, stop-action final scene, melodramatically revealing that "the cornered one" is Coigne, Willet's twin brother. But, ironically, both Will and we in the audience have known or at least suspected this for a long time. The real suspense surrounds other questions, which are never answered: Was Leland shot by mistake? What were the original events evoking the woman's desire for revenge? Why did she choose Will to help in her pursuit? What was the relationship between Will and Coigne? Who is the woman? What is her relationship with Billy Spear? And, most ironically, the question that is obscured by the slow-motion and stop-action techniques in the final gun battle: Who, besides Billy Spear, survives? The film calls attention to suspense, yet almost parodies it by leaving unanswered these teasing questions and undercutting the final revelation of Coigne's identity.

The chase through the desert, which comprises most of the film's action, departs from its usual prototype in several important ways. Instead of thundering upon each other's heels, camera cutting between pursuer and pursued, these people move with painful slowness despite the woman's efforts to increase the pace. Although they are the pursuers, they in turn are followed by a mysterious figure, later identified as Billy Spear.

[2] Beverly Walker, "Two Lane Blacktop," *Sight and Sound* (Winter 1970–1971), p. 34.

When the abandoned Coley finds a horse and rides to warn Will against Billy, a long shot shows the three men riding around in a huge circle in the desert, creating a chase-within-a-chase, underscoring the symbolic nature of the basic situation. For Willet, the chase embodies the existential dilemma that underlies many good westerns. He does not know where he is going, what he will encounter along the way, or why he wants to get there, though he says obscurely, "I've got my reasons." Coley, the "wise fool," enters the experience with a different mode of participation: He goes because he has put his life in Will's hands; he is glad to be along because he falls in love with the woman; finally, with naive courage, he pursues the trio in order to save Will's life. Yet his earnest engagement bears no better fruit than Will's existential detachment, for the chase leads to Coley's death. Billy is a chaser by profession, but at the end of this one his "occupation's gone," for a gunman with a smashed hand is a man without identity. Since the woman instigates and plans the chase, presumably she knows its purpose; yet she is defined as a character not by her goals but by what she does along the way. Thus, *The Shooting*'s unconventional use of the chase implies that a man's life is shaped not by his goals or values but by what he does and what happens to him. An audience from a complex and fragmented culture often goes to see a western in which a lone hero in a stripped-down environment, through independent strength and judgment, can prevail against evil forces of men and nature. This film's view of man's diminished control over the events of his life ironically denies this conventional satisfaction.

The familiar "wide open spaces" of the western are exaggerated in Gregory Sandor's powerful shots of the endless desert, its vastness broken only by the moving people, carefully positioned in relation to the horizon or to a solitary shape in the foreground. This use of space presents man unadulterated by the complexities of environment, throwing into strong relief his strengths and weaknesses and emphasizing his isolation in the universe. Even the barrenness of Willet's home and the town they visit suggests the difficulty with which man establishes himself in the physical universe. As Coley tells Willet of Leland's death, the camera shoots from both inside and outside the tent, through its triangular opening, emphasizing the strong contrast between blinding outdoor light and the darkness of the interior, suggesting that neither extreme is hospitable to man. During the chase, the camera cuts to shots of the burning sun, which, despite its deadly threat, appears like a beautiful abstract painting "pasted in the sky like a wafer." As in *The Red Badge of Courage,* nature looks down at human struggles with detachment.

In the indifferent universe of *The Shooting,* characters play out archetypal roles. Willet Gashade is the strong, silent, natural man (a type frequently played by Henry Fonda and Gary Cooper) who does whatever has to be done. Aware of his own vulnerability and limitations, he knows he cannot match Billy's prowess with a gun. Yet he acts with deliberation, as his name implies. In other films, this sort of character marshals his will with steady self-control, building schools and towns in the face of danger. One of these dangers is Woman, whose sexual, financial, and emotional irresponsibility pervades the western; she is the Eve who destroys the pastoral innocence of the frontier. Millie Perkins' unmotivated malevolence is so exaggerated that it virtually parodies this sexist view. The only character whose name we never learn, "the Woman" is first seen from an upward-angle shot as she appears mysteriously at the top of a hill, dressed in black like the symbolic death figure in Cocteau's *Orphée.* The next shot places her with Will and Coley, the fast cut implying that she has arrived there magically, without moving through the space that separated them. Unfortunately, Perkins' acting lacks the power to develop the

The Shooting

potential irony and force of this archetypal role. Jack Nicholson successfully develops the irony of the character Billy Spear, who combines (as his name implies) the childlike outlaw Billy the Kid with the gloved professional killer of *Shane,* dressed like Jack Palance in the sinister elegance of black leather. Coley, the comic sidekick, has his roots in characters like Gabby Hayes and California in the Roy Rogers and Hopalong Cassidy westerns respectively and in the wise fools of Shakespeare and Dostoevsky. It is to the credit of Will Hutchins' performance and Hellman's direction that the character narrowly but consistently avoids the dangers of sentimentality and ludicrousness implicit in the stereotype. When he gives the abandoned man with the broken leg a game with which to pass his time as he waits to be rescued, Coley demonstrates his humanity, but the game itself (getting buckshot into a hole) represents the pointlessness of their journey and of all human enterprise in the world of *The Shooting.* Coley's language includes many archaic phrases and provides much of the wit and humor that add the comic to the film's mixture of tones. When asked whether he thinks his films are funny, Hellman replied, "Yes, *The Shooting* set out to be a comedy . . . and I still think it is." [3]

One of the ways in which we evaluate these characters is through their relationship with horses and other animals, whose traditional importance in the western is self-consciously exaggerated. The film's first image is a close-up of a horse. The woman's presence is signaled by gunshots; later we learn that she has shot her gorgeous white horse only to force Will to guide her, though she claims the horse was lame. During the chase, she gets rid of a mule and exhausts several horses, abandoning them as she does Coley and the man with the broken leg, who are no longer useful to her either. In contrast, Coley's loyalty and attachment to his old horse, which he discovers in the town, are almost sentimental. When he tries to please the woman by calling her attention to a singing bird, she responds by shooting it, as Billy later casually shoots a rabbit. Will's attitude lies somewhere between these extremes, condemning the woman for shooting her horse and later combining practicality with respect as he refuses to ride double.

The symbolic dimension of this film is deepened by its incorporation of other mythic elements, particularly Christian. The name Coigne, close to Cain (which is actually used in Hellman's other western, *Ride the Whirlwind*), suggests the biblical struggle between the bothers Cain and Abel, which is acted out in the final gun battle. Like Eve, the woman is associated with a snake, both beau-

[3] Monte Hellman, quoted in *ibid.,* p. 37.

The Shooting

tiful and deadly, and her temptation, like the snake eggs of which Will tells her, can eat a man up from inside. The magical number three is important in symbolic communications with her accomplice killer and in shots of three figures riding across the desert.

The mythic dimension is also achieved by highly controlled visuals—the muted tones of the desert, the artfully designed compositions of every shot, and the carefully modulated editing pace. The film's texture seems lean and spare, while at the same time it is rich and dense in meaning. Like *Woman in the Dunes,* this film has the mythic quality of being both simple and profound, of selecting elemental aspects of experience that recur in every cultural context.

Many of the mythic elements in *The Shooting* recur in Hellman's *Two-Lane Blacktop* (1971). Although it is a road picture rather than a western, it treats the same basic situation in the same style. A strong silent man and his sidekick are approached by a mysterious woman who appears from nowhere and whose motives and behavior are unpredictable. Together they travel across the barren American desert, racing with a comic character (this time played by Warren Oates) who pursues them. As the goals and direction of their journey become increasingly vague, they focus on the mere

295

process of going; the journey ends abruptly with the ambiguous image of burning film. These elements seem to be essential to Hellman's mythology:

> There is a confusion in people's minds about what the essential elements of a movie are. We create "genres"— the road picture, the melodrama, the western. . . . I don't think those are good categories. Certain movies are made over and over again, each through a different director's vision. . . . They are all the same story, told against a different background. . . . I guess every film I've made has been either *The Maltese Falcon* or *Outcast of the Islands*.[4]

BONNIE AND CLYDE (1967)

Bonnie and Clyde explores the mythic roots of the American gangster film that flourished in the 1930's, seeing it as a psychological and social response to impotence caused by the Depression and the condition of American society. Its playful allusions to movies suggest that cinema was the most potent vehicle for expressing the American mythology and that it reciprocally shaped and was shaped by the society in which it flourished. In self-consciously metamorphosing the historical figures of Clyde Barrow and Bonnie Parker, who in real life were dubious heroic material, the film demonstrates the power of cinema as a mythmaking medium and comments upon the society that eagerly believed in that mythology. The social dimension is presented subtly, mainly through the desolate landscapes, the FDR posters, and the authentic signs of poverty, which provide the background for the story; nevertheless, these images are powerful in evoking the historical milieu that underlies the myth.

The line of mythic influence extends beyond the United States. *Bonnie and Clyde* was influenced by the French new wave, particularly films like Godard's *Breathless* and *Bande à Part* and Truffaut's *Shoot the Piano Player,* which combine comedy and violence and which in turn are based on the American gangster film. Newman and Benton, who wrote the original screenplay, tried to get Truffaut and Godard to direct the film before they turned to Arthur Penn.

Bonnie and Clyde are presented as two young people who are partially shaped by the myths around them and who consciously engage in a mythmaking process as a way of escaping from me-

---

[4] *Ibid.*

diocrity and impotence. They, as well as the other members of their gang, frequently allude to the movies. For example, when C. W. Moss is introduced to Clyde's brother Buck and his wife, his first comment is to ask Blanche whether the movie magazine in their car has a picture of Myrna Loy, his favorite star. After Bonnie, Clyde, and C.W. have committed their first murder, the film cuts to a movie theater where they are watching Busby Berkeley's production of "We're in the Money" (from *Gold Diggers of 1933*), with a long line of show girls dancing in front of huge gold coins with the words "In God We Trust" clearly legible. Within the inner movie, there is also an audience watching the musical number, which is interrupted by the arrival of policemen on screen, underscoring the parallel with the Barrow gang's situation. Bonnie is so deeply engrossed in the fantasy world of the film that she tells Clyde and C.W. to be quiet, though they are talking about a murder they committed just a few minutes earlier. The impact of the film is carried over into the next scene, in their motel room, as Bonnie stands in front of a mirror and sings "We're in the Money" as she arranges a gold coin necklace. The irony is that *Bonnie and Clyde* had the same impact on the 1967 audience. The costumes in the film dominated the fashions for the year and posters of the authentic Bonnie and Clyde and of Faye Dunaway and Warren Beatty appeared in head shops and bedrooms all across America.

The mythic quality is also expressed through still photography. The Barrow gang members are always eager to have their pictures

Bonnie and Clyde

taken—especially Bonnie, who brazenly poses with cigar and gun, as if aware of the Freudian symbolism, in contrast to the coyly feminine Blanche, who must be coaxed in front of the camera. It is Bonnie's idea to take a picture with Frank Hammer, the captured Texas Ranger, as if trying to use the gang's mythic power to ridicule him, and she succeeds because he becomes the villain in *their* story.

The brilliant camera work of Barnett Guffy also evokes the photography that documented the Depression in rural America, particularly that of Dorothea Lange, Walker Evans, and other photographers who comprised the Photographic Unit of the Farm Security Administration between 1935 and 1941. The images of the family piled in their car, ready to leave a house that has been foreclosed by the bank, and of the poor family who shares their meager food and clothing with the shot-up remains of the Barrow gang are particularly reminiscent of Lange and Evans. The titles of the film also use still photographs to suggest authenticity and to evoke nostalgia for rural family life (in one picture we see the whole family eating watermelon) and the innocence of the period. However, this innocence is called into question by the lettering of the names, which turn from pure white to blood red, and by a clicking between the photographs that sounds like a slide projector, camera, or gun.

The bond between Bonnie and Clyde is primarily based on their attempts to mythologize each other, yet their modes are quite dif-

Bonnie and Clyde

ferent. Like Patricia and Michel in *Breathless,* she fantasizes about the future or lingers nostalgically over the past, while he focuses on present action and is willing to take any risk. Yet both action and imagination are essential to myth. The opening sequence, presenting the meeting of Bonnie and Clyde, demonstrates these qualities quite clearly. Opening with a close-up of her freshly painted lips, the camera focuses first on Bonnie dreamily admiring her own sensuous reflection in a mirror and fantasizing about the future, yet with her childhood dolls in the background. She communicates nonverbally that the present holds only frustration as she pounds her fist against the bed post. When she happens to see Clyde lurking around her mama's car in the yard, she throws on her clothes and goes hastily down to join him; the camera at the bottom of the stairs shoots up at the soles of her feet as she clumsily runs downstairs to meet her destiny. One of his opening remarks is, "I bet you're a movie star." But he knows very well she is a waitress. Clyde's power lies in his ability to see reality; he knows the story of her life, including her romantic fantasies, just by looking at her. And this recognition of what she is and may become and of how she differs from the other country girls around her ("I knew it the minute I saw you . . . you may be the best darn girl in Texas"), more than the promise of adventure and wealth, makes Bonnie run off with him. Clyde, with his focus on present action, represents for Bonnie a chance of making her fantasy life come true. He tells her how he chopped off two of his toes when he was in prison to get out of hard labor, and later we learn that he was paroled the next week. He wastes no time on regrets but merely exclaims with a smile, "Ain't life grand!" He is willing to take a risk and pay the price. When she dares him to prove he is a criminal, he smiles and says, "You just keep your eyes open and wait right here," and he casually walks off to pull a robbery. But just as Bonnie is limited by living primarily in fantasy, Clyde's action is limited by his sexual impotence. The link between his action and sexuality is blatantly shown as the camera shoots Clyde in upward-angle close-ups drinking Cokes out of the bottle, with a gas pump on the side and a match dangling out of his mouth. As he takes out his gun to show Bonnie, he clears his throat and wiggles the match; she sensuously strokes the gun that is lying between his legs and then goads him into action.

The mythic bond between them is also revealed in the scenes where they are farthest apart and closest together, which take place in the open fields. In the first, they are in a desolate field arguing over Bonnie's hostility toward Blanche. Clyde asks, "What

299

makes you any better?" and denies the vision of her unique value that made her run away with him. She strikes back by mocking his impotence. Later, in an idyllic picnic scene Bonnie reads Clyde the ballad she has written about their adventures. Reminding her that he had promised to make her somebody, he says, "You told my whole story, right there . . . you made me somebody they're goin' to remember." At this point in the story they finally succeed in making love, for their two modes of mythmaking finally merge: Bonnie uses her powers of fantasy to transform his action into the ballad, a folk form of mythic tale. They confirm each other's sense of identity; his action has drawn her into reality and her imagination has rendered him potent. Yet later in bed when they muse on how they would change things if they had it all to do over, Bonnie still longs for lost innocence while Clyde would merely alter his strategy.

In mythologizing each other, they also have a powerful effect on others. They make the poor believe that there is an alternative to their passive acceptance of poverty. They inspire C. W. Moss to follow them into action, but, perhaps more significantly, he believes that Bonnie and Clyde are gods, incapable of being captured. Ironically, this belief, which makes it easy for his father to betray them, is shared by some of the lawmen. When a hospital guard confides to Frank Hammer that they expect the Barrow gang to rescue Blanche, Hammer mockingly retorts, "All two of them?" Hammer wants to destroy their mythic power because it threatens to destroy the people's fear and respect for the law and because it negates the myth of the Texas Rangers. Yet when he supervises the killing of Bonnie and Clyde, his men riddle their bodies with hundreds of bullets, as if they doubt whether they really are human. Clyde sees himself as a Robin Hood who steals from the rich, impersonal banks and gives to and is helped by the poor. Thus after their first encounter with violence, when Clyde is attacked from behind with a meat cleaver, he naively tells Bonnie with childlike bewilderment, "He tried to kill me. I didn't want to hurt him, I ain't against him . . . I was just trying to get something to eat." Their interaction with the poor is best revealed in one of their successful, comic bank robberies, where a jauntily costumed Barrow gang altruistically allows a poor man to keep his own money and shoots warning rather than wounding bullets at the bank guard. As they are leaving, Buck says with a cheerful smile, "Take a good look. I'm Buck Barrow." Their pride in their profession is apparent. The film then cuts to a farcical Keystone Kop chase scene in which harmless police cars roll over and nearly collide while the Barrow gang escapes across the state line, a scene that demonstrates the gang's comic buoyancy. Intercut with this humorous chase are quick shots back to the witnesses in the bank who are being interviewed by the press. The bank guard dramatizes his experience ("There I was, staring straight into the face of death."); the poor man shows his gratitude ("Clyde Barrow did right by me . . . I'm bringin' flowers to their funeral"). Both are photographed as they point to the bullet hole in the wall. This is a proud moment in their lives, for they are participating in the myth of Bonnie and Clyde.

Newspapers inform people of the gang's exploits—things they actually do and things they are said to have done. They also carry Bonnie's ballad to the masses. Both the newspaper and the ballad are popular forms that shape folk vision and culture through a straightforward, largely unembellished recounting of events. Although the film is also a popular medium that shapes culture, it is able to express the experiential richness that lies behind the simple ballad form, primarily through a masterful control of tone. Like Renoir's mixture of tones in *Rules of the Game,* the alternation among farcical comedy, poignant romance, and violent tragedy implies a complexity that prevents the story from being reduced to a single mode. Yet unlike Renoir's film, *Bonnie and Clyde* contains a constant underlying tension or hysteria that erupts suddenly into laughter or violence, an alternation emphasized by the film's structure and sound track.

The structure alternates between various actions and tones, a pattern that provides the repetition and variation that are basic to the ballad with its chorus and verses. The main incidents are robberies, meetings, visits, gun battles, and love scenes, each having its own tonal development. The robberies have a circular pattern, beginning with their comic failure when Clyde tries to rob a bank that has gone broke and moving to the first violence, in the grocery store, to the first murder, and finally to the last job, which is a comic success. Although the meetings always have comic elements, they grow increasingly disruptive as they go from the building of the Barrow gang (first the magical union between Bonnie and Clyde, then the addition of the admiring C.W. and of Buck and Blanche, who introduce disharmony) to the encounter with hostile forces (Frank Hammer, the Texas Ranger, and Eugene, the mortician, who both forebode death). The visits also grow ominous, moving from the idealized visit with Bonnie's mother, in which they first realize their alienation, to the desperate visit with C.W.'s father, who ultimately betrays them, and ending with Hammer's visit to Blanche in the hospital, where he exploits her hysteria in

301

Bonnie and Clyde

order to discover C.W.'s name and Bonnie and Clyde's where-
abouts.

The most dramatic downward trend occurs in the gun battles
with the police, which accelerate in death and destruction. Despite
the bullets flying in the first shoot-up, no one in the Barrow gang
is wounded, an indication of comic resourcefulness. However, the
gang is very vulnerable to the horror of the second battle, which
leads to the death of Buck and the wounding of everyone else except C.W. Although the final shoot-up is romanticized through the
slow-motion photography and the symbolic image of the birds, it
results in the massive overkill of Bonnie and Clyde and gives a
tragic ending to their story. This downward trend is partially balanced by the tonal development of the love scenes, which move
from Clyde's initial comic refusal to his poignant failure when he
first tries to make love to Bonnie after their first murder, to an ultimate comic success after she reads him her ballad; the growing
power of their love story is carried even into the final slaughter in
the momentary look they exchange before their bodies are riddled
with bullets.

As a transition between these various actions and tones, there is the recurring comic image of the Barrow gang's driving down the road to the banjo music of Flatt and Scruggs's "Foggy Mountain Breakdown," which becomes the visual and audio chorus for their adventures. It concludes the opening sequence when Bonnie and Clyde first meet and marks the boundaries between sequences. Its absence underscores the disappearance of the comic tone, both in the playful bank job, which ends with the first murder, and in the hilarious encounter with Eugene and Vilma, which ends with the gloomy discovery that he is a mortician. In both cases the Barrow gang drives off down the road in silence. After Buck has been killed by the police, and C.W. manages to steal a getaway car for the wounded Bonnie and Clyde, the music starts very softly and assures the audience that the horror is over, at least for a little while, and that the surviving members of the Barrow gang are on their way to escape and recovery. This musical cue implies that they have the comic resourcefulness to bounce back like cartoon characters who survive all kinds of extreme violence. The automobile is also a symbol of their mythic resourcefulness, for it alludes to other kinds of films with a variety of tones: The effortless changing of one stolen car for another emphasizes the characters' mobility and implies a false sense of longevity, both also present in *Breathless;* the significant role of the automobile in the robberies and gun battles is a strong convention of the American gangster thriller. Finally, the playful chase scenes in the open countryside evoke the world of the Keystone comedies, where precise timing and chance repeatedly enabled the heroes to escape impending doom.

Tension is sustained by abrupt shifts in tone, which make the film unpredictable. Violence and horror frequently develop from a scene that begins with playful jubilance. For example, a butcher's attack with a meat cleaver is immediately preceded by Clyde's asking, as if he were a regular shopper, "Are you sure you ain't got no peach pie?" The startling first murder is preceded by the hilarious incident where C.W., pulling off his first job, foolishly parks the getaway car and then has trouble getting it out. Similarly, the three police battles follow poignant scenes between Bonnie and Clyde that usually stress her childlike vulnerability. In the first, she is proudly reading the others her poem like a precocious child; in the second, she is curled up, describing her loneliness to Clyde; and in the final scene, she is dressed in white and is playing with a fragile pink doll.

The frequent alternation between silence and shrieking also contributes to the sustained tension, implying that hysteria is always just below the surface of the action. In a scene where Clyde and Buck are reunited after years of separation, the nervous tension is staggering; they drive around in circles, scream, spar, hit each other to relieve it. When they go inside the house to "talk," the strained silence is finally interrupted when Buck shrieks, "OOoooeee, we're goin' to have ourselves a time, boy!" and playfully hits Clyde on the shoulder a little harder than they both expect. The general tone of hysteria is largely dependent upon Blanche, whose terrified screams run throughout the film and are as grating on the nerves of the audience as they are on Bonnie's. They are handled most effectively in the hospital scene, where they are supported by the visuals. Dressed in a white gown, her head swathed in bandages, Blanche is seated alone in silence in a totally white room. Frank Hammer noiselessly tiptoes into the room and suddenly lays his hand on her shoulder, causing her to shriek in terror. This visual image helps us to understand Blanche's behavior; she has been walking blindly through the world in false innocence, constantly frightened by unpredictable events. As Hammer shrewdly sympathizes with her as the daughter of a preacher, Blanche pours out her self-pity in flowing tears and a steady stream of garrulous talk. When he gets the information he wants, he abruptly leaves her still babbling blindly in her isolated white world. After Buck and Blanche have been shot, the Barrow car is full of chaos. Bonnie shouts for silence, a request that is granted in the next quick scene as they stop to steal another car. Then we see C.W. alone in the second car quietly weeping, before cutting back to the other vehicle filled with moans of anger, fear, and pain. Finally the silence is restored as they stop for the night in an open field, but at dawn it is broken by the police who surround them, screaming like Indians as they set the Barrow car ablaze and resume the shooting. The steady alternation between silence and hysterical screaming creates the emotional horror of this violent scene.

The mythic dimension of the film and the skillful merging of various tones are also achieved by the visual qualities, particularly in a sequence where the Barrow gang visits Bonnie's mother. A shift in the mode of reality is signaled by the use of special lenses and filters, which give the image a soft focus and a hazy quality and suggest that this scene offers an alternate myth (as opposed to the Bonnie and Clyde legend). This rural family picnic is in a Garden of Eden (ironically barren because of the social and economic conditions of the period), the community for which Bonnie

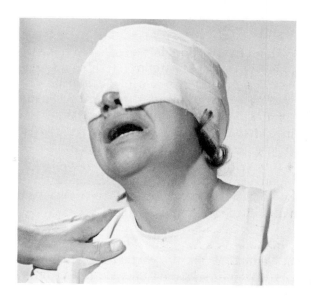

Bonnie and Clyde

longs in her darkest moments, made distant by the filters and to which the alien criminals can never return. Clyde frankly admits to Mrs. Parker, "At this point we're not headed to . . . we're runnin' from." The muted colors, the soft hazy focus, and the slow-motion shots of children playing cops and robbers, which anticipates the fate of Bonnie and Clyde—all these characteristics create a poignance that has a painful double quality. This visit is idyllic, yet its comfort is temporary. The use of authentic country people rather than actors contributes to the mythic simplicity and poignance we attach to lost community and to the tragic Depression period. In this encounter Bonnie fully realizes her isolation. In the next scene, Clyde tries to comfort her; she is feeling like an abandoned child:

> Clyde:　Is it what your mama said?
> Bonnie:　What mama? She's just an old woman . . .
> 　　　　　I don't have no mama, no family . . .
> Clyde:　I'm your family.
> Bonnie:　At the beginning I thought we were goin'
> 　　　　　somewhere, but we're just goin'.

This sense of outcast alienation from the whole species, the recognition that one is alone, is the deepest mythic note sounded by the film, a theme common in the western and the gangster genres and central to other Penn movies, such as *The Left-handed Gun* and *Mickey One.* The primary value of *Bonnie and Clyde* is that its structure and its visual and audio qualities reexpress this traditional theme with innovative power, rendering it heroic through various forms of mythmaking characteristic of American culture.

ROSEMARY'S BABY (1968)

Rosemary's Baby transforms the conventions of the horror film, and combines them with other qualities to transcend the usual limitations of the genre.[5] As the titles appear, a childlike voice sings the "La La" of a lullaby, but in an ominous minor key. The opening shot presents a highly ornate, convoluted fountain in which the water spouts from lilies, the flower of death. The conventional haunted house becomes an apartment building (formerly occupied by notorious modern witches and cannibals) with dark corridors and sinister cellar transformed into a laundry room but still frightening to the occupants. The process of luring a young innocent into being the subject of devilish experiments is transformed as the friendly old neighbors lure the aspiring actor (as Faust was lured) with promises of worldly success. When Rosemary (Mia Farrow) and Guy (John Cassavetes) first look at the apartment, they casually mock the traditional signs of witchcraft left by the former occupant. Of the sinister looking herb garden, Guy quips, "What? No marijuana?" Mysterious drugs and potions are worn in jeweled charms, eaten in chocolate mousse and frothy drinks made in the blender, and prescribed and injected by a famous doctor. Rosemary's taste for raw meat emerges slowly out of the natural protein hunger of her pregnancy. Old ladies pet black cats, and crosses hang upside-down in a context that touches these signals with irony.

These horror conventions are used in unique ways so that they become part of a complex film about a girl trapped in a reality in which she cannot believe. She must choose between not believing what appears to be real and believing what cannot be real. Paradoxically, Rosemary finally believes the fantastic because Roman Polanski gives it the texture of undeniable reality, however bizarre.

Based on a novel by Ira Levin, the film takes the traditional myth of the Messiah and dresses it in its equally traditional satanic disguise. The film's myth parallels the New Testament with the Divine Figure as Father of the Child and with Rosemary as the chosen vessel; the name Rosemary, the starting of the new era with the birth of the Messiah, and the adoration of the Child support the myth. We are forced to accept its literal truth because Polanski gives us evidence that is far more tangible than any yet offered on

---

[5] This discussion is based on an essay entitled "Rosemary's Baby" by Beverle Houston and Marsha Kinder, originally published in *Sight and Sound* (Winter 1968–1969), pp. 17–19.

behalf of Christianity. The film skews our perspective on various mythologies that underlie our culture.

Concern with the nature of reality is expressed in the film's style, tone, imagery, and structure. Visually, it presents a highly complex and textured surface usually linked to realism or naturalism and usually not found in horror films. The environments are crowded with objects, colors, textures. But, upon examination, these details arouse conflicting responses to what is being perceived. In a scene where Guy has gone to the Castevets' for the second evening, Rosemary is alone in the apartment. She is wearing a very bright, long plaid skirt, predominantly red. The fabric is of a nubby and uneven weave. On the sofa are two pillows of green and yellow that appear to be crewel work, so thickly embroidered that large flowers stand out in clear relief. Polanski brings these two very strong colors and textures together as Rosemary lies down on the sofa touching the pillows. Then the two older women, Minnie and Laura Louise, enter the apartment, and their colors and the movements and texture of their knitting complicate the scene and usurp the focus. This purely visual conflict builds toward the dramatic content of the scene, where the two women interrupt the already visually doomed serenity of Rosemary's evening.

During a scene in which Rosemary and Guy first dine with the Castevets, Minnie's costume, wildly whimsical, creates great tension as the green, purple, orange, and pink swirls of her dress contend against the sequinned pink organdy apron she wears over it. Elements of the costume fight for dominance and all lose. Visual reality has no focus. Ironically, in several scenes the blues and yellows of the costumes of Guy and Rosemary create a Bobbsey Twins togetherness that is being proved spurious with every development of the plot. This conflict also extends to the make-up. When we first see the Castevets coming down the street toward the camera, their weird costumes and make-up elicit a dual response. On the one hand, the flat pallor of their faces suggests the werewolf and the vampire, but the color in their make-up and dress is exaggerated just enough to become clownish and grotesque. Minnie Castevet's circles of rouge and the streaked lipstick on her wrinkled mouth are both ludicrous and pathetic. She is the living dead, but harmless.

Many of these techniques for creating conflict about perception are used in contrasting the two apartments. We move rapidly from the filtered gold and white of young love to the winey and cluttered, deceptively warm browns, reds, and greens of middle-European decadence. To heighten the contrast, Polanski allows us to see the young couple transform the browns and yellows of the old apartment as they redecorate it in what they mistakenly believe to be their own image. The contrast becomes ironic when we begin to see that these surface differences cannot hide the similarity of horrors going on in both apartments. Yet it is hard to believe that supernatural horror can take place in an environment so brightly decorated in the sunshine colors of yellow and white; the mythology of advertising and of magazines like *House Beautiful* has strongly implanted this idea in the consciousness of Rosemary and the audience. She promises her child that it will be born in a nice "clean" hospital, as if cleanliness will ensure its godliness. The audience shares Rosemary's temporary beguilement by false appearances in the scene where she awakens after the delivery; the camera focuses on the clean white ceiling and then slowly pans downward to Guy, smiling serenely at Rosemary, who is tucked into freshly ironed yellow and white striped sheets. We hear the regular ticking of the clock. Taken in by this vision of orderliness, she asks, "Is it okay?" He falsely replies, "Yes, fine."

A parallel to the redecoration of the apartment is provided by the transformation of Rosemary's appearance from that of a healthy, blooming young newly-wed to an emaciated, pain-ridden "piece of chalk," a metamorphosis greatly facilitated by a fashionable Vidal Sassoon haircut. In this case, the appearance confirms rather than denies the reality that something is wrong. The scene in which we first see her beginning to regain her health and bloom after the pain has stopped opens with a shot of decorators wallpapering the nursery; both Rosemary and the room are once again harmoniously coordinated in white and gold.

Camera angle also aids in creating this conflicting and elusive reality. For example, in the dinner scene the camera peers down over Mrs. Castevet's shoulder from what could be a neutral viewpoint. But both position and lens exaggerate her already mannered eating style, creating the grotesque by distorting the realistic. Shots from below insist on the mundane reality of feet, floors, thresholds, and legs; yet these are imbued with a pointless significance as they are distorted by the bizarre angle. If God looks down on his children from above, perhaps these angles provide a "devil's-eye view" of reality. There are several effective depth focus shots of Rosemary and Guy at the end of a long hallway. The most intriguing is a shot into the hall with Guy in the foreground as Rosemary disappears into the bedroom to receive the phone call that informs her of her friend Hutch's death. In the deep back-

Rosemary's Baby

ground is the kitchen window with yellow Dutch curtains, through which we see a lit window in another building that looks like a mysterious eye peering into their apartment; the camera holds this shot as if to give the audience plenty of time to discover this strange phenomenon.

The heightening of the realistic, which contrasts with the horror myth, is reinforced by allusions to the world outside the film. Repeatedly we see familiar products (Pall Mall cigarettes, Yamaha motorcycles, *Time* magazine) and hear well-known names (Albert Finney, Vidal Sassoon, *Luther, Open End, The New Yorker,* Lipton's tea), and recognize familiar settings (the Time-Life Building, where Rosemary is to meet Hutch, and the Bramford Building itself, which is really the well-known Dakota). These familiar touches anchor the events concretely in time (1966) and space and suggest that the characters inhabit our world. Like the gold and white decor, they also make it difficult for us to believe in the supernatural horror. When her girl friends at the party call Dr. Sapirstein a monster and urge her to consult another obstetrician, Rosemary naively replies, "No, he's very good—he was on *Open End.*" Dr.

Hill has a similar attitude, for Sapirstein's reputation finally persuades him that Rosemary must be crazy. They both believe very strongly in the American myth of success through advertising and television.

These techniques impart a strange tone to the film. They create the impression that never did the details that make up real experience receive greater attention; never were things so clearly seen, so "real." Yet at the same time exaggeration, conflict, and distortion insist that these events are grotesque, that this perception of reality is not to be believed.

This tone is also expressed in the acting style and development. Most of the characters operate in at least three modes of reality—as stereotypes from the horror movie, as characters from domestic comedy, and as actors representing different styles. To demonstrate, we shall examine John Cassavetes (Guy Woodhouse) and Ruth Gordon (Minnie Castevet). Cassavetes is at once Guy, a man who has sold his wife to the devil, a "sensitive young husband," and a "method" actor whose style is to seem as if he is not acting —yet ironically in this film he plays an actor. Ruth Gordon is at once a blood-drinking witch, a nosy old vulgarian with too much make-up, and an actress whose style is explicitly mannered. Polanski exploits the fact that the acting styles represent opposite extremes in creating theatrical reality. He actually calls attention to the difference in their styles when Cassavetes (as Guy Woodhouse the actor) mockingly imitates Ruth Gordon (as Minnie Castevet). In the scene where Rosemary drops the knife when she sees her baby and the reality of witchcraft is at last confirmed, Minnie rubs the knife scratch on the floor so it will not be so noticeable. Through this little domestic detail, the witch is once again transformed into a fussy housewife. Thus Polanski demonstrates how difficult it is to choose among various and sometimes conflicting perceptions. He created a similar effect in *Cul de Sac,* where the three main characters, on one level, were stereotypes from three kinds of films—the sluttish young wife of French sex films who takes off her clothes at every opportunity, the tough but purtianical hood from the American gangster movie, and the eccentric English gentleman from the "weekend in the country" film. All three are conventional characters, but their identities change when they inhabit the same world and are forced to interact.

The dream sequences are particularly effective in blending various modes of reality, for we can recognize their roots in Rosemary's experience. Her first dream takes place after the suicide of Terry (a young girl whom the Castevets have taken in and "rehabilitated") and after her first meeting with the Castevets. The camera pans over Rosemary's head to the yellow floral wallpaper and dissolves to a quick cut of Terry's dead body before dissolving to the dream. We see a nun in a black habit speaking but hear Minnie's voice. Since the image and voice are out of synch, we do not know whether the words are being dreamed by Rosemary or merely overheard through the walls. Then there is a shot of a huge white room, which is probably a Catholic school but bears a striking resemblance to the Woodhouse apartment; a workman is sealing windows with bricks (clearly an association to the process of decoration and to the mystery of the hidden closet). Rosemary mumbles as if trying to exonerate herself from a childhood guilt: "I told Sister Veronica about the windows and how it would disqualify..." Thus, the dream combines distant memories, recent experience, a generalized feeling of guilt, and actual sensory experiences in the room.

This process also takes place during the conception scene, in which many modes of reality and myth are combined into a powerful cinematic experience. The images of Rosemary's half-drugged waking vision are rooted in her past and immediate experience as well as in the fantastic reality of the witches' coven. The overexposed scene on the boat changes from a cocktail party to a religious experience, as the Kennedy-like captain turns around and is transformed into Hutch, making a gesture like the Pope as he blesses a large crowd, an image bound to remind us that just before Rosemary passed out, Guy was watching the Pope at Yankee Stadium on television. Later, when she asks the captain whether Hutch can come along even if he is not a Catholic, he responds in a voice that sounds amazingly like that of John F. Kennedy, a modern mythic figure who believed in Christianity. Shots of the familiar floral wallpaper merge into Renaissance murals, particularly Michelangelo's *Creation of Adam*. Later on the boat, Rosemary walks naked toward the black man at the wheel, who looks like the black elevator operator at the Bramford Building and who functions in the dream like Charon, the ferryman of the River Styx; his comment supports both realities: "You'd better go down below, Miss." The film cuts to Rosemary descending a ladder into a hellish dungeon; she lies down on her bright floral mattress and is surrounded by a group of grotesque naked people, including the Castevets and Guy. Suddenly the fantastic reality of the witches' coven has completely merged with her dream. As the motherly woman in white chiffon steps forward to comfort Rosemary, we recognize that her voice belongs to one of Minnie's friends. Minnie's allusion to the mousse ("She can't be awake if she ate the mousse.") is transformed by Rosemary into a line that also refers to the rape: "It's only the mouse bite." The combination of Christian and demonic mythology, the past and the present, dream and witchcraft, prepares for the actual conception, where Guy merges with the devil, who rapes her and causes her to scream, "This is no dream; this is really happening!" Then Rosemary is approached by the Pope, who says, "They tell me you've been bitten by a mouse." As in the previous dream, she plaintively asks, "Am I forgiven, father?" "Oh, absolutely," he replies, and extends his hand so that she may kiss his ring in the traditional manner. As the camera moves in for a close-up of the ring, we recognize the devilish charm with the tannis root. Ironically, the events that trigger the uncertain reality of Rosemary's dream are just as fantastic as the dream itself.

But whatever reality we chose to believe, it would not remain constant, for one of the controlling structural elements of the film is a recurring reversal of belief on the part of characters and audience. In the beginning, Rosemary is the sole Christian among disbelievers who mock the Pope. She does not yet believe in witchcraft, when both Hutch and the audience are beginning to. When she finally is convinced of its reality, she tries to get help from Dr. Hill, who questions her sanity. For the first time, the audience considers that Rosemary may be mad; after all, her explanation is fragmented and hysterical. Yet the audience hopes urgently for Dr. Hill's belief, for if Rosemary is mad and witchcraft is not real, then we in the audience have also misperceived the entire experience up to that point. To doubt Rosemary's hold on reality is to doubt our own. But we know that her narrative to Dr. Hill could not begin to communicate the subtleties and nuances of the reality that we and Rosemary have experienced through the visual texture of the film. We have watched Rosemary's private suffering and experienced the tension of her growing panic as one avenue of escape after another is cut off. We despair at the defeat of her last hope.

After this scene, the audience eagerly awaits indisputable confirmation of witchcraft's reality, a consolation that Rosemary does not need. We are more relieved than she is when finally she confronts the witches and the child. But Rosemary's old way of believing serves her in this new situation. Here is a child real enough to mother; she either accepts or ignores its mythic evil. This time she has evidence of the myth's reality—evidence of a kind completely different from any available for her in Christianity. The innovative combination of horror film conventions and realistic texture forces us to experience the film at several levels. Frightened and tense with sympathy for Rosemary, we must also confront the problem of our own hold on reality.

three films from fellini's mythology

Like parts of the Bible and Greek and Roman mythology, Fellini's films tell stories that in plot, setting, imagery, and tone reflect states of being common to man in his various stages of development. Fellini's work moves through a progression of themes, creating a cinematic language as he journeys through the psychic ontogeny of the individual. For this reason, Fellini uses myth differently in each film, sometimes disguising or displacing it with the trappings of realism or exhibiting it in frank abstraction, and sometimes reflecting in his approach the problem of giving concrete expression to the questions of being with which he is concerned. *Satyricon* (taken from the *Satyricon* of Petronius Arbiter, Roman satirist of the first century A.D.) reveals Fellini's mythic vision, mixing abstract and realistic, universal and particular in a unique combination to express the struggle for survival, which is the film's central concern. Using comparison in the ways invited by each film's particular qualities, we will contrast the development of closely related themes in *Satyricon* and *La Dolce Vita* and examine *The Clowns,* focusing on the process by which it merges all aspects of Fellini's mythology.

Le Dolce Vita records the quest of a sensitive individual for meaningful work and personal relationships in a decadent environment that is slowly sapping his real creative energy and offering, instead, a paradoxically sterile sexuality. In the world of *Satyricon,* so hostile is the universe, so baffling is experience, that the central figure must struggle for his very survival; questions of meaning or value seem an existential luxury. *The Clowns* returns to the problem of shaping a creative vision (earlier threatened in $8^{1}/_{2}$), this time in the context of declining values and a pervasive need to face the inevitability of death.

SATYRICON (1969)

In *Satyricon,* blond and earnest Encolpius (played by Martin Potter) moves through a series of episodes, often accompanied by

Ascyltus (Hiram Keller), his dark and sneering friend, in almost all of which his life or freedom is threatened. He is able to survive because, unlike Ascyltus, he knows himself, offers no disguises, and can acknowledge his weakness and vulnerability. When the Minotaur is about to kill him in the labyrinth, he weeps and says, "There should be a gladiator here, not I, who am a student. . . . I don't know how to use a sword as one needs to use it here. Have pity on Encolpius." As Lichas is about to squeeze him to death on a ship, his very helplessness and beauty inspire Lichas' love, and he is spared. Yet events in his bitter universe are charged with irony. The Minotaur saves him only for the terrible shame of sexual failure, and Lichas spares him so that he must endure the humiliation of a mock marriage. And Ascyltus, whose code of expediency ("Friendship lasts as long as it is convenient") would seem to assure his survival, is murdered in the most unpredictable, almost offhand way: The camera glances briefly out the window to see someone assaulting him. Though the murderer can be identified as the boatman who brought them to the dwelling of the witch Oenothea, this recognition requires a second viewing of the film and careful attention during the few seconds of the action. The boatman's motives are never revealed. Encolpius recognizes the irony of Ascyltus' death as he comments, "Where is all your joy now, all your arrogance. . . . You who only a little time ago were showing off for us your thoughtless bravery." Thus Fellini makes a nondiscursive statement about the random power of violence in this universe through his choice of victim (the adaptive "modern" boy) and through the pacing, which offers only the most fleeting glance at this matter of life and death, as it is to dwell unevenly on events throughout the film. We get only brief or fragmented revelation about things like the gallery, the murder of young Caesar, and Encolpius' restorative encounter with Oenothea, but spend a great deal of time on the banquet scene at Trimalchio's, the encounter with the Minotaur, and the elaborate failure at the Garden of Delights.

The uneven use of time heightens the baffling quality of experience in this surreal vision and emphasizes the fragmented and bizarre in ironic contrast to the most mundane and realistic details. The structure is characterized by extreme narrative discontinuity. The film cuts from one major episode to another with almost no expository linking, confusing movement in time and space. For example, after Encolpius and Eumolpus talk dreamily of nature while lying in a field, the film cuts suddenly to Encolpius awakening, bound and a prisoner, on a beach where a boat awaits him. After the encounter with the Hermaphrodite, we suddenly find Encolpius being pushed down a dirt slide into an arena. Though Encolpius acts as narrator, only occasionally does he give us information, apparently at random. We are more baffled by such narration than we would be by none at all. Fellini said, "I want to take all the narrative sequence of traditional cinema out of the story, to give it an unremitting harshness." [6]

As sequences neither unfold nor conclude but rather start and stop, almost nothing is complete or whole. We see the huge head of a broken statue being drawn through the streets at night, and later, in the Minotaur's arena, Encolpius' impotence is displayed before the statue of a female figure whose head is broken off. People, particularly the leader in the Minotaur sequence, laugh in short bursts and screams that end suddenly. Bodies are dismembered, appearing without heads and limbs. In the gallery, paintings and sculptures are partial and broken; there is an unfinished mosaic on the wall of Trimalchio's house, and the film ends with the camera fixed on fragmented murals of the main characters. The discontinuities and fragments heighten our sense of the bizarre and abstract, making it extremely difficult to determine the mode of reality in which events take place and creating a deep sense of disturbance, which underlies the fantastic visual texture dominating the film.

Seldom in the history of cinema have plastic effects—particularly make-up and setting—been developed with such innovative brilliance. The characters' faces painted bright red, blue, green, yellow, gold, and white, the women's hair piled high in fabulous arrangements—these extremes reassure us that we are watching a fantasy, a decadent circus going mad. But not all the make-up is so extreme. Prostitutes and upper servants often wear a cruder, less elaborate version of the aristocrats' embellishment, and streets, kitchens, and galleys are full of the unadorned poor. This range awakens the uneasy sensation that a whole culture is being represented with historical accuracy. Fellini emphasizes the artful, nonrealistic face of Lichas by peering at it through cracks in a wall and shadowing it carefully, arousing our curiosity before he gives us the chilling shock of the glass eye. But what do we know of the treatment of such wounds in Roman times, especially in this vision designed to enhance mystery? Perhaps such apparitions walked the streets of Rome. The film offers a catalogue of gro-

---

[6] Federico Fellini, quoted in *Fellini's Satyricon* (New York: Ballantine Books, 1970), p. 20.

Satyricon

tesques such as might inhabit a sideshow designed by Hierony-
mous Bosch: midgets, cripples, and hunchbacks, the hugely fat
and painfully thin, those without arms and legs, old toothless
whores with darting tongues and young ones with whips or tattooed faces, the oversexed, the sexless, and the androgynous—
the population of a nightmare, combining the grotesques of the
earth with those of fantasy. Yet along with their extreme, bizarre
characteristics, these people are often given business to do that
is at once realistic and more mystifying than their appearance.
When Giton leaves with Ascyltus before the collapse of the Insula
Felicles (the apartment-like building at the beginning of the film),
his stylized hand gestures suggest some commonly known Roman
form of communication, but their meaning is completely inaccessible to us. Giton repeats these gestures in the hold of Lichas'
ship when he meets other prisoners. At the feast, Trimalchio's
wife Fortunata receives a female friend who makes similar gestures. This repetition causes the audience to speculate like ar-
cheologists or historians—perhaps this is a form of greeting
authentic to the period and with a range of variations—and enhances the surreal mix of styles. The list of details exhibiting
this mysterious realism can be drawn from anywhere in the film.
In the prologue and throughout, words and numbers of graffiti and

advertising appear scrawled on the walls; two painted, costumed little boys play and scuffle at Trimalchio's mock funeral, the strange context rendering artificial their commonplace behavior; Fortunata and her visitor peck at each other's lips in some unfathomable version of a kiss, whether of lust or greeting is unknown; Giton plays a strange little instrument that might or might not have really existed. One of the most successfully jarring of these effects is the film's mixture of languages, including forms of German, French, Latin, Greek, Italian, and a gloriously bizarre clicking tongue spoken by a slave girl at the sucide villa.

These people act out their strange realism in a physical universe that is at best inhospitable and at worst frightfully hostile. Again the effects are achieved through a mix of the bizarre and realistic. Lichas' ship and the one that conquers it are covered with huge metal anchors and other strange instruments bristling with steel points and spikes. In Oenothea's cave, we see a sculptured figure studded with large nails or spikes. After Lichas' defeat, we see a montage of cruel, smoking machines of war and torture, crucifixions, spears, and severed heads. (This montage is followed by the only welcoming environment in the film, the suicide villa, enhancing the ironic structure just described.) These nightmare props exist side by side with the realism of an unhealthy and repellent world; many people are crowded into small spaces, especially in the hold of Lichas' ship, where ledges and openings are too small or too oddly shaped to allow comfort. Such is the sense

Satyricon

of confinement that it is a surprise to see the open skylight of the Insula Felicles. The air is fetid with pollution, as in Trimalchio's house. Nature itself is hostile, offering the burning sun of the valley and the stinging wind of the plains.

The artificial sets, perhaps more than any other characteristic, lift *Satyricon* out of time and space, distorting its mode of reality as Fellini ignores film conventions for his special purpose. Large budgets, technical improvements, and a popular taste for verisimilitude have accustomed us to a high degree of realism in film. If a scene takes place outdoors, we expect the contemporary filmmaker to go outside and shoot it. While several exterior sequences are indeed filmed outdoors, many more are shot before highly artful backdrops, making a surreal contrast with the strange signals of realistic behavior. The sequence in Vernacchio's theater (which is the first to follow Encolpius' prologue) makes good metaphoric reference to this relationship. Before a crudely artificial backdrop, dressed in bizarre masks and costumes, the players suddenly and actually (in the play within the play) cut off a man's hand. The visual shock of Fellini's realistic treatment of the actual severing is deepened by the dawning notion that Roman theater indeed included such actions. After Encolpius and Eumolpus leave the gallery, the film cuts to the overripe red of a painted sunset before Trimalchio's house, its exaggerated coloring enhanced by the flickering golden light of candles held by scores of bathers in steaming pools. After the meast, poet and hero lie in a plowed field offering one of the closest horizons since the invention of perspective. Barren sticks, unaccountably planted in orderly rows, stand behind the wagon of the nymphomaniac. Even the pinks, grays, and beiges of the suicide villa, while suggesting the soft, pleasing colors of certain rocks and sand, are too clean to be natural, the setting of the waterfall too perfect, and the greenish shrubbery not quite recognizable. The sound track also seems too clean, offering only the faintest chirp of birds and trickle of water. The frank artifice of setting is frequently complemented by the composition of scenes. In the foreshortened depth of the cannibal sequence, Eumolpus' body, lying on a platform, is surrounded by his heirs, who carefully distribute themselves in back, middle, and foreground, as if making conventionally correct use of stage space.

The narrative discontinuity, fragmentation, and combination of the frankly bizarre and mysteriously realistic together lift the film out of time and space and call into question the mode of experience being presented. This ambiguity is the basis of one of the film's strongest effects: It permits an analogy with contemporary life that is strongly felt but in a way not seen. Freed from the bonds of authenticity and verisimilitude, the film invites us to seek causes, motives, and values from our own culture. In other words, like a vacuum, it demands that we rush in with what we know to occupy a kind of allegorical space left vacant by the mystery. Though the film can be experienced primarily as a visual artifact, the vacant spaces allow us to receive certain cultural signals in the subject matter. Like the Romans who worship freaks and corrupted gods, we live in a time of bizarre cultism where God is said to be dead, as he had not yet made himself felt in the Rome of *Satyricon;* his presence looms outside the film, anticipated by the audience but unfelt by the characters. The fragmented state of art and the harkening back to Greek culture remind us of our own apprehension about the health of the arts. The episodic life style of Encolpius and Ascyltus suggests not only the lives of many traveling and uncommitted young people today; the two of them embody conflicting moral attitudes in the contemporary world. Life is controlled by the money-hungry and corrupt (Eumolpus: "By means of little swindles and little deals I've become master of the town.") who seem eminently recognizable to a civilization that may itself be dying of imperialism, vandalism, warmaking, and other ills that many blame on exclusive dedication to the profit motive. Fellini (like Swift in "A Modest Proposal") renders explicit this cannibalism in the final sequence, where the heirs cannot inherit Eumolpus' fortune unless they consume his corpse. Like civilized men, they justify their horrific action with a too-familiar argument: So has man always been, and so shall I be:

First Heir:	In certain races, even today, it's usual for the defunct to be eaten by his relatives.
Fat Heir:	I'm not worried about my stomach turning. It'll follow orders if, after an hour of nausea, it is promised such a heap of good things.
Wise Heir:	When the Sagutines were besieged by Hannibal, they ate human flesh and they weren't waiting for an inheritance.
Young Heir:	I am ready to conform.[7]

[7] *Ibid.,* p. 272.

LA DOLCE VITA (1961)

The relationship between artifice and realism in *Satyricon* is reversed in *La Dolce Vita.* A realistic surface dominates the latter film, but the bizarre or surreal emerges in important sequences. This difference in visual texture provides the strongest distinction between the two films and allows each to express its particular theme. In *Satyricon* order and meaning are no longer viable, and the central problem is to survive in the disoriented chaos of this universe. In *La Dolce Vita,* however, the conflict between order and chaos, between meaning and despair, is alive and is reflected in the order and predictability implicit in a realistic style.

The bizarre images in *La Dolce Vita* reveal another dimension of the decadence of modern Rome. Things have become so extreme there that they are difficult to relate to one's previous experience (hence the difference in visual mode) and suggest the beginning of a madness (on the part of Marcello and his culture) into which the world of *Satyricon* completely descends. The film opens with the first of these surreal images, a statue of Christ slung from a helicopter and casting a shadow on the blank, white wall of a modern apartment building. In the next sequence, a Roman night club presents three masked and painted "Siamese" dancers who combine the highly stylized movements of a refined civilization with a primitive, muscled sensuality. When Marcello and his father go to the Kit Kat Club, the girls are costumed as cats, contrasting sharply with the poignance of the clown who blows a sweet trumpet that draws a group of balloons along behind him. In the night club, which was once the Caracalla Baths, we meet Frankie, a dancer who has purposely altered his appearance so that he seems the living embodiment of a satyr. At the party in Steiner's apartment, the civilized, cosmopolitan variety of the guests is exaggerated to the point of freakishness, which is also true of the party at the castle, with the difference that the former group are intellectuals and the latter aristocrats, encompassing two important aspects of culture that are on the decline. In the final orgy at the beach villa, which attracts various hangers-on from the movie world and the Via Veneto, Marcello completely descends into decadence by leading the revels and pretending cruel metamorphoses as he rides a girl as if she were a horse and then tries to turn her into a chicken by covering her with feathers (evoking the grotesque ending of *Freaks*).

Despite the different emphases in theme and style, many important similarities invite comparison of *La Dolce Vita* and

La Dolce Vita

Satyricon. Both use a highly episodic structure in which a young hero, without family or alienated from it, moves through a series of adventures, including parties, unsatisfactory sexual encounters, meetings with disillusioned artists (Eumolpus and Steiner), experiences revealing the corruption of religion (the hermaphrodite and the "miracle"), and confrontations with grotesque monsters from the sea. Both films develop themes important in modern life—the problem of communication and of the corruption of life through financial exploitation. In *La Dolce Vita,* Marcello's attempts to talk to someone are repeatedly thwarted by the sounds of helicopters, telephones, music, and the sea. People speak a variety of languages, as they do in *Satyricon.*

Certain episodes central to the development of each film are strikingly similar, yet important differences distinguish the two films' views of experience. Both include a suicide that takes place in a setting that at first appears to be an oasis in the cultural chaos. Both men are married and have children, and in both cases the motives for their suicide are left to conjecture. But each man's attitude toward his suicide and the way in which he involves his family are very different. Steiner, the modern man, assumes his suicide to be a private act and waits until his wife is out of the house, but, with bitter irony, he takes his children with him, implying that they must be spared the terrible experience of life itself. We get some insight to his motives in the party sequence where he is compared to a Gothic steeple in his serenity and search for perfection; he puts his children to bed behind filmy gauze curtains, as if to shelter them in perfect sanctuary from the hidden danger of chaos. When Marcello learns of Steiner's death, he reaches the apartment by climbing a spiral staircase, ringed with onlookers, suggesting a whirlpool into which everyone will be drawn. Ironically, he finds Steiner as neat and orderly in death as he was in life, wearing a tie, his impassive face marred only by a tiny bullet hole. Throughout *La Dolce Vita,* Steiner has been an important symbolic figure for Marcello, to whom he can relate better than to his own father and who has kept alive Marcello's hopes of literary artistry. Steiner's suicide implies that beneath an orderly appearance may be the same incipient chaos and madness with which Marcello is struggling and of which Steiner was aware:

> Sometimes the night, this darkness, this calm, weighs on me. It is peace that makes me afraid. . . . I feel that it's only an appearance, that it hides a danger. Sometimes, too, I think of the world that my children will know. They say that the world of the future will be wonderful. But what does that mean? It needs only the gesture of madmen to destroy everything.[8]

Steiner's artificial order has failed to sustain him, and there is only one hope for sanity—to plunge into the chaos of life, as Marcello tries to do. Suicide, then, is a terrible disillusionment rather than the elegant and reasonable choice it appears to be in *Satyricon.*

With ironic pessimism, every aspect of the suicide scene in *Satyricon* enhances its aura of calm wisdom. Servants and children are sent away, and the double suicide is an agreement between adults, imposed on no one else. The act is preceded by rituals of food and drink and by loving glances between the married couple. With a smile on his face, the husband cuts his wrists and weakens slowly from loss of blood before his wife follows. Although this is the only scene in which this man appears, he has

[8] Federico Fellini, *La Dolce Vita* (New York: Ballantine Books, 1961), p. 136.

a startling relationship with the author of *Satyricon,* Petronius Arbiter, who committed suicide in exactly the same way. This connection also supports the view that in this no-exit universe suicide is a reasonable choice for those who are accustomed to the values of humanistic serenity and love presented in this scene. Unlike Marcello, Encolpius and Ascyltus are not disillusioned when they encounter the suicides, not only because they are strangers, but because these values are not part of their experience and, as we have seen, would actually impede their survival in this universe.

The second important distinction between the films lies in their attitudes toward the existence of alternative positive values. *La Dolce Vita* is more hopeful. In it, past and present are often juxtaposed to show that although humane values have deteriorated, they are at least still possible. Marcello has gone from creative writer to journalist to public relations man, but this trend is not necessarily irreversible. The decline is shown visually in the contrast between the gracefully arched San Felice aqueduct and the stark sterility of the apartment building and in the Baths of Caracalla, which has become a night club that caters to the old and bored. When we see the Roman baths in *Satyricon,* steaming and dirty and sheltering the cruel Ascyltus, we realize that the attitude toward the past implied in *La Dolce Vita* is at least partially naive and sentimental.

This difference in attitude is subtly revealed in the closing sequences of the two films. Both heroes have come to the sea, which is at once an end and a forced beginning, as in *400 Blows.* Both have just left a scene of degradation: Marcello has dehumanized the girl whom he rides and feathers; Encolpius has witnessed cannibalism, the primeval act of inhumanity. Both are beckoned by a figure who could be seen as offering a positive alternative. In *La Dolce Vita* the beckoning figure is Paola, whom Marcello met at his emotional high point, right after Steiner's party; she is linked to his fondest hopes (she even reminds him of "one of those little angels in the churches of Umbria") and promises a reawakening of his ideals. However, Marcello cannot hear her, for the sea drowns out her voice, and he turns away with a shrug of resignation. But the final image of the film is her angelic face, smiling as if to suggest that the hope she offers still exists. In *Satyricon* the idealized figure toward whom Encolpius yearns has been transformed, emerging as Giton, the beautiful heartless young boy who affects a graceful innocence. However, he is not the one who beckons at the end; instead, a black servant laughs and leaps with joyous energy, implying that any hope for the future lies not in spiritual regeneration but in the rejuvenating power of youth. In short, Encolpius gets on the ship as he has entered all other experiences—simply because it is there. Finally, it will take him to some unknown place, distant from his culture, which no longer offers any possibility. Although Encolpius is able to respond to the beckoner and Marcello is not, the ending of *La Dolce Vita* seems more optimistic by traditional standards. The world of *La Dolce Vita* prepares us for Marcello's potential artistry; in the world of *Satyricon* hope lies in the unknown.

THE CLOWNS (1971)

Made for television, *The Clowns* appears to be a documentary concerned with the passing of an art form, but upon closer scrutiny it offers an autobiographical statement by Fellini, an exploration of the ways in which art combines various modes of reality, and a confrontation with old age and death. *The Clowns,* like most of Fellini's films, and particularly *Satyricon,* has the power to re-shape the audience's vision of reality. One emerges from the theater into a neighborhood that seems to have been decorated and cast by Fellini and his people. Whereas the problem of integrating experience is the central focus of $8^1/_2$, *The Clowns* successfully merges childhood memories, the present, fantasy, images and musical themes from each of Fellini's previous films, and various cinematic styles. Access to this kind of integrated experience makes it possible for a man to face with some degree of equanimity the slow process of old age and death.

The film, like a three-ring circus, is divided into three parts, which offer three different styles of cinema with which to pay homage to clowns—an autobiographical account of childhood memories, a documentary of the past glory and present remnants of circus clowning, and a fantastic recreation of a clown act. Part one opens as a little boy (dressed in white as in $8^1/_2$) is awakened by the sounds of grunts, ominous and unidentifiable until he goes to the window and discovers that a circus tent is being raised in the eerie light of a fire. His first circus frightens him with its knives and sledge hammers, grotesque faces, violent behavior, and especially the bottled Siamese twins, whom the circus master shows to him and asks, "You see them, little boy, aren't they nice?" Even if we in the audience do not share the child's fear, we can understand it because, as yet, we do not recognize the conventions of clowning, and to us, as to the child, the violence appears pervasive and unpredictable. This first circus scene introduces images and patterns that run through the film—the red drapes of the circus ring, the parody of other circus acts by the midgets, the rebellion of clowns disguised as animals, the hammer routine, the traditional make-up and costumes of Augusto and the white clown, and, perhaps most important, the breakdown of distinction between audience and performers. The sequence also integrates images that remind us of other Fellini films—the basic circus situation of *Variety Lights* (the first film he directed), the strong man from *La Strada,* the circus music from *La Strada* and *8¹/₂,* the Indian fakir from both *8¹/₂* and *Juliet of the Spirits,* the cannibalism from *Satyricon,* the fascination with bizarre make-up from *La Dolce Vita* and *Satyricon,* and the image of his mother as laundress, a role his wife played in the harem fantasy in *8¹/₂.* The Amazons, Matilde and Miss Tarzan, are reminiscent of Saraghina from *8¹/₂,* here rendered comically aggressive, their power mocked through exaggeration. To underscore the connection, Fellini again uses the music he used in the harem fantasy (Wagner's "Ride of the Valkyries") as the accompaniment for the struggling behemoths.

The basic movement of the first part is a merging of memories from two aspects of the past—the reenactment of a child's first visit to the circus and an adult's narration of how this experience reshaped what he saw around him. As Fellini's voice off-screen tells us, "The night ended badly . . . they frightened me . . . those twisted, crazy masks . . . they reminded me of other clowns," we realize the autobiographical link to the same consciousness that created the "twisted, crazy masks" of *Satyricon.* Whereas *Satyricon* affects our private experience by forcing us to create our own analogies with the film, *The Clowns* provides us with new categories by which to organize what we encounter in the real world. As Fellini describes his memories of the "town clowns," we distinguish between the Augustos (the lecherous Big John; the whining, drunken husband whose wife fetches him in a wheelbarrow; and the stuttering Giudizio) and the white clowns (the insane midget nun, the mutilated war veteran who knows Mussolini's speeches by heart, and the stationmaster). The final scene with Giudizio is most effective in creating a complex analogy between real life and clowning. The inflated amorous gestures of the local sheik, bescarved and groomed (who could have come right out of *I Vitelloni*) are deflated by Giudizio with comic obscenity. Developing the iconoclasm of the Augusto figure with poignance, Giudizio plays mad war games through the streets of the town, suggesting (as does the mutilated war veteran) that Mussolini and all war lovers are insane white clowns. The onlookers are touched as he concludes his act by playing "Taps" on an imaginary trumpet. The raspberries of the children on the train have a similar function in deflating the costumed and prancing stationmaster, who must call in a Fascist official to protect his white clown's dignity. Another kind of complexity is introduced by the exotic blond, wrapped in white fur, who is fancied by all the locals in the poolroom; she anticipates the later appearance of Anita Ekberg, also draped in white fur, and parodying her role as the feline femme fatale in *La Dolce Vita.*

Part two turns from private experience toward the unique process by which Fellini makes this "documentary" on clowning, and at the same time parodies cinema vérité's assumption that film can objectively record reality. It opens in Fellini's offce, where he introduces his film crew, another clown act that includes Gasperino, the cross-eyed little grip; Lina, the moon-faced wardrobe mistress; and Maya, the decorative but barely functional scriptgirl. They make faces, bump heads, and try on funny hats as they are directed by Fellini, the ringmaster in his private circus, but they also function as a warm and enthusiastic audience for everything they see.

Throughout his search, Fellini repeatedly encounters the inadequacy of film to capture "what remains of these clowns of my childhood." As he visits the old clowns, they bring out their scrapbooks that offer blurred fragments of former comic glory. In the sequence where he visits film director Pierre Etaix and his wife (who is part of the famous Fratellini family), Etaix promises to show him a "rare documentary," which we do not see because the projector breaks and burns the film. This failure is contrasted with a brief shot in which a picture of Buster Keaton appears among Fellini's crew, as if to imply he is one of them and the spirit of clowning is still alive. Fellini's search for documentary evidence from the past becomes increasingly futile, culminating in his descent into the "vast funeral atmosphere" of the Paris studio where he is to see a film about Rhum, the only existing record of one of the greatest clowns of all. The crass film editor who shows "Mr. Bellini" the film has never heard of Rhum and refers to the film only by number. The film is short, grainy, and completely unsatisfactory. Fellini sadly concludes, "It's as if our journey has led us nowhere . . . maybe Remy is right that the clown is really dead."

Yet even within the "documentary" of part two, Fellini's unique process of merging personal memories with fantasy offers an alternative to cinema vérité that is much more successful in cap-turning the spirit of clowning. His interviews document not the past glory for which he has been vainly searching but the present pathos of these men's lives. The last two visits to Loriot and Bario (both Augustos) provide a subtle but important contrast. Bario, ironically dressed in jaunty plaids, is trapped in aging hopelessness: "It only breaks my heart to talk about the circus. . . . I spent sixty years there and then I came home . . . the circus was my whole life." Although he still has the companionship of a protective wife who hovers around him, she too can only look backward: "You always miss the past . . . and your youth." We see Bario for the last time as he peeks out of an upstairs window, and one of Fellini's crew remarks, "Damn, old age is terrible." In contrast, Loriot tries to make fruitful use of his limited life, still working from time to time, though "in Rome, nobody laughed." Although his wife is dead, her momeory seems to offer him more comfort than Bario can draw from his living wife. As he drinks "to her precious memory" he says, "We were together fifty-three years . . . that's not just a day, you know." Of all these old clowns, Loriot comes closest to the integration Fellini seeks, combining memory, imagination, and present experience to help him face old age and death.

These visits also record the decline of the art form, which is developed ironically in the audition of Baptiste, a psychiatrist who wants to revive clowning. His feeble efforts, lacking energy and imagination, are made more pathetic by the fact that his assistant is the daughter of cinema's greatest clown, Charlie Chaplin. At this point Fellini clowns with the documentary form itself as we wonder whether Baptiste (the actor Jean-Baptiste Thierrée, who played Bernard in Resnais's *Muriel*) is in real life a psychiatrist turned clown and whether Chaplin's daughter is really his assistant. The scene calls into question the role of cinema vérité in this film: Which scenes are staged and which are authentic? Are the old clowns played by themselves, like Fellini and Ekberg, or have they been effectively re-created by other actors, as in the inset reconstructions of the old clown routines?

These reconstructions allow Fellini to express the clowning spirit most successfully by using his imagination to integrate fantasy and data from the real world. Fellini transcends the expert's argument about who made the clowns' costumes by insetting a parade of white clowns trying to outdo each other in glitter and design as they mince along a runway. As the camera moves in, it focuses on one clown whose tufted hair, bright red ears, and protruding tongue remind us of the harsh grotesquery of *Satyricon*. As the white clowns argue shrilly, the camera cuts back abruptly to the cafe, re-creating the argument exactly, but this time it is among the bickering experts. This visual transition is also used at the Fratellinis' home, where a photograph of the three brothers dissolves into a live action shot as they move out of exactly the same position to begin a performance, once again transcending the limits of the photographic record by an imaginative re-creation. They perform before audiences of the retarded, the sick, and the mad (reminding us of Gelsomina's performance before the idiot child in *La Strada*), their mutual grotesquery breaking down the distinction between audience and performer as the inmates rise to imitate psychiatrists and ringmasters. This merging is made more complex in the re-creation of the dying act of Guillon (the "first-class artist" who created the character of Augusto) as he sneaks out of his hospital, past a snoring mustachioed nun to take his place among the audience watching Chocolat and Footit. He and the heavily rouged lady next to him do a little act in the audience as, sympathetic, she watches him die laughing, using his last energy to applaud the art that was his own.

In part three Fellini offers an emotional richness that far transcends the limited documentary by drawing upon all the elements present in the film—memory, fantasy, and research; audience, performers, and crew; allusions to earlier films; elements from previous clown acts; and the various tones in which all this material has been presented. Continuing the parody, Fellini's final act, ostensibly a wake for the death of clowning, is performed with such exuberance and energy that it actually celebrates the continued life of the comic spirit.

The first part of the act parallels the viewing of the body and allows the clowns to gather and develop the comic ineffectuality that is part of their traditional stance. Lina's attempts to sew the hemline of the widow's dress lead into a hatpin battle of deflation, which reminds us of the struggle between Matilde and Miss Tarzan. There is a merging of audience, crew, and performers at several levels while the cameraman of the film that we are actually watching shoots Fellini's cinematographer shooting a clown photographer shooting a group portrait of clowns. A breakdown in Fellini's film equipment (which reminds us of the earlier broken projector) brings forth a crew of bumbling clown carpenters, including Fellini's grip and sound man (who perform the familiar hammer routines) and an explosion from a prop table marked "special effects." The comic defiance of death is stressed as an old clown, bearded to the floor, rushes to the corpse, weeping,

The Clowns

"Papa, why did you leave me all alone?" The implication is that if clowning lived long enough to have such an aged son, it is probably immortal. Unimpressed by a pompous lawyer who reads the will, the clowns respond by nibbling at it, a comic reversal of the cannibalism of *Satyricon*. On the sidelines, amidst this simultaneous chaos, a critic earnestly asks, "Signor Fellini, what message are you trying to give us here?" In answer, buckets fall on the heads of Fellini and the critic, reminding us of the attack on the intellectual writer in *8½*, and of Remy, this film's clown expert, and suggesting that the traditional ineffectuality of the clowns extends to Fellini and to critics like us.

The second part of the act, paralleling the funeral procession and oration, accelerates the pace, intensifies competition between authoritarian white clowns and rebellious Augustos, and further develops the film's attitude toward death. The hearse arrives, driven by a wonderfully unique white clown with an English accent, who, like the stationmaster, struggles to subdue rebellion among the ranks. Like the children on the train, his horses are defiant; one of them lifts his tail and lets fly a stream of water, a traditional weapon of the downtrodden Augusto. As an Augusto buzzes a parody of a prayer, a white clown delivers an oration that contains outrageous sarcasm: "He died an untimely death at the age of two hundred ... we all mourn that he died now instead of the minute he was born;" comic philosophizing: "His soul flew out his left ear ... he no longer lives ... luckily I still do;" and an occasional poignant truth: "In his long dishonest life he was dedicated to getting pails of water in the face . . . he made other children laugh but his own children cry." The traditional funeral procession, accompanied by the familiar circus music from earlier films, is transformed into the circus finale that provided an ending for *Nights of Cabiria* and *8½*. As the procession accelerates, some of the old clowns cannot keep up with the pace and drop out to become spectators like Giullon. Augusto is comically reborn as he is shot from a champagne bottle and flies from the ceiling (like the Fratellini butterflies) amidst a shower of brightly colored streamers, while everyone dances below. Abruptly the music stops, and the only sound we hear is the rustling of paper as Augusto swings through the streamers. We are reminded of one of the early fantasy images in *8½*, where Guido descends from the sky. The ailing white clown on the sidelines turns to Fellini and says, "I liked it very much." Fellini replies, "Turn it off, it's over."

However, Fellini adds a kind of epilogue, in which the white clown tells a story that becomes a parable of the film's effort to transcend the death of clowning. The clown describes his act, which centered around his search for Fru Fru, his dead partner. Refusing to accept the death, he asks continually, "Where can I find him. . . . I'd call him and call him." Then the scene dissolves

The Clowns

to a re-creation of the circus ring from the childhood memory early in the film. The camera follows the spotlight as it pans between a lone Augusto and a white clown moving slowly toward each other as they play "Ebb Tide" on their trumpets, which reminds us of Giudizio playing "Taps," of the trumpet music awakening Zampano's love in *La Strada,* and of the clown's solo in *La Dolce Vita* luring the balloons. In a final image very much like that of *8¹/₂,* the camera cuts to an overhead shot as the two clowns, finally joining each other in the center of the ring, magically vanish.

From the perspective of *The Clowns,* we see how Fellini has transformed the circus from a powerful childhood memory into the central metaphor for his mythic vision—one that insists, with its simultaneous three-ring structure and mixture of tones, on a comic acceptance of the chaos and contradictions of experience. It is this comic acceptance that Steiner cannot reach and that is Marcello's only hope in *La Dolce Vita;* it is the solution that Cabiria, Guido, and Juliet discover at the end of *Nights of Cabiria, 8¹/₂,* and *Juliet of the Spirits;* it makes *Satyricon* tolerable to watch; and it is the only perspective that makes survival possible.

This all-embracing acceptance derives from a complete integration of the various aspects of one's experience, an integration that is reached not through reason and logic but through intuition and imagination. Particularly important for Fellini is the combining of his roles as artist and individual, a process he explores in most of his films but especially in *8¹/₂,* arriving at a whimsical solution in *The Clowns.* Fellini achieves this integration primarily by keeping the past alive in the present (his childhood memories, his past films, and the social and mythic past of the culture) and by combining fantasy and realism in a way that frees his creative impulses from the conventional limitations of either mode.

Fellini's films are marked by characteristics that integrate them into a kind of mythological system. Like all mythologies, they are concerned with the basic questions of existence—survival in an unpredictable universe, dangerous extremes of madness and order, struggle with religious belief, and the need for a viable attitude toward death. In film after film similar characters appear, wearing the faces of fantasy, moving through a circus-like world to Nino Rota's haunting music, and confronting these archetypal problems at the various stages of their psychic development. Any subject Fellini treats becomes uniquely his, transformed by the comic energy and chaotic richness that inform his vision.

8

the shape
of politics
in film

Here we will explore films that, because of their politics, raise certain problems in evaluation. A relativistic approach meets a special challenge in dealing with films that have a political focus, whether they be those dealing with present revolutionary issues and goals (such as *Punishment Park, La Chinoise, The Battle of Algiers, Z,* and *Zabriskie Point*) or those developing broad issues of political power and morality in a context more distant in time and space (such as *The Damned, The Wild Child, Walkabout,* and *The Conformist*).

Of all filmmakers and critics, Godard is most insistent that all films have conscious political goals; if they do not, by implication they will support the status quo. He has attacked *Z, The Battle of Algiers,* and *Zabriskie Point,* as well as his own early work, as bourgeois films pretending to be radical:

> *The Battle of Algiers* was produced, as a matter of fact, by Italy's biggest producer, with the help of the Algerian movie office, which is still using nonrevolutionary ideology. ... It does not show the way the present Algerian regime is dealing with its complex problems, so it is really harmful to the Algerian revolution and a victory for Hollywood.

> Gavras is objectively an ally of the Greek government. In his film, he does not speak at all of what the real situation is in Greece today. It's not by chance that *Z* won an Oscar. After all, who financed the coup d'état? The CIA. And who gave the prize to a Greek film? Hollywood. *Z* got an Oscar from the same people who silenced the Greek people.[1]

> *Zabriskie Point* is more reactionary than a picture like *Young Mr. Lincoln.*[2]

Godard's attacks are obviously based on certain implicit assumptions: Subject matter must deal with contemporary political situations (what is happening now in Algiers and Greece); style must be realistic (this is hard to reconcile with the style of his own work and reveals a special conception of realism); external conditions (who made the films, who financed them, what prizes they won) are important criteria in evaluating the films themselves.

Godard's statements contain important ideas, which need to be fully understood. Art cannot be separated from politics; any work of art has political implications, even a western or a Hollywood musical. Yet political and esthetic approaches differ; any work, indeed any action, can be viewed as an esthetic construct, as well as for its political implications. The emphasis of an esthetic approach, is centripetal, focusing on the relationship of the parts and the work's fulfillment of its goals. The emphasis of a political approach is centrifugal, focusing on how the work relates to power relationships in the extensional world. Films with a political subject tend to elicit critical responses that are primarily centrifugal. The political content of a film is partially determined by the artistic form. Jean-Pierre Gorin, Godard's colleague, asserts, "You can't express a revolutionary content if you haven't got a revolutionary form." This oversimplifies the problem, for it is possible to create ironic incongruity: Use of traditional form might imply the historic roots of revolution or the inadequacy of that form to express revolutionary ideas. But it is certainly undeniable that form always has political implications.

Unlike Godard (who often ignores esthetic considerations), we insist that in evaluating political films, the artist must be granted his *donné,* or subject just as in any other film. The question is how

---

[1] Jean-Luc Godard, quoted in Guy Flatley, "Godard Says Bye-Bye to Bardot and All That," *New York Times Magazine* (May 17, 1970), p. 11.

[2] Michael Goodwin, Tom Luddy, and Naomi Wise, "The Dziga Vertov Film Group in America: An Interview with Jean-Luc Godard and Jean-Pierre Gorin," *Take One,* Vol. 2, pp. 22–33.

effectively he deals with the subject he chooses, how he transforms the medium in order to express his subject. Of course we in the audience bring our own knowledge and experience to bear on the evaluation—our knowledge of politics, of historical background, of other films that deal with similar issues. Yet this knowledge should be used to understand the unique way in which the artist treats his material rather than to dictate the subject, style, or focus. Godard's conception of revolutionary cinema would dismiss the political value of films like *The Conformist.* An approach that is more esthetically inclusive will help to clarify the political role and implications of such a film.

Using the comparative method, we will examine the conception of revolution in *Battle of Algiers* and *Z* and we will discuss its relationship to the formal structure of each film in order to determine how the structure heps to define the political position. Such analysis will reveal why *Battle of Algiers* is successful and *Z* is not, in both political and esthetic terms. Focusing on the relation between form and content in *Zabriskie Point,* we will show that the film's strengths and weaknesses cannot be explained in terms of this dichotomy. *The Conformist* reveals a broader conception of the ways in which a film can be political, in this case through concern with issues like freedom, order, and sanity, which lie behind all political thought and action. This concern is given unique expression in the film's innovative visual form.

THE BATTLE OF ALGIERS (1967)

Godard seems to imply that the conventional form of *The Battle of Algiers* exposes the fact that it is not so radical in content as it pretends to be. But actually the film suggests, primarily through its structure, that the success of a revolution depends on moral idealism, effective strategy, and historical inevitability. The film is divided into three parts, each emphasizing one of these factors. As a strategic prologue, the film offers a written statement (presumably from Pontecorvo) that not one foot is newsreel or documentary footage. While explicitly acknowledging that this is a "fiction" film, the statement calls our attention to its verisimilitude and objectivity and plants the idea in our head that it is to be viewed like a documentary, an idea that is immediately supported by the grainy black and white photography. Throughout the film, Pontecorvo moves back and forth between documentary and fiction.

the battle of algiers

The first part stresses moral idealism. The film opens in 1957 at the military headquarters of the French, after they have successfully tortured an Algerian to get information about Ali, an FLN leader about to be captured. We see the trembling victim, subdued like a frightened animal, his eyes glazed with fear, pain, and shame, and the insensitive French soldiers who force him to come along for the capture, allowing him the honor of wearing a French uniform as a disguise. These images immediately lead us to sympathize with the revolutionary Algerian victim and to condemn the French oppressors. Yet the film starts in the middle of an action, and the shots are not carefully composed, suggesting cinema vérité rather than melodrama, so we are led to feel that our moral evaluations are impartial. Once we see the close-up of Ali's face and then cut to a flashback to 1954, revealing the story of how Ali became a revolutionary, the film shifts to dramatic fiction. From this perspective, the opening now seems to be the heroic convention of starting *in medias res.* This flashback also makes us focus on Ali's individual contribution to the revolution and consider him as a possible hero of the film. When he is in prison and watches a fellow Algerian being guillotined, the camera work makes us identify with his point of view. Ali's story is one of moral regeneration. Like Malcolm X, he is transformed from an aimless criminal into a selfless, dedicated, courageous leader. The opening stresses the moral justifications for the revolution and clearly makes the audience side with the Algerians.

As we move into the second part, we see that Ali is not a hero in the traditional sense but is merely being used as a case study. His story is only one step in a strategy of building an effective revolutionary organization. The second part provides a blueprint for revolution—recruiting good men (like Ali) who must be tested, purging the ghetto of the "garbage" until only the committed remain, murdering police to demonstrate the power of the FLN and the vulnerability of the government. The structure no longer follows a dramatic plot but is comprised of carefully selected episodes that illustrate a practical handbook for revolution. The revolutionary tactics lead to an escalation of violence. The French respond by bombing the Casbah, killing innocent women and children and radicalizing large masses; the FLN responds with well-coordinated bombings to avenge the Algerian people. The bombings induce the French to call in paratroopers under the heroic leadership of Mathieu (which is deflated by the music). When Mathieu reviews the pyramid structure of the FLN for his men and begins to outline his counter-strategy of police action, he suggests that revolution is a game in which tactics and organization are all-important. Unlike those in the first part of the film, the moral lines in the second part are no longer so clear-cut. Mathieu is not a melodramatic villain; he had a distinguished record with the French underground during the Second World War. Although the killing of women and children was begun by the French, it is practiced by both sides. Both assume that the end justifies the means, and each is convinced that its end is morally superior. Both sides have the problem of getting the support of the majority of their people behind them. Moral commitment is also dependent upon strategy.

In a scene where Mathieu is briefing his troops, they look at moving pictures of Algerians crossing the checkpoints into the European section of the city. This "documentary" footage reveals the image of one of the women who was carrying a bomb in her purse, a fact that is known to us in the audience but not to Mathieu and his men. Perhaps Pontecorvo is suggesting the limitations of the straight documentary and showing the need for interpretation, which his own film provides.

The third part, which introduces the concept of historical in-evitability, comprises two specific actions and is concerned with evaluating their success. It begins with the strike called by the FLN. We see the strategy on both sides: The FLN members are trying to assess their own strength and demonstrate it to others (to the French and to the United Nations); Mathieu uses the strike to identify supporters of the FLN and to start breaking the pyramid. The press conference demonstrates the importance of interpreta-tion and the ambiguity of trying to assess the success of an action. There was strong Arab support, yet the United Nations fails to act, and Mathieu succeeds in breaking some links of the pyramid. The question remains unresolved.

Growing out of the strike is the offensive move by the French to "cut off the head of the FLN tapeworm." The strategy is "Nothing comes from nothing"; once the leadership is destroyed, the rev-olution will be over. We watch the French capture four groups of leaders, the last including Ali. We realize that the film began not in the beginning or in the middle, as we at first suspected, but at the end—with the capture of the last of the FLN leaders, which seems to confirm the success of the French. The plot or game seems to be over, but this view is based on the limited assumption that strategy alone makes a successful revolution.

The film unexpectedly presents us with an epilogue—a flash forward to 1960, when the people suddenly rise up with thousands of flags against French tanks. Only now can we determine the success of the earlier events. The news commentator who is narrating this supposed newsreel footage ironically says there is no motive or explanation for this action: Not even the FLN leader in exile can account for it; the people must have made the flags the night before. The time is finally right for the revolution to take place, but he seems to deny any casual connection with the earlier revolutionary action. The French may have won the strike and the battle of Algiers in the short run, but those victories could not deter the revolution. It is Pontecorvo's strategic decision to omit the years of rural warfare that took place during the time-gap between early failure and later success. Like *Mother* and *Battleship Potemkin,* this film seems to imply that nothing can impede a revolution that is presented as growing out of moral necessity. We are reminded of the reply by the captured FLN leader in the press conference when he was asked if he thought the movement really had a chance of beating the French: "At least as good a chance as the French had of fighting the tide of history." We also recall his earlier prediction to Ali that their efforts would ultimately result in this kind of mass action, and we have witnessed the escalation of violence, from the torture of one man to the killing of many. All three justifications of revolution—moral idealism, effective strategy, and historical inevitability—are merged in the final image of a woman tauntingly dancing forward, waving her flag at the French soldiers as the rest of the Algerians scream for freedom. We can read on her face that she believes that freedom is only a matter of time, that soon Algeria will be free because it is right. This kind of self-fulfilling prophecy is the ultimate strategy.

Pontecorvo sees revolution as a historical movement with strong roots in the past. His reworking of traditional conventions of cinema does not contradict his political perspective, as Godard implies, but rather is an effective objective correlative. Pontecorvo builds his conception of the sources of revolution into a three-part structure, which is analogous to the strategy of the FLN, which used the three-man cell to build a successful revolution.

Z (1969)

Unlike *The Battle of Algiers, Z* has a structure incongruous with its political content. Costa-Gavras takes the political situation in Greece and turns it into adroit melodrama. Both the film and the novel *Z* (the latter is by Vassilis Vassilikos) are based on the actual political murder of Gregory Lambrakis, a socialist politician, in 1963. One might argue that Costa-Gavras was trying to generalize the situation, to make it apply to the Kennedys in the United States and to Ben Barka in Algeria. But even if this is the case, Costa-Gavras' decision to gloss over the political issues and divide the characters into stylized heroes and villains seriously weakens the film. He has insisted that the primary function of cinema is to inform:

> I believe very little in the cinema as propaganda. My films have been intended more to inform about a situation than to carry a message. . . . What I am trying to do in my films is to inspire an awareness of what is happening in this politicized world of ours, to present the problems, reveal the circumstances. I leave the spectator to find his own solutions.[3]

But how is it possible for the audience to reach its own solutions if Costa-Gavras gives little information about the actual political circumstances? We do not really discover the specific political motivations of Lambrakis or his murderers, nor do we learn the full ramifications of the assassination. Costa-Gavras believes in simplicity: "I think the issues in politics are not complex, even though politicians tell us so in order to convince us of their importance . . . and to keep us from criticizing them."[4] This desire for simplicity, however, here leads to a slick, highly manipulative structure, shallow characterization, and heavy-handed universalizing of the political issues.

The film's basic structure consists of a conventional separation into five major parts, or acts, followed by an epilogue arranged chronologically, often depending on the familiar technique of the ironic reversal. In act one we see preparations for the opposition rally, which in act two culminates in the murderous attack on the deputy. In act three, the rally's aftermath ends in the deputy's death. Act four presents the first objective phase of the magistrate's investigation, which he summarizes to the prosecutor. In act five, the magistrate valiantly pursues truth despite political threats and pressures, and his success is joyfully announced by the lawyer. The epilogue is a news summary of the actual results ironically defeating the lawyer's hopeful predictions. The final announcement works in almost the opposite way as the information at the

---

[3] Costa-Gavras, quoted in Merton S. Davis, "Agent Provocateur of Films," *New York Times Magazine* (March 21, 1971), p. 32.
[4] *Ibid.*

beginning of *The Battle of Algiers.* From the opening frame, the melodramatic style of *Z* emphasizes curiosity, suspense, and a clear distinction between good and evil, qualities that lead us to expect poetic justice. Yet in its knowing examination of conspirators in high places, of police-supported vigilante groups, and its casual reference to these evils all over the world ("It's safe to blame the Americans . . . they're always guilty of something if the truth were really known"), the film prepares us for the triumph of corrupt power. But melodrama requires a different kind of ending: The good must not appear defeated, the struggle must continue. So the epilogue concludes with a list of things banned in present-day Greece, including the letter *Z*, which means "he lives." The film seems to urge its audience toward indignation, presumably against the right-wing militaristic government of Greece. But, since it fails to explore the underlying political issues, the audience can sit back and self-righteously condemn the Greek government without really understanding the situation or doing anything about it; perhaps we feel vaguely grateful that things are not yet so bad in the United States. The film has not even provided us with enough information to distinguish between the real and the wished-for in Greece, let alone to draw meaningful analogies with political circumstances in the United States or elsewhere. As Gorin observed:

> A film like *Z* can be helpful in a very precise circumstance: if you don't know *anything* about Greece, maybe you learn that somebody was murdered whose name was Lambrakis. But the film is a flop unless you have a political friend sitting by your side, explaining to you what the real situation was in Greece, and why the colonels took power. The film explains nothing about the Greek situation.[5]

The film attempts to disguise its conventional structure through rapid editing and an extensive use of flashbacks. The editing moves so quickly that it appears to reveal a great deal of significant complexity, always showing new details of plot and counterplot, passion and deception. Yet it is carefully controlled, ensuring that we will be satisfied with our film entertainment, moving quickly enough so that we are always "excited" by trying to grasp everything, yet slowly enough that we will not become frustrated. The film is composed of so many brief scenes (which we often enter after the action has begun) that when we spend a great deal of time in the hospital with the witness, the change of pace seems

[5] Goodwin, Luddy, and Wise, p. 24.

disturbing and we are worried that we will miss so much of what is going on.

In the opening title sequence the camera cuts quickly from symbols of traditional authority (crosses, jeweled crowns, medals), to extreme close-ups of faces. Frequently the camera moves in for a tight close-up of an unidentifiable object and then pulls back to reveal it is part of someone's face, or the focus shifts abruptly from foreground to background. The effect is to make us notice faces and language carefully, and later we will recognize that all the men are part of the official conspiracy and that they bear marked similarities to actual figures in the Greek government. (One title announces with blatant irony, "Any similarity to persons living or dead is not accidental. It is intentional.") One man gives a speech on mildew, which is followed by the general's speech about the "political mildew" that is "infecting" the youth. The frequent recurrence of this metaphor becomes a clue that enables us to discover the conspiracy (the homosexual killer boasts with heavy-handed irony, "We're the good element in society, we're the antibodies, so we gave those perverts a beating."), the very same process that the magistrate employs to catch the general, when he says "as supple and agile as a tiger," the exact phrase used by the two killers. The frequency with which these phrases are repeated and the obviousness of the parallel make it difficult to take seriously this investigative technique.

The flashbacks, largely dependent upon fast cutting, achieve a variety of effects. When the deputy sees a girl putting a wig on a mannequin in a window, there is a quick cut back to an ambiguous incident. Presumably the deputy is in his medical office about to examine a pretty young girl who is just taking off her wig and blouse when his wife enters with a facial expression of doubt and suspicion. Costa-Gavras raises the unanswered question about the deputy's fidelity to the wife, as if suggesting, on the one hand, that he is going to alleviate the one-dimensional quality of character and action and yet implying at the same time that this is not the proper path for our curiosity. When asked about his wife, the deputy later says, "We have the same problems that anyone's bound to have after fifteen years of marriage." If the audience is still not satisfied with that answer and wants to know more about it, they will soon find their curiosity discredited by being associated with that of the reporters who callously ask his wife as she is arriving at the hospital, "Is it true you were about to file for a divorce?" or with the general who wants to smear the deputy by finding out whether he ran after women. Instead of developing

340

personal and moral complexity, this detail emerges as unsatisfying and somewhat offensive—an obvious manipulation adding a little sex to the violence. The flashbacks of the wife as she arrives at the hospital and after she learns of her husband's death are effective nonverbal communication of the onrush of confused feelings and the disorientation of time at that moment of extreme grief, a quality achieved also by Irene Papas' marvelous acting. The flashbacks during the magistrate's investigation fill in missing pieces of the action (like the lawyer's account of how the Volkswagen drove them to the hospital) or reconstruct in a distorted fashion (aided by slow motion and omission of key sounds) events that we have already seen. When we see these reenactments, we want to check them against the earlier footage and hence are given another reason for carefully scrutinizing each frame of the film.

Just as Costa-Gavras manipulates the structure and editing to control emotional response, he also dictates who are the villains and who are the good guys. The right-wing officials in the opening sequence are given a touch of comic madness that in conventional melodrama often is shown to accompany the assumption that God is on one's political side; the camera looks up at the face of one of the speakers from a mock-heroic low angle. The actual killers are a brutish, moronic but sly drunkard and a lascivious homosexual; their politics seem to spring mostly from economic self-interest and a taste for violence. Lest we miss the clichéd connection between homosexuality and pleasure in violence, Costa-Gavras underscores it for us many times and with a heavy hand. The homosexual killer is shown kicking a woman with great glee. After brutally clubbing someone, he ogles a young man standing in his underwear on a nearby balcony. So aroused by the violence is this man that, after making a pass at a reporter friend who has promised to get his name in the paper for "the boys," he rushes across the street to a pinball joint to lay hands on the first young boy he encounters. As for the good guys, we are led to assume that the deputy is wise and courageous not because of his ideas or actions but because of his glamorous physical appearance and the responses and actions of other. Yves Montand's personal elegance of bearing enhances the role as he walks, straight and dignified, in a well-tailored brown suit, off the airplane toward a group of obviously admiring students. Our feelings toward Montand are further manipulated by the rhythmic, happy music that accompanies his arrival. Later, in the midst of the crisis, as he stands before a window in a well-composed shot, the "objective" reporter summarizes his career as politician, doctor, and athlete but finally evaluates the man on the basis of his glamorous appearance: He cannot be a communist because "he looks like a winner." The opposition itself is also composed of stereotypes: the fiery Jewish radical, the traditionally conservative lawyer who is earnest in his desire to protect the group, the wife who brings the woman's touch—"He's dying . . . isn't that more to us than *your* politics?"

In the important role of the investigating magistrate, well played by Jean-Louis Trintignant, it seems that Costa-Gavras wanted to guard against stereotyping by showing the growth of the character toward moral strength. Early in the film he is quiet and unassuming, though clever in unearthing evidence and manipulating witnesses. His movement toward belief in the existence of a plot and his commitment to revealing it turn upon another heavy-handed word clue. Suddenly, after carefully referring to the murder as an "incident," he calls it "the assassination." After this change, he is shown to be much more forceful; as he himself says, he has "faced his duty."

The obviousness with which Costa-Gavras expresses his simplified vision is particularly clear in his attempts to universalize the moral and political implications. We never learn the name of the country in which the events take place (although it is obviously Greece), and the major characters are referred to by their titles— deputy, magistrate, general, prosecutor, lawyer, fig-seller, witness. The murderers, however, are given names that comically rhyme. Perhaps Costa-Gavras is trying to give a mythic dimension to the story, which he supports with occasional visual details like the opening montage of symbols of authority or a scene in the police station when the camera pans over the head of the colonel to show a world map and the photographs of a king and queen whose faces are conveniently obscured by spots of light. Unfortunately, however, these visual details are as obvious and ineffective as the verbal signals. There are also many attempts, both verbal and visual, to link the events with the decay that is happening all over the world, particularly in the United States and the Soviet Union. The deputy speaks against both Russian and American armaments; the Russian informer Dumas speaks against Russia as he is seated under a Canada Dry ad that says, "America is going Dry"; as the prosecutor leaves the Bolshoi, he quips, "The new Russian idea is to live just like the Americans." The contrast between the morality of those attending the Bolshoi and those attending the political rally is exploited to the point of exhaustion in an attempt to connect it to the polarity of decadence and activism in every nation. These attempts to universalize are further weakened by the watered-down peace politics of the opposition. The film remains a superficial melodrama, never reaching the level of astute political awareness to which Costa-Gavras aspires.

ZABRISKIE POINT (1970)

The separation of form and subject has occurred frequently in the critical response to Antonioni's *Zabriskie Point*. Many critics argued that the film was brilliant visually but that its contents had serious limitations, a trend that recently led Antonioni to observe:

> You cannot argue that a film is bad but that the color is good, or vice versa. The image is a fact, the colors are the story. If a cinematic moment has colors which appear right and good, it means that it has expressed itself, that it achieved its purpose.[6]

One can apply what Antonioni says about color to all formal aspects of *Zabriskie Point* as well as to his earlier films. *Zabriskie Point* deals with the conflict between the American establishment and the new left student radicalism. It does not offer new insights or answers to the political questions it raises, but it does make extremely effective use of visual techniques—especially the spatial composition of the panavision image and conflicts in scale—in order to explore and express the political conflict. The same could be said for Antonioni's earlier films that focused on personal relationships: They never offered solutions but innovatively used visual techniques to explore and express the nature of the problem in a very perceptive way, and by so doing they expanded the expressive possibilities of cinema. The reason this lack of a solution was attacked in *Zabriskie Point* and not in the other films is that people have different expectations for a "political" film. Antonioni saw the political conflict as the milieu in which two young people interact: "I think that this film is about what two young people feel. It is an interior film. Of course, a character always has his background."[7] The limitations of the film seem to lie in the presentation of the characters. The values result from examination of the environment.

[6] Michelangelo Antonioni, "Let's Talk About Zabriskie Point," *Esquire* (August 1970), p. 146.

[7] Antonioni, quoted in Marsha Kinder, "Zabriskie Point," *Sight and Sound* (Winter 1968–1969), p. 27.

Zabriskie Point is most reminiscent of *Eclipse* (supposedly Antonioni's favorite), especially in structure. Both films concern a young man and woman, associated with two contrasting worlds, who come together for a brief period, make love, and then separate. Both films have a plane sequence associated with escape from one's orbit. Each ends with a brilliant sequence that has the greatest visual impact of any in the film and that concerns the relationship of people and objects. In *Eclipse* objects have replaced people; in *Zabriskie Point* the objects are destroyed. In *Eclipse* the contrast between Piero's world of business and Vittoria's world of humanity is defined primarily by pace; in *Zabriskie Point* the contrast is expressed mainly through spatial compositions. Although their limitations may be caused by the outside world, human relationships are clearly the focus in *Eclipse,* but in *Zabriskie Point* the focus is on the world in which Mark and Daria live. However, Mark and Daria are presented as individuals, neither of whom really fits into the world he inhabits. Mark wants to be a radical without belonging to any radical organization; Daria works as a typist for the Dunes Realty Company, though her own life style and values are clearly in conflict with those of her employers. Their brief encounter in the desert, apart from their ordinary milieu, supposedly has a profound effect on Daria, but this is very difficult to believe because of the poor acting of Daria Halprin and Mark Frechette and because the dialogue is so banal. In earlier films, the sparse dialogue was compensated for by the extraordinary expressiveness of Monica Vitti, Jeanne Moreau, and Marcello Mastroianni, but here the gestures and facial expressions are as wooden and flat as the language. The two young people and their relationship are developed superficially.

Nevertheless, the film effectively explores the environment in which these two people exist. In a sequence where Mark is walking down a Los Angeles street to find a phone, the space is crowded with billboards, telephone poles, wires, and automobiles. Everything seems bigger than in real life. He passes a giant in an advertising display, which makes him look like a dwarf. The object-oriented culture alters one's self-image. It is hard to believe this is panavision because suddenly everything looks so cramped, as though one needed a larger image to fit everything into the shot. In the real-estate office the miniature model of the desert, complete with plastic people, fills the entire screen and alters the scale. Later, in an overhead shot of Daria's car driving along a desert road, she is reduced to the same scale as the plastic people. While these shifts dwarf Daria, they magnify her boss (played by Rod Taylor, the only known actor in the film). In his suite of plush offices he is set against many scales of reality—the miniature models and small television images before him and downtown Los Angeles seen through the window behind him. One close-up makes Taylor look as big as the Richfield Building. Later, a low-angle shot catches a corner of his desk and the view through the window, with Taylor in the center looming skyward like the giant whom Mark encountered on the street. Once Mark steals the plane, he soars above Los Angeles and reduces the houses and freeways to miniatures. But when he meets Daria, they transcend this size distortion with their game; the shadow of the plane on the desert is similar in size to that of the car. They are both in the same scale, which prepares us for their human encounter.

The establishment world is dehumanized. No character is individualized, not even Daria's boss. The people are interchangeable with each other, with objects, and with machines. Human voices are often distorted through some kind of mechanical device. The executives approach each other in opposing groups, all wearing the same kind of suit, and they murmur of marinas,

Zabriskie Point

dollars, and percentages. Their dialogue is as insignificant as the bland background music in their office building. They are defined not by what they say or do but by what they wear and where they are. Besides the business executives, the establishment world includes the robot-like cops in their ominous uniforms, set against the wire caging in their cars or in jail, holding their guns, wearing their plastic visors or gas masks, distorting their voices through loudspeakers, screeching their sirens, never without the paraphernalia that defines them. There is also the common man—the middle-class family driving their camper (which is pulling a boat) through Death Valley. The father is defined by the stereo-typed costume of the American tourist—bermuda shorts, camera dangling from his neck. The car is full of labels to prove they have been to see all the sights, as if an external record will compensate for the absence of internal experience. These images are very familiar; it is as if these people have intentionally modeled themselves after the clichés that advertising has sold them. The desert accentuates their absurdity.

As the setting for the brief interaction of Mark and Daria, the desert is contrasted with Los Angeles. The full potential of pana-vision is used to reveal its horizontal openness. Both its spatial vastness and its muted colors define its moral implications. Death Valley is not sterile, but neutral. In contrast to Los Angeles, it imposes no qualities, pressures, or clichés and thereby accentu-ates what is already there in the individual. The emotionally disturbed children who tease and frighten Daria are not wanted by the city, so they come to Death Valley. The desert does not undo the damage done by society but merely makes their perversity easier to perceive. They are still casualties of an object-oriented culture like the empty billboards and abandoned cars and piano that lie dead by the road.

Three key sequences in *Zabriskie Point*—the opening, the desert love scene, and the explosion—suggest two competing concep-tions of cinema: film as commentary on the contemporary scene versus film as autonomous fantasy. In the opening, which functions like a prologue, a meeting of student radicals is handled from both perspectives. During the titles we see a golden haze that gradually becomes a sharply focused image of an individual, then slips out of focus back into the haze while another person is selected for scrutiny. The colors are brighter than in most other shots, and the technique reminds us that we are watching a film. The audio is comparable to the visual as audible dialogue drifts in and out of electronic music. The sequence that follows treats the same subject and setting in a naturalistic, documentary style. We recognize a meeting of white and black radicals (including Kathleen Cleaver) in a rather small room. Unlike the title sequence, there is seldom a shot of an individual, for the room is overcrowded and people visually overlap as do their voices. Although it is difficult to follow what they say, some of the comments define the political issues of the film: What does it take to make a white radical? Does one have to fight guns with guns? When Mark says he is willing to die alone, suddenly there is silence and everyone looks at him. He becomes the central focus, and the film drops the documentary style.

In both the love scene and the explosion, the double perspective is fused. Although both scenes have clear revolutionary implications, they are presented as Daria's personal fantasies— or at least their reality status is ambiguous. These orgies of sex and destruction, which are so terribly threatening to the establishment, are presented in a style that is joyfully unconventional, both musically and visually, and that creates the most exhilarating moments in the film. In the desert love scene, we see sensuous bare skin on warm sand; like the golden haze, the sand accentuates the individuals. Unfortunately, however, the stilted acting style of Mark and Daria undermines the spontaneity necessary for the sequence and, indeed, creates a kind of embarrassment in the audience as they strive unsuccessfully for joyful freedom. Yet these qualities are achieved by the anonymous lovers, who become formal properties of the scene rather than having to express themselves as individuals. Antonioni knew that whatever his own intentions, and despite its esthetic power, this sequence would fascinate and horrify middle-class Americans who so greedily gobbled up the nasty innuendos about the victims in the Sharon Tate murder and the detailed descriptions of the accused Manson family's sexual activities in Death Valley.

The first explosion of the house in the final sequence is shocking, but as it is repeated from different angles we become more interested in it as an esthetic experience. There are no bodies, no blood, no physical violence. And once we move to the slow-motion explosion of objects out of context, the tone becomes jubilantly playful. A mind has been altered—not only Daria's but also Antonioni's (if we compare this sequence to the final montage of objects in *Eclipse)* and perhaps some of the minds in the audience. When books and newspapers are destroyed, we are suddenly reminded of the newsreel footage of book-burnings in Hitler's Germany or in *Fahrenheit 451.* Then Antonioni abruptly

Zabriskie Point

cuts back to Daria. The final shot is of a glowing desert sunset, which reinforces the double perspective. In color it is linked to the explosion and the golden haze; it may suggest that such revolutionary action is on the horizon. Yet the shot also alludes to the Bank of America billboard in Los Angeles and the establishment world of advertising, perhaps reminding us that the explosion is also an artificially constructed fantasy. On the other hand, the Bank of America is one of the chief targets of the student radical movement, which sees it as a symbol of the materialistic culture. The ambiguity is purposely unresolved.

In evaluating this film, it is not adequate to make a simple distinction between the success of form and the failure of content. Instead, we must recognize that the film attempts various combinations—between the external environment and inner lives of characters, between film as commentary on reality and as autonomous fantasy. Some of the film's aspects, then, are devel-

348

oped more successfully than others; the weakness of the main characters and of their relationship can be located in their poor acting, which fails to compensate for the sparseness and banality of parts of the script. Antonioni's understanding of a culture's visual statement about itself and his ability to create autonomous fantasy in film remain powerful despite the fact that he is working in an alien land. His conception of what is needed to express the inner lives and relationships of individuals in that culture appears inadequate and hence cannot be successfully realized in film.

THE CONFORMIST (1970)

Though Bertolucci's film (like *The Damned* and *The Wild Child*) does not deal with political issues in a contemporary setting, it nonetheless explores the roots of behavior that lie beneath all political thought and action. It focuses on the conflicts between entrapment and freedom, inner and outer reality, as protagonist Marcello Clerici struggles to conceal the madness in his background by seeking normality in the Fascist Party. The style that successfully expresses these conflicts is not the realism that Godard requires but an expressionism that, as in *The Cabinet of Dr. Caligari,* interprets the madness of an individual and a society. At times it incorporates the surreal, which, as in the films of Buñuel, reveals the incongruity of fascism with its rigorous conformity disguising an impulse toward madness. Despite these links to earlier films and its 1930's setting, *The Conformist* revitalizes form and theme both esthetically and politically.

Like *Blow-Up* and *Performance, The Conformist* on first viewing seems to have a random structure that uses flashback to move unpredictably through time. Yet on second viewing we realize that repetition and association provide a tight narrative control, implying that present and future are inevitably shaped by the past. Within a highly erratic series of flashbacks, the film establishes its time boundaries with the exact dates of three murders: For most of the film, the present is October 15, 1938, the day on which, at 4 P.M., Marcello participates in the assassination of Quadri, his old liberal professor, and his wife; the flashbacks take us to March 25, 1917, the day young Marcello thought he had murdered the chauffeur; the film ends in 1945, when Marcello goes out "to watch a dictatorship fall." Apart from the opening and closing sequences, the film's "present" takes place in the automobile carrying Marcello and Manganiello, his political accomplice, to the murder. The first flashback takes Marcello's mind back to a conversation with Italo Montanari, his blind Fascist friend, at a radio station, where he also speaks to a Fascist official. When the official asks him about his motives for joining the party, Marcello flashes forward (within the flashback) to his first visit to the Fascist minister, who is making love to a woman in black sprawled on his desk, to whom Marcello assigns the face of Anna, Quadri's wife (played by Dominique Sanda), whom the audience has not yet seen. Within this sequence, time shifts constantly among these three points.

At times the associative link between flashbacks can be fully understood only after one has seen the entire film. A number of consecutive sequences reveal Marcello's attempts to deal with his own pressing guilt, not only about his past experience but about the assassination, which, we in the audience do not yet know, lies at the end of his journey. First, he questions his mad father about his role in World War I and asks him if he feels shame. Then the film cuts to the present in the automobile, where Manganiello is telling a story about having committed four unnecessary murders when he failed to receive a counter-order. When Manganiello reminds him that it is too late to save Quadri's wife, Marcello gets out of the car, which follows along beside him, flashing his mind back to the scene that led to his shooting of the chauffeur. The association, however, is based not only on the concrete details of the car but on the pervasive sense of guilt, which leads his mind to the next flashback—the church confession required for his forthcoming marriage, in which he confesses the full details of the homosexual encounter and shooting. He arrogantly tells the priest that he has already repented for past sins: "Now I ask forgiveness from society . . . I'm confessing for the crimes I'll commit tomorrow."

While this flashback technique leads to great mobility in time and an exhilarating cutting pace, Bertolucci also uses frequent repetition and parallelism to make the narrative structure express a sense of inevitability. The first three sequences are strikingly parallel to the final three scenes set in 1945. In the opening sequence we find Marcello on the bed, apparently alone in a darkened hotel room, with a flashing neon sign lighting the room with intermittent bursts of red. As he leaves the room, we learn for the first time that someone is lying naked, face down on the bed, beside him. The last scene finds him once again in a darkened bedroom, with reddish lighting (this time provided by fire), as he looks over his shoulder at a street boy sitting on his bed in the makeshift

The Conformist

dwelling he has set up in the passageways of the Colosseum. On a phonograph the boy plays the song that was being sung in the radio station in the film's second scene. There he met Italo and flashed back to fragments of sculpture being moved about in the minister's palace. In the next to last scene, he also meets Italo and sees the broken head of a Mussolini statue being dragged through the streets. In the third sequence, Marcello goes to visit his fiancée Julia, whose black and white striped dress pattern is repeated in barred light from the venetian blinds. The 1945 sequence begins in the same apartment; Julia is again wearing stripes, this time vertical; though her mother is no longer there, her picture evokes her presence in the earlier scene; the lighting is again uneven, this time fading off and on as the chaos outside results in power failures. Both sequences include important shots from the same camera angle. The hallway and parlor of the apartment are divided by a wall that juts into the foreground like a wedge; the camera shoots directly at the wedge. In the first of these depth focus shots, Julia and Marcello are on the left in the parlor, and her mother, who is about to bring forth the anonymous letter about Marcello's dubious background, is on the right in the hallway. In the 1945 sequence, Julia is on the left and Marcello on the right. Just as she is about to tell him that she knows of his involvement in the Quadri murder, the camera moves up the hallway, making her disappear. Then she suddenly appears in the hall to tell him that her feelings for him haven't changed. This kind of repetition successfully expresses the ways in which one can be trapped by the past, inevitably living out its dictates. But unfortunately Bertolucci is not content with this structural statement; he reinforces it by having Marcello encounter Lino, the chauffer he thought he had killed, in a melodramatic dénouement that simplifies rather than deepens the relationship between present and past.

This repetition occurs not only in major sequences but in significant details throughout the film. The obsessiveness of Raul, the Fascist official, is expressed visually by the hundreds of walnuts arranged neatly throughout his white office; later Marcello develops the same characteristic, and the surfaces of his apartment are covered with rows of apples. In the first sequence, Marcello expresses mild distaste as he covers his wife naked buttocks, as later he covers his mother's naked thighs, suggesting the roots of his sexual ambiguity. Painted blue skies with puffy white clouds provide the artificial backdrop for several scenes. Often repetition takes the form of a visual enactment of a verbal statement. In the radio station, Marcello tells Italo of his fiancée: "Whenever we're alone together, she jumps on me." Later in her apartment, we see this acted out. On the train, as Julia tells Marcello how her six-year affair with Perpuzzio began, Marcello, voyeuristically aroused, re-enacts the seduction. To add another dimension to the repetition, Julia's confession of this early affair parodies Marcello's confession in the church, a parallel he ironically underscores when he pulls down the black shade, reminding us of the confessional, which darkens half the screen. The repetition extends to camera movement, as in the scene where Marcello goes to the hotel and surreptitiously observes lesbian play between Anna and Julia. As he walks down the hall to the room, the camera tracks backward, widening the distance. As he returns, he and the camera move toward each other, telescoping time and space and reminding us of a similar camera movement the first time we saw him leave this hotel in the opening sequence (which is, actually, later in "real" time). The repetition also occurs in the music, with motifs linked to specific characters or places, thereby providing possible associative links between flashbacks. The singing paraders in the Colosseum evoke memories of the violet vender singing the "Internationale," and the music from the street boy's phonograph recalls the trio (reminiscent of the Andrews Sisters) in the radio station singing "Who Is Happier Than I."

While repetition is extremely successful in developing thematic implications, probably the most striking characteristic of *The Conformist* is the consistently brilliant visual imagery, the extraordinary work of cameraman Vittorio Storaro. Rarely since *Citizen Kane* has a film appeared in which the visual composition of every shot is so carefully controlled. This quality has led some critics to charge Bertolucci with self-indulgence (a charge also frequently aimed at Welles), implying that the visuals are not integral to the film's meaning. But we would argue that the choice of environments, lighting, and camera angle are essential in expressing important elements of the film such as the conflict between narrow enclosed space and open expanse. While one might assume that the former is linked to entrapment and the latter to freedom, the dichotomy is not so simple. Two of the most striking open environments, white and expansive, are the huge official ministerial hall, which contains only the private secretary's desk in the middle of the room, and the insane asylum, which is like an open Roman amphitheater. The visual similarity between asylum and hall ironically implies the link between fascism and madness. The building in Ventemiglia where Raul has his office is particularly ambiguous. When Marcello enters, he pauses to look at a huge painting in the hallway. An ancient woman hurries him inside, telling him testily that this is no museum. The whore, whom he encounters inside the first room (again, in memory he has given her Anna Quadri's face), announces more than once that she is crazy. Beyond this lies Raul's large white office lined with walnuts. Bordello or museum, office or asylum? Or are these elements fused in a vision of institutionalized chaos? The link between open space and entrapment is comically presented in the scene where Marcello and Julia stand in the open square, with the Eiffel Tower in the background; he shrewdly gains his freedom to pursue Anna by entrapping Julia in the narrow confines of the taxi that carries her off alone to the tower.

Throughout the film the car is the main metaphor for Marcello's encapsulation; as he rides to his destiny, it is as if he is entrapped in the choices he has made in his rides with Lino the chauffeur and with Manganiello. When Lino carries the young Marcello off to his room, he leads him through hallways filled with hanging sheets, mysteriously animated by the wind. After the shooting, Marcello remains locked in the small room, in the fetal position, until he is released by the wind, which blows open the window and continues to blow at intense moments throughout the film—as in the scene, shot from an extreme upward angle as if from the leaves' perspective, where he walks with his mother through the leaf-strewn yard after having gotten rid of her chauffeur/lover.

In these encapsulated environments the camera frequently shoots through glass—both inside from without and outside from within, as if to accentuate Marcello's detachment from experience and the separation of inner and outer reality. In the radio station, for example, we first see Marcello's dark outline against the glass wall of a recording room. Although this studio is framed by the dark outer room, which contains Marcello and the camera, its dazzling whiteness and the lively animation of the singers with their black and white polka-dotted dresses and their curly red wiglets make it seem more expansive. A later shot shows Marcello pacing back and forth near the glass so that we cannot see its boundaries; he is telling Italo his father's story of how he met a lunatic who turned out to be Hitler. His movements almost make him seem a part of the song and dance number ("Who Is Happier Than I") that is going on behind him, a fusion enriched by the frequent use of superimposed reflections. As Italo broadcasts a propaganda speech about the Italian-German Alliance, Marcello's reflection is juxtaposed with Italo's image, suggesting that they are an embodiment of the "mutual alliance." This triple-layered imagery is a visual equivalent of the triple time scheme developed by the complex flashbacks already described.

The ambiguity about which side of the glass is enclosed is also developed in the honeymoon train sequence. Although logic tells us that Marcello and Julia are enclosed inside the train, as in the train scene in *La Chinoise,* when the camera shoots the outside world flashing by, the window seems like a two-dimensional framed motion picture screen. Later, as Marcello and Julia make love, the landscapes, tinted gold and blue, are like a romantic backdrop that they are projecting, an idea reinforced when the images are superimposed on their bodies and ironically undercut when we see their comically wiggling feet.

In the dance sequence the entrapment is treated as a romantic bewitchment that entices the characters as well as the camera. The sequence opens with the camera tracking after Anna and Julia as they run toward the circular ballroom and shooting at the inviting interior through frosted windows (on which we see a picture of Laurel and Hardy, adding a comic touch). Once inside, the camera pans around the room, resting finally on the strikingly costumed figures of Anna and Julia leaning against a booth in the left foreground and sizing up the ballroom before they take over. The women do a tango that draws the other dancers into an admiring circle around them. Marcello is frightened by their extravagant display, urging Quadri to "make them stop." The professor replies, "Why? They're so charming!" But that is precisely why Marcello fears them. Julia undergoes a magical transformation (which could be explained more mundanely by her drunkenness), shouting, "This is Paris . . . I'm a New Woman." Then the music shifts, and Anna and Julia lead the others in a circle dance. The camera follows the line of dancers as they carry off Quadri, leaving Marcello in his seat. As the line dances out the door, the camera remains inside and follows their circle through the window but pauses when it reaches Manganiello the incongruous, seated alone in a far corner. Then it cuts to an overhead shot of the almost empty room as Marcello walks across the dance floor to pass Manganiello information about the coming murder. As he is walking back to his seat, the dancers reenter and entrap Marcello as Manganiello

The Conformist

escapes out the door. The camera then peers down at the frightened Marcello, who draws himself in like a child as if to protect himself from the dancers who encircle him (as he was earlier encircled by Quadri's colleagues as they marched him into the study). Throughout this sequence, the camera's movements are almost choreographed, including both inner and outer space, and adding to the exhilaration of graceful motion.

But the enchanting vision of entrapment offered by the dance is completely reversed by the murder sequence that immediately follows. As Marcello and Manganiello drive toward the assassination, both offer fantasies that show their desire to escape from their inevitable task: Marcello describes a dream in which, after Quadri successfully restores his eyesight, Marcello runs off with Anna, who loves him (just as he had earlier asked her to run off to Brazil in the dancing school scene); Manganiello, who is angry with Anna because her presence complicates the murder, muses incongruously, "That's love for you . . . I just meant that sometimes love can work miracles." But their desire for escape is thwarted as the sequence brings together all kinds of entrapment imagery encountered throughout the film. The confinement of both victims and assassins is stressed by shots through the tiny rearview mirror and the windshield; the wipers try to clear the frost, which further isolates them. The camera looks through the back window into the gold and beige interior of Quadri's car; the calm muted colors belie the impending horror, as does the snow scene that surrounds them. When their progress is blocked by another car, they all pause, uncertain what to do; the camera offers a slow montage of shots through various windows, emphasizing the tense stillness broken only by the wind, which has accompanied violence throughout the film. When Quadri finally gets out of the car, there is a conventional shot of the sun's rays streaming through the trees as if to deny with its openness the entrapment of his situation. However, the forest produces a group of assassins who stab him ritualistically one by one and finally encircle him for the kill like a pack of wolves. As Anna flees from her car, she runs over to Marcello, who is seated impassively behind a closed frosted window, wincing only at the sound of gunshots. Screaming and whining in inarticulate terror, she claws against the window, the camera hovering close by to record their faces. When she finally realizes he will not help her, she runs off into the woods. Again the open spaces offer no sanctuary as the killers hunt her down like a wild beast, the hand-held camera moving along in agitated pursuit. We see her stumble and turn, her face covered with blood, and she

The Conformist

falls, like Lena in *Shoot The Piano Player,* against the deceptive softness of the snow. Marcello's terrible inaction, which results in Anna's murder, expresses the final gap between the chaotic desires of his own emotional life and the "normality" he seeks through the bizarre predictability of fascism. In denying Anna, who is so much like him in her sexual ambiguity and disguised intensity, he is actually denying himself and the last possibility of integrating his inner and outer life.

Like Anna, Marcello had been drawn to Quadri as a wise teacher who could possibly cure his distorted vision, both in his dream and in their first meeting in Paris. The scene in Quadri's study is one of the few in the film that explicitly treats the philosophical questions underlying Italy's political situation; it also presents the alternative course of action that Marcello could have chosen. As part of his own plan to prepare for Quadri's assassination, Marcello decides to stage a scene with his old professor. He begins by evoking the memory of their classroom days, when windows and doors were always shut so that Quadri's voice made the strongest impression. To enclose the office like the classroom and to act out his description of Plato's myth of the cave (the subject of his thesis, which he abandoned when Quadri left Italy for political reasons), Marcello closes a window, plunging the left side of the room into darkness. As the two men move in and out of darkness and bright silhouette the camera, too, alternates between them, stressing the tension between appearance and reality, vision and blindness. Quadri insists that in Fascist Italy they see only the shadows. When he tells

Marcello he is not really a Fascist, we at first wonder if Quadri has been fooled by the charade, but upon reflection we realize that indeed Marcello's fascism is only a political appearance that disguises the underlying psychological reality.

The Conformist (like *The Damned*) expands its political dimension through the incorporation of a variety of myths. In addition to Plato's myth of the cave, several other classical references are used ironically: Blind Italo, a corrupt Tiresias whose prophecy is Fascist propaganda, leads Marcello into the Dante-like inferno of the Colosseum; Quadri is murdered ritualistically like Julius Caesar, evoking power-hungry and decadent Rome; Anna and Julia, particularly in the dance scene, are like sirens, yet they are victimized by Marcello. An interesting and subtle reference is made to the form of classical drama. The time structure of the film creates an inverted dramatic irony: The protagonist knows more than the audience. Cinema itself has created myths to which the film alludes. As Anna poses with hands in pockets and cigarette dangling from her mouth, she evokes the strangely masculine sexuality of Marlene Dietrich. In turn, the authentic details of setting, costuming, automobiles, and music tend to mythologize the period (as *Bonnie and Clyde* did with the Depression). The most pervasive mythology, however, is Freudian. The basic Oedipus conflict is acted out in several ways: Contemptuous of a seductive mother, Marcello nevertheless gets rid of her chauffeur/lover; forced to reject his own father, he is both drawn to and hostile toward Quadri, seducing his wife and ultimately destroying them both; his unresolved guilt is expressed in a fastidious homosexuality, which he shares with other Fascists and which is overemphasized in his final lingering gaze on the street boy in the Colosseum.

Thus the characteristics of *The Conformist* result in an implicit political statement about fascism: It is at once the cause and effect of psychic entrapment; its appearance of compulsive, orderly normality covers a fear of madness. Finally, the film's plot and structure suggest that madness must inevitably follow from the unbridged gap between inner experience and outer behavior.

the
ultimate
performance

Personality is persona, a mask. The world is a stage, the self a theatrical creation: "The self, then, as a performed character, is not an organic thing...it is a dramatic effect arising diffusely from a scene that is presented...."

Norman O. Brown
Love's Body

The innovative complexity of *Performance* (1970), directed by Donald Cammell and Nicolas Roeg, requires us to explore it from many perspectives. Like the films discussed in Chapter 6, *Performance* is explicitly concerned with the arts of performing and of cinema itself and emphasizes in theme and development the value of a subjective, transforming vision. It suggests a Western version of *Woman in the Dunes* in which a man goes underground into what he thinks is a bizarre trap or hideout, only to have his mind altered and expanded to a new view of life. Concerned, like the films discussed in Chapter 7, with the mythic dimension of human experience, it traces the merging of two basic myths—of the gangster and the rock star—but goes beyond them to incorporate archetypal elements from literature, painting, and philosophy. Like *Bonnie and Clyde, Rosemary's Baby,* and *The Shooting,* this film takes a self-conscious attitude toward the genres of the gangster thriller and the trip movie, simultaneously parodying them both and greatly expanding their possibilities. Finally, the radicalism of its themes and techniques have raised extraordinarily difficult problems in arriving at an evaluation based on the film itself.

Performance has evoked both passionate approval and horrified contempt. Larry Cohen of the *Hollywood Reporter* believed that "in its own way, it's as great and disturbingly mature a work of art as we are likely to witness in 1970; the most compelling, mesmerizing visual experience of the year." Peter Schjeldahl of the *New York Times* praised its "organic unity and consistent energy" and calls it "that perfect poisonous cinematic flower." Leonard Brown of the *Los Angeles Free Press* applauded the film's honesty and moral health. With equal passion better-established critics have called it "a picture without a single visible excuse for its existence" (Arthur Knight, *Saturday Review*), "the most disgusting, the most completely worthless film I have seen since I began reviewing" (Richard Schickel, *Life*). John Simon in the *New York Times* asks: Is this "The Most Loathsome Film of All?" *Time* and *Newsweek* respectively assert that the film "alternates between incomprehensible chichi and flatulant boredom" and is "the ugliest, most contrived and self-indulgent film of the year."

Why all this intensity from the guardians of public taste in the mass circulation journals? This film, especially when misunderstood, evokes the strongest fears and defenses surrounding questions that have polarized our minds and hearts—questions of sexual identity and morality; problems of violence on the streets, in the counting houses, and in the bedroom; relationships between the individual and the groups on which he depends. These are problems we all confront in our search for survival, sanity, and the "good life." As the lawyer in the film asserts, "What's really on trial here are the ethics of a culture." We have come to believe that even the critics who claim the film has nothing to say are in fact reacting to the radical and disturbing position it takes on all these issues.

It is impossible to be neutral about a film that claims "Nothing is true—everything is permitted." *Performance* rejects all conventional distinctions, limitations, and preconceptions about identity and morality. At times it brings to mind some of the most innovative expressions of this radicalism in other media. For example, R. D. Laing, the existential psychologist, argues in *The Politics of Experience* that a man cannot live the free life until he has taken the ultimate risk of consciousness—the descent into madness. Like certain works by Norman Mailer—especially *Why Are We In Viet Nam?*—the film implies that the sources of creativity and destructiveness are inextricably fused. As in William Burroughs' writings, both the visual imagery and the language evoke a merging and metamorphosis of time, space, and flesh. But the works that offer the richest parallels with *Performance* are Norman O. Brown's *Love's Body,* Herman Hesse's *Steppenwolf,* and Jorge Luis Borges' "The South."

In *Love's Body,* Brown is concerned with the question of how man can break out of the sterility of his private life and the destructiveness of his public behavior. The book bases its program on a concept of archetypal or collective consciousness that develops out of the work of Freud, Jung, Melanie Klein, Geza Roheim, and others. Linking his ideas to poetry, mythology, and Eastern thought, Brown attacks rational classification of "real" phenomena because it denies the imaginative and symbolic connections the unconscious makes in its efforts to unify experience. According to Brown, we must accept life as a symbolic representation of the inherent nature and patterns of the unconscious mind. Brown exhorts us to question the ego-centered individuation on which we base our hopes for personal fulfillment and suggests that we reconsider the concept of the species as one body, linked together by powerful psychic ties that unify experience. Thus particular instances of time, space, personal identity, and indeed, life itself are not distinct from each other but are completely fluid, both continuous and interchangeable. From this reborn awareness will come life-oriented (rather than death-oriented) patterns of private and public behavior.

This belief in the fluid nature of identity and psychic life has also influenced contemporary thought through fiction, in the short narratives of Borges and in the works of Hesse, especially *Steppenwolf.* The basic characters, plot, and themes of *Performance* bear a striking resemblance to those in the Hesse novel. The central character in both works is a man who is fleeing death within his own world. In *Performance* Chas (James Fox) is a gangster; in *Steppenwolf* Harry Haller is an intellectual. Though each character is contemptuous of the bourgeois class, each is bourgeois. Each encounters a new world of unlimited possibilities where he meets three people in a *ménage à trois* who are all reflections of himself: a young, boyish girl to whom he is very much attracted (Lucy, the young French girl, in *Performance;* Hermine in *Steppenwolf*); a voluptuous blond who is sent to his bed by one of the others (Turner sends Pherber to Chas; Hermine sends Maria to Harry); and a beautiful, androgynous young man (Turner; Pablo). The young man is loved by both women yet is attracted to the man; he is associated with foreign lands—particularly the East—and is a wonderful musician capable of playing any instrument. He turns the man onto drugs and exhorts him to madness; he can transform himself into other images and acts as the main character's host in a magic ritual that reveals his multiple identities. After exploring these identities, the central character commits murder, at the request of the victim, who feels "stuck" and sees death as a "means of breaking into the beyond." In *Performance* the victim is Turner, in *Steppenwolf* Hermine. This act of murder allows the man to incorporate the victim into his own personality and to return to life within his own world, no longer fearing his inevitable death. The situations are parallel because they are vehicles for developing parallel themes: the concept of multiple identity in which one must destroy the single or dual personality in order to break through to the unlimited possibilities of being, which necessarily include violence and insanity

> Harry consists of a hundred or a thousand selves, not of two. His life oscillates, as everyone's does, not merely between two poles, such as the body and the spirit, the saint and the sinner, but between thousands and thousands, between innumerable poles.
> ... It appears to be an inborn and imperative need of all men to regard the self as a unit. However often and however grievously this illusion is shattered, it always mends again. ... And if ever the suspicion of their manifold being dawns upon men of unusual powers and of unusually delicate perceptions ... they have only to say so and at once the majority puts them under lock and key, calls science to aid, establishes schizomania and protects humanity from the necessity of hearing the cry of truth from the lips of these unfortunate persons.[1]

The connections with Borges are made explicit in the film through visual and verbal allusions. Borges' *Personal Anthology,* with his name and face prominently displayed on the cover, is clearly shown three times. During the stag-film sequence, there is a quick cut to one of the gangsters reading the book. During the titles at the end of the film, the book is one of the background shots. But the most important reference is the passage read by Turner (played by Mick Jagger), which helps to illuminate the theme of merging identities and the ambiguous ending of *Performance.*

Turner reads from a Borges story called "The South," about a

[1] Herman Hesse, *Steppenwolf,* trans. Basil Creighton (New York: Bantam Books, 1969), pp. 66–67.

362

man named Dahlmann, who, after reading *The Thousand and One Nights,* goes mad and is confined in a sanitarium where "they undressed him, shaved his head, bound him with metal fastenings to a stretcher; they shone bright lights on him until he was blind and dizzy, auscultated him, and a masked man stuck a needle into his arm." [2] This description reminds us of Chas, who has gone to Turner's Persian madhouse, where he is transformed. While in this "suburb of hell," Dahlmann "hated his identity." He seeks escape in *The Thousand and One Nights,* traveling with this exotic book into a new romantic adventure. Like Turner and Chas, "It was as if he was two men at a time"; simultaneously he was in the protective sanitarium and he was dreaming an adventure in southern Argentina where he encountered an oriental-looking young tough who "threw a long knife into the air, followed it with his eyes, caught and juggled it, and challenged Dahlmann to a knife fight." This is the passage that Turner reads aloud:

> From a corner of the room, the old ecstatic gaucho [his demon] . . . threw him a naked dagger, which landed at his feet. Dahlmann bent over to pick up the dagger, and felt two things. The first, that this almost instinctive act bound him to fight. The second, that the weapon, in his torpid hand, was no defense at all, but would merely serve to justify his murder. [3]

The story ends with Dahlmann's going out "into the plain" to encounter the romantic "death he would have chosen or dreamt."

Though Dahlmann could be compared with Turner and Chas, it is Turner, stuck in an identity he has grown to hate, who takes on Chas's challenge and becomes "two men at a time." One of the first images we see as the camera zooms into the hole Chas's bullet has blown into Turner's head is the face of Borges. When we see Turner's face in the white Rolls Royce instead of Chas's, we realize that Turner, like Dahlmann, has courageously gone "out into the plain" to encounter the death he has "chosen or dreamt." Throughout the film, Turner has used Borges' book in the way Dahlmann used *The Thousand and One Nights*—as a guide to his destiny and, more importantly, as a means of "suppressing reality" (the old lady in the train station says of Turner before we even see him, "He can't face reality"), offering in its place an expanded vision based on the transformation of myth, dream, and madness. Like Brown and Hesse, Borges offers a justification for fantasy, by

[2] Jorge Luis Borges, "The South," in *Ficciones* (New York: Grove Press, 1962), p. 168.
[3] *Ibid.,* p. 174.

means of which man can escape his limitations. Drawing on myths from many cultures, Borges stresses the potential multiplicity of psychic life, which can transcend death.

Performance ushers us into the future of film consciousness by presenting a vision embodying many of these radical concepts, and therefore it deserves careful attention. Essentially, the film is about unity, about the merging of life and death, reality and fantasy, sanity and madness, creativity and violence, male and female. *Performance* also merges the characteristics of the conventional gangster thriller and "trip" movie. The automobile, familiar symbol of power and mobility in the gangster film, is here elevated to a fairy-tale luxuriousness. Characters take revenge against enemies by spoiling the "tasty" finish of a gleaming black Rolls. The traditional moral distinction between the black and white horses of the western is ironically exaggerated as the white cars of the villainous Harry and Chas glisten and sparkle like jewels and the black car of the lawyer seems like an ominous trap. The first half of the film takes place in typical gangster settings: the bookie joint, gym, and night club, usually inhabited by Humphrey Bogart or George Raft. The important relationships are between men, implying that the homosexuality, which flares up in sado-masochistic violence, actually underlies the whole gangster world. Although the conventional moll is missing, she is suggested by Chas's bed partner, a night club singer, and by the silent black girl and the picture of the contortionist in the night club. The cockney slang, though frequently unintelligible to American audiences, is recognizable as an English counterpart to the special language spoken in gangster movies. In addition to playing with these conventions, *Performance,* like *Bonnie and Clyde,* explores the roots of the genre. In fact, a poster of Gene Hackman as Buck Barrow hangs on Chas's wall. The film establishes a bitter equation between big business and organized crime. It also explores the connections between the gangster and his exotic counterparts: the gaucho, the Persian bandit, and the Islamic assassin.

The second half of the film, which has been likened to the "trip" movie, actually avoids the clichés of this genre. Many of the characteristics conventionally used to portray the drug experience (fast cutting, strange camera angles, weird settings, heightened sexuality) are not limited to these scenes but are used throughout the film to define a world view. *Performance* develops an attitude toward drugs that suggests that they can teach and expand rather than merely distort. The mosaic table, which arouses Chas's new awareness of beauty, is indeed a gorgeous object. Jagger's performance of "Memo From T," which culminates the "trip," successfully merges aspects of the two worlds and corroborates Brown's argument for the unity of all experience.

The dialogue quickly establishes the film's central theme of merging in the context of social satire, where language is corrupted to disguise the interchangeability of business and crime. Both the bewigged lawyer and the fatherly gangster Harry Flowers have much to say about "merging" and "taking over." Since "business is business and progress is progress," the lawyer asserts that it is a "natural law" of business "to consolidate"; Flowers offers his Darwinian homily that "small business is against nature." Even more immediate than the message of the language is the cutting of the opening sequence, which visually merges sex, violence, money, and technology. But as the film progresses, the full range of cinematic techniques expresses this merging as a vision of how life is lived at a level of experience enriched by the collective unconscious.

Three techniques are particularly effective in the innovative development of this vision: point of view, cutting, and the repetitive and rhythmic use of visuals and audio. One of the most fascinating aspects of this film is its point of view. The opening sequence reveals both playfulness and well-controlled complexity. First we look at the powerful and beautiful jet plane as if we were on its level. Although we see the luxurious black Rolls from the same aerial overview, the effect is very different because of the distance. As the camera moves in, our experience with film conventions makes us asume that we are about to focus on an occupant of the car. When the film cuts to the sex scene in Chas's bedroom, we infer (wrongly) that we are getting a flashback from the consciousness of someone in the car. However, when we learn a little later that the car contains the lawyer and not Chas, we realize that we have been teased. Camera work and editing express not the motions of a single consciousness but a double or perhaps a multiple point of view.

A number of the film's shots are like free-floating perceptions, suggesting a consciousness that includes many perspectives and levels of seeing and knowing. For example, as Chas seeks a new identity for the passport photo, there is a quick flash of him as Turner. We see Chas in bed with Turner, who is quickly transformed into the young French girl. In whose consciousness do these changes take place?

Camera angles also contribute to the complexity of the point of view. As Chas enters Turner's house for the first time, the camera looks down at him from the top of the stairs. Who, if anyone, is seeing him from there? In the courtroom the camera mocks the heroic perspective by looking up at the lawyer's face from his toes. During the shooting sequence, the camera looks up at Chas from very low and down at Joey from very high. The wide-angle lens distorts Chas as it looks down on him in the telephone booth. From whose perspective do we see the highly magnified shots of the fly, the mushroom, and the mountainous nipple?

Thus we have a point of view for the camera that is omniscient in a new and powerful way. As in *Last Year at Marienbad,* past, present, future, and conditional are all accessible to the camera, but in this film they are not changed into the present time and personal vision of any individual character. Instead, the point of view is frankly clairvoyant, polymorphous in its perspective, and completely omniscient as its views phenomena. This point of view implies that all things may be known to a single encompassing consciousness (or perhaps to all minds). It suggests also that knowing is an experience far deeper and broader than our rational definitions would have us believe. Brown asserts in *Love's Body* that, "since the true psychic reality is the unconscious, the true psychic reality is collective; there is only one psyche, a general possession of mankind." [4] This view of the nature and importance of the collective psyche has developed quietly along with the more ego-oriented psychology of the last decades. The cross-cutting and camera angles of the point of view, which so many critics call purposeless, merely slick, or downright fraudulent, actually give controlled and effective visual expression to this aspect of psychic experience.

Cutting also prevents the separation of individual sequences that would ordinarily be perceived as remote in time, space, and concept. The sequence where Chas kills Joey demonstrates this merging function, which is significant to the structure of the film as a whole. It opens with cross-cutting between Chas driving up to his apartment and paint being flung onto its walls. As the paint (Godard red) splashes, it takes on the appearance of abstract expressionist painting. In this way, the destructiveness is linked to art and to "decorating," an important ambiguity in the film. Earlier, when Harry ordered the "decoration" of Joey's shop, the film quickly cut to the Brown boys breaking it up, which visually exposes the corrupt use of the term. As the violence in Chas's apartment becomes artful, we see the connotations of "decorating" expand so that the term is both corrupt and appropriate at the same time. Once Chas

4 Norman O. Brown, *Love's Body* (New York: Vintage Books, 1966), p. 86.

enters the apartment, the shots of the red paint are intercut with the bloody fight among Chas, Joey, and his friends, thereby strengthening the bonds between blood-lust and art and making the scene appear more violent than it really is. There is also a quick cut to Turner spray-painting a red wall, an image not recognizable until it is later intercut into the scene where Chas is dyeing his hair red. The identification between Chas and Turner is again underscored in red when, much later in the film, Chas washes out the dye, which drips down his face and makes him resemble the poster of Turner, to which the camera quickly cuts. Finally, when Joey is shot and dying, the entire screen turns red, as if to imply that death, the ultimate violence, is itself a red experience.

After Joey and his friend overpower Chas and begin whipping his bared buttocks, we cut back to the opening sequence, reestablishing rather blatantly Chas's sado-masochistic homosexuality. Then the film immediately cuts forward to Turner in his Persian paradise, suggesting the more subtle and complex homosexual

Performance

relationship that is to unfold. Before Joey dies, there is a flashback to Joey and Chas fighting as children (apparently the only conventional use of a flashback). After Joey's death, there is a quick cut to the back of Turner's head in his own bathroom, again taking the film forward in time and space, foreshadowing the symbolic complexity of the murder of Turner at the end of the film.

Other shots unify past, present, and future as they anticipate the final murder and reveal the extraordinary richness of the film's visual associations. As Turner sings his first song, he becomes three people as we see his seated black-clad body casting its shadow on the wall and reflected in the mirror. At the end of the song, he bends his head down in precisely the same way he does before Chas shoots him. The words of the song might allude to Chas's uncertain fate: "I might take ya down to the riverside, I might drown ya, I might shoot ya, I just don't know." Pherber adds another relevant chorus to the song in the scene where she tries to seduce Chas. She puts a small round mirror in the center of Chas's long-haired wig—at exactly the spot where the bullet is later to enter Turner's head. The wig is the one Turner is wearing when he appears as Chas in Harry Flowers' white Rolls. During the seduction scene, Pherber tells Chas that Turner has lost his demon; in the mirror flashes an image of the dying Joey, who also saw Chas as his demon. When Chas accuses Turner of poisoning him with the psychedelic mushroom, Turner replies that he has just bored a hole in his head so that he could get in there.

In the process of turning Chas on and altering his identity, Turner takes him backward and forward in time, supporting with visual imagery the movement of the cutting. Chas's first new identity, in pencil mustache and bowler hat, ironically takes us back to the earlier shots of the lawyer, whom Chas now resembles. When Chas puts on the wig and Persian robe that make him resemble Turner, he takes us back to the ancient image of the Islamic assassin but also moves us forward in the film to the final shot of Turner in the same wig. Supporting this double movement, Pherber says, "We've got to go much further out." Turner contradicts her: "We've got to go much further back." The concept of double motion is ironically corrupted in the courtroom scene where the lawyer, walking backward, declares, "Progress is progress." Like the child who walks backward in the final sequence, Turner wishes to move back with Chas, exploring the ancient roots of his "performance" —comparing him to the juggler for the king of Tuscany, naming juggling as the "third oldest profession," and telling Chas, "You've been on the road a million years." This association is emphasized by several allusions to other performers, like Van Gogh, James Dean, and Turner himself, whose acts are touched with madness and who meet an early death. The idea of timelessness projects beyond the film itself; the poster of Jim Morrison, which reads "It's over," not only suggests an artist who is stuck but actually prophesies his unexpected death. Turner's statement, "The only performance that makes it is the one that achieves madness," echoes Dahlmann's situation in "The South" and Pablo's speech to Harry Haller as he initiates him into the "magic theater" in *Steppenwolf:* "Just as madness in a higher sense is the beginning of all wisdom, so is schizomania the beginning of all art and all fantasy."

Another merging function of the cutting is to eliminate the distinction between the ordinary and the bizarre. After the initial sex scene, in which camera angles and cutting create ambiguity about the exact nature and extent of the violence, we cut to a series of shots that present the mundane quality of the morning after: the ringing alarm clock, the girl's face in the mirror with a drop of liquid rouge on her cheek, the plastic apartment with its Playboy-signed radio, the preparation of breakfast. Yet there is still another area between the bizarre and the banal, which is first shown to us as Chas does not ordinary calisthenics but isometrics, which suggest the tension of his life. As Chas gets dressed, we see that his back is crisscrossed with whip marks or scratches. Another linking occurs as we watch the girl dressing in the mirror and see her buttocks being encased in the rubber of her girdle. When Chas and the others "redecorate" by dropping acid on the lawyer's Rolls and shaving the chauffeur's head, we suddenly cut to a milkman, making his ordinary rounds, walking past a no-parking sign that says, "This garage is constantly in use," while the grotesque violence goes on behind the closed doors. A more complicated development of this contrast emerges as the camera cuts from the bizarre Turner house to Tony in his perfectly ordinary bedroom with his wife and child. The later cut to Tony at work suggests the masculine world of machinery and physical labor. When we see him next, he is in a gym, and the camera follows a boxer dressed in a lush blue satin robe, evoking a world where super-masculinity disguises latent homosexuality. The final scene in Tony's bedroom at first appears commonplace, but in an instant we learn that just out of camera range lurks the exotic presence of the gangsters. Once we discover Tony's betrayal of Chas, we also notice the Islamic dolls and camels, which visually relate back to the Persian paradise scene at the Turner house. The careful timing and cutting show us that the mundane can be touched unexpectedly with the bizarre

Performance

and grotesque. The film is teaching us a lesson that Brown, Hesse, and Borges would also have us learn: If we classify and try to fix the nature of phenomena, we close the mind to their potential relationships and are baffled by our experience.

The cutting also has a satiric function. In the courtroom sequence, for example, the film cuts from a mock-heroic upward shot of the jury through a merging of realities where color changes and a projector appears at the back of the jury box, to a screening of a pornographic film, the subject of which is similar to that of the opening sequence. The link is made among three audiences—the jury, which must judge the movie of life; the audience, which covertly watches the dirty movie; and we, the third audience, who watch *Performance.* The appearance of the projector implies that the jury is watching a movie in the courtroom, and when that movie turns out to be a sado-masochistic sex film, we realize the further implication that the trial in itself is a movie of perversion and sadism. This double context also develops visually the verbal play

370

on the words "merger" and "takeover" by linking their sexual and business connotations.

The final important technique of the film, dependent upon the cutting but actually subsuming it, is the innovative use of repetition and rhythm to integrate visual images and sound. The first component of this complex technique is recurring visual imagery, already illustrated in the use of the color red. Other groups of recurring images are automobiles, planes, doors, pictures, and mirrors. Perhaps most interesting is the mirror imagery, which we see for the first time in the opening sex scene, where Chas holds up a mirror to watch his partner going down on him. Here it is no more than a kind of sexual diversion. Later, in Harry's office, a painting of an obese man on horseback is repeatedly removed and returned to its place in front of a mirror. The apparently fixed images of painting are both interchangeable and superfluous. Refusing to buy a portrait, Turner acquires the empty frame to add to the collection in the closet, where his discarded body is stored after his murder. In contrast, the mirror provides a fluid series of images—an idea that is emphasized when Pherber films her own reflection with a motion picture camera. In the scene where Pherber and Chas are in bed, with Turner waiting in the wings, she uses a mirror to project her breast onto Chas's chest and his face inside her hair. She offers herself as a mirror to Chas so that he can see his female side, his *anima;* but she is also simultaneously functioning as a reflection of Turner. Pherber believes, like Hermine in *Steppenwolf,* that "we ought all to be such looking-glasses to each other and answer and correspond to each other."[5] When Chas asks what Turner wants, Pherber replies, "Maybe a little mirror . . . he lost his demon." Mirrors provide not merely a single reflection; rather, individual characters fluidly reflect different aspects of themselves and each other.

Repetition occurs not only with visual images but with whole scenes, frequently ritualistic in content—such as decorating, bathing, lovemaking, and killing—which link the two parts of the film's structure. All these actions are related, either visually or symbolically, to discovering or establishing identities. One of the strongest and most intriguing kinds of visual repetition is the temporary substitution of one individual for another in an important situation. In some shots, it is impossible to tell which of the characters (who can be made to look astonishingly alike) is being seen at a given moment. Sexual identity puzzles us as we get our first shot of

[5] Hesse, p. 200.

Turner in bed, naked beside a person whose sex we cannot determine no matter how carefully we peer. We still cannot tell the creature's sex through a long and active bathing scene, until she stands up and we see that it is a young French girl. The ambiguity of identity is given its strongest visual expression when we see Turner as Chas looking out of Harry's white Rolls in the final sequence.

At what level of experience does the film claim that this merging takes place? Hesse places it in the imaginative realm of the artist and the magical world of childhood (images of children pervade the film), "when the capacity for love . . . embraces not only both sexes, but all and everything, sensuous and spiritual, and endows all things with . . . a fairy-like ease of transformation such as in later years comes again only to a chosen few and to poets." [6] Brown goes further and suggests that there is a unity of the species such that we respond to our fellow creatures without sexual distinction: "If we are all members of one body, then in that one body there is neither male nor female; or rather there is both: it is an androgynous or hermaphroditic body, containing both sexes." He adds, "The tendency of the sexual instinct is to restore an earlier state of things, an earlier state of unity, before life was sexually differentiated." [7] This view of sexuality is difficult to understand, and its consideration does not imply acceptance, but the idea has a long history. Perhaps we are more willing to accept it in Plato's "Symposium" because there it is treated comically.

The theme of merging is also developed through recurring phrases in the dialogue that link the two parts of the film. Some of them also distinguish between the contexts in which they are uttered. In the night club scene, Dennis (Flowers' henchman) says that Chas is "an ignorant boy, an out-of-date boy." Harry and Dennis are condemning Chas because he has allowed his personal involvement with Joey to limit his ability to take orders and behave with the inhumanity necessary if he is to be valuable to Harry. Though Harry has often praised Chas for "enjoying his work" and "having the gift," these qualities threaten Harry's control. If Chas acts according to personal desire, he ceases to be a cog in Harry's machine, and Harry can no longer "push the buttons." Important in this argument is Harry's shouted question: "Who do you think you are?" Chas replies, "I know who I am, Harry." Thus the question of an individual's identity is linked to power and control. Later in the film, many of these phrases are repeated exactly or with subtle variations, as when Chas seeks a new

[6] *Ibid.*, p. 190.
[7] Brown, pp. 84–85.

372

identity for the passport photo. In this second context, these terms come to imply not a struggle for control of an individual's static identity but Turner's attempts to merge and expand the identities of himself and Chas. When Chas offers his new identity as the juggler Johnny Dean (a name perhaps suggested by the picture of James Dean in the basement), he asserts again, "I know who I am." Turner comments to Pherber that this boy is "a bit old-fashioned." Turner says that he knows that Chas "enjoys his work" and tells him, "You've got the gift." He calls Chas a "performer of natural magic" and "the lone ranger." Whereas Harry wants to limit Chas's involvement in his job, Turner wants to emphasize that Chas's "work" is a timeless acting out of an archetypal aspect of life. Turner says that he and Pherber "push the buttons"; unlike Harry, they do so (as they later push the magic mushroom buttons on Chas) to open, not close, the possibilities of Chas's identity. The contrasting meanings of a similar phrase in different contexts is perhaps most obvious in the repetition of "We'll find out tomorrow what's true and what isn't." For Harry, this means that anyone who doubts that reality is as he defines it will discover tomorrow the proof of his control. No one questions his assertion. When Chas later echoes this idea, Turner expresses the film's attitude toward reality by uttering "the last words of the old man on the mountain," which he has adopted as his personal motto: "Nothing is true—everything is permitted." What a contrast to Harry Flowers' motto, which ends with a clamorous "Me, me, me!"

Another playful kind of repetition is the extensive punning, developed both verbally and visually. We have already mentioned several examples—decorating, merging, dropping acid, pushing buttons. There are many others, of course, such as "Hairy" Flowers (remember the curls on Harry's naked arms), Rosie Bloom, and mind-blowing. In both parts of the film characters consciously pun. In the scene where Chas is shaving the head of the chauffeur, one hoodlum outrageously puns, "Hair today, gone tomorrow," which draws groans from his accomplices. After Chas appears with the red paint washed out of his hair, there is a head-spinning series of plays on "die," "dye," "died," "dyed," and "dead." The most powerful and significant pun of the film is developed with originality around the phrase "blow your mind." Just before killing him, Chas tells Joey who he is. "I am a bullet," he announces and proves his self-knowledge as he indeed shoots Joey. Later on, as he is about to go with Harry to be killed ("I've got to shoot off, now," he says), Chas takes his leave of Turner, who wants to go with him. In the context of merging identities established through-

373

out the film, Turner implies by this that he wants to go to the end of Chas's trip with him. Chas hesitates and cautions Turner, who claims that he knows what he is doing. Though Turner hesitates for a moment, Chas finally sees deeply into his need, abandons all sentimentality, and takes Turner on. He blows Turner's mind as Turner had earlier blown his. He gives Turner his identity—a bullet.

The movement of the actors, the motion of the camera, and the rhythmical pace of the cutting are integrated with elements of the sound track to form a highly controlled musical structure. In the night club scenes, flashbulbs explode rhythmically, freezing the shots and syncopating the dialogue. In Harry's bedroom, the exaggerated gestures and phrasing, the grotesque close-ups and sing-song delivery of the lines create the feeling of stylized opera. In the courtroom, the camera cuts and then zooms into the face of the defendant precisely at the moment when he purses his lips. In the trucking office, the electronic music belies the gangsters' claim that the equipment is "not maintained" and must be destroyed; the music carries over to the intercut scenes of the courtroom, ironically undercutting the lawyer's comment that "in this age of computers, words still have meaning." In his argument with Chas, as Harry says, "Me, me me!" the echoing sounds parallel exactly three backward movements of the camera as the office changes into an elongated green tunnel. In the scene where Turner performs a song, dancing with a long neon tube, and Chas also moves to the music, the editing keeps pace with the tempo, alternating between their faces with every beat; as Turner screams, the camera quickly cuts to the poster that presents a stylized version of his face with the same expression. The rhythmic pace is also varied by the use of several slow-motion scenes—Joey's death and the waitress serving the battered Chas in the train station. The slow-motion love scenes of the *ménage à trois* and between Chas and Lucy contrast sharply with the opening love scene in Chas's apartment, which is developed through fast cutting. Although Pherber tells the stoned Chas that "we just wanted to speed things up," the pacing of the second half is considerably slower than that of the first.

The rhythmic unity of pacing, imagery, and sound finds its best expression in Jagger's performance of "Memo from T." The sequence incorporates images that have appeared before—the drawer of bullets; the picture in front of the mirror, which will become the surrealistic portrait Turner refused to buy; the Musak, which now amplifies Jagger's rock and roll—transforming the parallel sequence in Harry's office early in the film. Jagger condemns the gangsters' inhumanity and their impotent lust for power as he tells Dennis, "You're the man who squats behind the man who works the Soft Machine." He warns them of their false view of identity: "Beware . . . of all the skins you breed." His exposure of these men is expressed visually as, strutting to the rhythm of his song, he strips them of their clothing. Though Dennis (who might have come right out of *Satyricon*) can be whipped up to a mockery of a musical freakout (snapping his fingers with artificial enthusiasm, mocking rhythm itself), he, like the others, is incapable of the real metamorphosis required by Turner's transforming power. Instead, these men are burned out by the song and lie, naked and lifeless, in the surrealistic, empty silence of the final shot.

Jagger's performance, in which he moves successfully through a variety of roles (the "faggy little leather boy from 1956," the

Performance

parody of Harry Flowers, and Turner/Jagger, the fabulous rock singer) is the film's strongest manifestation of its central concern—the value of the collective level of experience where all identities and performances are potentially accessible to everyone. But the ultimate performance is achieved by Cammell and Roeg in creating this film, which evokes such passionate responses by brilliantly expressing a radical view of human potentiality. Their performance liberates cinema by demonstrating in both form and content that "everything is permitted" to the creative imagination.

appendix 1
films
discussed

Ballet Mécanique (1924), Fernand Léger, France, 14 min., Museum of Modern Art.

The Battle of Algiers (1967), Gillo Pontecorvo, Italy, 120 min., CCM Films.

Battleship Potemkin (1925), Sergei Eisenstein, Soviet Union, 67 min., Museum of Modern Art.

Birth of a Nation (1915), D. W. Griffith, United States, 100 min., CCM Films.

Blackmail (1929), Alfred Hitchcock, England, 85 min., Museum of Modern Art.

Blow-Up (1967), Michelangelo Antonioni, England, 110 min., Films, Inc.

Bonnie and Clyde (1967), Arthur Penn, United States, 111 min., Warner Bros.

Breathless (1959), Jean-Luc Godard, France, 89 min., Contemporary Films.

The Cabinet of Dr. Caligari (1919), Robert Wiene, Germany, 50 min., Museum of Modern Art.

Un Chien Andalou (1928), Luis Buñuel and Salvador Dali, France, 20 min., Museum of Modern Art.

La Chinoise (1967), Jean-Luc Godard, France, 95 min., Leacock-Pennebaker.

Citizen Kane (1941), Orson Welles, United States, 119 min., CCM Films.

The Clowns (1971), Federico Fellini, Italy, 90 min., Levitt-Pickman Film Corp., 35 mm.

The Conformist (1970), Bernardo Bertolucci, Italy, 115 min., Paramount, Genesis Films, Ltd.

Contempt (1963), Jean-Luc Godard, France, 103 min., CCM Films.

The Damned (1969), Luchino Visconti, Italy, 150 min., Warner Bros.

La Dolce Vita (1961), Federico Fellini, Italy, 180 min., CCM Films.

Dream of the Wild Horses (1960), Denys Colomb de Daunant, France, 9 min., Creative Film Society.

8¹/₂ (1963), Federico Fellini, Italy, 135 min., CCM Films.

Faces (1968), John Cassavetes, United States, 130 min., Walter Reade, Inc.

The 400 Blows (1959), François Truffaut, France, 98 min., Janus.

Gimme Shelter (1970), Maysles Brothers and Charlotte Zwerin, United States, 90 min., Cinema V, 35mm.

The Great Train Robbery (1903), Edwin S. Porter, United States, 12 min., Museum of Modern Art.

Hiroshima, Mon Amour (1959), Alain Resnais, France, 88 min., CCM Films.

Hour of the Wolf (1968), Ingmar Bergman, Sweden, 88 min., United Artists.

The Immortal Story (1968), Orson Welles, France, 63 min., CCM Films.

Jules et Jim (1961), François Truffaut, France, 104 min., Janus.

Land Without Bread (1932), Luis Bruñel, Spain, 28 min., Museum of Modern Art.

Lapis (1967), James Whitney, United States, 10 min., Creative Film Society.

The Last Laugh (1924), F. W. Murnau, Germany, 80 min., Museum of Modern Art.

Listen to Britain (1942), Humphrey Jennings and Stewart McAllister, England, 20 min., Museum of Modern Art.

The Love of Jeanne Ney (1927), G. W. Pabst, Germany, 142 min., Museum of Modern Art.

M (1931), Fritz Lang, Germany, 90 min., Museum of Modern Art.

A Married Woman: Fragments of a Film Made in 1964 (1964), Jean-Luc Godard, France, 94 min., Columbia Cinemathèque.

Monterey Pop (1968), D. A. Pennebaker, United States, 72 min., Leacock-Pennebaker.

Mosori Monika (1970), Chick Strand, United States, 20 min., Los Angeles Filmmakers Cooperative.

Muriel, or the Time of a Return (1963), Alain Resnais, France, 120 min., United Artists.

Nanook of the North (1922), Robert Flaherty, United States, 55 min., Contemporary Films.

Night and Fog (1955), Alain Resnais, France, 31 min., Contemporary Films.

Nude Restaurant (1967), Andy Warhol, United States, 96 min., Magick Seal Films.

Open City (1945), Roberto Rossellini, Italy, 103 min., Contemporary Films.

The Passion of Joan of Arc (1928), Carl Dreyer, France, 61 min., Museum of Modern Art.

Performance (1970), Donald Cammell and Nicolas Roeg, England, 105 min., Warner Bros., 35mm.

The Rise to Power of Louis XIV (1966), Roberto Rossellini, France, 100 min., CCM Films.

Rosemary's Baby (1968), Roman Polanski, United States, 136 min., Films, Inc.

Rules of the Game (1939), Jean Renoir, France, 110 min., Janus.

Runs Good (1970), Pat O'Neill, United States, 15 min., Los Angeles Filmmakers Cooperative.

Satyricon (1969), Federico Fellini, Italy, 136 min., United Artists, 35-mm.

Shoot the Piano Player (1960), François Truffaut, France, 92 min., Janus.

The Shooting (1965), Monte Hellman, United States, 82 min., Walter Reade, Inc.

The Tempest (1968), Frank Olvey and Robert Brown, Canada, 7 min., Creative Film Society.

La Terra Trema (1948), Luchino Visconti, Italy, 160 min., CCM Films.

Trash (1970), Paul Morrissey, United States, 103 min., Cinema V.

Triumph of the Will (1934–1936), Leni Riefenstahl, Germany, 120 min., Museum of Modern Art.

2001: A Space Odyssey (1968), Stanley Kubrick, United States, 160 min., MGM, 35mm and 70mm, Films Inc., 16mm.

The Wild Child (1970), François Truffaut, France, 85 min., United Artists.

Woman in the Dunes (1964), Hiroshi Teshigahara, Japan, 130 min., Contemporary.

Woodstock (1969), Michael Wadleigh, United States, 183 min., Warner Bros.

Z (1969), Costa-Gavras, France, 127 min., Cinema V, 35mm.

appendix 1

Zabriskie Point (1970), Michelangelo Antonioni, United States, 112 min., Films, Inc.

Unless otherwise indicated, the films are available in 16mm.

appendix 2
distributors

CCM Films, Inc.
34 MacQuesten Parkway South
Mount Vernon, N.Y. 10550

Cinema V
595 Madison Avenue
New York, N.Y. 10022

Columbia Cinemathèque
711 Fifth Avenue
New York, N.Y. 10022

Contemporary Films–McGraw-Hill
330 West 42nd Street
New York, N.Y. 10036

Creative Film Society
14558 Valerio Street
Van Nuys, Calif. 91405

Films, Incorporated
38 West 32nd Street
New York, N.Y. 10001

Genesis Films, Ltd.
1040 North Las Palmas
Los Angeles, Calif. 90038

Janus Films
745 Fifth Avenue
New York, N.Y. 10022

Leacock-Pennebaker, Inc.
56 West 45th Street
New York, N.Y. 10036

Levitt-Pickman Film Corp.
505 Park Avenue
New York, N.Y. 10022

Los Angeles Filmmakers
Cooperative
P.O. Box 36563
Los Angeles, Calif. 90036

Magick Seal Films
9422 Mokihana Drive
Huntington Beach, Calif. 92646

MGM, Inc.
10202 West Washington Blvd.
Culver City, Calif. 90230

Museum of Modern Art
Department of Film
11 West 53rd Street
New York, N.Y. 10019

Paramount Distribution Exchange
291 South LaCienega
Beverly Hills, Calif. 90211

United Artists Sixteen
729 Seventh Avenue
New York, N.Y. 10019

Walter Reade, Inc.
241 East 34th Street
New York, N.Y. 10016

Warner Brothers Film Gallery
666 Fifth Avenue
New York, N.Y. 10019

index

Index

index

index

index

index

picture credits and copyright acknowledgments

A 2
B 3
C 4
D 5
E 6
F 7
G 8
H 9
I 0
J 1

395